Contemporary Issues in Quantitative Finance

Contemporary quantitative finance connects the abstract theory and the practical use of financial innovations, such as ultra-high-frequency trading and cryptocurrencies. It teaches students how to use cutting-edge computational techniques, mathematical tools, and statistical methodologies, with a focus on real-life applications.

The textbook opens with chapters on financial markets, global finance, and financial crises, setting the subject in its historical and international context. It then examines key topics in modern quantitative finance, including asset pricing, exchange-traded funds, Monte Carlo simulations, options, alternative investments, artificial intelligence, and big data analytics in finance. Complex theory is condensed to intuition, with appendices presenting advanced mathematical or statistical techniques. Each chapter offers Excel-based implementations, conceptual questions, quantitative problems, and a research project, giving students ample opportunity to develop their skills. Clear chapter objectives, summaries, and key terms also support student learning.

Digital supplements, including code and PowerPoint slides, are available for instructors. Assuming some prior financial education, this textbook is suited to upper-level undergraduate and postgraduate courses in quantitative finance, financial engineering, and derivatives.

Ahmet Can Inci is Professor of Finance at Bryant University in Rhode Island, U.S.A. He received his Ph.D. from the University of Michigan, Ann Arbor, in 2001. He holds an M.B.A. from Ohio State University, an M.Sc. in control systems from Imperial College – University of London, and a B.Sc. in electrical and electronics engineering from Bogazici University in Istanbul. Professor Inci's research interests include exchange rate dynamics, corporate governance, emerging markets, oil and energy, futures, contagion and flight to quality, the gender gap at the workplace, insider trading, intraday volatility, and market efficiency. He teaches innovations in finance, international finance and business, investments, corporate finance, foundations of financial theory, financial analytics, and financial engineering. He is a C.A.I.A. member, A.A.S.C.B. program consultant/reviewer, and editorial board member of numerous academic journals.

Routledge Advanced Texts in Economics and Finance

For more information about this series, please visit: www.routledge.com/Routledge-Advanced-Texts-in-Economics-and-Finance/book-series/SE0757

Contemporary Issues in Quantitative Finance

Ahmet Can Inci

Routledge
Taylor & Francis Group

LONDON AND NEW YORK

Cover image: © Getty Images

First published 2023
by Routledge
4 Park Square, Milton Park, Abingdon, Oxon OX14 4RN

and by Routledge
605 Third Avenue, New York, NY 10158

Routledge is an imprint of the Taylor & Francis Group, an informa business

British Library Cataloguing-in-Publication Data
A catalogue record for this book is available from the British Library

ISBN: 978-1-032-10115-6 (hbk)
ISBN: 978-1-032-10112-5 (pbk)
ISBN: 978-1-003-21369-7 (ebk)

DOI: 10.4324/9781003213697

Typeset in Bembo
by Apex CoVantage, LLC

Access the Support Material: www.routledge.co.uk/9781032101156

I am grateful to all my teachers and professors, without whom this work would not have been possible. I especially thank J.C. Allwright, Yorgo Istefanopulos, Kadri Ozcaldiran, Marcus Sandver, Tyler Shumway, and especially Nejat Seyhun. I greatly appreciate the editorial help from Amelia Bashford, Kate Fornadel, Michelle Gallagher, Chloe Herbert, and Natalie Tomlinson at Routledge.

This book is dedicated to the memory of my parents: my mother, Nebahat Inci, and my father, Ismet C. Inci.

Contents

About the Author

Ahmet Can Inci Bryant University, Rhode Island Ph.D.: University of Michigan Ann Arbor, 2001 M.B.A.: Ohio State University, 1996 M.Sc. Control Systems: Imperial College – University of London, 1994 B.Sc. Electrical Engineering: Bogazici University, 1993

RESEARCH

Ahmet Can Inci is a prolific researcher in finance. His research activity focuses on exchange rate movements, corporate governance, emerging markets, oil and energy, futures, flight to quality, contagion at markets and financial institutions, the gender gap at the workplace, insider trading, intraday volatility, and market efficiency. He has published in top journals, such as *Journal of Financial and Quantitative Analysis*, *Financial Management*, and *Global Finance Journal*. Social Science Research Network (ssrn.com) views: 26,200 Google Scholar citations: 448 ResearchGate score: 18.4 LinkedIn: www.linkedin.com/pub/a-can-inci/5/235/539/

TEACHING

Professor Inci teaches investments, financial management, international business, international finance, innovations in contemporary finance, securities analysis, finance for executives, corporate finance, and foundations of financial theory at the undergraduate and graduate level, including doctoral programs. He consistently received excellent student evaluations.

CONSULTING AND SERVICE

Professor Inci is a highly experienced higher education consultant with significant knowledge about the A.A.C.S.B. accreditation process for business schools in the U.S.A. He has worked with a number of quality assurance agencies, including the A.A.C.S.B., N.E.A.S.C., and E.Q.U.I.S. in Europe. Professor Inci has provided advice to universities on the assurance of learning, goal assessment techniques, design of program learning goals, collection of artifacts on critical thinking, problem-solving, and other skills, as well as the development of assessment processes. He has served on the Curriculum Committee, Faculty Development Committee, Institutional Review Board, Assessment Steering Committee, Graduate Faculty Committee-Business, University Committee on Scholastic Standing, and others.

CHAPTER 1

Introduction

History, Present, Future of Financial Markets and Securities

OBJECTIVES

- Evaluate the history of technology and mathematical/statistical modeling in financial investments.
- Outline the development of modern portfolio theory.
- Describe the incorporation of computers into research and trading from the 1970s onward.
- Evaluate the current technological environment with examples from artificial intelligence, fintech, and cryptocurrencies.
- The research techniques used to make investment, risk management, and portfolio formation decisions are mentioned.
- Categorize the financial securities and the characteristics of the forums that they are traded with an international perspective.
- Explain the commonly used research sources.

1.1 INTRODUCTION

The investments area of the finance field as a profession has grown at a tremendous pace since the 1950s. Traditional securities, such as stocks and bonds, had been the primary areas of investments for centuries, especially in common law countries, such as the United Kingdom. And the idea of putting all your eggs in one basket has been considered a risky strategy since those times. But investments as a field of study and a focus on a profession based on a scientific foundation started to take off in the 1950s. Portfolio optimization techniques were first introduced by Markowitz in 1952. Risk and return characteristics of different investment opportunities were formally and scientifically taken into account in developing optimal portfolios for the clients.

Stochastic calculus techniques from physics and mathematics started to be considered for the valuation of alternative investment opportunities. The commencement of options trading at the Chicago Board of Options Exchange, coupled with the presence of the Options Clearing

DOI: 10.4324/9781003213697-1

Corporation (O.C.C.) in 1973, coincided with the formal derivation of option pricing techniques by Fisher Black, Myron Scholes, and Robert Merton. The standardized exchange-traded call options enhanced portfolio components. Twenty-four-hour trading of futures contracts all around the world in 1992 with the electronic trading platform Globex was another contribution to enhancing portfolio components. Investors then had the means to trade various different types of securities more conveniently and easily.

By the late 1980s and early 1990s, trading mechanisms started to become available for investors. Information dissemination became easier and more accessible for traders. Internet-based brokerage firms started to appear as alternatives to traditional brokerage companies. As markets became more efficient due to the faster access to information and faster execution of trades, traditional frictions that prevented many different types of investors started to diminish. Increased globalization of international commerce and reduction of barriers to trade further helped with the reduction of frictions and started to enable trading activities and investment portfolios to become global. The international diversification benefits formally proven in the 1970s by Bruno Solnik and others became practical applications starting in the 1990s.

The growth in the subfield of investments, financial engineering, led to the creation and introduction of numerous derivative securities in the 1990s. Any item of value now had the potential to be converted into a tradable security for a wide range of anticipating investors all around the world. As the derivatives markets grew at an enormous pace in futures, forwards, options, swaps, convertibles, trusts, and real estate products, the decade of the 2000s culminated in the explosion of structured products in the mortgage industry. The housing market collapse demonstrated the dangers in the lack of knowledge about these structured products. As the deep recession of the financial crisis of 2007–2008 started to subside and as investors started to return to these investment opportunities with a more speculative eye, other investment opportunities started to appear: the publication in 2008 of the paper 'Bitcoin: A Peer-to-Peer Electronic Cash System' by the person(s) using the pseudonym 'Satoshi Nakamoto' jumpstarted a whole new asset class: cryptocurrencies in the 2010s.

Technological improvements in computing and communication techniques have led to algorithmic and ultra-high-speed trading, which started to take significant portions of trading activity in the 2000s and 2010s. Machine learning and robo-trading are some other examples of new trends taking place in the investments field in the 2010s.

As these new and alternative trends and techniques continue to develop and be part of the investments field, students, investors, professionals, academicians, regulators, and candidates of this profession must gain the knowledge and proficiency of these developments and techniques. This is the main goal of this book. And in this introductory first chapter, an overview of the derivatives area of finance and investments will be provided. Many of the discussions in this introductory chapter will be developed in much more detail in later chapters. But it is appropriate to understand the history and the characteristics of derivatives. After all, they are the end products of the previously mentioned new tools, trends, and techniques that are shaping modern finance and investments. An overview of a large chunk of these new investment alternatives and derivative products is provided in the following sections.

1.2 DERIVATIVE SECURITIES

1.2.1 What Is a Derivative?

A derivative is a financial security, an instrument whose value depends on or is derived from the value of another asset. From this perspective, a derivative security has nothing directly related to the concept of derivatives in calculus. Rather, we name this financial security as a derivative because the price of the security is derived from the price of another security. We call that other security as the 'underlying security'.

There are dozens, even hundreds, of derivative securities. We can collect them under groups such as futures, forwards, swaps, options, exotics, and so on. All kinds of new derivative products are created every day by technically savvy and creative analysts to satisfy the needs and desires of their clients. These specific analysts are also known as financial engineers, and the clients are from a wide spectrum of wealthy individual investors, professional investment agencies, and domestic or multinational companies. The clients express certain payoff/revenue streams in the future based on the values of certain financial securities. Financial engineers design strategies (many times by creating certain portfolios of various financial securities) to generate the matching revenues requested by their clients. This area of financial investments has been growing at a steady rate since the mid-1990s as the demand of clients increase.

One important fact about these derivative securities is that derivatives are known as zero-sum games. In any derivatives transaction, there is a buyer and there is a seller of that derivative security. These two investors on opposite sides of the trade have opposite views about the future. In order to act on their beliefs, they take opposite positions in the derivatives trade. In the end, one of these investors will be correct. The correct investor will end up with a profit, while the wrong investor will end up with a loss. The profit and the loss (negative profit) will add up to zero. That is why derivatives trading is referred to as a zero-sum game.

Although derivative products have exploded exponentially over the last 30–40 years in terms of numbers, trading volume, and interest, the history actually goes back all the way to the mid-1800s to forward contracts in the Midwest, more specifically in Chicago. Farmers and buyers of agricultural products started creating binding agreements starting from the 1800s for exchanging the coming year's crops at specific prices on certain dates. These contracts later became formal futures contracts and led to the creation of futures exchanges.

1.2.2 Derivative Instruments and Underlying Assets

The derivatives market consists of numerous financial securities that provide investors with many different types of return opportunities. We can broadly categorize these derivative products as follows:

(1) Forward contracts: These securities are signed and legally binding commitments to trade a specific underlying asset at a specific future date at a fixed price. Forward contracts are private agreements, and since the characteristics are non-standard, it is generally difficult to get out of the contract once committed.

(2) Futures contracts: These derivatives are similar to forwards, but the characteristics of the contract, such as the underlying asset, its size, and the date of contract fulfillment, are all standardized. The standardization enables futures contracts to be traded actively at secondary markets over-the-counter or organized physical exchanges.

(3) Options: These securities enable the owner the choice but not the obligation to trade an underlying asset at a specific price.

(4) Warrants: Also known as employee stock option plans (E.S.O.P.s), these securities are options provided by firms to their employees as a part of the compensation packages. If the share price of the firm increases in equity markets while the employee is holding the warrants, it will be advantageous to exercise the warrants and purchase the shares of the firm at the lower exercise price associated with the warrant.

(5) Swaps: These derivatives are legally binding agreements between two parties to swap the cash flow streams of investments/projects that the counterparties own. A follow-up second derivative tied to this is called *swaptions*, which are options to enter into a swap derivative at a fixed value in the future.

(6) Real options: These derivatives are embedded into the operations of a firm. Firm managements have access to utilize such options if the circumstances are favorable. Some examples are (a) tax timing options motivated by the tax code and (b) call provision options in order to pay off a corporate bond earlier than the maturity of the bond.

(7) Mortgage-backed securities: Such structured derivative products' payments are based on mortgage payments. These repackaged mortgaged products, such as asset-backed securities (A.B.S.) or collateralized mortgage obligations (C.M.O.), distribute the cash flows from a pool of regular mortgages based on certain rules.

(8) Convertible bonds: These corporate bonds have the possibility to be converted to equity shares if the investor chooses to do so.

(9) Forward rate agreements are private agreements that specify the interest rate to be used (and, therefore, the interest to be paid) at a fixed future date for a fixed notional amount.

(10) Collateralized debt obligations: These credit derivatives are financial securities that shift the risk of a pool of securities from one party to another party without transferring the actual securities. Different levels of risks assumed by the investors are accompanied by relevant compensating cash flows.

All these derivative securities have uniquely associated underlying assets that influence the values of the derivatives. The underlying asset can be anything that has a measurable value that changes dynamically with time and in an uncertain manner. The commonly seen underlying assets are (1) financial securities, such as stocks, bonds, stock/bond indices, and currencies; (2) commodities, such as different grades of oil, and agricultural products, such as wheat, corn, beef, pork, and orange juice; (3) precious materials, such as gold, silver, and platinum; and (4) exotic and unusual assets, such as electricity, carbon emissions, media bandwidth frequencies, and even the weather.

This derivatives instruments listed is by no means exhaustive. There are dozens, if not hundreds, of additional derivative products, and new ones are designed all the time by financial engineers. In terms of increased demand and popularity, however, it takes some time for a derivative product to become familiar to a wide variety of investors. Futures, forwards, swaps, convertible bonds, and options are the more popular derivatives in secondary markets, and consequently, more overview of these financial securities is provided in the following sections.

1.2.3 Forwards and Futures

Both forwards and futures are fundamentally contracts about the future delivery of an asset. There are three key pieces of information on the contract: (1) what will be traded; (2) the contract execution date, which is also known as the maturity date of the contract; and (3) the price at which the trade will be executed on that maturity date, the forward/futures price.

The party who commits to buy the underlying asset is known to have a *long position* in the contract. This trader is assumed to have *purchased* the contract. The counterparty who commits to sell the underlying asset is said to have a *short position* in the contract. This trader is also assumed to have *sold* the contract.

The underlying security in forward contracts is unique and is of interest to only a very small group of investors. As a result, forward contracts are not actively traded. They are highly illiquid and very tough to get rid of once committed.

Futures contracts, on the other hand, have underlying securities that are of wide interest and of high demand. Investors all around the world make futures actively traded and liquid securities. Many of the features in the contracts, such as the size of the underlying security or the maturity date, are standardized to make the contract easy to trade in an organized exchange. Many investors in futures contracts easily trade away with additional counter positions. Traders in futures only get the actual underlying asset 2% of the time. Most long positions are canceled out with an additional opposite short position, leading to a monetary profit or loss realization.

1.2.4 Swaps

Swap derivatives are agreements between two trades where each trader agrees to exchange (i.e., swap) the futures cash flows of two different financial instruments that the trades own. The ownership of the financial instruments does not change. The principal values of the financial instruments are equal. Only the cash flows of the instruments are swapped with the agreement. There are different types of swaps, depending on the type of cash flow exchange. Two major types are (1) interest rate swaps, which are exchanges of coupon payments of two different bonds held by two traders, and (2) currency swaps, which are exchanges of cash flows denominated in different mediums of exchanges.

There is an active over-the-counter market for swaps. As an interest rate swap example, consider a bond with a 5% fixed coupon rate held by the first investor and a bond with a variable coupon rate of 3% plus the 10-year Treasury yield held by the second investor. The first investor anticipates rising interest rates in the future and the second investor believes the opposite; the rates will decline in the future. The two investors with opposite views about the future get together and create a legally binding swap where they agree to exchange the payments of their bonds throughout the maturity of the two bonds. At some point, if one of the investors wants to get out of the swap obligation, the secondary over-the-counter market would enable the investor to *sell* the swap.

1.2.5 Convertible Bonds

Convertible bonds are debt instruments issued and sold by firms. These corporate forms can be converted into a pre-specified number of shares (conversion ratio) of the company at the choice of the convertible bond owner. This will be a viable choice if the conversion value (conversion ratio multiplied by the per-share price) is larger than the straight bond value.

As an example, consider that the conversion ratio is 50 shares of stock for a convertible bond. Also, assume that at that moment the annual bond has five years to maturity. The coupon rate of the bond is 6%, the face value is $1,000, and the yield to maturity is 6%. Since this is a par bond, the straight bond price is $1,000. (To double-check with a financial calculator, we would input N = 5, P.M.T. = 60, F.V. = 1,000, and Y.T.M. = 6 and find P.V. as $1,000 in absolute value). If the per-share price of the firm's stock is $22, this will mean that the conversion value is $1,100 (50 × $22 = $1,100). The true value of the convertible bond is whichever is higher between the straight bond price and the conversion value. This higher value is formally called the floor value of the convertible bond, and in this numerical example, the floor value of the convertible bond is $1,100. Under these circumstances, it is definitely advantageous for the holder of the bond to convert. It should be noted that this conversion is a one-way street. Once the bold holder converts, she becomes a shareholder of the company, and later on, the inventor cannot convert back.

Convertible bonds are attractive to a wide range of investors, from individuals to hedge fund managers. As a matter of fact, hedge fund managers commonly utilize convertible bond arbitrage by purchasing convertible bonds and shorting an appropriate number of shares of the same firm which leads to arbitrage profits (more on this strategy in the 'Hedge Funds' chapter).

1.2.6 Options

Options became popular in the mid-1970s, and today, the dollar volume of open interest in organized exchanges is larger than that of futures. There are numerous types of options. The two types that are in high demand are call options, where the owner of such options has the right but not the obligation to buy a certain underlying asset by a certain date for a certain price (called the strike price or exercise price) and put options where the owner that the right but not the obligation to sell the underlying asset by a certain date for the exercise price. Deciding to use an option is called exercising the option.

Options typically have a life of two years when they are created, but longer maturity or shorter maturity options are also available. An *American* option can be exercised at any time during the life of the option. *European* options, on the other hand, can only be exercised on the final day, the maturity date of the option. Options are traded as *contracts*. One option contract is 100 options.

An option is quoted with several of its characteristics. An I.B.M. Sept 100 Call would mean a call option with a $100 strike price, an expiration date as the third Friday of September, and an I.B.M. stock share as the underlying asset. The option might be trading at $45, but if you want to purchase this option, the minimum you could buy would be one option contract (100 options) worth $4,500 plus the transaction cost to your broker.

1.2.7 Where Are Derivatives Traded?

The first medium to trade derivative securities is through an organized exchange. Such a derivatives market fulfills a number of important functions. These exchanges are places where (1) traders can act on their beliefs about the future; (2) since buyers and sellers get together at these mediums, transaction costs and other frictions are reduced and efficiency increases; (3) firms, multinationals, and other professional investors can raise funds by selling claims against themselves; and (4) capital flows help increase productivity for the society.

For derivatives, Chicago has been the main physical location for such derivatives exchanges. The Chicago Mercantile Exchange (C.M.E.) (non-agricultural futures), Chicago Board of Trade (agricultural futures), and Chicago Board Options Exchange, founded in 1973, are some of these derivatives exchanges. Although there have been adjustments over the decades, such as the merger of the C.M.E. and Chicago Board of Trade in 2006, forming the C.M.E. Group and leading to the inclusion of the New York Mercantile Exchange (N.Y.M.E.X.) into the C.M.E. Group in 2008, internationally, there are other exchange centers for derivatives trading, such as Eurex (E-X) in Frankfurt, Germany, and Hong Kong Futures Exchange (H.K.F.E.) in Asia, but the size of trading volume and the spectrum of trading products are dwarfed by those in Chicago.

The second medium to trade derivative securities is through over-the-counter markets, essentially computer trading networks. These networks are not directly accessible to individual traders. Some of these electronic trading networks are limited, where only traders working for banks, fund managers, and corporate treasurers contact each other directly. Others are more accessible, mainly to all the major brokerage firms (and, therefore, indirectly to regular investors).

1.3 SIZE OF DERIVATIVES MARKETS

The size of derivatives markets is huge. Global interest in derivatives and associated underlying assets have increased dramatically since the late 1990s. The close correlations between the changes in the values of the derivatives and the changes in the associated values of the underlying assets make it substantially more practical to invest in derivatives instead of the underlying assets. For example, investors prefer to buy (have long positions) in gold futures than to buy actual gold if they believe gold prices will go up. Similarly, as one can imagine, it is substantially

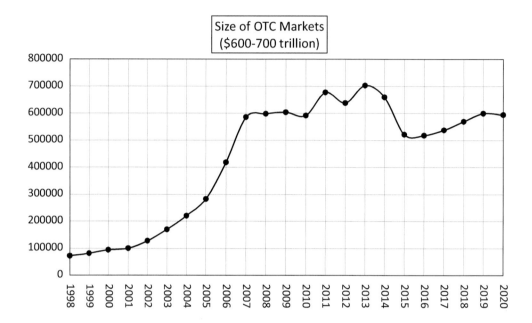

FIGURE 1.1 Size of the Notional Amounts Outstanding in Global Over-the-Counter Derivatives Markets in Billions of U.S. Dollars

Source: Bank of International Settlements Statistics

easier to long a futures contract on 5,000 bushels of corn than to actually buy 5,000 bushels of corn if an investor believes that corn prices will go up.

Figure 1.1 shows the outstanding size of existing derivatives in the over-the-counter markets worldwide since 1998. The exponential increase in the total size stabilized after the financial crisis of 2007–2008. The securities in the figure include all derivatives with all underlying assets: foreign currency derivatives, interest rates, equity-linked contracts, commodity contracts, credit default swaps, and others.

Figure 1.2 depicts the size of the open interest of the derivatives – futures and options – traded at organized exchanges around the globe since the early 1990s. We see a similar pattern in the dramatic increase in the contract sizes for options and futures until 2007. Then with the financial crisis, the increase in open interest slowed down significantly. The total size of open interest in notional principals for options is larger in general compared to those of futures. In December 2019, for example, the total open interest for options was $60 billion, while for futures, the dollar amount was $35 billion, making the total open interest in organized exchanges for futures and options close to $100 billion. The over-the-counter markets have been consistently larger for derivatives markets in terms of the size of outstanding trades, compared to organized exchange-traded markets. We also observe that the financial crisis of 2007–2008 had a negative impact on the overall growth of derivatives markets.

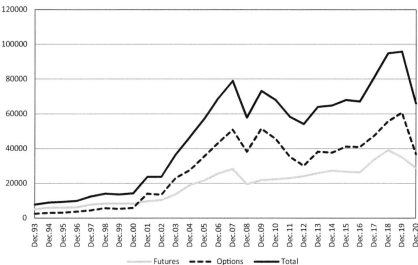

FIGURE 1.2 Open Interest in Notional Principals of Futures and Options Contracts in Exchange-Traded Markets in Millions of U.S. Dollars

Source: Bank of International Settlements Statistics

1.4 HOW ARE DERIVATIVES USED AND BY WHOM?

There are three general purposes of derivative securities trading. The first purpose is to consider them as typical financial securities to invest and, therefore, buy them at low prices and sell them later at high prices, or short-sell/write them at high prices and buy them later at low prices. The success of these strategies depends on the correct estimation of future price movements. The investors in this context are called speculators, and *speculation* is the first way to utilize derivatives.

The second reason derivatives are used is for risk management purposes. A specific example of risk management is *hedging*. Farmers want to reduce the uncertainty about next year's agricultural product sale prices. Therefore, they take positions in derivative products in order to lock in their future profits and eliminate the impact on price fluctuations. Such farmers will be willing to forego potential additional profits if selling prices increase, in return for protecting themselves from the potential losses if selling prices decrease. Similarly, cereal producers also hedge by entering into these derivatives contracts to protect themselves from the potential increase in purchase prices.

The third way derivative products are utilized is by a group of professional investors called arbitrageurs. Arbitrageurs constantly monitor financial markets for mispriced securities. When they detect such opportunities, they trade in order to lock in guaranteed, risk-free profits called *arbitrage profits*.

The three strategies, speculation, hedging, and arbitrage profits, are how market participants utilize derivatives. The types of investors participating in derivatives markets are categorized based on these strategies. Hedgers use derivative products in order to reduce their total risk exposure of their investments and businesses. Speculators have certain views on the future direction of securities and markets based on their research and knowledge. They trade and take risky positions in order to implement their future beliefs. If their beliefs are accurate, they generate profits; otherwise, they end up with losses. Finally, arbitrageurs try to lock in guaranteed arbitrage profits by constantly monitoring numerous markets to find mispriced securities.

Arbitrage opportunities stem from mispriced securities. These situations are not common, but once they are detected, arbitrageurs have very short windows of time to act on them. As an arbitrage example, consider that the stock of a multinational firm is quoted as £100 at the London Stock Exchange (L.S.E.) and $140 at the New York Stock Exchange (N.Y.S.E.). At that same time, the direct quote of the exchange rate between the U.S. dollar and the British pound is $1.42/£. Inspection of these values for a bit should tell us that there is something wrong in these markets – a mispricing – hence an arbitrage opportunity. In cases such as these, the proper approach for the arbitrageur would be buying (selling) the cheap (expensive) and round up the transaction by selling (buying) the expensive (cheap). In our numerical example, given the exchange rate, $142 is equivalent to £100. This tells us that the stock is trading at a lower price on the N.Y.S.E. Therefore, the arbitrageur buys the stock for $140 at the N.Y.S.E., then sells the stock at the L.S.E. and receives £100. The British pounds are immediately converted to U.S. dollars, providing $142. The arbitrageur started with $140 and ended up with $142. The risk-free guaranteed profit is $2 for each share traded.

There are several caveats we must consider. First, we have ignored the frictions for these trades, such as transaction costs. Second, we assumed that all the markets are perfectly connected with each other. Third, we assumed that the transactions took place almost immediately, one after the other, before the prices moved. In reality, for individual investors, these three frictions will make it practically impossible to benefit from an arbitrage opportunity. But for arbitrageurs at powerful investment companies, such as hedge funds with constant monitoring capabilities, negligible transaction costs, and fiber optic connections to access all markets globally, arbitrage opportunities provide great profits.

Investors who trade derivative securities can be tempted to shift from their original purpose to another quite easily, and that is very dangerous. For example, a trader whose primary purpose is to hedge might switch over to speculating related to his/her anticipations about the future. If those anticipations do not materialize, enormous losses might be incurred. Or an arbitrageur looking for guaranteed profits might become a speculator, and the trade positions might lead to significant losses. Unfortunately, this is not an uncommon occurrence. An example is the conviction of a high-position trader at the French investment company Société Générale because of conducting false and unauthorized trades leading to a loss of roughly €5 billion in 2008.

1.5 THE FINANCIAL CRISIS OF 2007–2008

The collapse of the inflated housing market starting in 2007 started a chain of negative events unseen since the Great Depression of the 1930s. Large sums of investments in a wide variety of securities based on the strategy of continued increases in housing prices led to enormous quick losses, insolvencies, and failures. Investment professionals and companies betting heavily on these housing price products were the first ones to declare bankruptcy. Lehman Brothers was the most famous of these companies. The bankruptcy filing by Lehman on September 15, 2008, was the biggest bankruptcy in U.S. history. Lehman was an active participant in the over-the-counter derivatives markets on financial securities that were known as mortgage-backed structures securities. The firm started to experience financial difficulties because of the huge positions taken in these collateralized mortgage obligations betting that housing prices would continue to increase. The collapse of housing prices revealed the highly risky positions undertaken by Lehman. The firm found it impossible to roll over its short-term funding obligations. Hundreds of thousands of transactions outstanding with about 8,000 counterparties remained unfulfilled. There was no other choice than to declare bankruptcy. Since then, unwinding these transactions has been extremely challenging for both the Lehman liquidators and their counterparties.

The Lehman bankruptcy was coupled with the demise of another highly recognized investment company, Bear-Stearns, around the same time. These two events started an avalanche effect with some of the giants of the finance industry, such as Washington Mutual, Merrill-Lynch, and Wachovia Bank, either going bankrupt or having been in such poor financial health that they had to be rescued or acquired by other banks during the financial crises. When the dust settled, some of the remaining finance and insurance pillars were Wells Fargo, Goldman Sachs, Bank of America, Citigroup, J.P. Morgan, Morgan Stanley, and American Insurance Group (though A.I.G. got substantial government assistance to stay afloat and to avoid the crisis become even worse). We will be discussing the 2007–2008 financial crisis in much more depth in Chapter 3, including its impact on the derivatives markets.

1.6 SUMMARY AND CONCLUSION

The field of financial investments has expanded exponentially over the last 40 years. Market participants are offered numerous new financial securities under the umbrella of derivatives. These derivative products are designed by financial engineers, and as demand for specific products perks up and persists, security becomes a permanent part of the investment spectrum.

It is very important to understand the risk and return characteristics of financial securities. Many investors have difficulty fully digesting all the characteristics of newly created securities. This leads to flawed funding commitments, and if the anticipations about the future do not materialize, huge losses are recorded. Lack of knowledge about new derivative products was one of the most important reasons behind the 2007–2008 financial crisis.

Market participants use derivatives markets for speculative, hedging, or arbitrage opportunities. It is very tempting and dangerous for investors to move away from their original purpose to another. Traders can frequently be tempted to switch from being hedgers to speculators or from being arbitrageurs to speculators. These types of decisions put the funds and portfolios of clients and firms in danger. The experience of Société Générale in 2008 is an example of what can go wrong.

Arbitrage as a strategy is a smart way of utilizing financial securities. Generating risk-free guaranteed profits is very enticing. However, market participants must be aware of several facts when pursuing arbitrage. First, many arbitrage strategies still involve some risk-taking.

However powerful a trader is with instant access to markets and with negligible trading costs, glitches and unanticipated frictions pop up, which might eliminate or backfire the arbitrage. Second, many smart investors and institutions are continuously searching for arbitrage opportunities, and this makes finding simple and straightforward opportunities especially rare. In academic circles, theoretical investigations usually assume that there is no arbitrage and that assets are fairly priced. When theory and practice diverge, the investigator/trader does not feel so bad because additional profit opportunities appear.

In conclusion, when trading financial securities in general and derivative securities in particular, the old standard of buying the cheap and selling the expensive rules. The absence of arbitrage is usually the accurate assumption. If arbitrage is detected by a professional investor with fast access to markets and negligible frictional costs, the opportunity should be utilized as quickly and as much as possible before the arbitrage vanishes. On the other hand, individual investors should be skeptical when arbitrage is detected: either they will not act fast enough to take advantage of or transaction frictions will be too much to generate profits.

REFERENCES AND ADDITIONAL READING

Bank of International Settlements Statistics. 2021. *BIS Derivatives Statistics*. www.bis.org/statistics/.
Black, F., Scholes, M. 1973. The Pricing of Options and Corporate Liabilities. *Journal of Political Economy*, 81, 637–654.
Markowitz, H.M. 1952. Portfolio Selection. *Journal of Finance*, 7, 77–91.
Merton, R.C. 1973. Theory of Rational Option Pricing. *Bell Journal of Economics*, 4, 141–183.
Nakamoto, S. 2008. *Bitcoin: A Peer-to-Peer Electronic Cash System*. https://bitcoin.org/bitcoin.pdf.
Solnik, B.H. 1974. Why Not Diversify Internationally Rather than Domestically? *Financial Analysts Journal*, 30, 48–54.

CHAPTER 2

Global Finance

OBJECTIVES

- Summarize the history of the development of the financial markets in different regions of the world.
- Justify the traditional case for international diversification with graphs and examples.
- Assess the new developments and the ebb-and-flow nature of the benefits of international diversification.
- Appraise the counterarguments of diversification.
- Justify the ultimate correct policy about international diversification.
- Design a three-step smart diversification strategy for a domestic investor with examples.
- Evaluate the challenges for analyzing multinational corporations with international projects.
- Contrast multicurrency international projects and devise selection solutions.

2.1 INTRODUCTION

International investment opportunities started to become accessible starting in the 1970s, first for large professional investment companies and financial institutions and then with the rise of the internet, lower transaction costs, and online brokerage firms for all market participants, including small individual investors. In this chapter, we will look at the evolution of the securities markets around the world. We will group countries into two: common law countries and civil law countries. Common law countries, such as the U.K., the U.S., Canada, and Australia, have traditionally favored the public participating in the trading of financial securities of business enterprises. Civil law countries, on the other hand, have been slow in the creation of organized securities exchanges. As a consequence, financial markets matured, and international trading became popular first in common law states. The documentation of the evidence

DOI: 10.4324/9781003213697-2

of financial markets helping the economy of a country eventually led to the establishment of financial markets for most countries around the world.

Starting from the 1970s, researchers such as Bruno Solnik proved unequivocally that international diversification increases profits and reduces risk at the same time. Domestic investors, even with their home bias, started to expand internationally. We will demonstrate the traditional case for international diversification with examples. We will also show that while international diversification is indeed beneficial, this is a dynamic phenomenon, and there are oscillations in the advantages associated with international diversification. We explore the reasons for these ebbs and flows. We also present the counterarguments about diversification. Regarding the pros and cons, the ultimate correct policy is to diversify in an intelligent manner. We will justify this view from the point of view of a U.S. domestic investor and will highlight the smart diversification strategy as a three-step process: (1) quantitative investigation, (2) qualitative investigation, and finally (3) the targeted diversification decision. We will provide an example of this strategic process for an equity investor and then for a fixed-income investor. The discussions are valid the domestic investors from any country, and the strategy can be applied by any investor around the world.

The final section of the chapter focuses on international corporate finance. Increasing international economic cooperation and globalization with easier access to capital across borders, decreasing frictions, and reduced tariffs and protections, multinational corporations have increased tremendously in number and in total capacity within domestic and international commerce. International projects with multiple currencies have become the norm of operations for these multinational firms. We investigate the decision criteria along with the challenges of analyzing and correctly choosing such international projects.

2.2 HISTORY OF INTERNATIONAL COMMERCE: COMMON LAW AND CIVIL LAW DIFFERENCES

Rafael La Porta, Florencio Lopez-de-Silanes, Andrei Shleifer, and Robert Vishny detail the financial differences between civil law countries and common law countries in their seminal work, *Law and Finance*, in 1998. Common law countries, such as the U.K., U.S., Canada, and Australia, have historically encouraged financial markets and exchanges. This early start has spilled over to international commerce and trade. However, as the advantages and profits of international trade became clear, all nations have moved toward the establishment of the rules, regulations, procedures, and organizations for globalization.

Studies in economics and finance have shown unequivocally that internationalization and global diversification reduce risks and increase profits at the macro level and at the micro firm level. Most nations, with common law countries leading the helm, have enabled firms and investors to trade internationally by reducing tariffs, restrictions, frictions, taxes, and costs. However, globalization is not an unfailing process without any drawbacks. There are many opponents of globalization who have not been convinced of the advantages dominating the disadvantages. The opposition to globalization appears in various formats. One fundamental manifestation of standing against globalization is called home bias.

Home bias is the tendency of investors to place a higher than necessary portion of their funds in their home country securities even though a more diversified portfolio has more profit and less risk. Rationally, this strategy is not sensible; that is why home bias is considered an anomaly. Interestingly, home bias has been documented for different markets, such as equity markets and fixed-income security markets, and different types of investors, ranging from individual to professional. Higher tax rates for foreign investors, higher transaction costs for foreign transactions, and tariffs are other examples of opposition to international investments. Even with all these frictions and biases, the case for international diversification remains strong, as explained in the next section.

2.3 THE CASE FOR INTERNATIONAL DIVERSIFICATION: STOCK MARKET CAPITALIZATION

Our justification for international diversification starts with stock market capitalizations around the world. Figure 2.1 depicts total equity market capitalizations in three different regions of the world denominated in U.S. dollars. Spanning a period of 45 years from 1975 through 2020, the total capitalizations for European equity markets are represented with the top bars; for Asian markets, with the middle white bars; and for the American equity markets, with the bottom bars.

There are several important observations from the figure. First is the steady growth in equity markets all around the world from one decade to the next. While there are some short declines, such as the beginning of the 2000s (World Trade Center attacks) and 2008 (the financial crisis of 2007–2008), the continual increase in the sizes of capital markets in all regions of the world is clear. Second, at any point in time, we see that the American equity markets

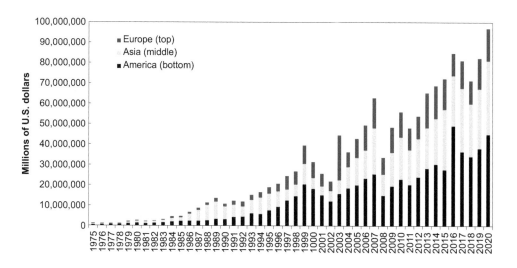

FIGURE 2.1 World Equity Market Capitalizations in Different Regions

(essentially the U.S. stock exchanges) take about half of the share of the total world stock market capitalization. Although the U.S. stock exchanges are the largest in the world, there is no question that at least half of the equity capitalization is outside of the U.S. This clearly indicates numerous substantial investment opportunities for U.S.-based investors to look for outside their home turf. This is also obviously correct for Asian and European investors. There are plenty of opportunities outside the familiar local exchanges. Third, although all three major regions are growing substantially, we can detect that European markets are becoming more and more stable, while Asian markets are growing at the fastest pace. In recent years, Asian and American equity markets together have become larger than European equity markets.

The existence and substantial growth of equity markets with various interesting profit opportunities in different regions of the world certainly make a case for international diversification for all investors using stocks in their portfolios.

2.4 THE TRADITIONAL CASE FOR INTERNATIONAL DIVERSIFICATION

The fundamental reason for international diversification has been firmly established in the 1970s by the seminal work of Bruno Solnik (1974). He has documented that foreign investments allow investors to reduce the total risk of the portfolio while offering additional return potential. This is an extremely difficult goal to achieve. Reducing risk and increasing profits at the same time is the traditional case for international diversification, which has been confirmed over many follow-up studies. By expanding the investment opportunity set and the spectrum of securities to be included in portfolios, international diversification helps to improve the risk-adjusted performance of a portfolio.

The low international correlations across markets and securities of different countries allow for the reduction of the risk (i.e., volatility) of a global portfolio. The risk accumulated at the country level is diversified away with the help of including portfolio securities from other countries around the world.

When it comes to international diversification, there are a wide variety of candidate countries to pick from depending on the risk tolerance level of investors.

(1) Developed country markets: These countries are highly advanced and developed. They have well-established financial markets and sophisticated economies. Countries such as the U.K., Germany, France, Switzerland, and Japan are examples of developed countries.

(2) B.R.I.C.(S.) countries: These countries are considered by many as the next superpowers. Brazil, Russia, India, China, and South Africa have fast-growing G.D.P.s, large populations, significant natural resources, and numerous economic and financial opportunities for the future.

(3) M.I.S.T. and M.I.N.T. countries: These countries are believed to be the successors to the B.R.I.C.(S.) countries. Mexico, Indonesia, South Korea, and Turkey, according to Goldman Sachs researchers, and Mexico, Indonesia, Nigeria, and Turkey, according to Fidelity researchers, are countries with rapid economic growth but also with significant risk sources.

(4) Emerging countries: These economies have significantly high risk but also enormous profit potential. The economic and financial performances of these countries are unstable. While one year can be a definitive success, the next might lead to significant losses.

(5) Frontier countries: A frontier economy is a country that is less established than the emerging markets because of its very small size, high internal risk, or substantial frictions, such as high illiquidity, to be considered as an emerging market. Clearly, these countries have the highest risks.

(6) Least developed countries: Unfortunately, these countries do not have the infrastructure, natural resources, or know-how to provide financial markets or securities that can be part of the portfolio of a global investor. These alternatives are to be avoided currently or in the short term.

Although this classification is a well-founded guideline for the global investor, which category a specific country belongs to can be determined from Fitch sovereign ratings. The complete Fitch sovereign ratings history or the Fitch ratings website (www.fitchratings.com) provides rankings and letter grading of sovereign risk characteristics and investment potentials.

As the first numerical example of the traditional case for international diversification, we consider a two-stock international portfolio. The expected return (profit) of this portfolio is

$$E(R_p) = w_d E(R_d) + w_f E(R_f), \tag{2.1}$$

where the expected return of the portfolio is the weighted average of the expected return of the domestic security and the expected return of the foreign security, and w_d (w_f) is the weight of the domestic (foreign) security.

The risk of the international portfolio is represented by the standard deviation

$$\sigma_p = (w_d^2 \sigma_d^2 + w_f^2 \sigma_f^2 + 2w_d w_f \rho_{df} \sigma_d \sigma_f)^{1/2}, \tag{2.2}$$

where σ_d is the standard deviation of the domestic security, s_f is the standard deviation of the foreign security, and ρ_{df} is the correlation coefficient between the returns of the domestic and foreign securities. Assume that the standard deviations of the domestic and foreign assets are $\sigma_d = 12\%$ and $\sigma_f = 20\%$, respectively, with the correlation of $\rho_{d,f} = -0.2$. If the portfolio is equally invested in the domestic and foreign assets, the standard deviation will be

$$\sigma_p = [(0.5)^2 (0.12)^2 + (0.5)^2(0.20)^2 + 2(0.5)(0.5)(-0.2)(0.12)(0.20)]^{1/2} = 10.58\%.$$

We observe that the international portfolio has less risk than either the domestic security or the foreign security. Although the example focuses only on one dimension, the risk, and although the numerical values lead to this particular conclusion, this is consistent with the generally observed conclusion of the risk advantage of international portfolios.

For a more comprehensive view of the financial performance of an investment, both characteristics, risk and profit, must be taken into account. We all know that we prefer high-profit investments and we also prefer low-risk investments. But there are many high-profit and high-risk investments. Also, there are many low-risk and low-profit investments. Consider

Investment A with a 10% profit potential and 12% standard deviation. Also consider Investment B with 12% profit potential and 15% standard deviation. Which investment is superior?

This is a commonly encountered issue in investments, and a good parameter that takes into account the attractiveness of profits and the unattractiveness of risk is the Sharpe ratio (S.R.), developed in 1966 and named after William Sharpe. The S.R. is defined as

$$Sharpe \ Ratio = \frac{E(R) - r_f}{\sigma}, \tag{2.3}$$

where $E(R)$ is the expected profit of the investment, r_f is the risk-free rate in the economy, and σ is the standard deviation, i.e., the risk of the investment. The S.R. is also known as the risk-adjusted return or the reward-to-risk ratio because the numerator is the excess return or the risk premium of the investment over the risk-free rate of return. And the denominator is the risk measurement, the standard deviation. The S.R. of an investment is supposed to be high because that would be indicative of high profit (the numerator is high), low risk (the denominator is low), or both. Money market managers, along with other types of investors, attempt to maximize the S.R. of their investments.

The S.R. is used to better compare domestic, foreign, and diversified global investments. As an example, assume that investment A is a domestic investment. Therefore, $E(R_{doemstic})$ = 10%, $\sigma_{domestic}$ = 12%, and $r_{f \ domestic}$ = 4%. Investment B is a foreign investment with $E(R_{foreign})$ = 12%, $\sigma_{foreign}$ = 15%, and $r_{f \ foreign}$ = 4%. Clearly, foreign investment has a higher profit potential, but it is also risky with a higher standard deviation. As a third investment alternative, consider a global investment with half of the funds invested in the domestic and half invested in the foreign opportunity ($w_{domestic}$ = $w_{foreign}$ = 0.5). The correlation coefficient between the returns of the domestic and foreign investments is $\rho_{dom,for}$ = 0.55. Given this information, we can calculate the S.R.s for the domestic and for foreign investment alternatives as

$$SR_{domestic} = \frac{0.10 - 0.04}{0.12} = 0.5000 \ \text{and}$$

$$SR_{foreign} = \frac{0.12 - 0.04}{0.15} = 0.5333 \ .$$

As for the global diversified portfolio, expected profit and risk from equations 2.1 and 2.2 are as follows:

$$E(R_{global}) = (0.5)(0.10) + (0.5)(0.12) = 11\%$$
$$\sigma_{global} = [(0.5)^2(0.12)^2 + (0.5)^2(0.15)^2 + (2)(0.5)(0.5)(0.55)(0.12)(0.15)]^{1/2} = 11.91\%$$

Then, the S.R. of the global investment is

$$SR_{global} = \frac{0.11 - 0.04}{0.1191} = 0.5888 \ .$$

We should note that the average risk-free rate for global investment is the weighted average of the risk-free rates in the two economies, (0.5)(0.04) + (0.5)(0.04), and it is 4%.

The quick inspection of the three S.R. values demonstrates the globally diversified invest-ment as the best investment alternative. This example again exemplifies the classic case for international diversification. While the numbers in the example helped obtain the highest S.R. for the globally diversified portfolio, empirical studies continually reach this same conclusion as a stylized fact. Investing in foreign assets allows to reduce risk and/or increase profit at the same time for a purely domestic investor.

The risk and return trade-off of internationally diversified versus domestic portfolios can be seen in Figure 2.2. The x-axis represents risk, while the y-axis represents expected return, or profit. In the context of the figure, the desirable investment is as much in the northwest direc-tion as possible because such a position would indicate low risk and high profit at the same time.

If only domestic securities are used, investors end up with a northwest limit called domes-tic efficient frontier in Figure 2.2. For a given standard deviation or risk level, an investor will come up with a portfolio with the highest possible profit, and the risk-profit combination will be a point on the domestic efficient frontier. When all domestic and international securities are available for an investor, the efficient frontier shifts more in the northwest direction because of additional investment opportunities and a larger spectrum of securities.

The global efficient frontier consists of superior portfolios compared to the domestic effi-cient frontier portfolios with higher profits for a given level of risk, lower risk for a given level of profit, or higher profits and lower risk at the same time. For example, global portfolio B in the figure has the same risk but a higher profit compared to domestic portfolio C. Or global portfolio A has the same profit but lower risk compared to portfolio C. Any portfolio on the global efficient frontier between A and B has a higher profit and lower risk combination and is superior to the domestic portfolio C. This is the classic benefit of international diversification.

Figure 2.2 considers all securities traded domestically and globally. Sometimes investors would like to choose certain asset classes, such as only equities or only fixed-income securi-ties. Even then, there are international diversification benefits. When an investor shifts from a

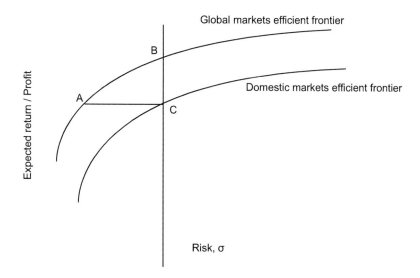

FIGURE 2.2 International Portfolios Versus Domestic Portfolios

domestic equity portfolio to an international equity portfolio, the first rule of thumb is to focus on an equity market whose returns have negative or low-positive correlations with the domestic equity market. Then the international portfolio will have a better profit-to-risk combination than that of the domestic portfolio.

Examination of the correlation characteristics to pick a foreign equity market involves quantitative analysis, and it is the first step of the strategy in creating a superior international portfolio. At the end of this first step, international equity candidates are determined. In the second step, the qualitative investigation follows. Potential candidates from the first step are evaluated from different perspectives, such as the history of the equity market, and the cultural, political, and economic conditions in the country and the region. All combined, the qualitative investigation pinpoints an ideal foreign equity market for international diversification. In the third step, the targeted investigation of quantitative and qualitative factors is finalized with the diversification decision. Such a three-step strategy can be applied to any asset class.

In table 2.1, correlations between the returns of developed equity market pairs are listed using monthly returns over the last five years. The three-step strategy for a U.S. equity investor wishing for an international equity portfolio starts by looking at the first column of the correlations between the U.S. equity market and foreign equity markets. Some candidates for international diversification are the Italian, Japanese, Hong Kong, and Swiss equity markets with low correlations. After the quantitative step, each candidate is qualitatively investigated. While the lowest correlation of the Japanese stock market is really attractive, the Japanese economy has been in continual stagnation since the late 1990s. The remarkable growth in the Japanese economy after the Second World War has turned Japan into one of the largest economies, but the growth has diminished. The Japanese government has lowered interest rates to almost zero and even to negative rates to literally force bank depositors to withdraw and use for innovative projects. The education system has been overhauled to promote creativity while continuing with the traditional goal of perfection. However, the markets remain stagnant and high-level profits are not experienced. Given these observations, perhaps the Japanese equity market is not the first choice.

The next candidate is Hong Kong. As a major hub of foreign direct investment, Hong Kong has been a finance center in Southeast Asia for decades, with major investment firms and multinational companies having a significant presence. But after the unification of China, some of the business rules and regulations have become more controlled. The original goal was to leave the economic system in Hong Kong autonomous, but the recent stricter controls and changing rules have led to local unrest. As a consequence, international investors have become hesitant, and other finance centers, such as Singapore, Seoul, Taiwan, and Bangkok, have started to take over. While the low correlation is certainly attractive, the political conditions lead to seeking an alternative.

The third candidate is the Italian equity markets. Italy is renowned for its creativity in design, art, fashion, luxury items, and automotive products, and the tourism industry is the best in the world. But there are serious economic problems. Italy has borrowed extensively over the years, and the danger of sovereign insolvency becomes a possibility from time to time. The financial crisis and global economic slowdown around 2007–2008 made matters worse. The inconsistency of the governing administration, numerous elections, short-term coalitions, and continual disagreements have made financial markets highly volatile. Perhaps the Italian equity market is not the first choice as a successful international alternative, even with a low correlation.

The next candidate in the qualitative analysis is the Swiss equity market. Switzerland is unique for many reasons. It is not part of the European Union, it takes a neutral stance on many political and economic issues, and it is considered to be a very safe and reliable county for banking services and fixed-income securities. The Swiss economy and political system are very stable. The higher education system guarantees quality professions for graduates. Swiss food items, tourism, and luxury products are known all around the world. These unique characteristics make the Swiss equity market an ideal choice for U.S. equity investors for international diversification.

Following the quantitative investigation and the qualitative investigation steps, the final step for the targeted investment decision is the Swiss equity market. It should be noted that the three-step decision process does involve subjective judgment, perhaps not for the quantitative analysis, but certainly for the qualitative analysis. A good finance professional must have the technical tools for quantitative investigation but also the knowledge, insight, and expertise for subjective qualitative investigation. With all of these combined together, the final targeted investment decision is made and successfully defended.

Similar analyses can be conducted for other types of financial markets. It is also important to note that even though the diversification analysis was based on the U.S. as the domestic country, similar principles can be applied to any investor with a different home country base. The quantitative step generates the correlation matrix and potential candidates. The qualitative step examines each candidate from political, economic, historical, cultural, regional, and global perspectives. The candidates are narrowed down, and in the third step, the targeted investment choice is finalized.

2.5 THE CASE AGAINST INTERNATIONAL DIVERSIFICATION

Even though the traditional case for international diversification is quite strong, investors have still not fully subscribed to globalization and to internationally fully diversified portfolios. Home bias puzzle (i.e., the tendency of investors to overweight their portfolios with domestic securities) is commonplace. Why is this so? In this section, we examine the case against international diversification and consider the reasons why international diversification may not be preferred.

2.5.1 Integration of Markets Around the World

One of the most important reasons behind international diversification has been the different characteristics inherent in foreign markets. Such differences, due to geographical locations, political and economic systems, types of industries and companies, and products and production processes, have led to low and even negative correlations leading to high profits and low returns observed in internationally diversified portfolios.

But over the last few decades, as economic cooperation has increased around the world, international frictions, such as tariffs, tax disadvantages, and customs fees, have been lowered. These closer relationships have led to increased integration of markets around the world. Markets that used to be segmented and different have become more similar to each other. Capital mobility across the border has increased substantially, especially among developed countries. International correlations between markets have increased substantially as a result of these similarities and further deregulation, free trade, and globalization of corporations.

TABLE 2.1 Correlations of Global Equity Markets (Using Monthly Returns from January 2010 through December 2020)

	US	Australia	Hong Kong	Italy	Japan	Holland	Sweden	Switzer-land	UK	Canada	France	Germany	EAFE	World
US	1.0000													
Australia	0.7070	1.0000												
Hong Kong	0.6382	0.5431	1.0000											
Italy	0.6551	0.6394	0.5005	1.0000										
Japan	0.6787	0.5230	0.4121	0.5942	1.0000									
Holland	0.7711	0.6203	0.5391	0.7818	0.6619	1.0000								
Sweden	0.7731	0.6379	0.5968	0.6828	0.6525	0.8073	1.0000							
Switzerland	0.7029	0.5711	0.3906	0.6464	0.6295	0.7321	0.6571	1.0000						
UK	0.7672	0.7041	0.6215	0.7041	0.5735	0.7448	0.7159	0.6725	1.0000					
Canada	0.8073	0.7598	0.6040	0.6312	0.5133	0.6499	0.6781	0.5748	0.7391	1.0000				
France	0.7877	0.7299	0.6073	0.8833	0.6777	0.8771	0.8361	0.7192	0.8252	0.7375	1.0000			
Germany	0.7847	0.6569	0.5888	0.7857	0.6831	0.8437	0.8503	0.6812	0.7516	0.7086	0.8949	1.0000		
EAFE	0.8760	0.7430	0.7097	0.8049	0.7169	0.7790	0.7835	0.6949	0.8225	0.7462	0.8714	0.8247	1.0000	
World	0.9742	0.7520	0.6964	0.7401	0.7104	0.7943	0.7981	0.7136	0.8138	0.8149	0.8464	0.8240	0.9597	1.0000

Source: Compustat Global Data M.S.C.I. Indices

Even more interesting, correlations between international markets tend to increase during crisis periods. International diversification benefits diminish when most needed. This phenomenon is called correlation breakdown.

While the correlation breakdown, i.e., increasing correlations between markets has reduced and has sometimes eliminated diversification benefits in recent years, the counterargument is its dynamic and evolving nature. As markets become highly correlated and diversification benefits vanish, traders shift from international to domestic portfolios. And when market segmentations begin, the differences between markets start to emerge again, making international markets attractive again: traders shift from domestic to international portfolios. Then markets start becoming correlated; the ebbs-and-flows cycle continues. For more information on this subject, an interesting article in the *Wall Street Journal* is recommended (www.wsj.com/articles/falling-correlations-spell-opportunity-for-investors-1487241004?reflink=desktopwebshare_permalink).

2.5.2 Barriers to International Investment

There are additional reasons that work against international investments:

(1) Lack of knowledge about foreign markets: Many international markets have unique characteristics. Differences in the language, culture, customs, trading systems and procedures, time zones, and reporting requirements all make it difficult for an outside investor to choose a foreign market. Professional investors hire locals to deal with these issues.

(2) Political risk: Many international financial markets are in countries with different political traditions and systems. While some are welcomed for diversification, unstable political, economic, or monetary environments are undesirable.

(3) Market inefficiencies: Many international markets have inefficiencies, especially if they are not from developed countries. Liquidity problems because of a lack of enough market participants, delays and costs of capital flows and fund transfers across borders, and deviations of security prices from their correct values for long periods are some examples.

(4) Insider trading: There are regulations all around the world that prohibit insiders from trading shares of their companies using private information. Unfortunately, lack of reinforcement results in unfair and unethical treatment, keeping international investors away.

(5) Currency risk: International investments involve the conversion of funds into a foreign currency. When the international investment concludes, the proceeds are converted back into the domestic currency. Exchange rates are dynamic and foreign investments are subject to currency risks. The currency movements sometimes enhance foreign investments and sometimes reduce profits. The uncertainty in currency movements presents an additional challenge to global diversification.

(6) Regulations: Foreign investors, foreign direct investment, multinational companies are generally subject to additional layers of regulations. It is sometimes tougher to transfer funds from domestic to foreign markets and back. The investment periods may be mandated to be longer than the investor wishes. The foreign investor may have to keep a portion of the profits within the foreign country, may have to hire local help and/or open a local office, and may be required to visit the foreign country regularly.

(7) Taxes: International investors, multinational enterprises, and foreign corporations may be subject to stricter and heavier taxation. This can happen either in their domestic countries, foreign countries, or both.

(8) Transaction costs: It has become convenient to access foreign financial markets over the last couple of decades with globalization, the rise of the internet, and online brokerage companies. These days it is easier to research and learn about foreign financial markets and companies. Trading foreign securities have become easier as well. However, transaction costs can still be higher because of additional fees in international research, communications, data subscriptions, and differences in accounting systems.

Barriers to international investments are numerous indeed. Two decades ago, they were more substantial. Today, they are less formidable. In the future, they will become minimal.

2.6 EMERGING MARKETS

A large group of alternatives for international diversification is emerging markets and, to a lesser extent, frontier markets. Emerging markets are fast-growing countries with robust economies and financial markets. These countries have a lot of catching up to do to reach developed countries. The G.D.P. growth rate of these countries is indeed very high, but this growth rate is not consistent. A few years of high G.P.D. growth might be followed by a significant negative growth rate. These differences and variations lead emerging markets generally to have positive but low correlations with developed markets.

Overall, expected profits are potentially very large in emerging markets. But so are local risks stemming from the volatility of economic performance, additional liquidity problems, political uncertainties, and highly fluctuating financial markets. For all practical purposes and from recent history, investment risk in emerging economies often springs from financial crises and government policy decisions. Two currency-related crises are the Mexican peso crisis of 1994 and the Asian financial crisis of 1997. In the former, the sudden devaluation of the peso led to extreme inflation, the collapse of the banking system, the flight to quality away from Mexican financial markets, and the spread of the crisis to other emerging economies. In the latter, the sudden collapse of the Thai currency baht led to a chain reaction in other Southeast Asian countries, ultimately triggering abnormal debt-to-G.D.P. ratios, collage of credit markets, and substantial capital flights away from the region.

Before deciding to diversify into emerging markets, we need to explore emerging market risks, emerging market profits, the overall performance of emerging market financial markets relative to developed markets, and different categories of emerging markets.

2.6.1 Emerging Market Risks

Emerging markets are associated with additional sources of uncertainty. These additional sources automatically push emerging markets as higher-risk alternatives. The first source of additional risk is the non-uniformity and asymmetric nature of returns and profits. A few years of reasonable positive returns might be followed by an enormous loss. Or reasonable returns might be followed by an abnormally high-profit year with no apparent reason. The second additional risk is due to the fast growth in emerging markets. Existing infrastructure often cannot keep up with economic activity and may limit growth. It is sometimes seen in China, for example, that miles of transportation vehicles are waiting for the end of the new highway construction. The third source of additional risk is the unfortunate higher probability of corruption and lack of enforcement of the law. The fourth source of additional risk may be the poor regulation of the financial, banking, and economic systems, often leading to distrust and undercapitalization. The fifth source of additional risk is the high volatility of currency dynamics. The state of the economy and political decisions generate accentuated volatility in financial markets and currency movements.

2.6.2 Emerging Market Returns

Emerging country economies grow faster than those of developed nations. As barriers have declined, liberalization of international trade regulations, political reforms, capital flows, and foreign direct investment increased the demand for emerging financial markets and securities.

Emerging markets have also increased in efficiency over the years with the enforcement of rules and regulations. Increased interest and research activity on financial securities, coupled with the application of stricter standards of market supervision, all contributed to efficiency. This, in turn, has increased the confidence of foreign investors to participate in emerging markets.

Regulators generally recognize the importance of being part of the global financial community in attracting foreign capital. Therefore, many emerging country administrations have adopted international accounting standards, procedures, and regulations. Furthermore, many financial securities have been repackaged into investable funds or indexes commensurate with international standards.

It is true that there are still a lot of risks and restrictions in emerging markets. Foreign ownership is restricted, repatriation of income and funds is limited, discriminatory taxes are unpleasant, and the need for authorized local representatives is costly. But even with these restrictions, emerging markets provide great returns and more than compensate for the restrictions and risks.

To verify that emerging market returns and profits are indeed higher than alternatives, the performance of developed markets and the performance of emerging markets are depicted in Figure 2.3, both denominated in U.S. dollars. The M.S.C.I. Emerging Markets Index is based on more than 25 emerging markets, with the Shanghai Stock Exchange having the dominant weight (more than 40%). The M.S.C.I. Developed Markets Index consists of 25 developed markets, with the U.S. equity markets having the dominant weight (more than 65%). The graphs cover the last two decades. The higher cumulative wealth generated from emerging markets is clear. The developed equity markets have generated a return of 165%, while emerging markets have provided 316% return during the last 20 years from May 2001 to May 2021.

The definite conclusion is that emerging markets should be used for international diversification purposes. Emerging markets are highly risky, but over time, they provide much higher profits. We should also keep in mind that for shorter time periods, returns fluctuate, and developed markets might generate higher returns. Also, the indices in the figure did not take

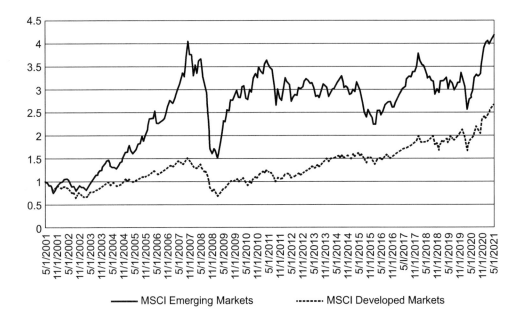

FIGURE 2.3 Performances of Developed Markets and Emerging Markets

dividends into account. Overall, we can confidently say that emerging markets should be part of international diversification, with long investment horizons, such as 20 years.

2.6.3 Emerging Market Alternatives

Emerging markets have a wide range of characteristics. Some of them have more risk than others. Some are expected to generate sooner, while others are expected to generate large profits further ahead into the future. Some markets are smaller, while others a quite large.

The first group of countries, known as B.R.I.C.(S.), is assumed to be fully developed financially and economically in the very near future. Brazil, Russia, India, China, and South Africa have fast-growing economies. These countries provide good profit opportunities with tolerable levels of risk compared to other emerging countries.

The second group of countries follows B.R.I.C.(S.) countries. Mexico, Indonesia, Nigeria, South Korea, and Turkey (M.I.N.T. and M.I.S.T.) exhibit rapid economic growth but with occasional severe crises. Risks are significantly higher, but profit potentials are also significantly high, expected to materialize 10 to 25 years down the road.

The third group exhibits the standard risk and return characteristics of emerging markets. These countries encounter significant growth in one year, then substantial losses the following year. High risks are accompanied by high potential profits. In the long term, up years dominate the down years.

The last group of frontier countries represents very small and highly illiquid markets. Even though the economic and financial infrastructures may be well-established, they also have the highest risks compared to other emerging countries. Investors who have a tolerance for risk and are looking for speculative opportunities with high-profit potentials would prefer this group.

2.7 FUTURE TRENDS IN INTERNATIONAL FINANCE

Finance academicians and researchers around the world occasionally get together in large conferences to meet, network, and present their ideas, innovations, and novel research. One of the most important such conferences is the American Finance Association (A.F.A.) Conference. At the 2017 A.F.A. Conference in Chicago, one panel titled 'Nobels on Where Is the World Economy Headed' was really unique. All five participants were Nobel laureates: Angus Deaton, Roger Myerson, Edmund Phelps, Robert J. Shiller, and Joseph E. Stiglitz presented their views about the globalization of the world economy, the current state and the future changes in artificial intelligence and machine learning, and the upcoming shift of the workforce to skill-based creative professions as automation replaces traditional manual labor. The link to the video for the session is www.aeaweb.org/webcasts/2017/nobels, and it is a great webcast to learn the views of the best researchers about the future of global finance and international economics.

Financial securities markets and exchanges have investors from all over the world these days. The exchange hours are widening to accommodate traders in different parts of the world. For example, the New York Stock Exchange has added after-hours trading to answer such requests. Securities are offered in multiple markets so that interested investors can trade them at locations closer to their time zones. As Asian physical exchanges close for the day, European exchanges open up for trading, and as these exchanges reach their closing time, American exchanges start to operate for the day. And as American securities exchanges stop trading for the day, Asian markets start to open with a couple of hours of delay.

The secondary markets using computer networks have much more flexibility in terms of opening hours or trade executions from around the world. For example, futures markets have underlying securities that are interesting for everyone around the world, such as precious metals, agricultural food products, and energy sources. These financial securities are traded all around the world 24 hours a day through an electronic trading platform called Globex.

2.8 GLOBAL MARKET PARTICIPANTS, INVESTMENT STRATEGIES, PERFORMANCE MEASUREMENTS

2.8.1 Global Financial Markets Participants

There are different types of investors who choose international markets. The first group is *private investors*. These wealthy individuals and entities are specialized in international investments and generally use their own funds to finance diversified global investments. The second group represents *institutional investors*. These powerful organizations, such as pension funds, endowments, foundations, and insurance companies, construct portfolios and strategies utilizing global markets. The third group is highly sophisticated and knowledgeable professional investors managing mutual funds or hedge funds. Their primary responsibility is to enhance the financial welfare of their clients, and they design strategies that include global markets and opportunities.

There are other participants in global financial markets as well. For example, *brokers* enable international transactions and order execution. Sell-side brokers/analysts conduct research to provide international recommendations to the clients of their brokerage companies. Buy-side brokers/analysts work for professional or institutional investors and invest globally for them. *Consultants and advisors* who are experts in the area of global financial markets and international opportunities. They charge substantial fees for their advice, services, and recommendations. Similarly, *custodians* are financial institutions or individual experts with legal responsibility for their clients' international investments.

2.8.2 Global Investment Strategies

The tactical decisions related to global investments are not much different than standard investment strategies and tactics. Some common international investment philosophies are as follows:

(1) Passive approach: The goal is to create the international portfolio and keep it stable and as is over a long period. This way, transaction costs due to frequent trading are avoided.
(2) Active approach: The international investor frequently buys and sells international securities. The transaction costs are substantially higher, but the profits are supposed to more than offsets such costs.
(3) Balanced versus specialized: The investor picks a variety of international investment opportunities from a wide spectrum of securities with roughly equivalent weights. In the specialized approach, the investor concentrates on only a few dimensions. Perhaps investing in only one type of financial security.
(4) Industry or country approach: Depending on the expertise of the investor, securities of only one/two countries or of one industry (technology) are picked.
(5) Top-down or bottom-up approach: In the top-down approach, the investor investigates the world's economic/financial conditions, followed by the analysis of the country, then the industry, and finally the specific security in that industry. If the overall analysis is positive, the investor purchases the security or otherwise sells or short-sells. In the bottom-up approach, the order of analysis is reversed.
(6) Currency: Some investors are specialized in currency dynamics and understand how certain factors affect future currency values. Taking long positions in currencies that appreciate in the future and taking short positions in currencies that depreciate in the future consistently generates profits for investors such as George Soros. Quantum Fund and Soros Fund Management design strategies based on currency movements.
(7) Quantitative versus subjective: The quantitative approach uses sophisticated mathematical models and algorithms to design international investment strategies. The subjective approach uses qualitative factors, such as experience; cultural, political, or economic perspectives; and interviews with policymakers, regulators, and corporate managers to develop international trading strategies. The holistic approach of using both quantitative and subjective approaches jointly would be the best strategy.

Whatever the global strategy and whomever the global investor, there will always be constraints and limitations. Liquidity requirements are one of these constraints. If a British investor needs cash urgently, it would not be wise to buy a condo in Spain because real estate is not a liquid asset class. Time horizon is another constraint. If the investor will need cash in three years, the investment horizon is limited to three years. Tax concerns limit the investment spectrum. Someone in a high tax bracket looks for opportunities associated with lower taxes. Legal and regulatory factors may be another constraint – foreign investors are often subject to extra layers of rules. Finally, unique circumstances may influence international decisions. For example, an investor may prefer not to invest in a country with human rights problems.

2.8.3 Global Performance Evaluation

International investments need to be evaluated regularly so that adjustments can be made. During these performance evaluations, the chief performance measurement is profits or returns. But the risk associated with the investment must not be ignored. Under normal circumstances, on average, riskier investments must provide higher profits to compensate for the extra uncertainty. These contrasting factors, profit and risk, are jointly taken into account in the Sharpe ratio. The investment with the higher Sharpe ratio has a better performance compared to other investments.

Another method for global performance measurement is to compare the returns and profits of international investment with a proper benchmark. The proper benchmark would be an alternative with the same risk characteristics and with similar assets. There are numerous international benchmark indexes created and maintained by research companies, such as Ibbotson Associates, now part of Morningstar.

Finally, when measuring the performance of international investments, attributions of the performance must also be considered. The unique investment decisions taken by the decision-maker and the subjective and qualitative criteria used throughout the decision processes must be examined to get the full picture of global investment performance.

2.9 INTERNATIONAL CORPORATE FINANCE

Multinational corporations constantly make investment decisions regarding international projects. These decisions involve net present value (N.P.V.) analyses of those projects, but in an international context, the currency dynamics add a complicating layer. In picking and choosing the most profitable projects, two different N.P.V. approaches are used, but one is superior.

Consider a U.S. firm analyzing a project in the Netherlands. The U.S. firm starts with local U.S. dollar funds and converts to euros for the investment outlay. The future cash flows will be in euros. How do we evaluate the project? There are two ways to calculate the N.P.V.:

In method 1, common with many multinationals, the U.S. firm organizes all the capital budgeting calculations in U.S. dollars. The investment cost and the estimated future euro cash flows are converted to U.S. dollar equivalents using the spot exchange rate and projected exchange rates at each future cash flow time point. The future dollar cash flow estimates are discounted to the present using the U.S. dollar cost of capital to determine the N.P.V.

Method 2 calculates the N.P.V. entirely, focusing on euros. The future euro cash flows are discounted using the euro cost of capital. Once the euro N.P.V. is calculated, the U.S. dollar N.P.V. is found using the then spot exchange rate. Method 2 avoids having to make forecasts and projections of the exchange rate. And this is the superiority of method 2. Forecasting exchange rates is notoriously difficult, and method 2 bypasses the need to forecast future exchange rates. Therefore, the N.P.V. calculation using method 2 is more reliable. Method 1, on the other hand, uses the projected exchange rates that contain significant estimation uncertainty. This causes the N.P.V. calculation using method 1 less reliable.

2.10 SUMMARY AND CONCLUSION

International finance is an exciting and fast-growing area of investment. In this chapter, we explored several important perspectives on international investments. After a quick history of international commerce differences due to different legal systems, the chapter focused on the main issue: international diversification of investments. The rich availability of alternative international investments outside of the U.S. for an investment was followed with a detailed examination of the traditional case for international diversification. To complete the full picture, the counterarguments against international diversification, such as increased integration of markets around the world and barriers to international investments, were described.

A large area of international investments involves emerging markets. The chapter discussed emerging markets in detail with the risk and return characteristics and different alternatives of emerging markets. The future trends in international finance, the characteristics of global market participants, strategies, and performance measurement tools are explained. Finally, international corporate finance and project investment decisions of multinational enterprises are outlined.

REFERENCES AND ADDITIONAL READING

La Porta, R., Lopez-de-Silanes, F., Shleifer, A., Vishny, R.W. 1998. Law and Finance. *Journal of Political Economy*, 106, 1113–1155.

Sharpe, W.F. 1964. Capital Asset Prices: Theory of Market Equilibrium. *Journal of Finance*, 19, 425–442.

Sharpe, W.F. 1966. Mutual Fund Performance. *Journal of Business*, 39, 119–138.

Solnik, B.H. 1974. Why Not Diversify Internationally Rather than Domestically? *Financial Analysts Journal*, 30, 48–54.

Solnik, B.H., McLeavey, D. 2003. *Global Investments*. 6th edition. Boston, MA, Pearson – Prentice Hall.

CHAPTER 3

Financial Crises

Reasons, Consequences, Lessons

OBJECTIVES

- Categorize the common characteristics of financial crises.
- Analyze the 2007–2008 financial crisis. Summarize the history of the events leading to the crisis, and assess the derivatives created from subprime mortgages.
- Categorize the characteristics, advantages, disadvantages, flaws, and lack of transparency in the creation and marketing of mortgage-backed securities.
- Appraise the great recession; relate the consequences/aftermath of the financial crisis.
- Justify the countermeasures by the Federal Reserve, the U.S. government, and the largest financial institutions; the new rules, regulations, and policy decisions; and the lessons learned by financial institutions, large multinational companies, and investors.
- Evaluate how risk management must change in order to avoid future crises.
- Categorize and compare the list of infamous global, domestic, firm-based, and industry-/economy-wide financial disasters.

3.1 INTRODUCTION

Financial crises have been part of the history of markets. Market participants are assumed to be consistent, rational profit maximizers. But we humans are complex organisms. We do not always act rationally. In fact, we act irrationally quite frequently, not only with financial decisions but in all aspects of life, both as individuals and as a society. We are not robots; we have complicated psychological characteristics.

Our irrational behaviors manifest in different ways. For example, a positive event, such as a profitable investment decision, may lead to knowing it all: we are experts in financial markets! This is known as irrational exuberance. On the opposite end, one wrong decision may lead us into a depression: we know nothing at all about markets! This is irrational sadness.

DOI: 10.4324/9781003213697-3

Society at large may exhibit these types of irrational psychological behaviors. In fact, Warren Buffett terms this as 'the nutty stock market'. On a typical day, the stock price of a company constantly ticks up and down. The primary reason is the arrival of new information – positive news pushes the price up, and negative news pulls the price down. But another important reason is the overreactions and underreactions of market participants to new information. Thus, the price constantly readjusts. When the majority of market participants irrationally and unjustifiably become optimistic, demand across the board increases, prices go up, and bubbles form. And when bubbles burst, we have a financial crisis.

There are many examples of these financial crises. In the late 1980s and early 1990s, high-yield and high-risk bonds (junk bonds) became very popular. The high demand from individuals, professional investors, and even pension funds pushed the prices to unprecedented levels. The irrational aggregate demand ignored important characteristics – namely, the high risk associated with the bonds. The slowdown in the economy in the early 1990s started a chain reaction: the inability to pay the high coupons. The collapse of the junk bond market is known as the savings and loan crisis (S&L crisis). About one-third of the savings institutions and pension funds collapsed, and many others significantly suffered.

Another example of the bursting of the irrational exuberance bubble is known as the 2000–2001 dot-com bubble. Many internet companies, communication firms, and high-tech organizations related to the rise of the internet were irrationally given extraordinarily high valuation. Even without any positive earnings estimates and with the then current large losses, the high demand appreciated prices. Once the economic slowdown started, the bubble burst and a large number of these internet companies went bankrupt in a very short time span.

The third example is the main theme of this chapter, the 2007–2008 financial crisis stemming from the collapse of the highly inflated real estate market in the U.S. Starting with the 2000s, low interest/mortgage rates and irrationally high demand for houses pushed real estate prices to unseen levels. When the real estate bubble started to burst in 2006, the chain reaction was the collapse of financial securities based on housing prices and mortgages and the bankruptcy of financial giants, institutional investors, and individual investors that had heavily invested in these financial securities. The crisis turned into the severest recession in the U.S. since the Great Depression of the 1930s and expanded into a global recession.

The psychological characteristics of market participants and over-/underreactions at individual or aggregate levels have led to the creation of a new field: behavioral finance/economics. The forefront researchers have been Amos Tversky and Daniel Kahneman. While the chapter touches on the exciting field of behavioral finance, the primary focus will be the discussion of the financial crisis of 2007–2008.

The brief history of the events, the securitization process, financial securities created from subprime mortgages, and the misuse and misrepresentation of securitized products will be discussed. The evolution of risk management to avoid future crises will be explored.

3.2 REAL ESTATE MARKET IN THE U.S.

The valuations of the U.S. real estate markets have been measured by the well-known Case-Shiller Index. This index was created in the 1980s by Allan Weiss, Karl Case, and Robert

Shiller. There are different versions of the index, such as the national home price index and the 10-city and 20-city composite index. These index data are available at the St. Louis Federal Reserve F.R.E.D. (Federal Reserve Economics Data) system (https://fred.stlouisfed.org/series/CSUSHPINSA). The U.S. real estate prices based on S&P/Case-Shiller U.S. National Home Price Index (1987–2021) are in Figure 3.1.

Real estate prices started to increase at an exponential pace, starting with the 2000s, reaching a peak in the middle of 2006, and then took a nosedive. Why did housing prices rise at such a dramatic pace in the first half of the 2000s? And why did the bubble burst?

Starting in 2000, mortgage creators started to relax their lending standards in the U.S. This created large numbers of subprime/risky/low-quality mortgages for first-time home buyers. The relaxed lending standards combined with very low interest rates increased the demand for real estate. The construction and homebuilding sectors could not keep up, so housing prices rose significantly. Mortgage companies and lenders continued to relax their lending standards further to continue to attract first-time buyers and keep on creating mortgage loans. These activities kept prices increasing further. There came a point in the mid-2000s when the main features of mortgage loans had become

(1) 100% mortgages: Normally, mortgage agreements require the home buyer to make a down payment of 20–30% of the house value and borrow the remainder in the form of a mortgage. But in the mid-2000s, down payment requirements were often bypassed, and the buyer could borrow the entire value of the house.

(2) Adjustable rate mortgages (A.R.M.s): The monthly mortgage payments fluctuate with these A.R.M.s. The mortgage rates are tied to certain interest rates. As interest rates fluctuate,

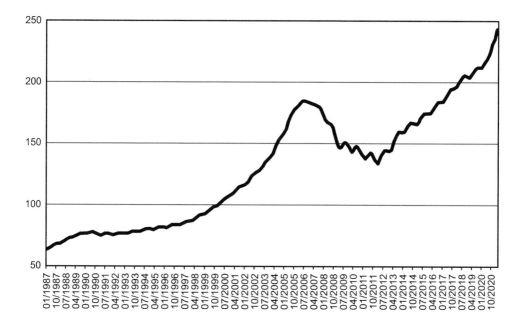

FIGURE 3.1 S&P/Case-Shiller U.S. National Home Price Index Data from F.R.E.D. St. Louis

so do the mortgage payments: an extra layer of risk to the homebuyer. As monthly mortgage payments fluctuate because of changing rates, budget planning becomes difficult. And if interest rates go up across the board, so do the mortgage rates and the mortgage payments. Low and attractive initial A.R.M.s become extremely unattractive. The home buyer may even end up foregoing the house because of the inability to pay the high monthly mortgages.

(3) Teaser rate mortgages: These mortgages can be treacherous. The initial rate may be very low for the first few years of the life of the mortgage. The house buyer may be focused on the low rates since the initial payments after the house purchase would be based on them. Once the teaser rate period is over, the rest of the life of the mortgage would be associated with substantially and sometimes unreasonably higher rates. This information would be part of the mortgage agreement but would be lost in the fine print or within the multitude of loan documents. The buyer would happily pay the monthly mortgage during the teaser period but might eventually have to give up the house during the higher rate period.

(4) N.I.N.J.N.A. loans: When someone buys a house, the mortgage lender conducts a thorough search about the financial reliability of the buyer. The buyer is expected to have a reliable job, stable income, good credit standing, and additional assets. In the mid-2000s, all these reliability requirements were put aside. Mortgage loans known as N.I.N.J.N.A. (no income, no job, no asset) had become commonplace. Mortgage firms were giving out loans to financially unstable buyers.

(5) Non-recourse loans: Most mortgages are known as non-recourse loans. The collateral asset mentioned and recorded in the loan process (i.e., the house) is the only asset that can be claimed by the lender. These types of non-recourse loans are favorable to borrowers. If the homebuyer can no longer keep the mortgage payment obligations, the lender can only get the house in the non-recourse loan, even if the house value at that point is much less than the remainder of the remaining balance of the mortgage. The lender would have no claim, the other assets of the homebuyer. It seemed as though the mortgage companies put themselves at further risk by limiting claims to collaterals if home buyers reneged on mortgage agreements.

The common denominator of these mortgage characteristics in the mid-2000s was that mortgage companies were willingly placing themselves in extremely risky positions by giving out loans to potential buyers who did not have financial reliability. The characteristics of the loans made them difficult to pay off fully by the borrowers. In case of a default, the mortgage company could only claim the house. If the value of the house were higher at that point compared to the remaining balance of the loan, that would have been financially okay for the mortgage company, and many times that was the implicit assumption. On the other hand, if the house value at default were significantly lower, that would have been a serious detriment for the mortgage company. The latter possibility materialized during the second half of the 2000s and during the financial crisis.

Why were the mortgage companies following highly risky lending policies in the mid-2000s? The reason was that these speculative mortgage loans were repackaged and converted into different financial products and securities. And these new products were sold to other investors. The high risks associated with the mortgages did not stay with the original lenders; the mortgage firms essentially became conduits and intermediaries of the mortgage loan process. Home buyers were effectively borrowing from other investors.

Under this setting, the securitized mortgages had to be attractive to other investors. Even though the original mortgage had extremely risky characteristics, they were not accurately reflected in the risk characteristics of the new securitized product. Investment companies, banks, and professional investors found it profitable to invest in these new products because the A.A.A.-rated portions promised significantly higher returns than those offered by standard A.A.A.-rated bonds. The demand for structured products, especially for the A.A.A.-rated portion, continued to increase at a dramatic pace until the real estate bubble burst from the middle of 2006 into the beginning of 2007. With the collapse of real estate prices, many home buyers found their houses worth much less than the outstanding parts of the mortgages. These home buyers opted to stop the mortgage payments and left their houses. Additionally, when the teaser rates ended, many home buyers could not afford to make their mortgage payments. The houses were abandoned, and mortgage banks reclaimed them. These foreclosures increased the supply of houses just as the demand was slowing. House prices continued to decrease, and the real estate market continued to collapse in this vicious cycle.

The structured products that were in high demand because of their seemingly safe and A.A.A.-rated nature stopped providing their periodic income since the payments were tied to the then-vanished original mortgage payments. All of a sudden, the true high-risk characteristics of these structured products came to light. The collapse of the real estate market, the lethargic equity markets, and the slowdown of the economy commenced a mass movement of 'flight to quality'. Credit spreads increased to extremely high levels. The securitized products lost all of their allure. Companies and professionals heavily invested in these securities could not offload them and had to helplessly observe the value shrink. Huge losses led to financial insolvencies and eventual bankruptcies. The domino effect led to the collapse of other financially unstable firms. The U.S. failures triggered a global slowdown and a severe recession all around the globe.

Traditionally, the banking industry has always funded loans to small and medium enterprises, mom-and-pop shops, farmers, and other entities using customer deposits. Securitization has increased the pace of lending. The loan provided to the borrower (hence, the bond held by the bank) is repackaged into a different financial security and sold to an investor, and the proceeds are lent to a new borrower. The second loan is repackaged, sold, and the proceeds are lent to a third borrower. The 'lending – repackaging – selling the repackaged security' cycle is repeated theoretically indefinitely as long as the borrowers fulfill their responsibilities.

The new products should have the same risk and return characteristics as the original loans, but the bank has some leeway for adjustments. For example, a large group of original bonds of medium risk level can be packaged into three different structured product groups – low risk, medium risk, and high risk – where the weighted average of the risks will equal the original risk. Also, the weighted average of the new payments will be equal to the payments of the original loans. The restructured products are advertised and sold to investors whose risk and profit profiles fit the structured products. This way, the original borrowers owe to these new investors through the restructured products. The bank remains the intermediate, helping with the transfer of the payments.

If the borrowers cannot make their loan payments, this system will start to show cracks. And during a wider (national or global) problem, the entire system might crumble, which is what happened in the 2007–2008 financial crisis.

3.3 OPERATIONAL SETTING OF THE MORTGAGE ENVIRONMENT IN THE MID-2000S

To understand the full operational setting of the mortgage environment and the problems leading to the collapse, we can refer to the visual settings in figure 3.2 through figure 3.4. Figure 3.2 is about the initial transactions. Figure 3.3 is about the short-term performance of the system in a healthy and expanding economy. Figure 3.4 is about the long-term consequences once an economic slowdown or a real estate market dip occurs.

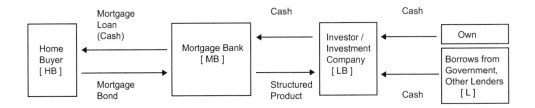

1. (a) HB purchases a house
   (b) Borrows from MB by:
   (c) Selling a Mortgage Bond to MB with 5% (for example) coupon rate

2. (a) MB gets the Mortgage Bond
   (b) Securitizes this mortgage into a Structured Derivative Product (SDP) through a Special Purpose Vehicle process and creates:
   Asset Backed Security (ABS) or,
   Collateralized Debt Obligation (CDO) or,
   Mortgage Backed Security (MBS) or,
   Collateralized Mortgage Obligation (CMO)
   (c) The SDP is
   Rated AAA (is the rating justified?)
   Offers 3% (for example) coupon rate (which is to be higher rate than other AAA products in the market)

3. (a) The SPD is sold to LB
   (b) LB loves, demands, and buys more of SDP with
   Own Cash
   Borrowed loan from Government
   Borrowed loan from Financial Institutions

FIGURE 3.2 First Movement – Initial Transactions

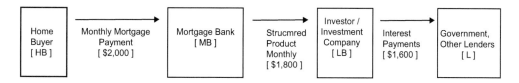

1. HB makes the regular monthly mortgage payment of $2,000 (for example) to the MB

2. (a) MB receives $2,000 from the HB
   (b) MB makes a payment of $1,800 (for example) to LB
   (c) MB always received more from HB than what it pays to LB. The difference is guaranteed profit for the MB
   (d) The payment for the Structured Product is higher than the payments of securities with similar risk in the market

3. (a) LB received $1,800 from the MB
   (b) LB makes a payment of $1,600 (for example) to the L
   (b) LB is happy with the Structured Product because the monthly income is higher from other securities with similar risk level.

4. (a) L is gets the interest income related to the loan provided to LB

FIGURE 3.3 Second Movement – Short-Term with Healthy and Expanding Economy

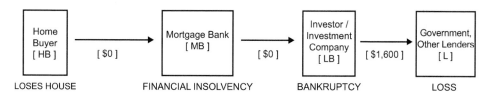

1. HB loses the house because:
   (a) HB did not have enough assets, income, or a job. The income stopped because the HM lost the job, and/or
   (b) End of teaser rates changed monthly mortgage payment from $2,000 to $3 ,000 which has become unaffordable, and/or
   (c) House Value now is less than the remaining mortgage balance
   Beginning: (1) Home value: $600k
   (2) Mortgage loan: $480k because the HM made a 20% down payment of $120k
   Now: (I) Home value: $350k (real estate market collapsed)
   (2) Mortgage loan: $400k ($80k of principal of the loan has been paid off)

2. MB had a neutral position as a conduit. But the misleading information on the Stntctured Product, especially about the risk characteristics led to severe loss of reputation and eventual fmancial insolvency (no-one wanted to do business with anymore)

3. LB went bankntpt because:
   (a) No income from the heavily invested Stntctured Product
   (b) Had to make regular payments to the L
   (c) No funds left within LB after a short duration

4. L had losses and therefore financial difficulty because LB could not make the interest payments on the loan
   (a) L takes LB to court; litigation costs; legal bankruptcy; funds divided amongst L entities

FIGURE 3.4 Third Movement – Long-Term with Economic Slowdown and Real Estate Decline

The figures explain the mortgage lending process, the restructuring and marketing of the mortgages, and the long-term consequences as the economy evolves from healthy to poor. Starting with figure 3.2, the crucial points to note are as follows:

(1) The mortgage bank gives a loan to the home buyer at a higher interest rate, while the structured product sold to the investment company is associated with a lower-interest payment. The difference is the net profit for the mortgage bank.
(2) The mortgage bank becomes a conduit, or intermediary, in this process. The entire risk of the original mortgage is shifted into the structured product and sold to the investment company.
(3) The first two points transform the mortgage company into a derivatives creator. The main purpose shifts into enticing home buyers of any quality to purchase houses by providing loans, converting the loans into structured products with any risk/profit assignments, and selling to investment companies and professional investors who are not aware of the actual features of the structured products.
(4) The structured product created by the mortgage bank has to have risk and profit characteristics that should be based on consistent mathematical models. But in the mid-2000s, following the rules became less important and assigning the characteristics of the structured product became arbitrary. For example, assigning an A.A.A. rating to a structured product derived from a subprime mortgage bond without any theoretical or mathematical justification is common.
(5) The structured derivative products (with higher payment given their risk) are attractive to investors and investment companies. Many investors use all their funds and borrow substantially from other lenders to invest even more.

Figure 3.3 provides details about how the setup works in the short term if the economy is expanding and the real estate market valuations continue to go up. In this setting, the home buyer makes the monthly mortgage payments. The mortgage bank receives the payment and, in turn, makes a smaller payment to the investment company for the structured product. The investment company receives the payment for the structured product and, in turn, makes a smaller interest payment for the loan obtained from the government and/or other lenders. Everyone is happy: the homebuyer enjoys living in the house; the mortgage company gets the difference between the high mortgage payment (received) and the structured product coupon (paid) with no risk; the investment company receives the payment for the 'safe' structured product, where that payment is higher those that provided by other investments of seemingly similar risk; the lenders get their interest payments for the loans they have provided.

Figure 3.4 presents the details of the 2007–2008 financial crisis. The home buyer has to leave the house for various reasons: losing the temporary/permanent job; initial low mortgage rates are now replaced with higher rates, making it impossible to make the higher monthly payments; the balance of the mortgage loan is higher than the declining value of the house due to the real estate market collapse.

Since home buyers stop payments to the mortgage bank, the structured product can no longer provide payments to the investment company either. The intermediary mortgage bank does not suffer since all the risk in the mortgage loan has been transferred and sold to the investment company. But once the true nature of the structured derivative risk comes out, all business reputation is lost. No one wants to deal with the mortgage company anymore. This leads to financial insolvency and the eventual failure of the business.

The investment company realizes that the structured derivative product has significantly more risk. Once the cash flows/coupons stop, the financial security loses much of its value. Nobody is interested in purchasing the security. The substantial investment in these structured products is now worthless. The lenders (government and others) demand their interest payments. After a short period, the investment company becomes cashless and declares bankruptcy. Litigations ensue, and parts of loans are recovered. Overall, lenders suffer losses. Every major party in the mortgage setting ends up with negative outcomes during the 2007–2008 financial crisis.

3.4 STRUCTURED DERIVATIVE PRODUCT

The problem area in the previous setting is the characteristics of the structured derivative product – how it has been created and marketed. The research divisions at mortgage companies have been responsible for converting standard mortgages into these structured derivative products through a process known as a special-purpose vehicle. The end the process is called structured derivative product, but there are many other names given to these financially engineered securities: Asset-backed security (A.B.S.), collateralized debt obligation (C.D.O.), mortgage-backed security (M.B.S.), or collateralized mortgage obligation (C.M.O.).

The conversion must be done in a systematic and mathematically sound manner. The total risk and return before and after the conversion should remain the same. In other words, the financial engineer should not create something from nothing.

In the example in figure 3.5, a mortgage bank has a $100 million outstanding standard mortgage principal. The bank creates a special-purpose vehicle, an autonomous division often with an independent balance sheet. The special-purpose vehicle converts the mortgage principal into three asset-backed securities (A.B.S.s): A.A.A. senior products ($70 million), B.B.B. mezzanine products ($20 million), and equity-type risky products ($10 million).

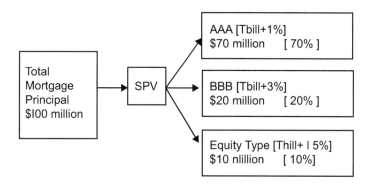

FIGURE 3.5 Asset-Backed Security by the Special-Purpose Vehicle

In this conversion, the total return and total risk should remain the same. The new products have different risk-return characteristics, but they must aggregate to the initial characteristics:

$$E(R_{mortgage}) = 0.7E(R_{AAA}) + 0.2E(R_{BBB}) + 0.1E(R_{EquityType}) + \text{mortgage bank profit, and}$$
$$Var(R_{mortgage}) = Var(0.7R_{AAA} + 0.2R_{BBB} + 0.1R_{EquityType}),$$

where $E(R.)$ is expected return, and $Var(.)$ is variance (standard deviation squared). Even though these two equations have to be satisfied, the financial engineer has some leeway in deciding the individual risk and return levels of the A.B.S.s. For example, the A.A.A. could be assigned an annual return of T-bill (or L.I.B.O.R.) + 1%, B.B.B. an annual return of T-bill (or L.I.B.O.R.) + 3%, and equity A.B.S. an annual return of T-bill (or L.I.B.O.R.) + 15%. This would, of course, mean that the original mortgages have a total return of T-bill (or L.I.B.O.R.) + [0.7(1%) + 0.2(3%) + 0.1(15%)] +2% = T-bill (or L.I.B.O.R.) + 2.8% +2%, where the last term in the total mortgage return, 2%, is the guaranteed profit of the mortgage bank.

With the creation of new A.B.S.s, investors with different risk and return preferences will be attracted to them. Investors who prefer safety will focus on A.A.A.-rated products, and investors with high risk tolerance levels will go for equity-like A.B.S.s. Once the A.B.S.s are sold to different types of investors, the payment flow from the mortgage loans will be transferred to the ABS_{AAA} investors first, then to ABS_{BBB} investors, and finally to $ABS_{EquityType}$ investors. In case some home buyers fail to make payments, the equity-type investors will suffer. But since these investors are informed about the riskier characteristics of their investment, this will not be a complete surprise.

Some of the new A.B.S. products will be in high demand, while others may not be as attractive. The actual experience from the mid-2000s has been a lack of interest in the mezzanine-level securities and a huge demand for A.A.A.-rated products. The B.B.B.-rated products were considered neither safe nor profitable. The common approach by the special-purpose vehicle authorities has been restructuring the B.B.B. products into A.A.A. and equity-type A.B.S.s. In the figure 3.6 example, 90% of the B.B.B. is converted into A.A.A., 5% is converted into equity type, and 5% remains the same. The total weight of A.A.A. products then becomes 70% + (0.9)(20%) = 88%, the total weight of equity-type products becomes 10% + (0.05)(20%) = 11%, and the total weight of the B.B.B. products drops down to 1%. Such restructurings were quite common in the mid-2000s as the demand for different A.B.S.s shifted and adjusted.

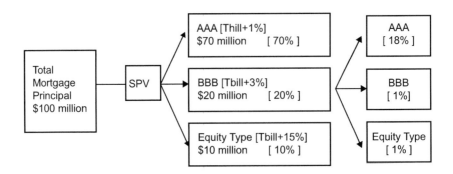

FIGURE 3.6 Restructured Asset-Backed Security by the Special-Purpose Vehicle

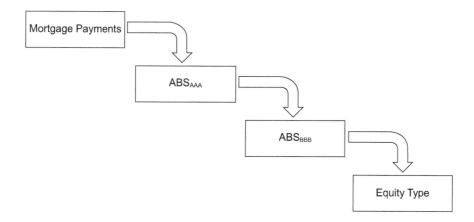

FIGURE 3.7 Cash Flow from Mortgage Payments to Asset-Backed Securities

In the restructuring process, the cash accumulated from the standard mortgage payments is distributed according to the risk order of the A.B.S.s. Like a waterfall, the safest A.B.S.s with A.A.A. ratings receive and distribute the cash to their investors, followed by mezzanine-level securities, and finally by the high-risk equity-type A.B.S.s as in Figure 3.7. The equity-type securities will be the first incapable of making their high-level payments if some home buyers stop making mortgage payments. The high risk assigned to the security makes this adverse situation a reasonable possibility.

Financial engineers assign the rating to the structured products at the mortgage bank. These ratings must be justified by independent agencies, just like corporate bond ratings. These ratings look similar to investors, but there are many important distinctions. Unfortunately, many of the differences were ignored in the mid-2000s when investment companies and professional investors took positions in structured derivative products.

3.5 RISK RATING DIFFERENCES BETWEEN STRUCTURED PRODUCTS AND BONDS

Risk characteristics of corporate and sovereign bonds are analyzed and summarized by independent rating agencies such as Fitch, Moody's, Standard & Poor's, and Duff & Phelps (Kroll) in the U.S. The analysts at these agencies investigate the company or the country from many different perspectives and produce a rating. The rating scale is different in each agency, but typically scales start with A.A.A. at the top (very safe) and down to C (implying default).

These rating agencies also offer risk measurements related to structured derivative products. Even though the rating scales are similar, there are significant differences between a B.B.B.-rated corporate bond and a B.B.B.-rated structured product:

(1) Bond ratings are based on a detailed investigation of the company (country), sound judgment, and objective analyses with sophisticated models. Structured product ratings are

supposed to be based on objective views and sophisticated models as well. But rating agencies had limited access and were provided muddled documentation, making it impossible to apply the sophisticated models during the mid-2000s.

(2) Structured products require an assumption about the correlation between the original asset and the final structure. Many times this fundamental assumption was ignored in the analyses. This was a crucial flaw.

(3) Ratings for the structured products often ended up to be 'negotiated'. The information independent rating agents sought was neither fully disclosed nor fully transparent. The special-purpose vehicle heavily influenced rating agents. If the rating was not favorable the first time, the ratings agent had much more difficulty accessing information next time. On the other hand, if the rating was favorable, a number of perks and advantages were provided to the ratings agent next time. There was implicit coercion throughout the process leading to inaccurate ratings.

(4) Related to the third point, structured products often end up with inflated ratings.

(5) As also mentioned in the third point, getting accurate information was extremely difficul. This was either (a) on purpose to entice a higher rating than deserved or (b) the messy documentation by the special-purpose vehicle made it impossible to understand and interpret the risk characteristics. As a consequence, the final rating was usually inaccurate.

Unfortunately, many market participants failed to recognize these distinctions during the 2000s. Investors who focused on structured derivative products had three wrong assumptions. The first was the consideration that similarly rated bonds, and structured products had the same risk. In reality, the structured products consistently had more risk.

The second mistake was assuming that the factors related to the structured products were symmetric and normally distributed. Especially for the tail-end events, the loss return distributions are not normally distributed at all, and they are very different from those of bonds.

The third mistake is also about stressed market conditions. Default correlations between regular mortgages and structured derivative products go up during poor economic conditions. The distributions are not only non-normal (the mistake in the second assumption), but additionally, the mezzanine-level B.B.B. tranche typically has 'all or nothing' binary loss distributions. This type of loss return distribution is very different from the loss tail-end normal distribution of B.B.B. bonds.

3.6 INCENTIVE STRUCTURES OF MARKET PARTICIPANTS

The incentive structures in the mortgage industry were full of wrong inducements in the early 2000s until the financial crisis. One of the outcomes of the 2007–2008 financial crisis has been the exposure of dysfunctional incentives in the industry so that they could be corrected. The wrong incentives can be grouped into four categories:

- Home buyers: Even though the home buyer did not have the financial capability, they were encouraged and to buy houses they could not afford. Many had to forego their houses once the real estate industry collapsed and/or their personal financial prowess weakened.

- Mortgage banks: Their primary focus shifted from verifying reliable potential buyers to giving out loans, receiving mortgages of any quality, securitizing these mortgages, and selling them to others. The incentive was the difference between the higher mortgage payments received and the lower coupons paid for the structured securities. Mortgage banks simply wanted to lend to any home buyer, since any risk would be directly transferred to the investors of the structured products.
- Independent rating agencies: The agencies were under constant pressure to provide higher ratings to the structured derivative products. Higher valuations and higher ratings ensured the status quo in the mortgage market. The rating agents received extra compensation, perks, and invitations for additional evaluations. With added benefits, rating agents were coerced into providing misleading higher ratings of structured products.
- Market makers and brokers: The intermediaries for structured product transactions were informed about the sellers, the buyers, and risk/return characteristics of the securities. Many experienced problems with structured products. But their primary concern was about maximizing the short- to mid-term compensation and bonuses and then moving on to another industry.

3.7 THE AFTERMATH

3.7.1 Repercussions

The collapse of the real estate market had a contagion effect. The mortgage industry and asset-based products collapsed in value and in demand. Investment companies and professional investors ended up with worthless securities in their portfolios. Unable to pay the interest rates on their loans, these investment companies started to declare bankruptcy one after the other. Some of the pillars of the U.S. finance and banking industry, such as Bear-Stearns, Lehman Brothers, Washington Mutual, Merrill-Lynch, and Wachovia Bank, went bankrupt. Bears-Stearns was the first to go with the last day of trade on June 2, 2008. The second was Lehman, with the last trading day of September 17, 2008. Washington Mutual had its last trading day on September 26, 2008. And January 2, 2009, was the last day for both Wachovia Bank and Merrill Lynch.

American Insurance Group (A.I.G.) did not go bankrupt only because of a rescue package by the U.S. government financed by taxpayers. Merrill Lynch was eventually acquired by Bank of America. So was Countrywide. The finance industry was experiencing a freefall, so much so that short-selling of the finance firms was temporarily suspended by regulators, with little effect.

The U.S. equity markets suffered significant declines. From the high of 14,164 on October 19, 2007, the Dow Jones Industrial Average dropped to a low of 7,882 on October 10, 2008 – close to a 45% decline in less than a year. On September 29, 2008, the Dow dropped 774 points (roughly 7%), the largest point drop in the index's history. The tremendous decline in the stock markets was followed by a severe U.S. economic recession and then a global economic contraction.

The crisis led to a number of corrections within the finance sector. Legislation was updated with an emphasis on the enforcement of the rules. The alignment of the interests of home buyers, mortgage banks, investment companies, and employees was achieved so that one group could not benefit at the expense of another. And third, the need for objective, transparent, and accurate mathematical models was acknowledged.

3.7.2 Regulatory Response to the Financial Crisis

The first legislation was the Emergency Economic Stabilization Act passed in October 2008, a fast and short- to mid-term response to protect the economy, the troubled firms, and consumers. The treasury was provided $700 billion to use in the Troubled Asset Relief Program (T.A.R.P.), where bank shares and mortgage-backed securities were purchased to relieve financially troubled American International Group, Bank of America, Citigroup, J.P. Morgan, General Motors, and others. Much of the funds used for the program were later recovered with interest.

The legislation to address the financial crisis long-term was the Dodd-Frank Wall Street Reform and Consumer Protection Act, signed into law in July 2010. The first of the four components was about the amendments to historical key legislations:

(1) Securities Act of 1933, where with the amendment, some assets of investors were given additional protection
(2) Securities Act of 1934, where significant improvements in the regulation of credit rating agencies, asset-backed securitization processes, and corporate governance/employee compensation plans were added
(3) Investment Company Act of 1940, where new oversight committees were added for consumer protection and disclosure requirements
(4) Investment Advisors Act of 1940, where registration requirements for independent investment advisors and hedge funds were enforced
(5) Sarbanes-Oxley Act of 2002, where new protections and incentives were added for whistleblowers

The second component of the Dodd-Frank Act was about the additional rules for the investments sector. Limits to speculative investments and to proprietary trading were imposed. Better enforcement systems for these rules were required.

The third component of the act was about better monitoring and enforcement. From a more holistic perspective at the government level, the Dodd-Frank Act required much better monitoring systems for too-big-to-fail financial institutions. Clearing houses for over-the-counter derivatives were granted more tangible and enforceable monitoring and disciplinary mechanisms. The Consumer Financial Protection Bureau was created as a monitoring and enforcement federal agency.

Finally, the fourth component of Dodd-Frank was about the liquidity and capital flows of the banking sector. Banks were required to do the following:

(1) Hold more capital so that liquidity problems were lessened and panic situations were averted.
(2) Satisfy a number of liquidity ratios to demonstrate their ability to stand a potential slowdown or an unexpected crash.

(3) Emphasize stress testing and utilize historical data from stressed market conditions. The aim was to investigate how banks would survive stressful economic conditions, declining markets, and panic environments. The stress tests and their outcomes would be used to implement better protections to survive disastrous economic situations and to stay aloft.

While some countries introduced additional regulations (for example, in the U.K., additional taxes were required for bonuses in the finance sector), some parts of the Dodd-Frank Act were eventually relaxed through the Economic Growth, Regulatory Relief, and Consumer Protection Act in 2018. But overall, the Dodd-Frank Act has provided a lot of adjustments to the finance sector to reduce the probability of a similar financial crisis in the future.

3.7.3 Alignment of Interests: Home Buyers, Mortgage Banks, Investors, Employees

The extreme divergence of the interests of market participants had to be aligned. There was ample evidence that mortgage banks used unjustifiably lax lending standards to create huge quantities of subprime mortgages only to securitize and sell them to others. The high risk of subprime mortgages was completely passed over to the securitized derivative products, and none of the risk remained within the original lenders.

For a fair, ethical, and sustainable mortgage industry, it was necessary to align the interests of mortgage banks with the interests of investment companies and professional investors. Researchers and regulators proposed that mortgage banks keep a certain percentage, around 20%, of the securitized products within the mortgage bank. The risks embedded in the securitized products would be shared by both investment companies and by the mortgage banks that created these securities. Therefore, the interests of mortgage banks and investment companies would be properly aligned. Additionally, mortgage banks were required not to convert all original mortgages into structured products. The interests of home buyers and mortgage banks would also be aligned this way. Both parties would want the mortgage transaction to be successful and stable.

The final alignment has been on designing better compensation plans. Until the end of the financial crisis, short-term compensation, such as end-of-the-year bonuses, was the dominant portion of compensation plans. Such short-term biases for decision-making and risk choices ignored the long-term consequences. Employees with such compensation schemes focused on maximizing salaries for a short period and moving on when long-term problems started to emerge. In other words, long-term performance was sacrificed at the expense of short-term gains.

To eliminate this problem, proposals for compensation systems to be aligned with long-term performance have been introduced and implemented, such as year-end bonuses spread over five to ten years. With such compensation plans, everyone would want the business environment to continue to be successful in the long term.

3.7.4 The Need for Better Mathematical and Statistical Models

Most financial institutions did not have the proper mathematical and statistical models for the securitization process throughout the late 1990s into the late 2000s. Different tranches and types of structured products were created arbitrarily. So were the valuations and risk distributions. Many special-purpose vehicles did not follow their own procedures. Without structured rules and valuation models, risk management was virtually impossible. Rating agencies could not get tangible data to provide correct ratings. Investment companies and professional investors were misled into buying products they really did not want.

Full transparency is now required in the creation of structured derivative products. Objective models and statistical analysis are properly implemented. Rating agencies access the necessary information to generate more reliable ratings. Institutions are required to emphasize stress testing. Senior management is expected to be involved in the development of different stress test scenarios. Value at risk (VaR) models with an emphasis on worst-case scenarios are now commonly used by financial institutions and throughout the banking sector.

3.8 SUMMARY AND CONCLUSIONS

Economic and financial crises will always occur because we as human beings frequently act irrationally. Such behaviors generate bubbles in financial markets, and when those bubbles burst, crises materialize.

In this chapter, the focus was on the 2007–2008 financial crisis. The root causes are examined with (1) how and why subprime mortgages dominated the decade of the 2000s, (2) how subprime mortgages were erroneously converted into structured derivative products and sold to investors, and (3) the consequences when the real estate bubble burst. The legislative measures, the efforts to align the interests of the relevant parties, and the need for better mathematical and statistical models are explained so that better levels of transparency, accuracy, objectivity, and ethical and rational expectations are achieved.

Even with all these countermeasures, uncertainty remains. Systemic risk, engulfing the entire economy, continues. There are large periodic swings in the U.S. economy and in other economies. For example, the unexpected Covid-19 pandemic extensively hurt all the economies of the world from 2019 through 2022. The efforts by central banks, the Federal Reserve, government agencies, and regulators to eliminate systematic risk have not been successful. But there are still useful actions to take: Regulators need better ways of monitoring systemic risk. International cooperation during times of crisis is necessary. Trying to avoid irrational exuberance or panic behaviors individually or as a society is key.

There are lessons to remember from previous disasters so that similar future disasters can be avoided. For the investors of derivatives and structured products, (1) risk must be quantified and limits must be established; (2) exceeding risk limits should not be acceptable even when there are profits; (3) monitoring mechanisms should exist for everyone, even for star traders; (4) diversification in investments is the key goal; and (5) worst-case scenario testing and stress testing are paramount for longevity.

For corporations and organizations, there are additional lessons: (1) investment firms should not give limitless power to star traders; (2) proper monitoring by separating front, middle, and back divisions is necessary; (3) new financial products must be treated rationally with reasonable expectations for success; (4) such products must be advertised ethically to clients; (5) risk management must always be tracked; (6) herd behavior of following the same strategy without justification should be avoided; and (7) employee incentives must be properly managed. Moreover, finance divisions in corporations should understand the derivative products they trade, not switch from hedgers to speculators, and refuse the task of becoming a profit center.

REFERENCES AND ADDITIONAL READING

Dodd, C., Frank, B. 2010. *Dodd – Frank Wall Street Reform and Consumer Protection Act.* www.cftc.gov/sites/default/files/idc/groups/public/@swaps/documents/file/hr4173_enrolledbill.pdf.

Kahneman, D. 2011. *Thinking, Fast and Slow.* New York, Farrar, Straus and Giroux.

Sarbanes, P., Oxley, M.G. 2002. *Sarbanes – Oxley Act.* www.govinfo.gov/content/pkg/PLAW-107publ204/pdf/PLAW-107publ204.pdf.

CHAPTER 4

Trading Ecosystem
History, Speed, Orders, Intraday, E.S.G.

OBJECTIVES

- Evaluate the general history of trading financial securities from ancient times until the present.
- Critique the technological innovations and advancements in the trading infrastructures, networks and cloud systems, and the global integration within the financial markets. Evaluate trading mechanisms executing trades at the speed of light through fiber optic network systems and intraday trading using ultra-high-speed technologies.
- Appraise the types of trading orders and intraday trading patterns in developed and developing financial markets with a focus on volatility smiles and smirks. Weigh the market efficiency consequences.
- Justify the rules and policy decisions taken by regulatory authorities, with corporate social responsibility and ethical governance perspectives.

4.1 INTRODUCTION

The last two decades have witnessed the integration of enormous technological advancements into the trading infrastructures of financial markets. Trading mechanisms enable the execution of trades at literally speeds of light these days through fiber optic network connections and communication systems. In this environment, intraday trading using ultra-high-speed means has become quite widespread. Developments in this area are examined, and the academic and practitioner research results are explored. The presentation of a brief history of financial securities and organized exchanges is followed by technological advances in financial markets and securities trading. Order types, secondary markets, intraday volatility, and the rules/regulations for corporate social responsibility are the other topics of exploration in this chapter.

DOI: 10.4324/9781003213697-4

4.2 BRIEF HISTORY OF FINANCIAL SECURITIES AND ORGANIZED EXCHANGES

Evidence of companies with transferable shares dates all the way back to classical Rome, but these were usually not long term, and no considerable secondary market existed. During the earlier Roman Republic days, private business was financed by banking and a market for private mortgages on estates came about but disappeared during the Roman Empire days. The emperors did not borrow using long-term government bonds because they used the proactive power of the state to deal with rebellions, wars, natural disasters, and infrastructure. Nevertheless, by extending the privileges of Roman citizenship throughout the empire, extensive trade within the empire and beyond were financed with contracts protected by the state. The extension of Roman citizenship stretched the mercantile practices of the Greeks and Phoenicians to the entire Mediterranean world and into northwestern Europe.

In the Near East, the Ottoman Empire sidestepped Islamic law and the prohibition of interest by using the system left by Eastern Roman Empire from Eastern Europe. Centralized regulation allowed local elites and merchants to create a financial system until the integration with international financial markets during the Crimean War of 1854.

In the Far East, the Chinese Song dynasty (960–1276) and Yuan dynasty (1271–1368) established the world's first paper currency, progressive taxation, and state monetary and credit instruments. The Ming dynasty (1368–1644) began with an anti-commercial policy until it reversed course in the 16th century. The Qing dynasty (1644–1911) refined financial institutions, but the weak central state led to multiple currencies throughout the country. China's silver standard led to export-led growth until the Boxer Rebellion (with root causes going back to the Opium Wars of the mid-1800s), which ended the Qing dynasty. China's role in the international economy suffered from the subsequent civil war, Japanese occupation, and complete isolation with the communist regime until 1978, after which the controlled opening of the economy started.

Modern financial capitalism began with the initiatives of the Italian city-states, particularly Genoa and Venice. In the middle of the 13th century, Venetian bankers began to trade in government securities. Bankers in Pisa, Verona, Genoa, and Florence also began trading in government securities during the 14th century. These independent city-states were ruled by a council of influential citizens. Italian companies were also the first to issue shares. Companies in England, Belgium, and Holland followed in the 16th century, and joint stock companies owned by multiple shareholders emerged.

The lenders of Europe filled the gaps left by banks. These traders transacted with each other, bought government debt issues (Venetians were the first to trade securities from other governments), and started in the 1300s selling debt issues to individual investors (Venetian and Genoese were the first). The Genoese institution of Casa di San Giorgio (created in 1407) and the Venetian Banco di Rialto (1587) served as models for city-states in northern Europe in the following centuries, such as the Duchy of Milan. The financial practices of the papacy were regularly serviced by bankers from Florence, Venice, and Genoa until the secularization of church properties during the Napoleonic wars.

The financial aspects of American silver were felt most directly in Spain and the areas under Spanish influence under Charles V and Philip II. The Spanish kings used their supplies of American silver to finance their constant wars, but even they had to rely on the services of Genoese bankers to borrow and frequently default. These defaults led to financial innovations, such as equity stakes and perpetual rents on state properties to compensate lender Genoese lenders.

In late-13th-century Bruges, Belgium, commodity traders would gather at a market square of an inn owned by Van der Beurze, which became an informal meeting area in 1409 called Brugse Beurse. In Holland, such meeting areas also took hold. The word 'Beurzen' came to define the place for stock market exchange by international traders: Italians (borsa), French (bourse), Germans (börse), Russians (birža), Czechs (burza), Swedish (börs), and Danish and Norwegian (børs). The Latin word for 'money bag' is *bursa*. In the 1500s, brokers and lenders in Belgium would regularly meet to deal with business, government, and individual debt issues.

The new Dutch Republic, influenced by the innovations in Belgium and Italian provinces, created both central government debt and consolidated debt by the major provinces, especially that of Holland and the city of Amsterdam. The first modern stock, for the Dutch East India Company, was traded in Amsterdam in 1602, followed by the trading of the first derivatives (options and repos) and the distribution of the first dividend distributions following several years later. Futures trading and short-selling were also invented in Amsterdam in these early years. In the 17th and 18th centuries, the Dutch pioneered several financial innovations that helped lay the foundations of the modern financial system.

To lessen the risk of a lost ship to weather, poor navigation, or piracy, it became common practice to seek investors who would put up money for the voyage – the early examples of limited liability companies lasting for only a single voyage. They were then dissolved, and new ones were created for the next voyage. Investors spread their risk by investing in several different ventures at the same time. These early financial innovations evolved into East India companies issuing stock that would pay dividends on the proceeds from all the voyages undertaken rather than voyage by voyage. These first modern joint-stock companies demanded more for their shares, built larger fleets, and with royal charters forbidding competition, generated larger profits for their investors.

The British public finances were improved by adopting Dutch practices. The obvious successes of the Dutch and English in public finance, combining both a public bank responsible for the payments of taxes and expenditures by the central government and a body of long-term government debt that was managed by private individuals of sound reputation and available for investment by outsiders, led to the similar initiatives in France.

Because the shares were issued on paper, investors could sell the papers to other investors. The lack of a stock exchange is used to force investors to track down brokers to carry out the trades. In England, most brokers and investors did their business in the various coffee shops around London. Debt issues and shares for sale were written up and posted on the shops' doors or mailed as newsletters.

In the 1600s, the emergence of various East India companies that issued stock led to financial ups and downs. The British East India Company had a government-backed monopoly. With large dividends and higher share values, demand increased dramatically. Other companies emerged with similar charters, and without any regulations or rules, numerous shares were issued and sold in blind pools. Inevitably, the bubble burst when the new companies failed to pay any dividends. The ensuing crash led the government to outlaw the arbitrary issuing of shares until the early 1800s.

In the newly formed republic of the United States of America, Alexander Hamilton recognized the merits of English public debt markets, the inspiring effects of bank chartering, and the ideas about the potential developmental contribution of the government to finance. He improved on these examples successfully.

The first stock exchange in London was officially formed in 1773, about 20 years before the New York Stock Exchange. While the London Stock Exchange was limited by the high degree of restrictions, the New York Stock Exchange freely dealt in the trading of stocks since its inception. Philadelphia was actually the first location with a stock exchange in the United States. Chicago and Los Angeles have also had stock exchanges. But the N.Y.S.E. – formed by brokers at the favorable location of Wall Street in lower Manhattan as the heart of all the business and trade coming to and going from the U.S. and as the domestic base for most banks and large corporations – quickly became the most powerful stock exchange. By setting listing requirements and demanding fees, the N.Y.S.E. became a very wealthy institution. Many countries developed their own stock exchanges, but domestic companies used them as stepping stones to the London Stock Exchange and then to the N.Y.S.E.

In 1971, N.A.S.D.A.Q., a network of computers that executes trades electronically, was formed. This electronic exchange has forced the N.Y.S.E. to evolve toward higher efficiency. There are now stock markets in virtually all developed and most developing economies, with the world's largest markets being in the United States, United Kingdom, Japan, China, Canada, Germany, France, South Korea, and Holland.

4.3 TECHNOLOGICAL INNOVATIONS IN FINANCIAL SECURITIES MARKETS

Technology has had an enormous impact on the functioning of the stock markets, communication systems, research capabilities, and the execution of trades. To be successful in securities trading, market participants must embrace technology. There are many different ways that technology influences stock markets, and in this section, a quick review is presented.

The earliest major technological invention in financial markets was in 1832, when Samuel Morse invented the telegraph. This achievement in communications led to the first financial newsletters. Western Union was founded in 1856, and people outside of Wall Street started placing orders. However, for a trader from outside the city, the transaction costs associated with using the telegraph frequently made it more convenient to use a local exchange.

The first successful quotation device, which printed the gold prices on a continuous basis, was invented in 1866. Edward Calahan and Thomas Edison improved the device for stock quotations and named it a 'ticker'. Investors anywhere could have up-to-date information for stock prices at a reasonable cost.

The telephone made its first appearance on Wall Street in 1878, and just as the ticker transmitted price information, the telephone could be used to buy and sell securities. By 1920, there were 88,000 telephones in service in the Wall Street area. A central quotation system for reporting bid and asked prices was established, and a high-speed ticker service was initiated at the New York Stock Exchange in 1929.

The arrival of computers in the 1970s and 1980s and the availability of the internet starting from the 1990s have revolutionized trading by introducing electronic markets and automatic order execution. This resulted in lower fees, more efficient markets, excellent research capabilities, and greater information and transparency for investors all around the world.

In the past, traders at financial exchanges would shout out orders back and forth through the open outcry system at trading pits in order to reach a consensus on the trading price. Nowadays, traders can easily get the best trading prices through automated computer quotation systems with the help of their brokers. The use of advanced computers has made it easy to buy and sell stocks. Incidences of human errors in transactions have been reduced significantly. Most of the transactions are now executed through advanced computers.

Research on financial conditions, markets, and securities has greatly improved. In the past, information could be accessed from libraries by reading printed financial literature or by directly contacting companies. These days, all the information is readily and mostly freely available on the internet. Rather than relying on others' analyses and recommendations, one can now download company reports and reach own judgments and informed decisions.

Online brokerage firms can be accessed easily through computers. Moreover, various financial security trading apps have been developed and are now ubiquitous. These apps can be installed on mobile phones and have made it easier to access the stock markets with drastic reductions in fees. As market conditions change, investors learn about them very quickly and can act on these changes rapidly through online trade executions. Market participants can trade anywhere and anytime.

High-speed trading is becoming more and more important. When a new piece of information comes out, a market participant would want to act on that information before anyone else and before the price of the security adjusts to that information. Investment companies, hedge funds, and professional investors physically want to be close to the stock market computer mainframes and want to be connected to these systems through fiber optic networks where transaction orders travel at the speed of light. These days, high-frequency traders are using experimental types of cables to speed up their systems by billionths of a second, the latest move in a technological arms race to execute stock trades as quickly as possible. The hollow-core fiber is the next-generation version of the fiber-optic cable. Made of glass, such cables carry data encoded as beams of light. But instead of being solid, hollow-core fiber is empty inside, with dozens of parallel, air-filled channels narrower than a human hair. Since light travels nearly faster through air than glass, it takes about one-third less time to send data through the new technology hollow-core fiber.

The difference is just a tiny fraction of a second. But in high-frequency trading, that makes all the difference between utilizing arbitrage opportunities and ending up with profits or losses. High-frequency trading companies use sophisticated machine learning algorithms, artificial intelligence, and ultrafast data networks in order to execute rapid trades in securities.

Hollow-core fiber is the latest technological enhancement in works to outpace the competition. In June 2010, Spread Networks laid out a fiber optic cable route for a straight connection between Chicago and New York for roughly $300 million so that traders would be able to send and receive data in just 13 milliseconds. Within a few years, microwave networks reduced the transmission time to less than nine milliseconds. The race for higher-speed communications and transactions continues with full force.

4.4 TYPES OF ORDERS

Traditionally, before someone can give a trading order, a brokerage must be chosen, and an account with that brokerage company must be opened. All brokerage firms will earn commissions on executed trades. But there are additional concerns. Choosing a broker is a tradeoff between the services provided and the costs of those services that must be paid. *Full-service brokers* offer order execution, useful information on markets and firms, and valuable investment advice. The fees are significantly high, but the information provided is of great use. The other types of brokers are *discount brokers*, *deep discount brokers*, and *e-brokers*, or *online brokers*.

As we scan these different brokerage firms, we notice that the services provided and quality decreases, but the fees and costs also decline. Online brokers, or e-brokers, are the least expensive brokerage firms. There is minimal unique information to act on, although there are plenty of publicly available facts, figures, material, and analysis. On the upside, the transaction costs are minimal. For someone who conducts his/her own research, online brokerage companies are excellent for accessing financial markets and executing trades.

Once a brokerage company is picked, an account needs to be opened. There are different types of accounts to choose from. The standard and easiest account is a *cash account* where the investor pays the entire purchase price for each transaction with cash out of pocket (i.e., the cash already deposited into the account). The more popular and proficient account is the *margin account*. With margin accounts, investors can borrow a part of the purchase price from the broker. In general, the most that can be borrowed is the total own cash deposits to the margin account (set by the Federal Reserve in 1974). This means an investor can double the investment by financing half with their own cash and the other half by borrowing from the brokerage firm. Borrowing is not free, but it is cheaper than borrowing from another financial institution.

In margin accounts, something called *actual margin* is calculated by the brokerage firm continually. Actual margin is a ratio: the equity (i.e., total assets in excess of liabilities in the account) divided by the value of the investments in the account. The higher this actual margin, the larger the portion of the investments that truly belongs to the investor. If the investments' values decline, then the actual margin decreases. If it goes below a maintenance margin percentage set by the brokerage firm, the investor is required to deposit additional funds into the account in order to push the actual margin above the maintenance margin level. Overall, the margin account is highly desirable for investors because it provides extra flexibility by allowing them to borrow from the broker to magnify an investment.

The third type of account is called an *asset management account*. This is a comprehensive account with banking services such as checking and savings accounts, debit and credit cards, and checks. Excess deposits are reinvested at the money market rate. Additionally, there is a margin account for securities trading. The fourth and final type of account is called a *wrap account*, which is exactly the same as an asset management account. The only difference is, all the fees and costs are combined into a single periodic fee in wrap accounts.

Once a brokerage firm is picked and an account is opened, it is now possible to give trading orders. There are three fundamental order types:

(1) Market order: This is the typical order given to brokers. The trade will be executed by the broker immediately at the best possible price for the investor.

(2) Limit order: This is an order generally given when there is no hurry to execute a trade. A limit price is provided to the broker at which the trade is to be executed. Additionally, the number of shares to be traded is also specified. If the spot price of the security changes and reaches the limit price, the limit order is activated. Limit orders at that price by other clients are executed first, then the investor's limit order is executed. If the spot price changes to an unfavorable value before the investor's trade is executed, the order becomes an inactive limit order again. On the other hand, if the spot price changes to a more favorable value while the limit order is active and while the prior limit orders are executed, then when it is time for the investor's trade, it will be executed at the more favorable spot price than the limit price.

Limit orders can be day orders or open orders (valid for six months). Limit orders can also have additional features based on the size of the order. For example, (a) all or none is about the execution of the whole order or no part of it when the limit order becomes active; (b) immediate or cancel is about the immediate execution of the entire or a portion of the active limit order when it is time, and the cancellation of the remaining portion; (c) fill or kill is about the immediate execution of the whole order when it is time for the activated limit order or the cancellation of the order.

The bottom line for limit orders is to buy at or lower than the limit price or sell at or above the limit price. The goal is to make a larger profit by buying at a lower price (limit buy order) or by selling at a higher price (limit sell order).

(3) Stop order: This is an order where the goal is to stop something from getting worse. There is a spot price movement against what the investor wishes. The investor provides a stop price to the broker. When the spot price reaches the stop price, the stop order turns into a market order and is executed immediately around the stop price. In a stop-buy order, the investor will buy at a higher price than the spot price when the stop order was placed. The investor is not necessarily happy to be buying at the higher stop price, but at least the purchase is not executed at an even higher price than the stop price. In a stop-sell order, the investors will sell at a lower price than the spot price at which the stop order was given. The investor is not happy to be selling at a lower price, but at least the sale will not take place at an even lower price than the stop-sell price.

Overall, the stop orders are open orders without a time limit. The goal is to stop something from getting worse. In stop-buy orders, the goal is not to buy at a higher price. And in stop-sell orders, the goal is not to sell at a lower price.

There are also two-tiered orders, namely *stop-limit* orders, which are day orders. In a stop-limit order, once the stop price is reached, the order turns into a limit order (instead of the usual market order). The limit price can be different. In stop-limit orders, more precision is achieved compared to a stop order.

4.5 SECONDARY MARKETS

Whatever order is given to the broker, it eventually ends up at an exchange where the security is traded. In general, there are two types of securities exchange markets. The first type is the auction market, and the most famous is the New York Stock Exchange (N.Y.S.E.). Orders in auction markets are executed mostly from matched public buy and sell orders. The matching is accomplished by a group of professionals called specialists. Each specialist is responsible for five to ten different securities. The orders for these securities arrive at the specialist. The specialist matches the orders by establishing a fair price based on the volume of buy orders (demand) and the volume of sell orders (supply). There are situations where there will be an order imbalance. In those cases, the specialist plays a more active role. If there are too many buyers but not enough sellers, the specialist becomes a seller from the pool of securities that have been provided. As the price adjusts, other sellers start to appear and the specialist pulls away from the active selling role. On the other hand, if there are too many sellers but no buyers, the specialist becomes the buyer using the funds provided for the specialist position. Again, as the price adjusts, other buyers start to appear, and the specialist mitigates the active buying role. Thus, a very important function of the specialist is to make a market for the securities assigned to her/him and to keep the market functioning in an orderly manner. The specialist keeps track of the limit and stop orders as well. For all these responsibilities, electronic computer support is necessary. For the N.Y.S.E., the computer system used to be the designated order turnaround (D.O.T.) in the mid-1970s. D.O.T. was upgraded to the SuperDOT system to route market orders and limit orders from investors and their brokers to specialists and to transmit orders electronically. SuperDOT was replaced in 2009 by the N.Y.S.E. Super Display Book (S.D.B.K.) system to process orders, and in 2012, a more efficient system called the Universal Trading Platform (U.T.P.) became the standard. These electronic systems have helped with the recording, reporting, routing, and matching of orders. Moreover, preopening buy and sell orders are matched, and the imbalance is reported to a specialist so that opening prices can be established. With each new version of the electronic system, the functions have become more effective.

The second type of securities exchange market is the over-the-counter market, or the dealer market. The most well-known example is the National Association of Securities Dealers Automated Quotation (N.A.S.D.A.Q.) system, founded in 1971. In these securities markets, there are multiple independent dealers for each security. The broker acting on behalf of the client, find the best dealer with the highest bid price (if the goal is to sell for the client) or with the lowest ask price (if the goal is to buy). The dealers make a market for the securities by buying them at the bid price and selling, then at the ask price. The bid-ask spread (which is the ask price minus the bid price) is always positive and represents the profit for a dealer. The dealer always buys at a low price (bid) and sells at a higher price (ask). The fact that there is more than one dealer for each security keeps the spread in check because the dealers compete with each other to attract customers, and a high spread will make the dealer or the trader choose another dealer.

In the old days, this type of market used counters between the dealers and the traders. Over time, the counters have been replaced by computer terminals and electronic networks.

An individual trader cannot directly access these systems. But all brokerage companies have direct access, and therefore, the investors will have indirect access with the help of the broker.

There has been a desire in financial markets to integrate globally and to serve traders and customers nonstop all around the world. To this end, there have been multiple acquisitions and spin-offs. The N.Y.S.E. merged with Euronext (European Securities Exchange Group, consisting of Amsterdam, Brussels, Dublin, Lisbon, London, Milan, Oslo, and Paris) in 2007. The American Stock Exchange (A.M.E.X.) was acquired in 2008. A further merger attempt with Deutsche Börse was not successful. The Intercontinental Exchange (I.C.E.) acquired N.Y.S.E. Euronext in 2013, which ultimately led to the spin-off of the Euronext division. On the other hand, N.A.S.D.A.Q. acquired the O.M.X. exchange in 2008. But all the subsidiaries of the N.A.S.D.A.Q. exchange are known more commonly as N.A.S.D.A.Q. Nordic (Copenhagen, Stockholm, Helsinki, Iceland, Tallinn, Riga, and Vilnius stock exchanges).

4.6 INTRADAY TRADING PATTERNS OF VOLATILITY

Trading activity at the intraday market microstructure level often leads to price runs and momentum movements/reversals independent of new information. Trading based on non-information-related motivations is considered noisy trading activity. Such noisy trading may cause the price discovery process to become less efficient. Noisy trading leads to temporary price changes, which in turn leads to increased short-term volatility. This *accentuated volatility* is not a desirable property in the markets because it leads to (1) inefficiencies, (2) added difficulty in price discovery, (3) illiquidity, and (4) discouragement of market participants from engaging in trading.

Studies investigating intraday volatility in developed country markets have consistently documented a U-shaped curve in volatility, a *volatility smile*, during the day. The consensus formed by researchers both in the academic and professional areas for the reason of the volatility pattern is that the opening period (5, 15, up to 30 minutes) in the morning and the closing period (5, 15, up to 30 minutes) for the trading day exhibit accentuated volatility, compared to the middle of the day time period. This implies that price discovery seems to be much more difficult right after the market opens in the morning. There is hectic trading activity once the market opens, and the trades are all over the place. The common explanation for the heightened intraday volatility during the morning open is that the information accumulated overnight while the markets are closed is not fully absorbed by the market participants. The interpretations are not homogenous. The increased uncertainty culminates in significant noise trading during the opening period leading to accentuated volatility in the opening hours.

Eventually, the traders reach a consensus on the accumulated information and the prices. Trading activity settles down, and so does the volatility. Intraday, the commonly seen observation is settled trading activity. Of course, there will be sudden and sharp price changes, but mostly rationally, as a result of the arrival of an important piece of information. The market mostly exhibits efficiency throughout the middle of the trading day.

This intraday pattern of the short-term volatility during the closing period is similar to that of the morning period, but for different reasons. The consensus interpretation is that market-makers and traders want to close out the open positions from the unfulfilled orders by their clients or complete the realignment of their portfolios for appropriate risk management before the market closes. The increased time pressure and stress of the need to execute the trades before the close of the market lead to hectic trading activity and, consequently, to accentuated volatility right before the market closes for the day. The overall volatility pattern is the U-shaped short-term intraday volatility smile typical as in Figure 4.1.

These findings have been documented in dozens of studies for the developed country stock markets. For developing countries, similar principles hold for the *accentuated volatility* during the opening and closing time periods. However, additional insight is obtained because trading hours differ in developing country stock exchanges – most have a midday break. Therefore two volatility patterns, one for the morning session and one for the afternoon session, are generated. A quick examination of some of the intraday trading behavior studies from around the world illustrates the following:

(1) The Chilean stock market, the second largest equity market in South America behind that of Brazil, depicts the typical volatility smile intraday in Figure 4.1.
(2) The Korean stock exchange has opening price movements more volatile compared to those at other times of the day. The volatility pattern exhibit an L-shaped volatility smirk. The heightened volatility when trading begins eventually subsides and stays at low levels throughout the day, as in Figure 4.2.
(3) The Shanghai stock exchange also demonstrates two intraday L-shaped volatility patterns – volatility smirks – one for the morning trading session and one for the afternoon trading session, as seen in Figure 4.3.
(4) The Istanbul stock exchange in Turkey exhibits an L-shaped volatility smirk in the morning session and a U-shaped volatility smile in the afternoon session. The market close in Istanbul coincides with the opening of the U.S. exchanges. A lot of information spills over from the U.S., causing additional noisy trading during the closing minutes in the Istanbul stock exchange; hence, the volatility smile in the afternoon session. Day-of-the-week results in the Istanbul stock exchange reveal that Monday morning intraday volatility is the highest for the entire week, implying the added difficulty of market participants in understanding the information accumulated over the weekend. There is an L-shaped volatility curve in the morning and a U-shaped curve in the afternoon for every trading day, as in Figure 4.4.

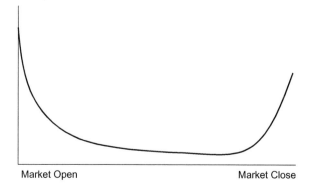

Market Open   Market Close

FIGURE 4.1 Intraday U-shaped Volatility Smile in Most Developed Countries

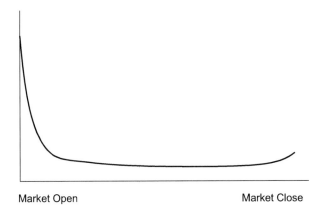

FIGURE 4.2 Intraday L-shaped Volatility Smirk in South Korea

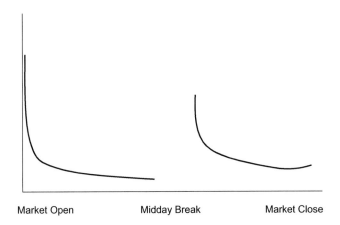

FIGURE 4.3 Intraday L-shaped Volatility Smirk in Shanghai

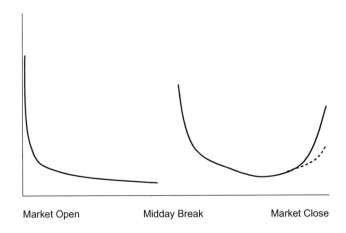

FIGURE 4.4 Morning Smirk and Afternoon Smile in Istanbul

Why are intraday volatility patterns important? Accentuated volatility due to noise trading is indicative of inefficiency. The price discovery is hampered significantly. If the securities prices deviate from the correct valuations in a financial market, this may lead to some traders taking advantage of other less informed traders. Therefore, many small investors stay away from that market. Given a volatility smile intraday, the recommendation for professional and well-informed traders is to focus on the morning and closing sessions because profits can be enhanced for such professionals. On the other hand, for the many small investors who are not highly sophisticated, the recommendation would be to trade during the middle of the day when the markets are calm, and the prices are more efficient.

Exchange regulators and policymakers would want everyone to access and utilize markets comfortably without the fear of being taken advantage of. Implementing tools and techniques that would reduce noise trading, reduce the associated accentuated volatility, and make markets more efficient would be highly desirable for these regulators. The next section explores such techniques.

4.7 RULES AND REGULATIONS FOR FAIRNESS, ETHICS, AND CORPORATE SOCIAL RESPONSIBILITY

A noisy financial securities exchange reduces efficiency and makes price discovery difficult. Incorrect asset prices cause many market participants to be taken advantage of when they trade securities. Such a trading ecology will be considered unfair, unethical, and undesirable. Such designations will be the basis for market participants to stay away.

Exchange regulators and policymakers would not feel comfortable with such a trading environment. It is the corporate social responsibility of securities exchange directors and regulators to introduce regulations to eliminate the conditions that may cultivate unfair and unethical behavior. Good corporate governance necessitates such policies. The main culprit in this context is the accentuated volatility due to noisy trading activity. Investigation for finding a remedy has led to the introduction of auction systems by exchange regulators in order to reduce noise-related volatility.

Many developed country exchanges have already implemented an opening auction system. Before official trading begins at an exchange in the morning, there is a short five-to-fifteen-minute period for the auction mechanism. During this time, all the accumulated buy and sell orders overnight for each security are considered altogether in order to establish a value-weighted average trading price for every security that would be fair and accurate for all the buyers and sellers. The trades are matched accordingly and are executed at the end of the auction period when trading begins. With the introduction of the opening auction system, intraday volatility levels during the market open have subsided substantially. Currently, the highest intraday volatility is still right after the morning open. However, if the auction system were nonexistent, the opening volatility levels would have been much higher. Currently, almost every exchange in developed and developing economies has an opening auction system in one way or another.

Exchange regulators have also focused in recent decades on the closing time accentuated volatility. Many times, the volatility is because of trading mechanisms – the desperate and frantic attempts to close out open positions or to rebalance portfolios for the risk management strategies of clients. Thus, many exchanges have implemented a closing call auction system. After trading stops for the day, unfulfilled buy and sell trades for every security are considered altogether to establish a fair value-weighted average trading price. The market makers are provided a short five-to-ten-minute opportunity to make the trades and close out the positions.

Such closing auction mechanisms have helped reduce accentuated volatility around the close of the market, as demonstrated by various academic and professional studies. For example, the closing call auction system was implemented by the emerging Istanbul stock exchange regulators in March 2012. Closing time volatilities have declined statistically significantly after the implementation of the closing auction mechanism (as depicted with the dashed line in Figure 4.4). The knowledge of an alternative outlet for order execution, even if the regular trading is missed, has helped markets to cool down and market makers to stick with rational trading. All developed securities exchanges and most developing exchanges have implemented a closing auction system.

Efforts to reduce noise trading continue at exchanges. Research continues, and new innovations are experimented with. One of the recent endeavors has been initiated by the Deutsche Börse and London Stock Exchange as the intraday auction in the middle of the day as part of a theoretical continuous auction model. The purpose of the intraday auction is the 'growing potential for strong price discovery' according to Deutsche Börse regulators. This will enhance welfare maximization, market efficiency, continuous access to market liquidity, capacity allocations, and congestion relief. Such auctions during the day act like pressure valves and also help deal with anonymous dark-pool-related large trades originating from investment companies and other financial institutions.

The introduction of the auction system in the open, in the close, and at midday helped check the intraday volatility from getting more accentuated as ultra-high-speed trading mechanisms, machine-coding-/artificial-intelligence-based automated trading protocols, and intraday market timing strategies are continually implemented. The volatility smiles and smirks have not gotten more pronounced or diminished as the counter forces of increased noise trading and auction mechanisms neutralize each other.

4.8 SUMMARY AND CONCLUSIONS

Financial securities and organized exchanges have existed for over more than seven centuries. They have developed at a naturally slow pace, along with developments in domestic trade and international trade. In this chapter, we examined a very brief summary of the history of financial securities and organized financial exchanges around the world, from the classic Roman era, the Middle Ages in Europe, the age of discovery, the Industrial Revolution, and the modern era. We got a glimpse of the development of stock exchanges from the coffee shops in London to the London Stock Exchange, then the New York Stock Exchange and beyond. We have also learned about the most recent technological innovations in trading mechanisms and research. The name of the game is speed. Every market participant wants to trade faster than the others. This has led to the arms race to establish the fastest connections to the trading platforms so that when news arrives or when an arbitrage opportunity appears, the trader with the fastest network benefits the first and the most.

The chapter provided information about the types of orders that can be given to a broker and about the modern secondary markets – auction and over-the-counter – where these orders are executed. Intraday trading patterns at these exchanges are explored internationally. Intraday volatility patterns of smiles, smirks, and trading strategies for different kinds of investors are examined.

Financial securities exchanges are large, sophisticated corporations. The administrators and regulators of these exchanges have the responsibility to the society to develop good corporate social responsibility policies. In this day and age, any discrimination is unacceptable. Discriminations based on race, age, religion, ethnic background, sexual orientation, or gender have no place in the finance world. Good environmental, social, and governance (E.S.G.) practices must be implemented by the administrators. Any discriminatory or unethical behavior must not be tolerated, and any such evidence of these must be taken very seriously.

REFERENCES AND ADDITIONAL READING

Bodie, Z., Kane, A., Marcus, A.J. 2021. *Investments*. 12th edition. New York, McGraw-Hill.
Inci, A.C., Ozenbas, D. 2017. Intraday Volatility and the Implementation of a Closing Call Auction at Borsa Istanbul. *Emerging Markets Review*, 33, 79–89.
Isaacson, W. 2014. *The Innovators: How a Group of Hackers, Geniuses, and Geeks Created the Digital Revolution*. New York, Simon & Shuster.
Lewis, M. 2014. *Flash Boys*. New York, W.W. Norton & Company.

5

Asset Pricing Models

OBJECTIVES

- Categorize popular asset pricing models in a pedagogically unifying and comprehensive style.
- Investigate the practical ways how the models are used.
- Develop the empirical evaluation and comparison of the C.A.P.M. model and the Fama-French three-factor, Carhart four-factor, and Fama-French five-factor models.
- Construct the empirical verification and comparison of different asset pricing models.
- Apply the primer about how to run regressions in Excel.
- Design and organize the practical details about how to download stock data and market data from popular internet websites and from the Ken French website.
- Analyze the regression results for different asset pricing models, and formulate convincing evidence about the inferiority of the C.A.P.M. model in predicting the returns of stocks compared to other asset pricing models.

5.1 INTRODUCTION

The asset pricing literature has been part of finance and investments since the 1950s. The main purpose of the research has been to predict security prices in general, and stock prices in particular. In the prediction models, the endogenous independent variable is the expected return of the security. The natural question is, if all the statistical models are predicting the expected return, why are they called asset *pricing* models? The answer to the question is really simple. Once the future expected return is predicted by the model, it is used to calculate the future price. Thus, the asset pricing models do indeed figure out future prices of the securities, simply in an indirect manner.

DOI: 10.4324/9781003213697-5

As a numerical example, the expected return of a stock is 2% for the next week. Also, the stock's spot price is $10 per share currently. Then the future price of the stock one week from today will be calculated from $[P_1 - P_0]/P_0 = R_1$ by substituting in the numerical values accordingly: $[P_1 - 10]/10 = 0.02$, and $P_1 = 2+10 = \$12$. Thus, even though the direct focus in the asset pricing models is the expected return of the asset, the ultimate variable of interest is the future price.

5.2 EXPECTED RETURN

The expected return, $E(R)$, has several different interpretations and practical uses. The first interpretation is that expected return indicates the profit (or the loss) associated with the asset for the coming period. Based on asset pricing model and the considered factors, the asset's capacity to produce the profit or the loss is called the expected return. The expected return is one of the two important variables associated with an investment (the other is the risk of the investment).

The second purpose of estimating the expected return is to find the future price of the security, as explained in the previous section with a numerical example. While the return (profit or loss as a percentage) is of great importance for investors, learning about the future price of the security is also quite informative.

The third interpretation of the expected return is the discount rate that is used to calculate the present values of futures cash flows of the asset. In a similar vein, the future values of cash flows related to the asset are calculated by using the expected return as the compound rate. Therefore, the expected return is known as the discount rate or the compound rate in present/future value calculations.

The fourth interpretation for the expected return is the required rate of return for an asset. From the stakeholder's viewpoint, the investor demands a minimum return to commit funds to an asset. This minimum return or the required rate of return of the investor is the expected return suggested by the asset pricing model.

The fifth interpretation of the expected return is from the firm's viewpoint. While investors want the return on their equity investment to be as high as possible, from the managers' perspective, this is a huge burden: the managers and all the employees must work really hard using the resources of the firm in order to generate the profits and returns demanded by the investors. Thus, the expected return from the point of view of the managers of a company is called the cost of equity. When managers finance their projects by issuing equity (as opposed to issuing preferred stock or issuing bonds), the cost of getting the funding through equity securities is equal to the expected return suggested by asset pricing models.

The asset pricing models provide an important service to different fields of finance when they suggest an accurate value for the expected return.

5.3 THE LIST OF THE ASSET PRICING MODELS

There are two approaches to finding the expected return. The first approach is a collection of asset pricing models, also considered equilibrium models. The second approach starts with the expected return of another security and builds up to determine the expected return of the specific security.

A. Asset Pricing Models Approach

(1) Capital asset pricing model (C.A.P.M.): The C.A.P.M. model is considered to be the oldest asset pricing model that is out there. It was developed in the 1950s.

(2) Fama-French three-factor model: In their 1992 *Journal of Finance* article, two finance professors, Eugene Fama and Kenneth French, proposed that the expected returns of securities are influenced by the general movements of the market, the size of the firm, and the stock price per share to earnings per share ratio (the P/E ratio) of the firm the security is affiliated with.

(3) Carhart four-factor model: As the Fama-French three-factor model became popular, the finance researcher Mark Carhart introduced the Carhart four-factor model with momentum as the fourth factor in the estimation of the expected return.

(4) Fama-French five-factor model: More than 20 years after the publication of their paper on the subject, Fama and French published a series of papers on asset pricing models from 2015 through 2018. In addition to their original three factors, the fourth factor is the profitability of the firm. Robust profitability enhances expected return, while weak profitability hurts the expected return. And the fifth factor is capital investment. A conservative investment policy helps, while an aggressive investment policy hurts the expected return of the security. Debate and empirical investigation continue on the Fama-French five-factor model and on other models.

(5) Arbitrage pricing theory – Chen, Roll, and Ross model: Arbitrage pricing theory was first introduced by Stephen Ross in 1976. According to this theory, the expected return of a security depends on the linear combination of a number of factors. The factors are left undefined, and therefore, arbitrage pricing theory models are fairly flexible. Any researcher can develop an arbitrage pricing theory model by choosing macroeconomic, microeconomic, and financial factors. The challenge is convincing market participants about the validity and usefulness of the model through econometric and empirical tests and analyses. Indeed, hundreds of arbitrage pricing theory models have been proposed, but only a few have survived the empirical verification process and the test of time. One of those is the 1986 Chen, Roll, and Ross model. The C.R.R. four-factor model uses four macroeconomic factors in order to predict the expected return of a financial security:

   (a) The change in industrial production
   (b) The difference between the yields of long-term and short-term government bonds
   (c) The difference between low-grade corporate bonds and long-term government bond returns
   (d) Surprises or changes in the inflation rate

(6) Arbitrage pricing theory – Burmeister, Ibbotson, Roll, and Ross model: Another arbitrage pricing theory model that has stood the test of time is the 1994 B.I.R.R. five-factor model, introduced by Burmeister, Ibbotson, Roll, and Ross. The five macroeconomic factors are as follows:

   (a) Confidence risk as a difference between corporate and government bond yields
   (b) Time-horizon risk as the difference between long-term T-bond and short-term T-bill rates

(c) Inflation risk as the difference between actual and unexpected inflation rates

(d) Business-cycle risk as the difference between actual and expected business activity

(e) Market timing risk: part of the stock market return that cannot be explained by the first four macroeconomic factors

B. Bond Yield Plus Premium (B.Y.P.R.P.) Approach

The second approach for finding the expected return of a security starts with the expected return of another security that has a connection to the original security. The expected return of the other security is augmented with a risk premium to account for the risk differences.

A common example is about finding the expected return of a stock of a company. Starting with the yield of the fixed-income securities issued and sold by the company, a risk premium reflecting the additional risk characteristics of the stock is added. Typically, the risk premium is 3–4% or more (2% for the annual inflation and 2% for the annual G.D.P. growth rate).

Overall, the B.Y.P.R.P. approach is used less frequently than the first approach of asset pricing models. Because it provides a different perspective, B.Y.P.R.P. is utilized in the robustness analysis of the expected return and, therefore, finds its place in the reports to enrich the analysis by providing a different viewpoint. In the following sections, we investigate the asset pricing models in more detail.

5.4 THE CAPITAL ASSET PRICING MODEL (C.A.P.M.)

The C.A.P.M. model is an equilibrium model derived from the principles of modern financial theory. The foundations of modern portfolio theory on which the C.A.P.M. model is built on go back to Harry Markowitz's work in the 1950s. The C.A.P.M. model is credited to several researchers who independently obtained the formula for the model in the 1960s. Although more of the credit goes to William Sharpe (1964) and John Lintner (1965), two additional researchers, Jack Treynor (1962) and Jan Mossin (1966), are also recognized for their contributions.

5.4.1 Assumptions of the C.A.P.M. Model

The C.A.P.M. model has a significant number of assumptions. Some of these assumptions end up being detrimental to the practical application of the model. Nevertheless, the assumptions build up the theory, which in turn produces the C.A.P.M. model.

The first assumption is that investors are price takers. No individual or entity manipulates or influences prices. While this assumption is sensible for rational equilibrium, price manipulations and large trading positions initiated by powerful investments often change prices.

The second assumption is that the investment horizon is a single period. While this helps with the theoretical development, in reality few investors tend to consider a single period as an investment horizon. Most investors tend to retain positions for multiple periods.

The third assumption is that investments are limited to traded financial assets. While this is a sensible assumption, in reality nontraditional assets, such as real estate, art, precious materials, undeveloped land, and natural resources, can be part of an investment portfolio.

The C.A.P.M. model assumes there are no taxes or transaction costs. While transaction costs have declined, they still exist and sometimes impact investment decisions. Tax rates change by government policy, and they cannot be ignored.

Another assumption is that information is costless and is available to all investors. While the internet and communications technology have reduced costs and enabled fast access to information, trading speeds have also increased. Milliseconds are crucial in placing orders and in accessing the early places in the order queues. Most investors are not equipped with the capabilities of ultra-high-speed trading networks. Many investors will access information with a slight delay compared to professionals, and that slight delay will make all the difference. Overall, this assumption stays as a theoretical ideal rather than a practical reality.

The C.A.P.M. model assumes that all investors are rational mean-variance optimizers. This is hardly true. We frequently act irrationally, and irrationality impacts our trading decisions. We display herd behavior frequently, move with the crowd, and become part of the bubble. When the bubble bursts, our investments suffer. Our psychology affects our trading behavior. We become unreasonably euphoric after a seemingly successful investment decision. We become irrationally depressed if our trade turns out to be a failure. Many investors do not know about modern portfolio theory or about optimization. Most trading decisions are not the result of detailed analysis utilizing mean-variance optimization principles.

The C.A.P.M. model assumes homogenous expectations. This assumption mostly stays at the theoretical level. Each investor has a unique level of knowledge and access to analysis tools, resources, time, liquidity needs, investment horizon, tax liabilities, and personal needs. These perspectives lead to differences in expectations. Thus, the correct assumption is heterogeneous expectations on the part of investors.

Overall, many of the assumptions in the theoretical derivation of the C.A.P.M. model are inconsistent with reality. And these seemingly unimportant differences ultimately account for the poor empirical performance of the C.A.P.M. model.

5.4.2 The C.A.P.M. Equation

The C.A.P.M. equation is actually quite elegant. The expected return of an asset is the sum of two components: (1) the risk-free rate prevalent in the market, which any security must provide at a minimum and (2) the additional return because of the risk involved with the security, called the risk premium. This risk premium starts with the market's risk premium, which is the expected return of the market in access to the risk-free rate, $[E(R_M) - R_f]$. This average risk premium in the market is then multiplied by an amplification or shrinkage factor called the beta of the security, β.

Beta for an average stock, for the market portfolio, or for the market is normalized to 1. All other individual security betas are scattered around 1. If the security belongs to a firm more affected by the general movements in the market, then the beta of the security will be bigger than 1 (the market risk premium is amplified to represent the risk premium of the security). On the other hand, if a security is not affected much by general market movements, then the beta will be less than 1 so that the resultant risk premium of the security will be less than the average market risk premium. Therefore, the risk premium of the security is represented with (β) $[E(R_M) - R_f]$.

The C.A.P.M. model is the combination of these two components:

$$E(R_i) = R_f + \beta_I [E(R_M) - R_f] \tag{5.1}$$

The theoretical setting for the C.A.P.M. assumes rational mean-variance maximization, which means that an investor is expected to form a well-diversified portfolio and get rid of the unnecessary risk exposures of the individual securities. The remaining risk that cannot be eliminated is measured by beta. Therefore, while σ represents the total risk of a security (which one faces if all the capital is invested in that particular security), β represents the relevant risk that cannot be diversified away.

Finally, the beta of the security is formally defined as the normalized covariance between the returns of the security and the returns of the general market. The normalization is achieved by dividing the covariance by the variance (standard deviation squared) of the market returns. Therefore, the equation for beta for security i is as follows:

$$\beta_i = \frac{\text{cov}(R_i, R_M)}{\text{var}(R_M)} \tag{5.2}$$

These returns are supposed to be contemporaneous to accurately represent the current beta value. In practice, the historical returns of security i and the historical returns of the market are used to calculate the beta. In statistical calculations, the goal is to have as many observations as possible. But in finance, and especially in the beta calculation, using returns from 20 years ago would not be a good idea because, at that time, the firm would have different characteristics and risk and return features and, thus, a different beta. Therefore, to calculate a proxy for the contemporaneous beta, five years' worth of historical data are typically used.

5.4.3 Security Market Line and the C.A.P.M. Equation

The graphical representation of the C.A.P.M. equation is called the security market line (S.M.L.). As seen in figure 5.1, the x-axis represents risk measured by beta, and the y-axis is the expected return of the security. The S.M.L. is described by the C.A.P.M. equation. Therefore, for a riskless security (with $\beta = 0$, as well as $\sigma = 0$), the expected return is simply the risk-free rate. As the beta value increases, so does the expected return. The expected return of a security with a $\beta = 1$ would be the expected return of the market, $E(R_M)$, according to the S.M.L. and the C.A.P.M.

Any security above (below) the S.M.L., such as the point represented by point C (D), would be considered as an undervalued (overvalued), inexpensive (expensive), or attractive (unattractive) stock because, given the relevant risk, the stock would be providing a higher (lower) return than the one suggested by the C.A.P.M. Either C or D would imply an inefficient market. Such points will not stay away from S.M.L. forever. Once the market participants identify the inefficiency and the arbitrage opportunity, they will trade in such a way that the point will be pushed toward the S.M.L., and the inefficiency will disappear relatively quickly.

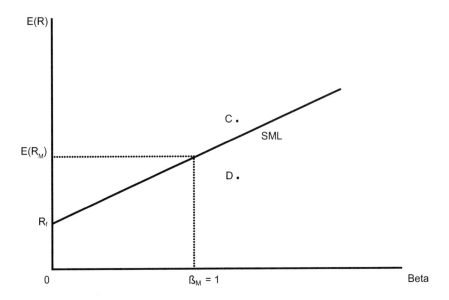

FIGURE 5.1 The Security Market Line

Some examples of the S.M.L. and the C.A.P.M. equation connection are as follows:

Example 1: If the market risk premium is 8%, the risk-free rate is 3%, and the beta of a
security is 1.25, what is the expected return of the security?
Answer: Using the C.A.P.M. equation for the S.M.L., we get the following:

$$E(R) = R_f + b \ [E(R_M) - R_f] = 0.03 + 1.25 \ [0.08] = 0.13 = 13\%$$

Example 2: Following up on example 1, if the beta of the security is 0.6 instead of 1.25,
what will be the expected return of the security?
Answer: Using the C.A.P.M. equation for the S.M.L., we get the following:

$$E(R) = R_f + b \ [E(R_M) - R_f] = 0.03 + 0.6 \ [0.08] = 0.078 = 7.8\%$$

Example 3: Following up with example 1, what is the expected return of the security if
beta is 1?
Answer: Using the C.A.P.M. equation for the S.M.L., we get the following:

$$E(R) = R_f + b \ [E(R_M) - R_f] = 0.03 + 1 \ [0.08] = 0.11 = 11\%, \text{ which is the expected}$$
return of the market

Example 4: Following up with example 1, what is the expected return of the security if
beta is 0?

Answer: Using the C.A.P.M. equation for the S.M.L., we get the following:

$$E(R) = R_f + b\,[E(R_M) - R_f] = 0.03 + 0\,[0.08] = 0.03 = 3\%, \text{ which is the risk-free rate}$$

5.4.4 Estimation of the Components of the C.A.P.M. Equation

If an investor wishes to utilize the C.A.P.M. equation to determine the expected return of a security that is of interest, what should be the process? From the right side of the C.A.P.M. equation, three components must be instituted to calculate the expected return: the risk-free rate, the beta of the security, and the market risk premium.

The first component of the C.A.P.M. equation is the prevalent risk-free rate in the economy where security exists. For a security that is based in the U.S., the common proxy is the ten-year U.S. government bond yield. One easy access resource is finance.yahoo.com/bonds for this rate. The risk-free rate is the ten-year government bond yield and not the short-term three-month T-bill yield. For equity investors, the creation of a well-balanced and well-diversified portfolio is not a trivial task. Such investments should be retained for the long term, typically in the range of ten years. Of course, an investor can decide on a different horizon, and in that case, the government bond yield with the matching horizon should be used as the risk-free rate.

The second component of the C.A.P.M. equation is the market risk premium. The market risk premium should be based on the expectations of all the market participants. Pablo Fernandez at I.E.S.E. Business School and his co-authors periodically send an email to market participants, academicians, and investment professionals in dozens of countries. The email asks two simple questions: 'What do you think will be the market risk premium in your country?' and 'What do you think will be the prevailing risk-free rate in your country?' The answers are compiled and summarized with statistical measures. The results are provided in a working paper at the Social Science Research Network website (ssrn.com), freely available to download. The average expected market risk premium provided by the market participants in each country (in the most recent working paper, 88 countries were covered) is the ideal market risk premium. In the June 2021 publication of the working paper, the market risk premium for the U.S. was 5.5% (5.8% for France, Germany, and Holland; 5.6% for the U.K.; 5.2% for Switzerland).

The third component of the C.A.P.M. equation is the beta of the security. Beta cannot be observed directly. Therefore, it must be estimated statistically, typically with a linear regression model. The regression is known as the market model, the statistical version of C.A.P.M.:

$$R_{i,t} - R_{f,t} = \alpha_i + \beta_i[R_{M,t} - R_{f,t}] + \varepsilon_t \tag{5.3}$$

In the regression, the excess returns of security i are regressed on the market excess return over a time period of observations. The regression estimates the intercept coefficient, $\hat{\alpha}$, and the slope coefficient, $\hat{\beta}_i$, the third component of the C.A.P.M.

Running regressions with software programs such as Microsoft Excel is quite easy, as explained in the primer chapter05Addentum1_primerRunningRegressions.doc. Following the instructions, running a regression of the daily excess returns of Microsoft on the daily excess

SUMMARY OUTPUT

Regression Statistics	
Multiple R	0.8281306
R Square	0.6858003
Adjusted R Square	0.6855505
Standard Error	0.0096428
Observations	1260

ANOVA

	df	SS	MS	F	Significance F
Regression	1	0.255314902	0.255315	2745.82	0
Residual	1258	0.116972658	9.30E-05		
Total	1259	0.37228756			

	Coefficients	Standard Error	t Stat	value	Lower 95%	Upper 95%	Lower 95.0%	Upper 95.0%
Intercept	0.000656	0.000272157	2.410205	0.01609	0.00012202	0.00119	0.00012202	0.00118989
XSMarketReturn	1.16912	0.022311196	52.4006	0	1.1253487	1.212891	1.1253487	1.21289121

FIGURE 5.2 C.A.P.M. Regression Output for Microsoft Stock for the Period from June 29, 2016, to June 30, 2021

returns of the market using Excel generates the regression output in Figure 5.2. Three pieces of information are important:

(1) The estimated coefficients: The intercept coefficient is estimated as $\hat{\alpha} = 0.000656$. And the beta coefficient is estimated as $\hat{\beta} = 1.16912$. The beta coefficient is the third component of the C.A.P.M. equation in estimating the expected return of the security.

(2) The statistical significance of the estimated coefficient: The point estimates of the estimated coefficients are important. But they must be statistically significant. Otherwise, they can be assumed practically as zero. The *t-stat* reported in the table reveals the statistical significance of the estimates. The absolute value of the *t-statistic* is supposed to be higher than a critical value to conclude that the estimate is statistically significant with a certain level of confidence. A level of confidence makes the statistical significance reliable. Typically, 95% significance is considered a high enough level of confidence. The corresponding *t-statistics* value for the 95% significance level is 1.960. Therefore, if an estimated variable has a *t-statistic* whose absolute value is larger than 1.960, then we conclude with 95% confidence that the variable is statistically significant. If the researcher is looking for a 99% (90%) confidence level, the corresponding t-statistic is 2.579 (1.645).

Both the intercept coefficient and the beta coefficient are statistically significant at a 95% level in Figure 5.2 because the intercept coefficient t-stat is 2.41, and the beta coefficient t-stat is 52.40. Thus, the beta estimate is indeed the third component in the C.A.P.M. model. As for the intercept coefficient, the statistical significance indicates that the Microsoft excess return is not explained by the market excess return factor alone. There are quite likely other factors that influence the excess returns of Microsoft. This is the interpretation of a statistically significant intercept coefficient.

(3) The third useful piece of information from the regression output in Figure 5.2 is the adjusted R-squared. Adjusted R-squared measures the proportion of the variation in the dependent endogenous variable, excess Microsoft returns, which is explained by the

independent exogenous factor variables in the regression. A regression model is more powerful, better performing, and preferable if the adjusted R-squared is high and closer to 1.

Furthermore, the adjusted R-squared takes into consideration the number of exogenous variables in the regression. A regression model with many independent variables is penalized in the adjusted R-squared calculation in order to have a level playing field for models with lower numbers of independent variables.

These characteristics of adjusted R-squared make it possible to compare different regression models with different independent factors. The best model would be the one with the highest adjusted R-squared value. In the regression output in Figure 5.2, the C.A.P.M. model has an adjusted R-squared of 0.68555 for the Microsoft stock excess returns.

Once the regression is executed and the three components are determined, the C.A.P.M. model can be used to determine the expected return of the security. Continuing with the C.A.P.M. model for Microsoft equity security, we would predict the expected return of Microsoft stock as follows:

$$E(R_{MSFT}) = 1.239\% + 1.16912 [5.5\%] = 7.6692\%.$$

Here, the ten-year U.S. T-bond yield is used as the risk-free rate; the market risk premium is assumed to be 5.5%; the beta is generated as 1.16912 using the five-year returns.

It should be noted that estimating the beta coefficient through the regression model is a noisy process. Therefore, several issues need to be emphasized:

(1) The regression model should use a decent number of observations for the results to be statistically sound. Generally, the minimum number of observations should be 60 data points as the sample size.
(2) Ideally, in a statistical regression, the sample size should be as large as possible so that the power of the statistical tests and the statistical significance of the results are strong. However, in beta estimations, the characteristics of the firm/asset where the security belongs to should be current. In a practical sense, data samples covering the recent five years of returns are sufficient. Of course, this decision is subjective. If the researcher can make a valid case for using a longer/shorter time horizon, that would be fine.
(3) The security excess returns should be regressed on the excess returns of a value-weighted, well-diversified portfolio in representing the market returns, such as the S&P 500 index.
(4) As mentioned before, the beta estimate will only be acceptable if it is statistically significant. Otherwise, the beta coefficient is assumed as '0'.
(5) Many times, the researcher will adjust the estimated beta of the regression either up or down. The overall anticipation of the future of the beta is a mean reversion toward '1'. A new firm/company/asset/entity will always have significant uncertainty. Thus, the beta for such a security can be estimated as anything. But as the entity grows and stabilizes over time with additional lines of business, the characteristics will start to become similar to that of a large portfolio or to that of the overall market. Then, the estimated beta in the future will move toward '1'. The researcher may take this into consideration, and the calculated betas can be adjusted toward 1. This can be achieved by putting a weight of two-thirds

(67%) on the estimated beta and a weight of one-third (33%) on '1'. Such a weighting scheme would adjust beta toward '1'. In the previous numerical example, the estimated beta was 1.1796751. The adjusted beta according to the weighting scheme would indeed be closer to '1':

Adjusted β = 2/3 (Estimated β) + 1/3 (1) = 2/3 (1.16912) + 1/3 (1) = 1.1127433.

Of course, the specific weights for the adjustment process and whether to use the estimated beta or the adjusted beta are based on the policy of the institution or the discretion of the researcher.

5.4.5 Evaluation of the C.A.P.M. Model

Since the C.A.P.M. model was introduced in the 1960s, there have been numerous empirical tests on its validity and predictive ability. Unfortunately, as intuitive and as simple as the model is, the empirical performance has been consistently poor. The C.A.P.M. is flawed mainly because of the validity of its assumptions mentioned before. However, the C.A.P.M. continues to be a widely used model. It is easy to understand, easy to interpret and explain, and easy to formulate an investment strategy around.

Two fundamental principles related to the C.A.P.M. model are sound and valid. The first is that the systematic risk that cannot be eliminated is the one that matters. So even though the total risk measurement, σ, is important, the relevant systematic risk measurement, β, is more practical and useful. Cyclical sectors, industries, and firms focused on manufacturing expensive goods and services are affected more by the market movements and have higher β values. On the other hand, sectors, industries, and firms in stable defensive (food, utilities, etc.) businesses are not impacted much by the ups and downs in the markets and have lower β values. The second principle is that a well-diversified portfolio is suitable for many investors. A well-diversified portfolio where the unnecessary sources of risk are weeded out should be the goal for those who do not have the time or research resources. On the other hand, for professional investors with ample resources, time, and funds, there will be extra profits with additional research and modified portfolios.

5.5 THE FAMA-FRENCH THREE-FACTOR MODEL

The empirical problems and prediction flaws with the C.A.P.M. model were evident from the 1980s. Alternatives were sought, and in 1992, two well-known professors and researchers in finance, Eugene Fama and Kenneth French, published a paper, 'The Cross-Section of Expected Stock Returns' in the *Journal of Finance* as a substantial improvement to the C.A.P.M. model. They documented the following:

(1) Stock returns are negatively related to the size of a company (as measured by market capitalization). Fama and French have noted that small firms/companies tend to consistently generate higher expected returns than suggested by the C.A.P.M. On the other hand, large, stable, mature firms/companies tend to consistently generate lower expected returns

for their securities than suggested by the C.A.P.M. Thus, smaller-sized company securities have higher expected returns than larger-sized company securities. This factor is known as the size factor and is expressed as S.M.B. (small minus big − focus on smaller-sized firms, and avoid or short larger-sized firms).

(2) Stock returns are positively related to the ratio of the book value to market value of the equity of the company. The book-to-market ratio is practically the inverse of the better-known price-to-equity ratio. A relatively low P/E ratio company is said to have a value stock, while a relatively high P/E ratio company is said to have a growth stock. Value stocks are said to perform better than growth stocks. An imperfect but intuitively sensible view of value stocks is that the low P/E ratio is due to the low price in the denominator of the ratio. Such a low price will tend to go up in the future, generating a comparatively higher return. On the other hand, the high P/E ratio is due to the high price in the denominator. The price has already gone up significantly in the near past, and there is not much more room for further increase. Therefore, the price will stay at the same level or may even go down, generating a comparatively lower return. Overall, this intuitive train of thought (which makes sense but admittedly ignores the full details) says that value stocks with low P/E ratios lead to higher expected returns than growth stocks with high P/E ratios.

Fama and French focus on the book-value-to-market-value ratio, B.V./M.V. Therefore, the attractive low P/E ratio is equivalent to the high B.V./M.V. ratio. Similarly, the unattractive high P/E ratio is equivalent to the low B.V./M.V. ratio. High B.V./M.V. ratio securities consistently generate higher returns than the ones predicted by the C.A.P.M. Similarly, low B.V./M.V. ratio securities consistently generate lower returns than the ones predicted by the C.A.P.M. This factor has been known as the book-to-market factor and is expressed as H.M.L. (high minus low − focus on high B.V./M.V. firms, and avoid or short low B.V./M.V. firms).

Fama and French note that smaller firms and/or firms with high book-to-market (low P/E ratio) have higher stock returns than predicted by the C.A.P.M. model. According to the Fama-French three-factor model, the expected return of a security is related to the expected market risk premium, the size of the entity the security is affiliated with, and the book-to-market ratio:

$$E(R_i) = R_f + \beta_{M,i} \, [E(R_M) − R_f] + \beta_{SMB,i} \, [SMB] + \beta_{HML,i} \, [HML] \tag{5.4}$$

In the statistical interpretation, the excess return of the security is regressed on the excess market return, excess returns of small securities over big securities (S.M.B.), and excess returns of high book-to-market securities over low book-to-market securities (H.M.L.):

$$R_{i,t} − R_{f,t} = \alpha_i + \beta_{M,i}[R_{M,t} − R_{f,t}] + \beta_{SMB,i}[SMB] + \beta_{HML,i}[HML] + \varepsilon_t \tag{5.5}$$

The regression estimates the intercept coefficient, $\hat{\alpha}$; the market factor coefficient, $\hat{\beta}_{M,i}$; size factor coefficient, $\hat{\beta}_{SMB,i}$; and the book-to-market factor coefficient, $\beta_{HML,i}$.

Application of the instructions in the primer and running the regression of the daily excess returns of Microsoft on the daily excess returns of the market, the size premium, and the book-to-market premium using Excel generates the output in Figure 5.3.

SUMMARY OUTPUT

Regression Statistics	
Multiple R	0.8901247
R Square	0.792322
Adjusted R Square	0.791826
Standard Error	0.0078458
Observations	1260

ANOVA

	df	SS	MS	F	Significance F
Regression	3	0.294971625	0.098324	1597.275	0
Residual	1256	0.077315935	6.16E-05		
Total	1259	0.37228756			

	Coefficients	Standard Error	t Stat	P-value	Lower 95%	Upper 95%	Lower 95.0%	Upper 95.0%
Intercept	0.000513	0.000221581	2.314974	0.020775	7.8245E-Q5	0.000948	7.82E-05	0.00094766
XSMarketReturn	1.2468552	0.01852021	67.32403	0	1.21052124	1.283189	1.21052124	1.28318915
SMB	-0.354111	0.034545275	-10.2506	9.82E-24	-4218835	-0.28634	-0.4218835	-0.2863379
HML	-0.438972	0.025555471	-17.1772	1.45E-59	-0.48910807	-0.38884	-4891081	-0.3888358

FIGURE 5.3 Fama-French Three-Factor Regression Output for Microsoft for the Period from June 29, 2016, to June 30, 2021

The estimates are 1.2469 for the market factor, −0.3541 for the size factor, and −0.4390 for the book-to-market factor. All three estimates are statistically significant because the absolute values of the t-statistics are all larger than 1.96. The market beta of 1.2469 indicates that the expected return of Microsoft stock will be positively influenced by market movements and will be more pronounced than the market. The negative and statistically significant size factor tells us that the company is large and the size of the company is hurting the expected returns of the stock. The book-to-market factor is also negative and significant. This means the expected returns of Microsoft are reduced by the impact of the book-to-market factor. The P/E ratio of Microsoft seems to be higher than average, categorizing Microsoft as a growth stock whose price has grown significantly before but is now expected to decline in the future.

Finally, the adjusted R-squared for C.A.P.M. from Figure 5.2 is 0.68555, and the adjusted R-squared for the Fama-French three-factor model in Figure 5.3 is 0.79183. Even a tiny difference is important in deciding which model is superior for prediction purposes, and here the difference is vast. The Fama-French three-factor model is clearly better for predicting the expected return of Microsoft stock.

The proportion of the variation in the excess Microsoft return that is explained by the independent factors of the Fama-French three-factor regression is 79% as opposed to 69% for the C.A.P.M. Even after penalizing the Fama-French model in the calculation of the adjusted R-squared for using more independent factors, the model still ends up with a higher adjusted R-squared value.

5.5.1 Reception for and Problems with the Fama-French Three-Factor Model

When Eugene Fama and Ken French published their paper in 1992, the reception was lukewarm. It took more research, additional papers, and a large number of empirical tests for market participants to start feeling more comfortable. These days, most, if not all, research institutions, investment firms, and professionals prefer the Fama-French three-factor model over the C.A.P.M. But this does not mean that the Fama-French model is immune to criticism:

(1) The Fama-French model is an empirical model without an elaborate theoretical framework. The preference would be a sound theory, followed up with a detailed empirical analysis. Here, the focus has mostly been on the empirical side.

(2) Fama and French proposed the market premium, size, and book-to-market as the three factors. Will these variables continue to have predictive power in the future as dynamic changes take place in domestic and international markets? Are these three the only factors affecting expected returns? Ideally, a model should be sound enough to stand the test of time and answer these questions definitively, but in this context, the issues remain as open questions.

If anyone would like to employ the Fama-French three-factor model for regressions, where can the data for the size factor S.M.B. (the difference in returns between the small firm portfolio and the large firm portfolio as a time series) and the data for the book-to-market factor H.M.L. (high book-to-market portfolio return minus low book-to-market portfolio return as a time series) be obtained? The data are continually prepared, updated, and made available for interested researchers at the Dartmouth College – Tuck Business School website for Ken French: http://mba.tuck. dartmouth.edu/pages/faculty/ken.french/data_library.html. All the factor data with varying frequencies, along with the most recent values for the expected return calculations, are available, both for domestic analysis and for international market analyses. For example, using the market risk premium, size premium, and book-to-market premium from the Ken French website, and our regression output for the factor coefficients, we can estimate the expected return for Microsoft as

$$E(R_{MSFT}) = 1.239\% + 1.247 \ [2.79\%] - 0.354 \ [-0.22\%] - 0.439 \ [-7.70\%] = 8.176\%.$$

5.6 CARHART FOUR-FACTOR MODEL

As the Fama-French three-factor model became more mainstream in the 1990s, another researcher, Mark Carhart, came up with an extended version. The Carhart four-factor model, published in the 1997 *Journal of Finance* article 'On Persistence in Mutual Fund Performance', introduces momentum as the fourth factor. Securities that were up (down) in price movement in the near past continued to move in the up (down) direction in the near future, as momentum suggests. Up firms/companies tend to consistently generate higher expected returns than suggested by the C.A.P.M. On the other hand, down firms/companies tend to consistently generate lower expected returns. The momentum factor is expressed as U.M.D. (up minus down – focus on up firms, and avoid or short down firms):

$$E(R_i) = R_f + \beta_{M,i} \ [E(R_M) - R_f] + \beta_{SMB,i} \ [SMB] + \beta_{HML,i} \ [HML] + \beta_{UMD,i} \ [UMD]. \qquad (5.6)$$

Statistically, the excess return of the security is regressed on the excess market return, excess returns of small over big securities (S.M.B.), excess returns of high book-to-market over low book-to-market securities (H.M.L.), and excess returns of up over down securities (U.M.D.):

$$R_{i,t} - R_{f,t} = \alpha_i + \beta_{M,i}[R_{M,t} - R_{f,t}] + \beta_{SMB,i}[SMB] + \beta_{HML,i}[HML] \qquad (5.7)$$
$$+ \beta_{UMD,i}[UMD] + \varepsilon_t$$

The regression estimates the intercept coefficient, $\hat{\alpha}$; the market factor coefficient, $\hat{\beta}_{M,i}$; size factor coefficient, $\hat{\beta}_{SMB,i}$; book-to-market factor coefficient, $\hat{\beta}_{HML,i}$; and momentum factor coefficient, $\hat{\beta}_{UMD,i}$. Ken French's Dartmouth website provides the momentum data. The Carhart four-factor model regression results with Excel are presented in Figure 5.4.

The market, size, book-value-to-market-value ratio, and momentum factor are all statistically significant. The negative size factor indicates that Microsoft is larger than an average company and that the expected return of Microsoft is negatively affected. The negative book-value-to-market-value ratio indicates that Microsoft is a growth stock with a high P/E ratio and that the expected return of Microsoft stock is negatively affected. Finally, Microsoft stock has experienced statistically significant positive momentum in the near past (indicated by the momentum factor), which contributes positively to the expected return of Microsoft in the near future. The adjusted R-squared for the Carhart four-factor model is 0.79388. This is larger than the Fama-French three-factor adjusted R-squared value of 0.79183. Thus, the best asset pricing model for predicting the returns of Microsoft is the Carhart four-factor model.

When the Carhart model was introduced in the late 1990s, there was skepticism and hesitance. The adjusted R-squared value is not consistently better for the Carhart model when compared to that of the Fama-French model. Therefore, the superiority of the Carhart model over the Fama-French three-factor model has not been absolute. Fama and French themselves have not embraced the momentum factor, but they provide the data on their website.

SUMMARY OUTPUT

Regression Statistics	
Multiple R	0.8913647
R Square	0.794531
Adjusted R Square	0.7938761
Standard Error	0.0078071
Observations	1260

ANOVA

	df	SS	MS	F	Significance F
Regression	4	0.295794018	0.073949	1213.245	0
Residual	1255	0.076493542	6.10E-05		
Total	1259	0.37228756			

	Coefficients	Standard Error	t Stat	P-value	Lower 95%	Upper 95%	Lower 95.0%	Upper 95.0%
Intercept	0.0005416	0.000220625	2.454911	0.014227	0.00010878	0.000974	0.00010878	0.00097445
XSMarketReturn	1.2419559	0.018476989	67.21636	0	1.20570672	1.278205	1.20570672	1.2782051
SMB	-0.346853	0.034431482	-10.0737	5.26E-23	-0.41440272	-0.278205	-0.4144027	-0.2793035
HML	-0.356916	0.033847836	-10.5447	5.74E-25	-0.4233205	-0.29051	-0.4233205	-0.2905113
UMD	0.0965567	0.026286538	3.673238	0.00025	0.0449863	0.148127	0.0449863	0.14812711

FIGURE 5.4 Carhart Four-Factor Regression Output for Microsoft Stock for the Period from June 29, 2016, to June 30, 2021

5.7 FAMA-FRENCH FIVE-FACTOR MODEL

About a quarter century after introducing the three-factor model, Eugene Fama and Ken French published several papers from 2015 through 2018 on a new asset pricing model. The five-factor model includes two factors in addition to the market, size, and book-to-market ratio. The first is the profitability of the firm. Robust profitability enhances the expected return, while weak profitability hurts the expected return. Fama and French have designated the factor as R.M.W. (robust minus weak – focus on 'robust' firms, and avoid or short 'weak' firms). The second factor is the capital investment the firm undertakes. Large capital investments hurt the expected returns in the near future. Those investments may lead to successful outcomes, profits, and positive returns in the long term, but for the one-year or less short horizon, such aggressive investments are not helpful. Rather, a conservative investment strategy leads to better-expected returns in the near future. The investment factor is designated as C.M.A. (conservative minus aggressive – focus on firms investing conservatively, and avoid/short firms investing aggressively):

$$E(R_i) = R_f + \beta_{M,i} [E(R_M) - R_f] + \beta_{SMB,i} [SMB] + \beta_{HML,i} [HML]$$
$$+ \beta_{RMW,i} [RMW] + \beta_{CMA,i} [CMA]. \tag{5.8}$$

In these papers, Fama and French argue that the information in the momentum factor is absorbed by their five factors. They also report that the book-to-market ratio is not as significant as before.

The regression output of the Fama-French five-factor model is in Figure 5.5. All five factors are statistically significant. The market movements impact Microsoft stock's expected returns in a positive and amplified manner. Size and book-to-market have negative factor

SUMMARY OUTPUT

Regression Statistics	
Multiple R	0.8932593
R Square	0.7979122
Adjusted R Square	0.7971064
Standard Error	0.0077457
Observations	1260

ANOVA

	df	SS	MS	F	Significance F
Regression	5	0.297052784	0.059411	990.2447	0
Residual	1254	0.075234776	6E-05		
Total	1259	0.37228756			

	Coefficients	Standard Error	t Stat	P-value	Lower 95%	Upper 95%	Lower 95.0%	Upper 95.0%
Intercept	0.0004926	0.000218846	2.251091	0.024552	6.3297E-05	0.000922	6.33E-05	0.000922
XSMarketReturn	1.2249297	0.018845517	64.99846	0	1.18795746	1.2619019	1.18595746	1.2619019
SMB	-0.335697	0.035478439	-9.46201	1.44E-20	-0.405301	-0.266094	-0.405301	-0.266097
HML	-0.394316	0.031965912	-12.3355	4.43E-33	-0.4570282	-0.331603	-2.4570282	-0.331603
RMW	0.1819162	0.053889783	3.375708	0.000759	0.07619211	0.2876403	0.07619211	0.2876403
CMA	-0.333834	0.067107503	-4.97462	7.45E-07	-0.4654896	-0.202179	-0.4654896	-0.202179

FIGURE 5.5 Fama-French Five-Factor Regression Output for Microsoft for the Period from June 29, 2016, to June 30, 2021

estimates. Therefore, as before, the large size of Microsoft and the growth stock characteristic with a higher than average P/E ratio both hurt expected returns. The profitability factor is positive, which means Microsoft has been experiencing robust profits, enhancing expected returns. Meanwhile, the investment factor is negative and significant, implying that Microsoft has engaged in an aggressive investment policy, hurting short-term expected returns. The adjusted R-squared for the Fama-French five-factor model is 0.79711. Thus, the best asset pricing model for predicting the returns of Microsoft is the Fama-French five-factor model.

The Fama-French five-factor model has sparked a lot of interest in academic and practitioner circles. The model's predictive power is under investigation with out-of-sample tests and international applications.

5.8 SUMMARY AND CONCLUSION

The arbitrage pricing models use few assumptions and an unrestricted set of risk premiums added to the risk-free rate in order to predict expected returns. The risk premiums are amplified or shrunk with factor loadings (estimated beta coefficients). Over the years, a few arbitrage pricing models using macroeconomic risk premium factors have remained popular.

The C.A.P.M. and the follow-up asset pricing models are considered special arbitrage pricing theory models with more restrictions and more focus on company-specific attributes. The original Fama-French adds three (market, size, book-to-market), Carhart adds four (market, size, book-to-market, momentum), and the new Fama-French adds five (market, size, book-to-market, profitability, investment) risk premiums to the risk-free rate. The empirical regressions and estimations in the chapter were about the expected return of Microsoft stock. If another security is examined, the adjusted-R-squared values of the models might lead to a different order of the model's predictive ability.

Whatever model is picked, there will be scrutiny: (1) Model uncertainty – is the model really the correct one? (2) Input uncertainty – are the current values of the risk premium items (the factor values and the estimated beta coefficients/factor loading), including the risk-free rate, correct? (3) These sources of uncertainty remain because the characteristics of financial markets, securities, factors, and factor loadings are all dynamic. (4) One can add additional factors to explain the returns of the securities, but there needs to be a justification. (5) The explanatory variables might be related to each other. Such 'collinearity' problems adversely impact the model.

As the ecology of financial markets evolves, so do the models and the inputs. Therefore, finding the best model remains an open question. The goal should be to use the best model at that particular point in time to make predictions about expected returns while, at the same time, to continue to search for the superior model for prediction purposes.

REFERENCES AND ADDITIONAL READING

Burmeister, E., Roll, R., Ross, S.A. 1994. A Practitioner's Guide to Arbitrage Pricing Theory. In *A Practitioner's Guide to Factor Models*. Charlottesville, The Research Foundation of the Institute of Chartered Financial Analysts.

Carhart, M.M. 1997. On Persistence in Mutual Fund Performance. *Journal of Finance*, 52, 57–82.

Chen, N.F., Roll, R., Ross, S.A. 1986. Economic Forces and the Stock Market. *Journal of Business*, 59, 383–403.

Fama, E.F., French, K.R. 1992. The Cross-Section of Expected Stock Returns. *Journal of Finance*, 47, 427–465.

Fama, E.F., French, K.R. 2015a. A Five Factor Asset Pricing Model. *Journal of Financial Economics*, 116, 1–22.

Fama, E.F., French, K.R. 2015b. Incremental Variables and the Investment Opportunity Set. *Journal of Financial Economics*, 117, 470–488.

Fama, E.F., French, K.R. 2016. Dissecting Anomalies with a Five-Factor Model. *Review of Financial Studies*, 29, 69–103.

Fama, E.F., French, K.R. 2017. International Tests of a Five-Factor Asset-Pricing Model. *Journal of Financial Economics*, 123, 441–463.

Fernandez, P., Bañuls, S., Acin, F. 2021. Survey: Market Risk Premium and Risk-Free Rate Used for 88 Countries in 2021. *IESE Business School Working Paper*, IESE.

Lintner, J. 1965. The Valuation of Risk Assets and the Selection of Risky Investments in Stock Portfolios and Capital Budgets. *Review of Economics and Statistics*, 47, 13–37.

Markowitz, H.M. 1952. Portfolio Selection. *Journal of Finance*, 7, 77–91.

Mossin, J. 1966. Equilibrium in Capital Asset Markets. *Econometrica*, 34, 768–783.

Sharpe, W.F. 1964. Capital Asset Prices: Theory of Market Equilibrium. *Journal of Finance*, 19, 425–442.

Treynor, J.L. 1962. *Toward a Theory of Market Value of Risky Assets*. Unpublished manuscript.

6

Modern Portfolio Theory and Optimization

OBJECTIVES

- Appraise the fundamentals of modern portfolio theory established by Harry Markowitz.
- Defend 'putting all the eggs in one basket is wrong and that forming a well-diversified portfolio is beneficial for reducing risk and increasing returns'.
- Formulate the technical tools and the know-how to establish how much to invest in different securities to obtain the best portfolio – the optimal portfolio.
- Appraise the technical tools of optimization for an unrealistic two-to-three-security portfolio.
- Conjecture the full quantitative ecology for realistic multi-security portfolio optimization.
- Design the evaluation methods for portfolio characteristics and statistics utilizing Excel with the matrix algebra primer (chapter06Addentum1_primerMatrix Algebra.doc).
- Develop an understanding of the tools and techniques for a realistic optimal portfolio.
- Construct the optimal portfolio with Merton's (1972) proposition using Excel; design the concept of optimal weights of the securities of a portfolio.
- Develop concepts of minimum variance portfolio, efficient frontiers, and short-selling.
- Appraise the alternative way of generating the optimal portfolio with Solver in Excel.

6.1 INTRODUCTION

Forming portfolios is the sensible thing to do for most investors. If someone is absolutely certain about the superior performance of a single or a few securities, then the funds should be used for that security or those few securities. However, most of the time, market participants

DOI: 10.4324/9781003213697-6

are not absolutely certain about what will happen in the future. Therefore, forming a well-diversified portfolio of pre-researched promising securities if the proper approach. But then the question becomes, how much of the market participant's wealth should be invested in each security, such that the portfolio that is formed generates the best return and lowest risk at the same time? The answer is provided by the optimization tools and techniques introduced in the 1950s by the father of modern portfolio theory, Harry Markowitz, and followed up by other researchers, including Merton in the 1970s.

Before we learn about portfolio optimization, we first review the asset classes from which the securities of a portfolio come. Then we examine an unrealistic two-security portfolio and explore the basics of portfolio characteristics. We next explore realistic, multi-security portfolios with many securities. We do so with a primer on the matrix algebra theory and with the application of the theory using Excel for practical, real-life challenges. We then learn about portfolio optimization, minimum variance portfolios, and forming portfolios in markets where short-selling is/is not allowed. Finally, we examine whether an optimal portfolio can be adjusted by introducing subjective restrictions to accommodate the desires of investment clients.

6.2 ASSET CLASSES

Investors have a very large spectrum of alternative asset classes from which securities can be picked to form a portfolio. These asset classes offer a large variety of risk and return characteristics from global markets.

6.2.1 Money Market Instruments

Investors would like to keep a portion of their wealth as cash. When a great opportunity suddenly comes by for a limited time, the cash can be used for taking a position in that security. Or if there is a sudden personal need due to a medical emergency, for example, cash can be used for such personal reasons. Therefore, cash and cash-like securities make up the first asset class: money market instruments. Compared to other alternatives, these securities have the lowest risk but also the lowest returns and profits. They can be converted into cash very quickly and easily. Examples of money market instruments are certificate of deposit accounts (CDs); checking and savings accounts at banks; short-term debt securities issued by corporations (generally called commercial paper) and by governments (such as Treasury bills in the U.S.); Eurodollars (dollar-denominated deposits outside of the U.S.); Eurocurrencies (local currency deposits outside of the domestic country); trading of deposits between banking institutions, such as the federal funds (trading of U.S. banking institution deposits at the Federal Reserve in the U.S.); and international banks borrowing and lending to each other using the L.I.B.O.R. (London Interbank Offer Rate) rate.

6.2.2 Fixed-Income Instruments (Bonds)

Bonds constitute the second fundamental asset class. They are also known as fixed-income instruments because for most bonds, the interest, or coupon, payments are fixed amounts paid out at regular intervals. Bond is the official way of borrowing for an institution. When an entity borrows, the legally binding pieces of paper issued and 'sold' to lenders in exchange for the loan are bonds. These bonds act as proof of the loan and contain the conditions, such as the length of time of the bond, the interest rate associated with the loan (coupon rate), and the frequency of the coupon payments. There is a large and rich over-the-counter (through computer networks) secondary market for bonds. Bonds issued and sold by governments (sovereign bonds), by government agencies, by state and local city governments, by corporations, and by home buyers (mortgage bonds). There are also securities derived from bonds, such as S.T.R.I.P.S. (separate trading of registered interest and principal), where the payments of a bond are split into different securities or repackaged mortgage-backed securities.

6.2.3 Equities (Stocks)

The third asset class is the equity stocks issued and sold by corporations. When we think of capital markets, we first think of equity markets. There are different types of stocks. The first, common stock, is the ubiquitous equity, as its name suggests. Common stockholders have limited liability – the worst that can happen is the loss of the initial purchase value of the stock. Common stock represents the residual claim to the assets of a firm. In the event of bankruptcy, common stockholders are compensated last (and mostly at that point there is nothing left of the company). On the other hand, common stock owners can vote on important matters of the firm. Many companies share a portion of their profits with the common stockholders in the form of dividends. The dividend policy differs from one firm to the next. Some firms pay no dividends, many others pay dividends, and as the firm gets larger and more profitable over time, dividend distribution per share increases. The total return of a common stock investment is the capital gain/loss yield (the percentage change in the price of the stock share) plus the dividend yield (the total dividend received as a percentage of the purchase price of the stock share).

The second type of stock is known as preferred stock. Preferred stockholders receive very high dividend payments, but these payments generally do not increase over time. These are non-voting stocks but have priority over common stocks in bankruptcy. Preferred stock is considered to be something in between a corporate bond and a common stock.

The third type of stock is of a foreign firm trading in the equity market of another country – for example, a German firm's shares trading on the New York Stock Exchange. In the U.S., such shares are called A.D.R.s – American depository receipts – like the German firm's shares.

Equity exchanges where stocks are traded. The performance of the equity markets are measured and displayed by equity indices. The most famous index in the world is the Dow Jones Industrial Index – the Dow – for the U.S. stock market. Since its construction in 1896, the index has included the most important stocks (blue-chip companies). These contents were updated many times some industries were born and then emerged, while others became obsolete. Internationally, F.T.S.E. 100 for London Stock Exchange, D.A.X. for Frankfurt Stock Exchange, Nikkei 225 for Tokyo Stock Exchange, and C.A.C. 40 for Euronext Paris are some of the most important stock indices around the world.

6.2.4 Derivatives (Options)

There are various types of derivatives; however, some of them have become very popular for investors over time. Therefore, they have become asset classes themselves. One such derivative group is options. The choice but not the obligation to buy (sell) an underlying security – many times a stock – is a typical call (put) option. There are many other types of options and option-based securities. Altogether, options are high-risk and potentially high-return investments under the umbrella of the fourth asset class.

6.2.5 Derivatives (Futures)

The fifth asset class is futures. Futures contracts are agreements between buyers (purchaser of the contract – the long) and sellers (the short) to exchange a commodity at the maturity (expiration) date and at a certain price (contract price, or futures price). The commodities in futures contracts, such as oil and other energy products; corn, beef, wheat, and other agricultural products; gold, silver, platinum, and other precious materials; and currencies, indexes, and other financial products, are of enormous interest for investors. As a consequence, futures markets are huge in terms of the total dollar volume of agreed contracts. Investors can take very large and very risky positions in futures contracts, even with limited funding. If the positions are accurate, large profits are obtained, but if the positions are wrong, enormous losses are incurred.

6.2.6 Real Estate

Investing in real estate assets is another important portion of a portfolio. This sixth asset class involves taking investment positions in houses (including one's own house), apartments, condos, and commercial real estate properties, such as business/professional building complexes, shopping malls, hotels, and hospitals. International real estate opportunities are also plentiful. Market participants can either invest directly or indirectly through mutual funds, real estate investment trusts, and other real estate packages.

6.2.7 Cryptocurrencies

A recently emerging asset class is cryptocurrencies. The rules and regulations on the cryptocurrency industry are still not established, but the demand for and the supply of cryptocurrencies increase constantly. There are thousands of cryptocurrencies. Investors may include them in their portfolios under the seventh asset class.

6.2.8 Others: Art, Coins, Antiques, Undeveloped Land

As market participants become savvier and more knowledgeable, traditional asset classes are fully utilized in professional portfolios. The next step in developing better portfolios is the search for alternative investments and asset classes. Some alternative investments are undeveloped land investments, forest and timber investments, antique and historical objects, collectibles, historical coins, and artwork, such as paintings, sculptures, motion pictures, jewelry, and others.

It is possible to consider other asset classes to include in a portfolio in addition to these eight asset classes, such as precious materials (gold, silver, platinum, etc.). A portfolio can be enriched with domestic and international versions of the asset classes. Emerging country asset classes would add variety. Investing in professional portfolios such as mutual funds, hedge funds, and trusts as part of a market participant's portfolio would be further enrichments.

6.3 THE TWO-SECURITY PORTFOLIO

We first examine portfolio characteristics with a simplistic one with only two securities. While such a portfolio is almost never feasible or realistic, it will be a useful start to familiarize ourselves with the risk and return calculations, and it will be a good stepping stone to more realistic portfolios.

To calculate the expected return of this two-security portfolio, we need two sets of information. The first is the weight of each security in the portfolio. The weight of a security in the portfolio is the proportion of the total portfolio value invested in that particular security. The weights of the securities in a portfolio always add up to 100%. Thus, in a two-security portfolio, the weight of one security automatically tells us the weight of the other security (1 − the weight of the first security) since the two weights must add up to 100% (or 1).

The second set of information needed to calculate the expected return of the portfolio is the expected returns of each security. With these two sets of information, we can express the expected return of the portfolio as

$$E(R_p) = w_1 E(R_1) + w_2 E(R_2), \tag{6.1}$$

where w_1 (w_2) is the weight of the first (second) security and $E(R_1)$ ($E(R_2)$) is the expected return of the first (second) security. We keep in mind that $w_1 + w_2 = 1$.

Example 1: If the weight of the first security is 60%, and the expected returns are 9% and 11%, respectively, then the expected return of this two-security portfolio is

$$E(R_p) = (0.6)(0.09) + (0.4)(0.11) = 0.098 = 9.8\%.$$

The risk of the two-security portfolio is expressed with standard deviation, which is the square root of variance by definition. To calculate the standard deviation, we need three sets of information: the weights of the two securities, the standard deviations of the two securities, and the relationship between the returns of the security pairs in the portfolio, defined as the covariance. With these three sets of information, the standard deviation of the portfolio is

$$\sigma_p = \sqrt{w_1^2 \sigma_1^2 + w_2^2 \sigma_2^2 + 2 w_1 w_2 \, \text{cov}_{1,2}}, \tag{6.2}$$

where w_1 (w_2) is the weight of the first (second) security, σ_1 (σ_2) is the standard deviation of the first (second) security, and $cov_{1,2}$ is the covariance between the returns of the two securities.

While covariance measures how the returns of two securities are related to each other, its numerical value is easy to interpret. A more intuitive variable that describes the relationship between the returns of two securities is the correlation coefficient, rho, or $\rho_{1,2}$:

$$cov_{1,2} = (\sigma_1)\,(\sigma_2)\,(\rho_{1,2}) \qquad\qquad (6.3)$$

The correlation coefficient, ρ, is always a number between '-1' and '$+1$' (inclusive). A perfect positive correlation coefficient of '$+1$' indicates that the returns of the two securities change at the same time, by the same percentage, all the time. Such securities do not provide any diversification benefits in a portfolio. In fact, securities that are highly positively correlated should not be in a portfolio together. On the other hand, a perfect negative correlation coefficient, '-1', indicates that the returns of the two securities change in the exact opposite direction at the same time, by the same percentage, all the time. Such securities provide the maximum diversification benefit in a portfolio. If the correlation coefficient between two securities is '0', this means the returns of the two securities are not related to each other at all. If the returns are increasing in the first security, we would have no idea whether the returns of the security are increasing, decreasing, or staying flat.

In Figure 6.1.a, where the x-axis represents time and the y-axis represents returns, securities A and B have a perfect positive correlation. The resultant portfolio A.B. has similar risk characteristics as the two securities – no diversification or risk reduction is achieved. On the other hand, Figure 6.1.b depicts securities C and D with a perfect negative correlation. Total risk diversification is achieved in the resultant portfolio C.D. It is practically not possible to find perfectly negatively correlated securities. The goal of the portfolio creator is to find security pairs that are as negatively correlated as possible. If negative correlations cannot be found, then positive correlations as close to zero as possible should be preferred. When creating portfolios, the goal is always to avoid high positive correlations.

The correlation coefficients between the returns of the securities deeply impact the risk characteristics of portfolios. To see this more clearly, we can inspect Figure 6.2, where the x-axis represents standard deviation and the y-axis represents expected returns. Security 1 has an expected return of 10% and a standard deviation of 14%, while security 2 has an expected return of 15% and a standard deviation of 20%. We examine three different correlation scenarios. Under perfect positive correlation, as the weight of one security increases in the two-security portfolio as the weight of the other decreases, the portfolio moves along a straight line connecting the two securities. In the second scenario of zero correlation, as the weights change, the portfolio moves along a curved path. It is possible that the portfolio may have a lower standard deviation than either of the two individual securities. And in the third correlation scenario of perfect negative correlation, it is actually possible to end up with a portfolio that has zero risk, as depicted in the figure. While the two correlation extremes of '$+1$' and '-1' are not practically possible, they do demonstrate how dramatically the portfolio characteristics may be impacted by correlations.

For correlation coefficients between '-1' and '$+1$', such as $\rho = 0$ in Figure 6.2, there is a portfolio that generates the minimum risk (standard deviation, volatility, variance). Some investors would be interested in such a portfolio even though the expected return is not a dramatic

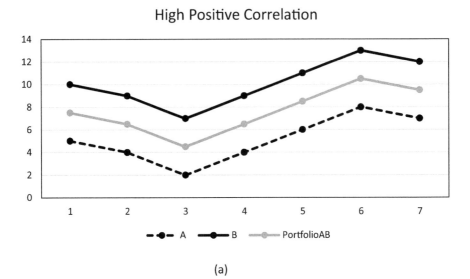

(a)

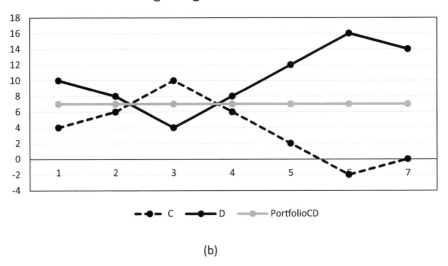

(b)

FIGURE 6.1 Correlations Impact Portfolio Risk Characteristics

consequence. For a two-security portfolio, the minimum variance portfolio weights of the two securities are defined as

$$w_1 = \frac{\sigma_2^2 - \text{cov}_{1,2}}{\sigma_1^2 + \sigma_2^2 - 2\text{cov}_{1,2}} \text{ and } w_2 = 1 - w_1. \tag{6.4}$$

Therefore, the correlation coefficient (or the covariance) and the variances of the two securities lead to the optimum weights to minimize the portfolio variance.

Example 2: Consider the two securities in Figure 6.2. With $\sigma_1 = 14\%$, $\sigma_2 = 20\%$, and $\rho_{1,2} = 0$, the optimal weights for the minimum variance portfolio are

$w_1 = (0.20^2)/[0.14^2 + 0.20^2] = 0.6711$, and $w_2 = 1{-}0.6711 = 0.3289$.

Then, from equations 6.1 and 6.2,

$E(R_p) = (0.6711)(0.10) + (0.3289)(0.15) = 0.1164$ and
$\sigma_p = [(0.6711)^2(0.14)^2 + (0.3289)^2(0.20)^2]^{1/2} = 0.1147$.

Example 3: If the correlation coefficient between the two securities is $\rho_{1,2} = 0.2$, instead of 0, then the optimal weights, expected return, and risk become

$w_1 = [0.20^2 - (0.2)(0.14)(0.20)]/[0.14^2 + 0.20^2 - (2)(0.2)\,(0.14)(0.20)] = 0.71$, and
$w_2 = 1{-}0.71 = 0.29$;
$E(R_p) = (0.71)(0.10) + (0.29)(0.15) = 0.1145$, and
$\sigma_p = [(0.71)^2(0.14)^2 + (0.29)^2(0.20)^2 + (2)(0.71)(0.29)(0.14)(0.20)(0.2)]^{1/2} = 0.1247$.

We see that as the correlation coefficient becomes more positive, the expected return of the portfolio decreases while the risk of the portfolio increases.

Example 4: If the correlation coefficient between the two securities is $\rho_{1,2} = -0.2$, then the optimal weights, expected return, and risk become

$w_1 = [0.20^2 + (0.2)(0.14)(0.20)]/[0.14^2 + 0.20^2 + (2)(0.2)\,(0.14)(0.20)] = 0.64$, and
$w_2 = 1{-}0.71 = 0.36$;
$E(R_p) = (0.64)(0.10) + (0.36)(0.15) = 0.1180$, and
$\sigma_p = [(0.64)^2(0.14)^2 + (0.36)^2(0.20)^2 - (2)(0.64)(0.36)(0.14)(0.20)(0.2)]^{1/2} = 0.1031$.

We see that as the correlation coefficient becomes more negative, the expected return of the portfolio increases and the risk of the portfolio decreases at the same time.

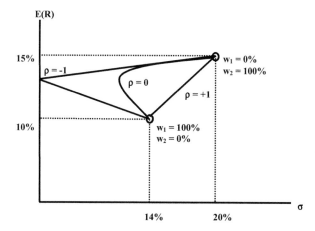

FIGURE 6.2 Two-Security Portfolios with Different Correlations

6.4 REALISTIC PORTFOLIOS WITH MULTIPLE SECURITIES

The previous section explored a portfolio with two securities. Such a portfolio is great to learn about the basic characteristics, but it is not realistic. Most investors, professional or individual, generally hold portfolios with many securities. This section examined such realistic portfolios.

There is a naïve and fast approach to creating a realistic portfolio. The investor is supposed to pick securities that are not closely related to each other; in other words, correlation coefficients should be low positive, or even better, negative. Stocks in different industries exhibit unrelated characteristics. So do securities from different asset classes. Including such seemingly unrelated securities will quickly eliminate unnecessary risk exposure, and the power of diversification will exhibit itself. Studies have suggested that having 20–30 securities will achieve as much risk diversification as possible, as depicted in Figure 6.3. However, the selection of the securities, asset classes, industries, and securities is subjective, without much statistical or mathematical justification. The expected return and profit are secondary in this approach. Ultimately, the Sharpe ratio of the portfolio from the naïve approach can be unimpressive.

Given a wide spectrum of securities from many asset classes, savvy investors try to pick the ones and combine them such that the portfolio that is created has the best expected return-risk combination. In other words, such a portfolio would generate the highest possible expected return for a given level of portfolio risk. These 'best' portfolios are known as *efficient* portfolios, and altogether, they form something called the *efficient frontier*. The efficient frontier portfolios are the dominant or superior portfolios compared to others. They are the best combination of securities to generate the highest returns for a given risk level or, alternatively and equivalently, to generate the lowest risks for a given expected return level. Graphically, it is easy to visualize these efficient portfolios and the efficient frontier. Following the similar structure in the previous figure, with the x-axis representing risk and the y-axis representing expected return, Figure 6.4 depicts the efficient portfolios constituting the upper half of the curve, the

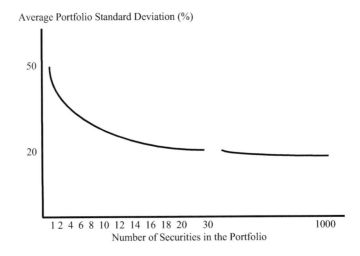

FIGURE 6.3 Naïve Diversification Approach in Creating a Portfolio

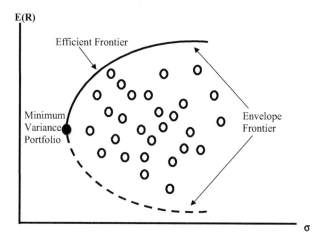

FIGURE 6.4 Realistic Portfolios with Many Risky Securities

efficient frontier. The entire curve is called the envelope frontier, which encompasses all the thousands of available securities from all asset classes. While the upper portion is the efficient frontier, the bottom half represents inferior or inefficient portfolios because, for each one with a specific standard deviation, there is an efficient portfolio in the upper curve that has a higher expected return for that same standard deviation. No investor would want a portfolio located in the lower dashed curve. The solid black dot represents a special efficient portfolio, the minimum variance portfolio. While the return of this portfolio is not necessarily special, the standard deviation is the lowest that can be achieved from the risky securities in the investment spectrum. Some investors would be interested in this minimum variance portfolio, and we will learn how to generate it. Finally, each circle in Figure 6.4 depicts a risky security with a certain expected return and standard deviation combination (to clarify the figure, only a few are provided here).

Investors want to choose investment points in Figure 6.4 that are as much in the upper-left position (or northwest position) as possible. Such investment points would provide higher returns and lower risks at the same time. It seems efficient frontier portfolios are the best for this purpose, but as a matter of fact, investors can do better.

Consider the risk-free security located on the y-axis in Figure 6.5. The straight lines starting from the risk-free asset and crossing the efficient frontier are known as capital allocation lines (C.A.L.s). They represent a new portfolio – one invested in the efficient portfolio (the intersection point) and in the risk-free asset. One of these C.A.L.s, the one that is tangent to the efficient frontier, which is depicted in the figure, is further known as the capital market line (C.M.L.). This is really special because the combination of the tangent efficient portfolio and the risk-free asset generates new portfolios on the C.M.L. that are actually superior to the portfolios on the efficient frontier. For example, portfolio A on the C.M.L. is superior to portfolio B on the efficient frontier because they have the same standard deviation, but portfolio A has a higher expected return than portfolio B.

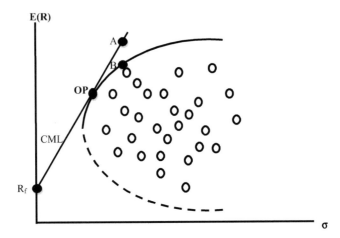

FIGURE 6.5 Optimum Portfolio and the Capital Market Line Versus the Efficient Frontier

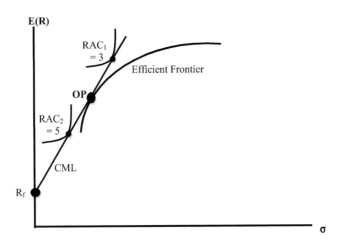

FIGURE 6.6 Utility Curves and Risk Aversion Coefficients

The C.M.L. dominates the efficient frontier. The slope of the C.M.L. is the largest of all the C.A.L.s, and it exactly measures the Sharpe ratio $= (E(R_{OP}) - R_f)/\sigma_{OP}$. For investors, professional or individual, the best portfolios are on the C.M.L. Which specific portfolio point an investor would choose on the C.M.L. depends on that investor's risk tolerance level, which is measured by the risk aversion coefficient, R.A.C. The higher the R.A.C., the more risk-averse an investor would be. Figure 6.6 depicts two investors defined by their utility curves and their risk aversion coefficients, $RAC_1 = 3$ and $RAC_2 = 5$. The first individual is more risk-tolerant, indicated by the lower value of R.A.C., and is willing to settle with a final portfolio that is further along the C.M.L. (with higher expected return but also higher risk). The second individual is more risk-averse, as indicated by the higher value of R.A.C., and is willing to settle with a final portfolio on the C.M.L. that is closer to the risk-free asset. These final portfolios for the individuals are decided by allocating the proper weights between the risk-free asset and the optimal tangent portfolio, O.P.

For the risk-tolerant investor 1, the weight of the optimal tangent portfolio might be 150%, and the weight of the risk-free asset −50%. The weights add up to 100%, as always. The negative weight indicates shorting the risk-free asset rather than buying it (this would be done equivalently by borrowing at the risk-free rate). The additional funds from short-ing (borrowing) are used to invest more on the optimal tangent portfolio so that the final portfolio for investor 1 is further up along the C.M.L. On the other hand, for the risk-averse investor 2, the weights might be 60% for the optimal tangent portfolio and 40% for the risk-free asset.

Ultimately, where the investor ends with the final portfolio on the C.M.L. is subjective and depends on the personality of the investor. Both investor 1 and investor 2 choose the same optimal, tangential, and well-diversified risky portfolio O.P. and the risk-free asset, but they assign different weights for each based on R.A.C.s. The responsibility of the professional financial advisor/investor is to objectively determine the optimal tangential portfolio (O.P. in Figures 6.5 and 6.6). The tangent portfolio that is both on the C.M.L. and the efficient frontier is a special portfolio. It is the optimal portfolio of risky securities that helps investors end up with their desired portfolios on the C.M.L. It can be figured out in a methodical and objective manner.

6.5 EXPECTED RETURN AND STANDARD DEVIATION OF REALISTIC PORTFOLIOS

To work with realistic portfolios of dozens or hundreds of securities, we need to know about matrix algebra. Please refer to the primer on linear algebra or matrix algebra and use Excel for matrix operations (chapter06Addentum1_primerMatrixAlgebra.doc). Once armed with the knowledge about matrices and how to use them in Excel, we can proceed with the risk and return characteristics of realistic portfolios.

To calculate the return and risk of a realistic portfolio, we need three matrices of a port-folio: (1) a column vector of expected returns of the individual securities of the portfolio, which is known as the *expected return vector (E(R))*; (2) a column vector of the weights of the securities in the portfolio, which is known as the *weight vector (W)*; and (3) a matrix of the risk characteristics of the securities in the portfolio, which is known as the *variance-covariance matrix (VarCov)*.

How do we obtain these three matrices? The expected return of each and every indi-vidual security in equation 6.5 can be obtained using an asset pricing model from Chapter 5. A faster way is using the average return of the security from the past. Although the past does not extrapolate into the future, the average historical return is an objective starting point (the data should not go too far back; the last five years of data would be sufficient). Using the return column for each security in Excel, we apply the 'average' function to each column to get the historical mean return of each security. The historical average of each security can then be shifted up or down depending on whether the researcher is optimistic or pessimistic about that security.

$$E(R) = \begin{bmatrix} E(R_1) \\ E(R_2) \\ \vdots \\ E(R_N) \end{bmatrix} \qquad (6.5)$$

The weight of each security in the weight vector of equation 6.6 is determined from the proportion of the total portfolio value allocated to that security. These weights can be determined from the wishes of the client, or they can be calculated using portfolio optimization techniques so that the portfolio has the maximum Sharpe ratio, as shown later.

$$W = \begin{bmatrix} w_1 \\ w_2 \\ \vdots \\ w_N \end{bmatrix}, \qquad (6.6)$$

where $w_1 + w_2 + \ldots + w_N = 1$.

The *VarCov* matrix represents the risk characteristics of the securities constituting the matrix. Each diagonal element is the variance of an individual security (standard deviation squared). The off-diagonal elements are covariances of the returns between security pairs. Since the covariance between securities A and B ($cov_{A,B}$) is mathematically the same as the covariance between security 2 and 1 ($cov_{B,A}$), the *VarCov* matrix is a square and symmetric matrix.

$$VarCov = \begin{bmatrix} \sigma_1^2 & cov_{1,2} & \cdots & cov_{1,N} \\ cov_{2,1} & \sigma_2^2 & \cdots & cov_{2,N} \\ \vdots & \vdots & \ddots & \vdots \\ cov_{N,1} & cov_{N,2} & \cdots & \sigma_N^2 \end{bmatrix} \qquad (6.7)$$

We use the data analysis function called 'covariance' to generate the *VarCov* matrix in Excel. The starting data that are necessary are the historical return values of each security in a column, and these columns should be next to each other. Then in Excel, under the 'Data' tab, we click on 'Data Analysis' and select 'Covariance' in the list. In the window that pops up, the Input Range is the return columns (if the first row has the labels for security names, the box for labels must be checked. The output range button is selected, and then a cell in Excel is picked as the upper-left corner of the *partial* variance-covariance matrix is generated. To get the *complete* variance-covariance matrix, we need to 'copy' the partial matrix, find a new location for the upper-left corner of the complete matrix, then paste special values, and after clicking on the upper-left corner cell of the complete matrix again, we paste special values one more time with the box for skip blanks and the box for transpose both checked. This process will generate the *VarCov* matrix for us.

Using these three matrices *E(R)*, *W*, and *VarCov*, we can express the expected return of the portfolio as

$$E(R_P) = W^T E(R) = \begin{bmatrix} w_1 & w_2 & \cdots & w_N \end{bmatrix} \begin{bmatrix} E(R_1) \\ E(R_2) \\ \vdots \\ E(R_N) \end{bmatrix},$$

(6.8)

which becomes $E(R_P) = w_1 E(R_1) + w_2 E(R_2) + \ldots + w_N E(R_N)$. In Excel, the formula is

$$E(R_P) = MMULT(TRANSPOSE(W), E(R))$$

(6.9)

As for the standard deviation of the portfolio, we have

$$\sigma_P = \sqrt{W^T VarCov W} = \sqrt{\begin{bmatrix} w_1 & w_2 & \cdots & w_N \end{bmatrix} \begin{bmatrix} \sigma_1^2 & \text{cov}_{1,2} & \cdots & \text{cov}_{1,N} \\ \text{cov}_{2,1} & \sigma_2^2 & \cdots & \text{cov}_{2,N} \\ \vdots & \vdots & \ddots & \vdots \\ \text{cov}_{N,1} & \text{cov}_{N,2} & \cdots & \sigma_N^2 \end{bmatrix} \begin{bmatrix} w_1 \\ w_2 \\ \vdots \\ w_N \end{bmatrix}}$$

(6.10)

In Excel, the expression for this formula is

$$\sigma_P = SQRT(MMULT(TRANSPOSE\ (W),\ MMULT(VarCov, W))).$$

(6.11)

As an example, in Excel, consider a five-security portfolio. With the expected return vector, weight vector, and the variance-covariance matrix, the expected return of the portfolio and the standard deviation of the portfolio are generated in Figure 6.7.

	A	B	C	D	E	F	G	H	I	J
1					**Five-Security Portfolio**					
2			**VarCov**				E(R)		W	
3	0.40	0.03	0.02	0.00	0.01		0.06		0.2	
4	0.03	0.20	0.00	-0.06	0.03		0.05		0.3	
5	0.02	0.00	0.30	0.03	0.12		0.07		0.1	
6	0.00	-0.06	0.03	0.10	0.09		0.08		0.1	
7	0.01	0.03	0.12	0.09	0.15		0.02		0.3	
8									1	=SUM(I3:I7)
9										
10	E(R_P) =		0.048	{=MMULT(TRANSPOSE(I3:I7),G3:G7)}						
11										
12	σ_P =		0.268626	{=SQRT(MMULT(TRANSPOSE(I3:I7),MMULT(A3:E7,I3:I7)))}						

FIGURE 6.7 Using Excel to Find Expected Return and Risk of Realistic Portfolios

6.6 OPTIMAL TANGENT PORTFOLIO, O.P.

Robert C. Merton, one of the most prominent finance academicians, published a series of articles in 1969, 1971, and 1972, where he proposed a construction where any portfolio on the envelope frontier in figure 6.4 must satisfy whether it is in the upper or the bottom portion of the curve. The expression finds the weight matrix of an envelope portfolio:

$$W = \frac{(VarCov^{-1})(E(R)-c)}{sum[(VarCov^{-1})(E(R)-c)]} \tag{6.12}$$

In this formulation, the inverse of the variance-covariance matrix is multiplied with the expected return vector after a constant, c, is subtracted from each element of the vector. The result is a column vector. The sum of all the elements of the column vector is in the denominator of equation 6.12. With this division, the column vector is normalized since each column vector element is divided, with the sum of all the elements of the vector. Here, the constant, c, is left undefined in the original Merton proposition. Each different c leads to the weight vector of another envelope portfolio. Graphically, equation 6.12 can be depicted in Figure 6.8.

With each c on the y-axis in the figure, there is a tangent line to the envelope frontier either in the upper efficient portion or in the lower inefficient portion. The tangent portfolio's weight vector, W, can be found from equation 6.12. Referring back to the five-security example presented in Figure 6.7, three sample tangent portfolios can be generated for $c_1 = 0$, $c_2 = 0.04$, and $c_3 = 0.14$, where equation 6.12 is used each time. For each tangent portfolio, the weight, expected return, and standard deviation are evaluated in Figures 6.9, 6.10, and 6.11.

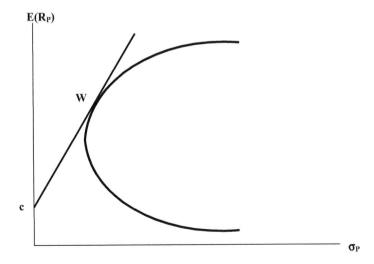

FIGURE 6.8 Finding Envelope Portfolios, W

	A	B	C	D	E	F	G	H	I	J	K
1					Tangent Portfolio 1 (c=0)						
2			VarCov				E(R)		c =	0	
3	0.40	0.03	0.02	0.00	0.01		0.06				
4	0.03	0.20	0.00	-0.06	0.03		0.05				
5	0.02	0.00	0.30	0.03	0.12		0.07				
6	0.00	-0.06	0.03	0.10	0.09		0.08				
7	0.01	0.03	0.12	0.09	0.15		0.02				
8											
9			-0.02749								
10			0.559479								
11		W$_1$ =	0.331529	{=(MMULT(MINVERSE(A3:E7),G3:G7-J2))/SUM((MMULT(MINVERSE(A3:E7),G3:G7-J2)))}							
12			1.273603								
13			-1.13712								
14			1	=SUM(C9:C13)							
15											
16		E(R$_{P1}$) =	0.128677	{=MMULT(TRANSPOSE(C9:C13),G3:G7)}							
17											
18		σ$_{P1}$ =	0.047396	{=SQRT(MMULT(TRANSPOSE(C9:C13),MMULT(A3:E7,C9:C13)))}							

FIGURE 6.9 Tangent Portfolio Calculation Using Merton Formula with c = 0

	A	B	C	D	E	F	G	H	I	J	K
1					Tangent Portfolio 2 (c=0.04)						
2			VarCov				E(R)		c =	0.04	
3	0.40	0.03	0.02	0.00	0.01		0.06				
4	0.03	0.20	0.00	-0.06	0.03		0.05				
5	0.02	0.00	0.30	0.03	0.12		0.07				
6	0.00	-0.06	0.03	0.10	0.09		0.08				
7	0.01	0.03	0.12	0.09	0.15		0.02				
8											
9			-0.02882								
10			0.562028								
11		W$_2$ =	0.335185	{=(MMULT(MINVERSE(A3:E7),G3:G7-J2))/SUM((MMULT(MINVERSE(A3:E7),G3:G7-J2)))}							
12			1.284106								
13			-1.1525								
14			1	=SUM(C9:C13)							
15											
16		E(R$_{P2}$) =	0.129513	{=MMULT(TRANSPOSE(C9:C13),G3:G7)}							
17											
18		σ$_{P2}$ =	0.047773	{=SQRT(MMULT(TRANSPOSE(C9:C13),MMULT(A3:E7,C9:C13)))}							

FIGURE 6.10 Tangent Portfolio Calculation Using Merton Formula with c = 0.04

	A	B	C	D	E	F	G	H	I	J	K
1					Tangent Portfolio 3 (c=0.14)						
2			VarCov				E(R)		c =	0.14	
3	0.40	0.03	0.02	0.00	0.01		0.06				
4	0.03	0.20	0.00	-0.06	0.03		0.05				
5	0.02	0.00	0.30	0.03	0.12		0.07				
6	0.00	-0.06	0.03	0.10	0.09		0.08				
7	0.01	0.03	0.12	0.09	0.15		0.02				
8											
9			0.003364								
10			0.500492								
11		W$_3$ =	0.246924	{=(MMULT(MINVERSE(A3:E7),G3:G7-J2))/SUM((MMULT(MINVERSE(A3:E7),G3:G7-J2)))}							
12			1.030578								
13			-0.78136								
14			1	=SUM(C9:C13)							
15											
16		E(R$_{P3}$) =	0.10933	{=MMULT(TRANSPOSE(C9:C13),G3:G7)}							
17											
18		σ$_{P3}$ =	0.071902	{=SQRT(MMULT(TRANSPOSE(C9:C13),MMULT(A3:E7,C9:C13)))}							

FIGURE 6.11 Tangent Portfolio Calculation Using Merton Formula with c = 0.14

Even though the constant c was left undefined in the original derivations, it resembles the interest rate of a risk-free security since it is on the y-axis with no risk. Indeed, when we focus on the optimal tangent portfolio, O.P., we will define c as such. With this additional definition, we can decide whether the tangent portfolio in Figures 6.9, 6.10, and 6.11 is efficient (in the upper part of the envelope curve) or inefficient (in the lower part of the envelope curve). If the expected return of the tangent portfolio is higher than c, the tangent portfolio is efficient. This is the case in the examples in figures 6.9 and 6.10. But in our third example in Figure 6.11, $c = 0.14 > E(R_{P3}) = 0.1093$. The tangent portfolio 3 is both risky and has a lower return than the 'risk-free' security represented by c. Therefore, the tangent portfolio 3 is inferior, and it is in the inefficient lower portion of the envelope curve.

These examples bring us to the purpose of this section; finding the optimum tangential portfolio, O.P., in Figure 6.6. The optimal weight of O.P. is directly found using the Merton equation 6.12. But there are two critical points. The first is the constant, c, is the prevalent risk-free rate, R_f. The second is to verify that the expected return of the tangent portfolio is larger than R_f so that the tangent portfolio is on the efficient frontier and is optimal. Then, indeed, the optimal weight vector W_{OP} of the efficient and optimal portfolio, O.P., has been found.

Referring back to Figures 6.9, 6.10, and 6.11, if we start each example by defining c as the R_f, then the tangent portfolio presented in each figure is the optimal tangent portfolio, OP, except for the last example because that portfolio is inefficient and inferior. In such a situation where the risk-free rate is extremely high, investing in risky assets does not benefit the client. The financial planner/advisor would advise the client to keep the funds in the risk-free security during those strange and somehow pathological economic conditions.

Another portfolio that may be interesting to some investors is the global minimum variance portfolio (G.M.V.P.). This portfolio is created from risky securities and has the lowest risk, as depicted in Figure 6.4. For the portfolio of two securities, equation 6.4 was used to find G.M.V.P. Now, for the realistic portfolio with many securities, the G.M.V.P. weights are similar in format to the Merton equation 6.12 with (E(R) – c) replaced by a vector whose each element is 1:

$$W_{GMVP} = \frac{(VarCov^{-1})\begin{bmatrix}1\\ \vdots \\ 1\end{bmatrix}}{sum\left[(VarCov^{-1})\begin{bmatrix}1\\ \vdots \\ 1\end{bmatrix}\right]} \tag{6.13}$$

Using the five-security portfolio in Figures 6.7 through 6.11, the G.M.V.P. weights, the expected return, and the standard deviation are calculated in Figure 6.12. The key takeaway is, as expected, the risk of the G.M.V.P. is lower than those of all the portfolios explored in the examples.

	A	B	C	D	E	F	G	H	I	J
1						**GMVP**				
2			**VarCov**				**E(R)**		**[1]**	
3	0.40	0.03	0.02	0.00	0.01		0.06		1	
4	0.03	0.20	0.00	-0.06	0.03		0.05		1	
5	0.02	0.00	0.30	0.03	0.12		0.07		1	
6	0.00	-0.06	0.03	0.10	0.09		0.08		1	
7	0.01	0.03	0.12	0.09	0.15		0.02		1	
8										
9			-0.0246							
10			0.553944							
11		W_{GMVP} =	0.323589	{=(MMULT(MINVERSE(A3:E7),I3:I7))/SUM((MMULT(MINVERSE(A3:E7),I3:I7)))}						
12			1.250796							
13			-1.10373							
14			1	=SUM(C9:C13)						
15										
16		$E(R_{GMVP})$ =	0.126862	{=MMULT(TRANSPOSE(C9:C13),G3:G7)}						
17										
18		σ_{GMVP} =	0.04706	{=SQRT(MMULT(TRANSPOSE(C9:C13),MMULT(A3:E7,C9:C13)))}						

FIGURE 6.12 Global Minimum Variance Portfolio Calculation

6.7 USING SOLVER TO FIND THE OPTIMAL PORTFOLIO, O.P.

There is an alternative method of finding the tangential optimal portfolio, *O.P.* As mentioned in the discussion of Figure 6.5, the *C.M.L.* from the risk-free rate to the tangent *O.P.* has a slope that is bigger than any other *C.A.L.* The slope of the *C.M.L.* is the Sharpe ratio = *SR* = $(E(R_{OP}) - R_f)/\sigma_{OP}$. To find the weight vector, W_{OP}, and hence the *OP*, the expression for the *S.R.* can be placed in an Excel cell, and it can be maximized by changing the weights of the securities in the tangent portfolio. After the maximization, the optimal weights for the W_{OP} will be found for the *O.P.*

The maximization is conducted with the *Solver* functionality in Excel. First, an Excel worksheet must be designed so that Solver can be applied. The three matrices for the portfolio must be specified: *VarCov*, *E(R)*, and *W*. Solver requires an initial condition for the weights in *W*; therefore, an arbitrary set of weights making sure that their sum is one can be picked (for example, equal weights or a weight of 1 for a security and weight of 0 for the other securities). There the formula for the expected return of the portfolio is typed in a cell. Additionally, the formula for the standard deviation of the portfolio is typed in another cell. Finally, the *S.R.* formula based on the previous two cells and the risk-free rate is typed in a third cell. The *S.R.* cell will be maximized by changing the weight vector cells. The constraint of the maximization problem is that the weights must add up to one.

Once the Excel file is set up as in Figure 6.13, Solver can be selected under the 'Data' tab. In the 'Solver' window, the 'Set Objective' cell should be the *S.R.* cell. The 'Max' button should be selected to maximize the Sharpe ratio. In the 'By Changing Variable Cells' section, the weight vector cells must be selected all together. In the 'Subject to Constraints' area, after clicking on 'Add', the 'Cell Reference' should be the cell that has the sum of the weights. This should be 'equal' to constraint '1'. Once these are input, the 'OK' button should be clicked.

Then the 'Solve' button can be clicked, and the 'Keep Solver Solution' should be selected. The O.P. weights, W_{OP}, will be available.

The Solver results are in Figure 6.13. The risk-free rate, R_f, is 0.04, as in Figure 6.10. As expected, the Solver resultant weights in Figure 6.13 are exactly the same as those in the Merton formula in equation 6.13 and presented in Figure 6.10. We notice that the first and the fifth securities have negative weights in the O.P. Such stocks are considered to be inferior, with dismal expected return and risk combinations. These stocks are not purchased; rather, they are short-sold: shares of the stock are borrowed and sold (to be covered and purchased back later potentially at a lower price) – hence the negative weights. The short-sell proceeds are used to purchase more of other promising stocks' shares. For example, the fourth stock in Figure 6.13 has a weight of 128.4%. This means the portfolio is invested in this really attractive stock. Additionally, some of the short-sell proceeds are also used to purchase more of this attractive stock, which results in a weight larger than '1' in the portfolio for this stock.

The Solver approach can be used to find O.P.s for a variety of situations where economic and market conditions or client requests lead to additional constraints. For example, some equity exchanges are lukewarm about short-selling. Borrowing and selling stock shares in anticipation of a decline in the price and covering the short position later by purchasing the shares back at a lower price (if the original anticipation turns out to be accurate) generate a profit for the short-seller. But these activities are considered unethical and unfair by some. Some market participants and regulators do not like short-sellers profiting from the decline in the share price and the demise of the company. Such short-selling may fuel others to short-sell, and the aggregate behavior may itself become the primary reason for the stock price decline. Several European Union countries, such as Belgium, France, Italy, and Spain, have banned short-selling, a practice that critics say can exacerbate market moves when there is panic-selling. The bans and restrictions can be permanent or temporary. For example, during the financial crisis of 2008, the S.E.C. temporarily restricted short-selling of financial sector stocks in the U.S.

	A	B	C	D	E	F	G	H	I	J
1					**Optimal Portfolio with Solver**					
2			VarCov				E(R)			
3	0.40	0.03	0.02	0.00	0.01		0.06			
4	0.03	0.20	0.00	-0.06	0.03		0.05			
5	0.02	0.00	0.30	0.03	0.12		0.07			
6	0.00	-0.06	0.03	0.10	0.09		0.08			
7	0.01	0.03	0.12	0.09	0.15		0.02			
8										
9			-0.02882							
10			0.562028				$R_f =$	0.04		
11		$W_{OP} =$	0.335185							
12			1.284104							
13			-1.15249							
14			1	=SUM(C9:C13)						
15										
16		$E(R_{OP}) =$	0.129513	{=MMULT(TRANSPOSE(C9:C13),G3:G7)}						
17										
18		$\sigma_{OP} =$	0.047773	{=SQRT(MMULT(TRANSPOSE(C9:C13),MMULT(A3:E7,C9:C13)))}						
19										
20		$SR_{OP} =$	1.87373	=(C16-H10)/C18						

FIGURE 6.13 Optimal Portfolio Weights Generated from Solver Maximization of the S.R.

	A	B	C	D	E	F	G	H	I	J
1		**Optimal Portfolio with Solver [Short-Selling is Restricted]**
2			VarCov					E(R)		
3	0.40	0.03	0.02	0.00	0.01		0.06			
4	0.03	0.20	0.00	-0.06	0.03		0.05			
5	0.02	0.00	0.30	0.03	0.12		0.07			
6	0.00	-0.06	0.03	0.10	0.09		0.08			
7	0.01	0.03	0.12	0.09	0.15		0.02			
8										
9			0.04233							
10			0.251367				R$_f$ =	0.04		
11		W$_{OP}$ =	0.060087							
12			0.646216							
13			0							
14			1	=SUM(C9:C13)						
15										
16		E(R$_{OP}$) =	0.071012	{=MMULT(TRANSPOSE(C9:C13),G3:G7)}						
17										
18		σ$_{OP}$ =	0.19951	{=SQRT(MMULT(TRANSPOSE(C9:C13),MMULT(A3:E7,C9:C13)))}						
19										
20		SR$_{OP}$ =	0.155439	=(C16-H10)/C18						

FIGURE 6.14 Optimal Portfolio Weights Using Solver Maximization (Short-Selling Not Permitted)

When short-selling is restricted, the weights of the securities cannot be negative. Then the portfolio optimization problem has additional constraints: each weight in the weight vector W must be larger than or equal to zero. With the Solver approach, this is easy to implement. Working with the previous example in Figure 6.13, as before, 'Solver' is selected under 'Data'. In the 'Solver' window, the 'Set Objective' is the *S.R.* cell. The 'Max' button is selected with 'By Changing Variable Cells' as the weight vector cells. In the 'Subject to Constraints' area, the first constraint is entered as the cell that has the sum of the weights set equal to '1'. At the point, instead of the 'OK' button, 'Add' is clicked to enter the next constraint. The 'Cell Reference' is selecting all the weight cells together. The relationship sign is picked as '>=', and the 'Constraint' is '0'. Once these are input, 'OK' is clicked, followed by the 'Solve' button. Keeping the Solver Solution generates the output in Figure 6.14, where short-selling is restricted.

As seen from Figure 6.14, all the five weights in the optimal portfolio are bigger than or equal to '0'. The fifth security is really inferior. If short-selling is not possible, then with a weight of '0', the security is not included in the portfolio. We also note that with additional restrictions, the *O.P.* generates an *S.R.* that is lower than the case with fewer restrictions.

6.8 FINAL REMARKS AND FURTHER IMPROVEMENTS

There are two specific improvements that need to be considered. The first is about the uncomfortable fact that in our examples throughout the chapter, the elements of both the expected return vector *E(R)*, and the variance-covariance matrix *VarCov*, have been based on historical return data for the securities making up the portfolio. Historical data can be poor predictors of the future. The length of the time series for the data should not be too short because it would lead to statistical problems. The length should not be too long either because the firm today is very different from 20 years ago. Thus, the returns from 20 years ago are not reflective of present returns. Generally, five years of historical daily returns would be an ideal length.

But trying to extrapolate the past into the future remains a problem. To resolve the issue, the E(R) and the VarCov can be updated by the researcher. Using additional fundamental analysis tools and techniques and utilizing personal expertise, experience, networking, and information, the elements of the two matrices can be adjusted for a better reflection of the future. Portfolio optimization is an important profession. Portfolio managers use quantitative technology, as in this chapter, but also art by adjusting the optimal weights up/down by incorporating their experiences, expertise, and subjective views.

The second improvement is about the O.P. weights. The optimization process frequently generates extreme weight positions. Optimization using historical data may produce large negative or large positive stock positions, as we have seen in our examples. Moreover, portfolio proportions are very sensitive to the inputs. Therefore, portfolio optimization researchers introduce additional constraints to eliminate the extreme weights. For example, constraints where the weight of each security can be at most 90% of the portfolio value can be imposed, or constraints where each security has at least a minimum weight of 3%. These restrictions eliminate the extreme weight positions from the optimization process. The sensitivities of the weights to E(R) and VarCov inputs are also curtailed a bit this way. The five-security portfolio is used one last time. The weights of the securities in the portfolio must add up to '1', as always. Short-selling is allowed, but two more restrictions are placed for the weight of each security: $0.03 \leq w_i \leq 0.90$ for i = 1, ..., 5. The implementation using Solver produces the output in Figure 6.15. As we see from Figure 6.15, the optimal weights now look more traditional.

	A	B	C	D	E	F	G	H	I	J
1			Optimal Portfolio with Solver [0.03 <= W <= 0.90]							
2			VarCov				E(R)			
3	0.40	0.03	0.02	0.00	0.01		0.06			
4	0.03	0.20	0.00	-0.06	0.03		0.05			
5	0.02	0.00	0.30	0.03	0.12		0.07			
6	0.00	-0.06	0.03	0.10	0.09		0.08			
7	0.01	0.03	0.12	0.09	0.15		0.02			
8										
9			0.04241							
10			0.235928				$R_f =$	0.04		
11		$W_{OP} =$	0.052837							
12			0.638825							
13			0.03							
14			1	=SUM(C9:C13)						
15										
16		$E(R_{OP}) =$	0.069746	{=MMULT(TRANSPOSE(C9:C13),G3:G7)}						
17										
18		$\sigma_{OP} =$	0.206321	{=SQRT(MMULT(TRANSPOSE(C9:C13),MMULT(A3:E7,C9:C13)))}						
19										
20		$SR_{OP} =$	0.144171	=(C16-H10)/C18						

FIGURE 6.15 Optimal Portfolio Weights Using Solver ($0.03 \leq w_i \leq 0.90$)

6.9 SUMMARY AND CONCLUSION

The portfolio optimization tools and models have evolved over the years, and research continues for better optimization processes. Portfolio optimization was examined in depth, but obviously, there is more to explore.

After the examination of different asset classes, a portfolio with two securities was analyzed. For a technical analysis of realistic portfolios, the primer on linear algebra or matrix algebra is utilized (chapter06Addentum1_primerMatrixAlgebra.doc). Implementation of linear algebra in Excel helped to practically deal with realistic matrices.

The expected return and risk of realistic portfolios, efficient frontiers, and calculation of the weights of the optimal portfolio using the Merton approach and using the Solver capability are established. Finally, restrictions from economic conditions, financial exchanges, client requests, and rules and regulations are considered in the formation of the optimal portfolio.

REFERENCES AND ADDITIONAL READING

Benninga, S. 2014. *Financial Modeling*. 4th edition. Cambridge, MA, MIT Press.

Bodie, Z., Kane, A., Marcus, A.J. 2021. *Investments*. 12th edition. New York, McGraw-Hill.

Markowitz, H.M. 1952. Portfolio Selection. *Journal of Finance*, 7, 77–91.

Merton, R.C. 1969. Lifetime Portfolio Selection Under Uncertainty: The Continuous-Time Case. *Review of Economics and Statistics*, 51, 247–257.

Merton, R.C. 1971. Optimum Consumption and Portfolio Rules in a Continuous-Time Model. *Journal of Economic Theory*, 3, 373–413.

Merton, R.C. 1972. An Analytical Derivation of the Efficient Portfolio Frontier. *Journal of Financial and Quantitative Analysis*, 7, 1851–1872.

CHAPTER 7

Hedge Funds, Mutual Funds, E.T.F.s

OBJECTIVES

- Examine and contrast the history, present, and future outlook of the hedge fund industry.
- Appraise the motivation behind the growth in the industry.
- Differentiate between the types of hedge funds and the strategies they follow is presented. Analyze some of the really popular strategies in more detail.
- Interpret the performance of hedge funds, the recent developments, the impacts of the scandals, and the popular viewpoints both in terms of conventional wisdom and in terms of the examples in print, digital, and broadcast media.
- Compare and contrast hedge funds with mutual funds.
- Evaluate the brief history, the current status, and the future outlook of the mutual fund industry, along with the characteristics, types, fee structures, and performance.
- Assess the characteristics, popularity, and future prospects of exchange-traded funds.

7.1 INTRODUCTION

Hedge funds are mostly unregulated investment portfolios that only issue securities privately to qualified investors. Alfred W. Jones was the first hedge fund manager. He formed a hedge fund in 1949 and followed a neutral non-directional strategy of buying promising stocks and short-selling others with poor prospects. Almost all hedge funds use a compensation structure under which the managing fund manager keeps one-fifth of the fund returns above a predetermined benchmark in addition to a 1–2% management fee, as summarized in the excellent discussion by the renowned academician Rene M. Stulz in the *Journal of Economic Perspectives*.

Hedge funds search for arbitrage opportunities, mispricings, and inefficiencies in financial markets and try to utilize them. The four popular ways of achieving this goal are through

DOI: 10.4324/9781003213697-7

long-short equity hedge funds, event-driven hedge funds, macro hedge funds, and fixed-income arbitrage hedge funds. Because the inefficiencies and mispricings are often small and of short duration, many hedge funds use substantial leverage to amplify the return on their decisions.

In the 1970s, most hedge funds specialized in a single strategy following the long/short equity model. During the recession of 1969–1970 and the 1973–1974 stock market crash, many hedge funds failed and had to close with heavy losses. They got renewed attention and popularity in the late 1980s, throughout the 1990s, and until the mid-2000s. The financial crisis of 2008 was a severe blow to the hedge fund industry, especially after the collapse of the well-known hedge fund, Bernard L. Madoff Investment Securities, L.L.C., which was created and managed by Bernie Madoff. However, since then, the recovery of the hedge fund industry has been steady, and its popularity has increased substantially. Hedge funds have become a significant part of the broadcast media with the hugely successful Showtime television series *Billions*.

Many hedge funds are geographically located in the southern Connecticut area. This is not a coincidence. Hedge fund firms are large and powerful investment companies with significant financial resources. They can negotiate transaction and research fees and easily bypass many of the intermediaries in financial transactions. The hedge fund manager and employees have vast mathematical and quantitative knowledge as well as intuitive and qualitative insight for good investment decisions. Most hedge funds are endowed with the most up-to-date computer mainframe systems, fiber optic communication networks, and trading platforms. Markets all around the globe are monitored constantly, and any arbitrage profit opportunities are utilized to the maximum. In today's ultra-high-speed trading ecology, nanoseconds matter to take advantage of mispricings by executing trades before others. Being geographically close to the largest equity markets in the world located in lower Manhattan and their computer mainframes located in New Jersey helps hedge funds execute trades before other investment institutions.

7.2 HEDGE FUNDS VERSUS MUTUAL FUNDS

Both hedge funds and mutual funds are giant portfolios managed by professional and highly knowledgeable managers. But the similarities pretty much stop right about there. Hedge funds and mutual funds are subject to very different rules and have very different characteristics.

Mutual funds are well-known in investment circles and by market participants primarily because they are advertised in order to attract customers. Mutual funds must disclose their investment policies in their fundamental document, the prospectus. The mutual fund manager must follow the specified investment policy at all times, even when there are really attractive and promising alternatives. In general, there is limited use of leverage allowed for mutual fund managers. And taking short positions in stocks in anticipation of price decrease is not possible in mutual funds. The investors in a mutual fund received shares as proof of their investments. These mutual fund shares reflect the changing value of the mutual fund over time. The shares are redeemable at practically any time at the then current value, reflecting the profit or the loss. Mutual funds are parts of retirement funds, pension plans, and small investors' alternatives for taking positions in financial markets. As a consequence, for stability, regulators have placed restrictions so that fund managers would not take arbitrary or highly risky positions.

Hedge funds are not subject to any of these constraints. The hedge fund manager need not disclose the investment policy. The policy can evolve over time, sometimes quickly, if highly profitable opportunities appear. Hedge funds use leverage, short-positions, and complex trading strategies and utilize derivatives for hedging, speculation, and arbitrage. Differences between hedge funds and mutual funds can be described as follows:

(1) Transparency: Hedge funds generally provide no information to the public and sometimes limited information only to their investors. This enables the hedge fund manager to pursue a profitable strategy without others jumping in and sharing the profits by following the same strategy. On the other hand, mutual funds are legally bound to be fully transparent.

(2) Investors: In a typical hedge fund, there are limited investors, often less than 100. The hedge fund manager typically prefers to collect the funding quickly from a few wealthy investors and not deal with hundreds/thousands of small investors. Participation in the hedge fund requires high dollar minimums. And consequently, the number of investors in the hedge fund is low, and they are very wealthy. On the other hand, the number of investors in a mutual fund is unlimited. Anyone, at any time, may contact the mutual fund manager and become part of the mutual fund.

(3) Strategies: Hedge funds may be created with the goal of pursuing certain strategies, but as financial markets evolve and other opportunities appear, hedge fund managers change plans and pursue whichever strategy generates the highest profits. There are no restrictions in choosing or changing an investment style or strategy. On the other hand, mutual funds must adhere to the prospectus and must follow the original investment policy or strategy.

(4) Liquidity: Hedge funds are not liquid at all. When wealthy investors provide the initial funding, they are subject to multiple-year lock-up periods. During the four-to-five-year period, the investor cannot access their original investments or the profits; many times, the original investment cannot be acquired back even if the investor is willing to suffer a significant penalty. Such a restriction enables the hedge fund manager to design trading strategies without worrying over the possibility that the investment may be pulled back by the backers. On the other hand, mutual funds are highly liquid. The shares can be redeemed on demand. The minimum tenure for mutual fund investments is one day (i.e., mutual fund shares can be redeemed the next day).

(5) Fees: Hedge funds typically charge more. In addition to the annual fee of 1% to 2% fixed percentage of assets, there is also an *incentive fee*: one-fifth of the profits above a threshold value go to the hedge fund manager. With this incentive fee, the hedge fund manager shares in the profits generated by the fund during the year. Such an incentive fee provides motivation to the hedge fund manager to try extra hard to make the fund profitable since a portion will be the manager's. This is good for hedge fund investors since their incentives and the manager's incentives are perfectly aligned. On the other hand, mutual funds generally typically 0.5% to 2% annual fee. There are extra one-time fees: front-end load at the beginning and back-end load when the shares are redeemed. Overall, hedge fund fees are larger.

7.3 CATEGORIES OF HEDGE FUNDS

When we examine different types of hedge funds or the different styles hedge funds follow, we can start with a broad categorization. We can divide hedge fund strategies into two groups: directional and non-directional:

(1) Directional strategies: Hedge funds that follow directional strategies generally take unhedged investment positions with the belief and hope that the position will be success-ful. For example, taking a long position in a sector of the economy will be beneficial if that sector outperforms. This is an unhedged bet on a price movement. Another example would be buying bonds in anticipation of an interest rate decline (which would increase the value of the bonds and lead to profits). These directional strategies produce net posi-tions in the hedge fund. If market conditions are favorable, profits are gained; otherwise, losses are incurred.

(2) Non-directional strategies: Hedge funds follow non-directional strategies in an attempt to arbitrage apparent mispricing. Ideally, the arbitrage opportunity should be risk-free and typically short. Hedge funds specialize in searching for and finding such arbitrage prospects. However, sometimes the arbitrage might have risk, and in non-directional strat-egies, some risk is present. For example, the spread between corporate bond rates and government bond rates may be perceived to be too large. The hedge fund would buy into corporate bonds (with high yields and low prices) and short-sell government bonds (with low yields and high prices). Overall, this is a neutral position – non-directional. There is no net long or short position. The fund does not demand interest rates will go up or will go down. The hedge fund manager creates a neutral position by investing accordingly with long and short positions.

Overall, directional hedge fund strategies are riskier. There is a net position, and market con-ditions must evolve accordingly for success. Otherwise, losses are incurred. Non-directional strategies are more flexible in terms of expected market movements, with comparatively lower risk. After this broad categorization, we can dig deeper and look at a more detailed list of hedge fund types and styles. These detailed categorizations are based on the types of securities that the hedge fund invests in or the investment strategies that the hedge fund follows.

7.3.1 Types of Hedge Funds

(1) Long/short equities: These hedge funds are equity-based positions with net either net long positions or net short positions depending on the manager's outlook on the economy and the market. The hedge fund may focus on a region of the world and take a net position in the stocks there, or the fund may focus on a sector or industry such as the technology, energy, or the discretionary industry and create the portfolio accordingly. Such hedge funds may also enhance their positions with derivatives (or sometimes derivatives are used to hedge the net positions).

(2) Convertible arbitrage: This is one of the most popular strategies used by hedge funds, regardless of whether as the original strategy or as a supplementary strategy of the hedge fund. In the convertible arbitrage strategy, convertible bonds and stock shares of the firm are jointly used.

A convertible bond is a company-issued bond which can be converted to a specific number of stock shares of the company (conversion ratio/rate) at the discretion of the investor. Such a convertible bond has a value that is the bigger of two prices: (1) conversion value (which is the product of conversion ratio and the stock price per share at that point in time) and (2) regular or straight bond price (the typical bond price calculated based on the time to maturity, the rate and frequency of the coupons, face value, and the yield to maturity). The holder of such a convertible bond will seriously think about converting if the stock price increases so that the conversion value becomes larger than the straight bond price. Once the conversion is done, the bondholder becomes a stockholder of the company, and there is no going back.

The convertible arbitrage strategy is buying the convertible bond and short-selling the proper number of shares of the firm. The short-sell proceeds are used for purchasing convertible bonds; therefore, the initial cost of the strategy is practically 0. This combination is repeated for many other companies that have convertible bonds. The stock price in each combination can perform in either one of two ways in the future:

(1) If the stock price increases, the convertible bond becomes more valuable. But at the same time, the short-sell position leads to a loss. The profit and the loss cancel each other out. The net result is 0. Overall, this possibility costs 0 and generates 0.
(2) If the stock price decreases, the convertible bond value stays the same as the straight bond price (conversion value declines with no material impact). At the same time, the short-sell position generates a profit. This possibility costs 0, and the net result is a profit.

The two possibilities combined together are an arbitrage opportunity. The initial cost is 0, and the future either generates 0 or a positive profit. For some combinations in the hedge fund, the future outcome will be 0; for others, the future outcome will be profit. Overall, convertible arbitrage is a great profit generator. The only issue with the strategy is that not all companies issue and sell convertible bonds. And because of the popularity of convertible bonds, they are tough to find.

As an example, consider the convertible bond purchased for $1,000 (depicted in bold lines) in Figure 7.1 with a $1,000 straight bond price (ten-year maturity, 10% coupon rate, 10% yield to maturity, $1,000 face value). Assuming that the conversion ratio is 25 shares and that the current share price is $40, the conversion value is $1,000 (25 times $40). The dashed line represents the profit generated from the short sale executed at $40 per share. If the stock price increases, there is a loss from the short sale, but the loss is eliminated by the gain from the conversion value. On the other hand, if the stock price decreases, there is a profit from the short sale, while the convertible bond value stays at the straight bond value. Having many convertible bonds and short-sell combinations of different companies overall leads to arbitrage profits.

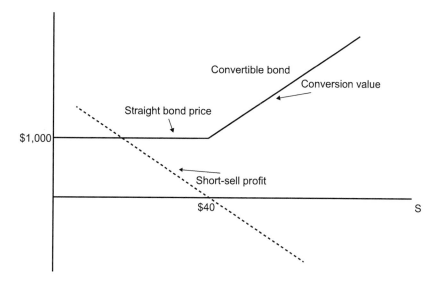

FIGURE 7.1 Convertible Bond Arbitrage Strategy

(3) Distressed securities: These types of hedge fund styles focus on firms and entities that are in financial trouble. The hedge fund manager is an expert in identifying the survivors and the ones that will fail. Survivors recover and thrive and thereby generate significant profits for the hedge funds. Another style of distressed securities involves breaking up the firm, extracting the valuable parts, restructuring and creating new, lean, and lucrative firms, and generating significant profits for the hedge funds. These hedge fund managers understand the inner workings of the corporate finance characteristics of distressed firms and design hedge fund types with the equity, fixed-income securities, and derivatives of such firms that have a high chance of getting out of the woods.

(4) Emerging markets: These international hedge funds focus on the firms, governments, and asset classes of emerging countries. Even though emerging markets have significant additional risk, the knowledge and expertise of the hedge fund managers reduce some of the risk and help select the emerging markets securities that will perform well. Different emerging markets perform in different ways over time. The hedge fund remains dynamic and expertly moves always from emerging markets that will perform poorly and shifts toward those that will perform well in a consistent manner. The inefficiencies in these markets are taken advantage of regularly by focusing on underpriced securities.

(5) Global macro: This hedge fund type is truly international. Securities from different countries and regions all over the world are used to create the hedge fund. The manager takes long and short positions in capital markets and derivatives markets from around the world. Major market conditions and broad economic trends are analyzed to take long or short positions in creating hedge funds. As expected, the portfolio positions are updated and adjusted dynamically as the economic and market conditions evolve.

(6) Merger arbitrage: These types of hedge funds are developed by managers who are experts in mergers and acquisitions. In a typical merger activity, the acquiring firm needs a long time to digest the merger. Typically, the share price remains sluggish or even declines for about five years after the merger. Also, typically, the target firm's share price goes up significantly when the merger/acquisition is announced and remains that way until the conclusion of the acquisition. The hedge fund manager is an expert in three perspectives. The first is in predicting accurately whether the announced merger will be successful or not. Many merger intentions fail, and positions taken in anticipation of a successful merger lead to large losses. The hedge fund manager successfully and consistently avoids these situations. Second, the hedge fund manager takes positions in the securities of acquiring firms to realize profits. These particular profits are generally (a) low, (b) based on short positions, and (c) realized over the medium term of around five years. Third, the prices of the securities of acquired firms go up considerably when the merger is announced. The hedge fund manager takes long positions before the announcement, after being fairly sure that the merger will be successful. The profits in these positions are substantial.

7.3.2 Hedge Fund Styles

While hedge fund types are categorized based on the types of securities the hedge fund focuses on, hedge fund styles categorization focuses on the main strategy a hedge fund is based on. It is true that a hedge fund manager can switch the style at any time, depending on the emergence of more profitable opportunities; however, the primary styles are important to go over. There is some overlap between the 'strategy-style' and 'type' categorizations. The concentration on a certain security (type) may also be related to a certain strategy (style).

(1) Dedicated short bias: This is a directional strategy hedge fund. The managers of this style of hedge funds are experts in and search for markets, sectors, industries, and companies with upcoming declines. The hedge fund manager takes short positions in the securities of these areas in anticipation of the decline. Here, the hedge fund only takes short positions (and no long position in any security), as opposed to a short exposure hedge fund, which would mean long and short positions in different securities with a net short resulting exposure. The short positions in dedicated short bias can be in any security around the globe.

(2) Equity market neutral: This is a non-directional strategy and involves taking positions in equity stocks. This hedge fund style uses both long and short positions and tries to generate hedge positions. The manager generally tries to control for factors such as industry, sector, size, and other exposures and creates neutral positions in order to take advantage of market inefficiencies. Longing an underpriced stock and shorting an overpriced stock belonging to similar-sized firms in the same industry is an example of the neutral position.

(3) Statistical arbitrage: A closely related hedge fund style to the equity-market neutral is called statistical arbitrage. Just like equity market neutral, statistical arbitrage is also a non-directional strategy with neutral positions. Statistical arbitrage is broader, involving all kinds of securities. The idea behind statistical arbitrage is (a) finding a sound investment idea that should be profitable, (b) taking positions reflecting the idea, and (3) repeating such positions many more times with other securities. Then by the statistical property of the law of large numbers, on average, the sound investment strategy generates guaranteed profits.

Statistical arbitrage style of hedge funds uses quantitative models and automated trading strategies. Starting from a simple and sound investment idea, the manager attempts to identify small mispricings in multiple securities. Small bets in hundreds of different securities for short holding periods (seconds, minutes, or a few hours) are placed. Using the hedge fund's technological advantages such as fast trading and low transactions costs, the mispricings are taken advantage of. Some of the hundreds of positions might not generate any profit or loss, but others would generate profits. By the law of large numbers, overall, the statistical arbitrage style leads to significant arbitrage profits. An example of this style is 'pairs trading', mentioned previously in equity market neutral. Finding two 'twin' stocks with very similar characteristics, shorting the high-priced one and buying the low-priced one, and doing this for many pairs in different economies, sectors, and industries generate arbitrage profits by the law of large numbers.

(4) Event-driven: This hedge fund style is about designing portfolios around important events and their consequences on certain securities. Events such as reorganization announcements, restructurings, bankruptcies, mergers, and acquisitions impact the values of the securities of the associated firms. The hedge fund manager is experienced in the positive and negative consequences of these events and takes positions to generate profits.

(5) Fixed-income arbitrage: This hedge fund style generates profits from market inefficiencies and mispricings in interest-related securities, such as government bonds, swaps, corporate bonds. Typical examples are arbitrage opportunities (a) in the yield curve (for example, long-term yields are too high, so buy the low-priced long-term bonds, and short-term yields are too low, so short the high-priced short-term bonds); (b) between the U.S. and non-U.S. government bond mispricings (after taking into account the sovereign risk of the foreign bonds); (3) in mortgage-backed securities; and (4) from swaps in interest rate discrepancies.

(6) Managed futures: This hedge fund style utilizes futures contracts with a variety of underlying securities, from commodities to currencies and other financial securities. The hedge fund manager mixes a variety of approaches, such as technical/quantitative analysis tools or subjective/qualitative research-based tools. These hedge funds utilize leverage and are generally high-risk. The expertise of the hedge fund manager attempts to counter the additional risk.

(7) Multistrategy: The hedge fund manager searches for and goes to where opportunities exist. As a consequence, there is no one specific style or strategy even when the hedge fund is established. As the economic outlook and financial conditions evolve, so does the hedge fund, shifting from one group of assets to another, potentially more lucrative group of assets.

(8) Fund of funds: This hedge fund style is about investing in a number of existing hedge funds. The hedge fund managers use personal networks and connections to reach agreements with existing hedge fund managers so that the investment amounts provided by the clients for the new hedge fund are invested in these few successful hedge funds. The double layer of fees in these funds of funds is the most unattractive characteristic of this hedge fund style.

In addition to the hedge fund styles mentioned earlier, there are a few more that have been covered in the hedge fund type section. The securities associated with the hedge fund type are intertwined with the style/strategy of the hedge fund. Some examples of these joint hedge fund types (securities) and styles (strategies) are convertible arbitrage, emerging markets, global macro, and long-short equity.

7.4 HEDGE FUND PERFORMANCE

Hedge funds are expected to perform well. The secretive nature, the sophistication of the hedge fund managers, the flexibility in the style, strategy, the type that the hedge fund policy can follow, the restrictions such as keeping the investment amount within the fund for a number of years, not being subject to the numerous rules and regulations like mutual funds, and the natural anticipation would be a better extra profit and/or a higher Sharpe ratio.

It is generally not easy to get data on hedge funds. However, through academic studies and through professional organizations such as the Chartered Alternative Investment Analyst Association (C.A.I.A.), important information has been compiled on hedge funds over the years.

We can inspect four pieces of academic research to inspect this issue.

An earlier study by Hasanhodzic and Lo (2007) found that after taking into account style and strategy differences, the adjusted alphas (extra profits) and Sharpe ratios are significantly greater than the measures for the S&P 500 for a large group of hedge funds. While this study claimed that hedge funds delivered higher profits after controlling for their risk and that hedge fund managers are highly skilled, the follow-up papers provided bleaker conclusions. For example, Aragon's (2007) study focused on the illiquidity characteristic of hedge funds with significant lockup period requirements and other redemption restrictions. Taking these frictions into account has eliminated the excess return, and thus, alphas became statistically insignificant. In a related work by Sadka (2010), hedge funds were exposed to generate significantly larger returns and profits in order to offset their illiquidity problems.

There has been evidence from reports and news analysis that the hedge fund performance has become less impressive, especially after the 2008 financial crisis. In a recent study by Bollen, Joenväärä, and Kauppila (2021), the hedge fund performance is compared to other asset classes over 20 years. For the second half of their time sample post-2008 financial crisis subsample, the researchers have found that hedge funds actually lag traditional stock and/or bond portfolios.

7.4.1 Hedge Fund Performance Measurement Problems

(1) Illiquidity and access restrictions: The research studies on the performance of hedge funds are affected significantly by the illiquidity problem. In such markets where trading is not liquid, prices become stale and are correlated with lagged, or previous, prices. The link between high serial correlations and high Sharpe ratios in hedge funds is interpreted as an implication of the high Sharpe ratio compensating for illiquidity. Moreover, serial correlations due to illiquidity are sometimes used by the hedge fund manager to depict a rosier fund performance than the true performance of the hedge fund. The fund values, rates of returns, and price estimates in such illiquid environments are generally evaluated in an optimistic manner during good times. A typical example is called the Santa effect. Hedge fund managers do not regularly report the performance of their funds, but when they do,

they tend to choose the month of December because average returns across the board tend to be higher at the end of December.

(2) Survivorship bias: Hedge funds are risky endeavors. Even with experienced and highly skilled managers, many hedge funds fail and cease to exist. Ignoring the funds that have failed and that have been removed from hedge funds databases leads to an unfairly positively skewed performance calculation. This is called the survivorship bias, considering only the surviving and successful funds in evaluating the hedge fund industry performance.

(3) Backfill bias: One of the fundamental problems with hedge fund performance is that the hedge fund manager chooses to report the activities of the hedge fund by choice. The manager may choose to skip reporting about the performance for years marked with sluggish or poor performance. On the other hand, the manager will be more tempted to report and boast about superior performance for a successful year. The flexibility about when to report leads to a positive bias about the performance of hedge funds.

(4) Factors and factor loadings (betas): Hedge funds are composed of all kinds of securities. Derivatives are certainly a large part of the composition of hedge fund portfolios. When the returns of hedge funds are evaluated statistically, linear regression models are generally utilized. However, many derivative securities, such as options, have nonlinear return characteristics. Trying to measure and predict nonlinear performance characteristics with linear regressions and straight-line fits cause measurement errors and inaccuracies in hedge fund performance values.

Another area of problem in the determination of the risk factors that influence hedge fund returns is the dynamic nature of the factors and factor loadings. Trying to use static measurement parameters and assuming constant risk levels are common but erroneous approaches because many hedge funds have variable risk levels and dynamic factors and loadings.

(5) Tail events: Hedge fund managers utilize sophisticated quantitative techniques and models with an empirical focus on the near-term history. Many hedge funds employ mathematical models that rely on near-term historical price data. Furthermore, a lot of hedge fund strategies work appropriately in low-volatility markets. The structures, styles, and strategies designed for hedge funds work well with average positive markets and with slight declines. However, in highly volatile markets with large positive moves or large negative declines, or with even rarer large market moves (tail events), the models and the techniques cannot keep up and accommodate. This is (a) bad during positive tail events because the hedge fund cannot generate large enough returns but (b) good during negative tail events because the hedge fund's negative returns are not as bad as those of the majority of the investment opportunities.

There are several key points of hedge fund performance. Academic and practitioner research studies during the past two decades have led to three fundamental conclusions:

(1) Under normal market conditions, hedge funds perform better than most other professional investment opportunities. During positive markets, the returns are slightly more positive, and during negative markets, the hedge fund returns are not as negative.

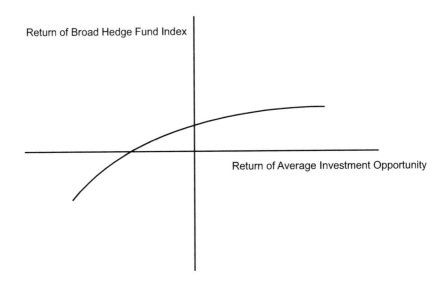

FIGURE 7.2 Hedge Fund Performance Over 20 Years in the 2000s

(2) During large upswings and aggressive bull markets (positive tail events), the hedge fund performance cannot keep up and tends to lag behind.

(3) During large downswings and depression-like markets (negative tail events), the hedge fund performance is poor and negative but not as bad as other investment opportunities. The hedge fund again cannot keep up with the negative tail event, but that is actually advantageous.

These three conclusions are summarized in Figure 7.2. The vertical axis represents average hedge fund returns after controlling for risk factors and loadings. The horizontal axis represents the overall market returns. Under normal conditions along the x-axis, hedge fund returns are positive and better than average returns. In extreme positive market conditions, hedge fund returns are not high enough. And finally, in the opposite extreme of negative market conditions, the hedge fund returns are negative but not as negative as the typical market returns.

7.5 HEDGE FUND FEES

The hedge fund fee structure is quite different from other professionally managed investments such as mutual funds. In addition to the typical fixed annual management fee between 1% and 2% of assets, there is also an incentive fee usually equal to 20% or more of the annual investment profits above a benchmark performance return.

The incentive fees can be substantial, but there is an important advantage to having them in a hedge. They place the interests of the hedge fund manager perfectly in line with the interests of the hedge fund clients. Any principal (owner, employer, client) – agent (manager, employee, advisor) problem is mitigated almost completely. The hedge fund manager practically becomes one of the investors and does the best to make the fund successful because the profits that are generated are shared; one-fifth belongs to the hedge fund manager.

One additional characteristic of the incentive fee is that it will be activated only when a 'high-water mark' is reached. Consider a fund starting with $100 million. At the end of the first year, the fund value is $110 million, and of the $10 million profit, 20%, or $2 million, is the incentive fee of the hedge fund manager. The high-water mark is recorded as $110 million. Suppose the second year is not successful, and the fund value is $105 million. Since there are no profits, naturally there are no incentive fees for the manager. Now, let us assume that the third year is successful and the fund value goes up to $109 million, generating a profit of $4 million for the third year. Even though the third year in and of itself has been successful because the high-water mark has not been surpassed, there will not be any incentive fees for the manager. Finally, consider the successful fourth year, where the fund value increases from $109 million to $120 million. Now that the high-water mark is surpassed, there will be incentive fees: one-fifth of the difference between the new high-water mark ($120 million) and the old high-water mark (which was $110 million) – and that is $2 million for the fund manager.

The high-water mark characteristic is a bit tricky. If a year during the life of the hedge fund is totally disastrous, it will be very difficult for the fund to recover from that substantial decline. Since the incentive fee is an important portion of the manager's compensation scheme, the lack of the incentive fee for the foreseeable future will discourage the manager. Hence, after deep declines in the fund value, the hedge fund is generally wrapped up with lost value. Whatever remains is shared among the investors, and the hedge fund manager moves on to create a new fund with a better chance of achieving high-water marks and incentive fees.

Overall, hedge funds have more fees. Incentive fees coupled with fixed annual fees lead to much larger costs compared to mutual funds. To counter the expenses, hedge fund managers suggest that they generate higher profits to more than cover those expenses.

The fees of funds of funds are worth exploring. Funds of funds are a special style of hedge funds. The clients' contributions are invested in popular existing hedge funds through the personal and network connections of fund managers. The advantage of funds of funds is that clients can become part of some of the most successful hedge funds. The disadvantage is the double layer of fees. This may cause strange situations, where the fund of funds loses value during a year, yet incentive fees are paid!

Consider the fund of funds in table 7.1 as an example. The fund of funds invests in two existing funds, $10 million each. Fund 1 is successful and rises up to $14 million at the end of the year. The incentive fee is one-fifth of the $4 million profit (i.e., $800,000). Fund 2 is not successful; the value drops sharply down from $10 million to $2.5 million. Clearly, there is no incentive fee for the second fund. Overall, the fund of funds starts with $20 million in the beginning and finishes the year with a value of $16.5 million. If this were a normal hedge fund, there would be no incentive fee. But because this is a fund of funds, and because the original funds making it up demand the incentive fee if they are successful like fund 1, there will be an overall incentive fee of $800,000, even though the fund of funds has lost value. Such strange fee consequences are not uncommon with a fund of funds.

In summary, funds of funds serve as feeder funds to the original ones. They allow clients easily diversify across popular hedge funds. But their extra layer of fees (first fee to original funds,

TABLE 7.1 Fund of Funds Fee Structure

	Fund 1	Fund 2	Fund of Funds
Commencement of Fund	$10 million	$10 million	$20 million
End of Year 1	$14 million	$2.5 million	$16.5 million
Gross Return Percentage	40%	−75%	−17.50%
Incentive Fee (20%)	$800,000	0	$800,000
Net End of Year 1	$13.2 million	$2.5 million	$15.7 million
Net Return Percentage	32%	−75%	−21.50%

second fee to the fund of funds manager) and the strange incentive fee situations in table 7.1 make them unattractive. Their reputation was badly damaged when it came out that many funds of funds were major investors in the Bernard L. Madoff Investment Securities hedge fund. It was a Ponzi scheme, and the fund of funds managers should have realized the problem.

7.6 FINAL REMARKS ON HEDGE FUNDS

The hedge fund industry grew at a healthy pace until the financial crisis of 2006–2008. The $50 billion Bernie Madoff Ponzi scheme scandal upset the trust in the industry. Bernard Madoff was a highly respected market professional and former chairman of N.A.S.D.A.Q. His Bernard L. Madoff Investment Securities hedge fund had a prestigious client book. Unfortunately, in his scheme, he would promise unreasonable high and stable returns to his investors, thereby attracting large funds, and would pay out attractive sums to his old clients, and these would, in turn, attract larger funds from new clients. During this vicious cycle, Madoff would skim some of the funds for his own use. The scheme would work until new funds started to slow down. During the financial crisis, that is exactly what happened. In 2008 redemptions intensified as clients needed money, and the scheme unwound. Madoff was convicted, sent to prison, and passed away there in 2021.

Lack of reporting requirements for hedge funds made the fraud possible, but there were several warning signs, as pointed out to the Securities and Exchange Commission in 2000 by Harry Markopolos, the financial fraud investigator: (1) the returns of the fund were too stable for too long, (2) the fund fee structure was too generous, (3) the audit firm verifying the fund transactions was not a major auditor and was susceptible to coercion from the fund, (4) contrary to the norm, all the assets of the fund were kept in house rather than with a custodian, and (5) there was no evidence of option investments whatsoever that Madoff claimed were behind the profits.

Even though the Madoff debacle is considered to be an isolated incident, trust in the system was damaged, at least temporarily. However, hedge funds and hedge fund managers continue to be the pioneers in the investments frontier. They use the most cutting-edge technology – hardware and software – to reshape the transaction and trade execution systems toward higher levels of effectiveness, improve communication systems, and influence financial market infrastructure.

They help move funds toward sectors, industries, and geographies that have the highest potential impact on the social and economic welfare of the world.

Considering all the positives (high profits) and the negatives (high fees, temporary loss of reputation) and the different perspectives mentioned, hedge funds continue to be one of the most exciting investment areas in contemporary finance.

7.7 BRIEF SYNOPSIS OF MUTUAL FUNDS

The mutual fund industry provides convenient opportunities for small and individual investors to take positions in sophisticated portfolios. Instead of an individual trying to form an internationally diversified portfolio of technology-based stocks, an investment in a mutual fund with that same objective is much more convenient and much less costly. Consequently, a mutual fund is one of the most preferred investment alternatives for small investors.

The global mutual fund size is roughly around $60 trillion in the early 2020s. With roughly half of that amount in total net assets, the U.S. mutual fund industry is the largest in the world. There are more than 100,000 mutual funds worldwide, and roughly one-tenth are in the U.S. In terms of asset size, the U.S.-based mutual funds are much larger. The biggest funds are in the U.S.

The largest mutual fund company in the world is BlackRock, with close to $10 trillion of assets making up the mutual funds. Vanguard Group, Fidelity Investments, Charles Schwab, State Street Global Advisors, Capital Group, J.P. Morgan Chase, Pimco, B.N.Y. Mellon Investment Management, and Goldman Sachs are the largest mutual fund companies in the world, all based in the U.S. The largest non-U.S. mutual fund company is Amundi, based in France.

The typical mutual fund is open-ended. Anyone who wants to be part of the fund contacts the mutual fund company and buys 'mutual fund shares' directly from the mutual fund company. Similarly, the shares are sold (redeemed) directly to the mutual fund company. These mutual funds are quite liquid. The share price is known as net asset value (N.A.V.):

$$NAV = \frac{TotalValueAssets - Liabilities}{NumberOfShares} \tag{7.1}$$

The second type of mutual fund is the closed-end mutual fund. In the U.S., 5–10% of the total number of mutual funds is closed-end funds. A closed-end fund issues a fixed number of shares through a single initial public offering (I.P.O.) to raise capital for the initial investments. Once the offering period ends, an investor can no longer be part of the closed-end fund. The existing investors cannot exit for a certain lock-up period. Afterward, closed-end shares can be traded in secondary over-the-counter markets through any brokerage firm.

Mutual funds are heavily regulated. They must be transparent; they must stick with the original investment objectives laid out clearly in the initial prospectus. They must be well-diversified (no security can have more than 5% of the total fund value). All the income through dividends or coupon payments must be provided to the mutual fund investors. They must have very limited or no use of leverage, derivatives, and short-selling opportunities.

As for mutual fund fees, there are (1) the front-end load (one-time fee paid when initially investing in a mutual fund), (2) the back-end load (one-time fee paid when redeeming and exiting the mutual fund), and (3) period fees such as management, administrative, 12b-1 (marketing, distribution, etc.). Finally, there are hidden costs due to the transaction fees paid for buying and selling securities while dynamically managing the mutual fund portfolio. If the turnover in a mutual fund is high, so will these hidden fees.

Investigation of the mutual fund performance leads to mixed results. Adjusting for the risk factors, the mutual funds do not perform better than the typical stock market index after considering the mutual fund fees. Focusing on successful funds in a given year and exploring consistency in the following year reveals that only half of the successful mutual funds continue to be successful the following year, while the other half performs poorly – not much different than tossing a coin in terms of consistency of mutual fund success.

While the performance of mutual funds overall may not necessarily be superior, the convenience of investing in a well-diversified portfolio directed by a professional manager continues to be a massive advantage for small and individual investors. There is an overall desire for a unified marketplace where the mutual funds created by different investment companies are altogether for comparison and trading purposes. For research purposes, the Morningstar website is an excellent source to get information about a mutual fund.

7.8 BRIEF SYNOPSIS OF EXCHANGE-TRADED FUNDS (E.T.F.S)

Exchange-traded funds allow investors to practically trade a financial index. For example, let's assume that an investor would like to invest funds to generate the same performance as the Dow Jones Industrial Average Index. The Dow consists of 30 blue-chip stocks – each of a fundamental company from a different industry. One way would be to purchase each stock and create a portfolio. But paying 30 transaction costs is quite costly. The more direct, convenient, and less costly approach would be to buy an E.T.F. designed to replicate the performance of the Dow: the Diamond E.T.F. (D.I.A.). This E.T.F. was introduced by State Street Global Advisors in 1998. The 'share price' of Diamond is one-hundredth of the Dow. As the index changes, so does D.I.A.

The E.T.F.s can be considered as a financial security in between a stock and a mutual fund. They are referred to as artificial stocks because they can be purchased and sold at any time, just like stocks. On the other hand, although the E.T.F.s have a fee as in other mutual funds, this annual fee is very low since there is almost no maintenance or active management needed compared to other mutual funds. E.T.F.s generally offer tax advantages compared to other mutual funds.

There are more than 7,500 E.T.F.s in the world, representing $8 trillion in assets, and the numbers continue to increase. One-third of the E.T.F.s are in the U.S., and these E.T.F.s are much larger (about $5 trillion worth of assets). The 20 largest E.T.F.s make up over half of the total asset value in E.T.F.s. Vanguard, BlackRock, and State Street Global Advisors are major E.T.F. providers.

The most popular E.T.F.s are S.P.D.R. (S.P.Y.), iShares Core S&P 500 (I.V.V.), Vanguard S&P 500 (V.O.O.), all replicating the S&P 500 index; Diamond (D.I.A.) replicating the Dow 30 index; Vanguard Total Stock Market (V.T.I.); Invesco Q.Q.Q. Trust (Q.Q.Q.) replicating N.A.S.D.A.Q.'s top 100 stocks index; Vanguard F.T.S.E. Developed Markets excluding the U.S. (V.E.A.); iShares Core M.S.C.I. E.A.F.E. – Europe, Australia, Far East (I.E.F.A.); iShares Core U.S. Aggregate Bond (A.G.G.); Vanguard Growth (V.U.G.); Vanguard Value (V.T.V.); Vanguard F.T.S.E. Emerging Markets (V.W.O.).

These popular E.T.F.s mentioned provide investors with the means to invest in sophisticated portfolios. World equity benchmark E.T.F.s help to invest in the stock market of a country or sector/industry. E.T.F.s enable choosing a diversified portfolio in a specific industry, such as technology, healthcare, and consumer staples. E.T.F.s based on specific financial securities such as bonds help access particular securities markets. Overall, E.T.F.s are extremely convenient professional portfolios that (1) are not costly, (2) are easy to access, (3) trade continuously, and (4) are associated with low taxes, especially for small investors. New E.T.F.s are continually created, including using leverage, inverse, short positions, and different securities. Such inverse or short E.T.F.s are used not only for investment purposes but also for hedging reasons. The future of the E.T.F. field is certainly bright with these innovations and creative constructions.

7.9 SUMMARY AND CONCLUSION

Professionally managed portfolios are convenient investment opportunities for many investors. Mutual funds have been the main attraction for decades. In a recent couple of decades, E.T.F.s have become extremely popular because of low costs, low taxes, and a wide spectrum of alternatives.

But hedge funds are the most exciting professionally managed portfolios. Hedge fund companies and managers use the most recent technological advancements in building their hardware infrastructures, computer mainframes, communications systems, and trading platforms. From fiber optic communication networks to the ability to monitor all the financial markets globally, from executing transactions at nanosecond speeds to consistently taking advantage of arbitrage opportunities, hedge funds fuel advancements and innovations in numerous areas of contemporary finance. Continually searching for and investing in ideas/companies on the frontiers of science and technology would ultimately lead to increased welfare of the global society. Therefore, hedge funds indirectly provide an important service by moving capital from where it is less useful toward where it is more useful for the global society.

REFERENCES AND ADDITIONAL READING

Aragon, G.O. 2007. Share Restrictions and Asset Pricing: Evidence from the Hedge Fund Industry. *Journal of Financial Economics*, 83, 33–58.
Bollen, N.P.B., Juha Joenväärä, J., Kauppila, M. 2021. Hedge Fund Performance: End of an Era? *Financial Analysts Journal*, 77, 109–132.

Hasanhodzic, J., Lo, A.W. 2007. Can Hedge Fund Returns be Replicated?: The Linear Case. *Journal of Investment Management*, 5, 5–45.

Markopolos, H. 2010. *No One Would Listen: A True Financial Thriller*. Hoboken, NJ, Wiley.

Sadka, R. 2010. Liquidity Risk and the Cross-Section of Hedge-Fund Returns. *Journal of Financial Economics*, 98, 54–71.

Stulz, R.M. 2007. Hedge Funds: Past, Present, and Future. *Journal of Economic Perspectives*, 21, 175–194.

CHAPTER **8**

Stochastic Calculus

OBJECTIVES

- Describe the historical perspective of where, when, and why stochastic calculus models were first developed and used in physics and mathematics.
- Justify the transition of the stochastic calculus model into the finance area.
- Interpret, critique, and clarify the technical terms and their fit within the standard financial concepts and models.
- Implement these stochastic models for practical investment analysis.
- Design Excel examples using real-life securities data to clarify the practical aspects, the advantages, and the increasing popularity of such models.
- Create and derive key financial and statistical variables using stochastic models for predictive purposes.

8.1 INTRODUCTION

Stochastic calculus is a highly sophisticated approach with equations that incorporate random variables. The solutions of these types of equations are always different due to the uncertain nature of the values related to the random variables.

Ordinary calculus is deterministic, and the solution is always the same. For example, in a simple algebra equation, $(2)(x) = 4$, the solution for the unknown, x, is always equal to 2. On the other hand, in a stochastic, or probabilistic, equation, the solution is always different. For example, in the simple stochastic equation, $(2)(x) = 4 + \varepsilon$, where ε is a normally distributed random variable with a mean of 0 and a standard deviation of 1, the solution for x will always depend on the value of ε: $x = 2 + \varepsilon / 2$. When we solve this equation now and draw ε as 0.2, the answer for x is 2.1. The next minute when we solve the equation again, we draw ε from the normal distribution as -0.4, for example, and the answer for x then would be 1.8.

Stochastic equations are ideal for describing situations, variables, and environments that have uncertainties. For example, if we are trying to describe the stock price movements in the future with an equation, the uncertainties about the future must be taken into consideration.

DOI: 10.4324/9781003213697-8

A deterministic equation would be simplistic and incorrect. On the other hand, a proper stochastic equation reflecting the stock's characteristics along with incorporating the uncertainties about the future would be ideal. That is why in recent decades, research in academia and strategy development at professional investment companies, hedge funds, and others have started utilizing stochastic equations.

In this chapter, the history of stochastic equations in physics, mathematics, and chemistry is examined. The transition into the finance field is explained. Different stochastic processes are investigated. Particular stochastic equations describing the dynamics of specific financial securities are presented and verified. Empirical validation of the models is outlined. Examples using Excel demonstrate the real-time application of these stochastic models and processes.

8.2 HISTORICAL BACKGROUND OF STOCHASTIC EQUATIONS AND PROCESSES

The history of stochastic variables and processes goes back to the late 19th century. Researchers in natural sciences, such as physics, mathematics, chemistry, and biology, have long desired to come up with structured models to describe the randomness in the dynamics of various phenomena in their fields. Examples such as heat transmission, particle movements, genetic expressions, computer science algorithms, formations of geographical phenomena such as rivers, manufacturing processes, radiation effects, color reproductions, musical compositions, and many others use stochastic processes. A stochastic process is defined as a mathematical object usually described with the help of a group of random variables. Many times the words 'stochastic' and 'random' are used interchangeably – even though the subtle difference is that 'stochastic' generally refers to the process or the model trying to describe the randomness, while 'random' is about the phenomenon itself.

Stochastic processes are widely designed as theoretical and mathematical models to describe systems and variables that appear to change dynamically in a random manner. As discussed in detail by Jarrow and Protter (2004) in their Institute of Mathematical Statistics research, efforts to formally design and introduce such stochastic models originate from three researchers in continental European in the late 1800s and early 1900s:

(1) Thorvald Thiele began using stochastic processes in time series analysis in Denmark in 1880.
(2) Louis Bachelier in France tried to model the dynamic characteristics of the Paris stock exchange using stochastic models in 1900. His attempts to model the market noise by proposing that stock price increments should be memoryless, independent, and normally distributed, satisfy the central limit theorem, and exhibit random walks were all innovative ideas and made him considered by many to be the founder of modern mathematical finance.
(3) Albert Einstein proposed to explain the motion of molecular-sized particles using stochastic processes in 1905.

These studies were independent of one another. Using mathematical models in economics and econometrics was not popular at that time; thus, of the three, Einstein's approach became tremendously and immediately influential in physics, mathematics, and other fields.

Einstein's approach laid the foundation for modeling the dynamic movements of tiny particles such as electrons, protons, and neutrons. Dynamics such as Brownian motion with continuous paths and Wiener processes developed in 1923 helped formally describe arithmetic and Brownian motions with continuous paths. The formalization of the structured expressions of the dynamic movements of random variables and phenomena continued until the 1940s through the invaluable contributions of researchers, such as Norbert Wiener, Andrey Markov, and Andrei Kolmogorov. Finally, in 1942, the Japanese researcher Kiyoshi Itô (1915–2008) started to synthesize the prior work and created the theory of stochastic differential equations, which describe the dynamics of random events. His additional publications in 1944 and 1951 completed the introduction of the stochastic calculus field. Itô is considered by most as the creator of the modern theory of stochastic analysis.

Stochastic processes became part of sophisticated research in many fields, including economics and finance, especially starting in the 1950s. The uncertain nature of stock price movements, and random characteristics of many dynamic variables in finance made stochastic processes a natural tool in the description of the movements of these financial and economic variables. Theoretical stochastic process models describing the evolution of these financial and economic variables became popular throughout the second half of the 20th century. With the advent of personal computers starting in the late 1970s, it became feasible to implement the theoretical stochastic models through empirical implementations, such as Monte Carlo simulations. In today's world of supercomputers and ultra-high-speed trading platforms, stochastic processes are primary tools of sophisticated investors and financial institutions in predicting the dynamic movements of economic variables and financial security prices.

8.3 STOCHASTIC PROCESSES AND FINANCIAL SECURITIES

Stochastic processes describe the way in which a variable, such as a stock price, exchange rate, or interest rate, changes dynamically through time. These processes incorporate uncertainties about the future into the security price movements.

These stochastic processes are more realistic than models using only deterministic variables. Any security whose value depends on future cash flows and on changes in domestic or international economic variables and political, economic, and market conditions can be described using models that take the ambiguous and vague characteristics of the future into account. Deterministic models unrealistically assume only one outcome about the future and do not reflect the true nature of financial security. Stochastic models have the sophistication and the flexibility to incorporate future uncertainties using random variables and reflect the future changes in the financial variables more accurately.

8.3.1 Markov Processes

Most stochastic processes used in contemporary finance have the Markov property. In a Markov process, the future movements depend only on the current value of the variable, not on the history of the movement to reach the current value. The commonly used phrase 'the past performance is not indicative of future performance' defines the Markov process.

Prices of financial securities (including stocks) are assumed to follow Markovian stochastic processes. We should, however, note that past patterns and security price behaviors should not be totally ignored. While they should not influence the dynamics of the stochastic processes and behaviors, they do provide a context about the risk and return characteristics of financial securities. If nothing else can be used to describe such characteristics, then past behaviors can be the starting points that can be adjusted empirically or subjectively to better distinguish the security.

As an example of a Markov process, consider a random variable. The current value of the variable is 30. The random variable follows a Markov process; therefore, how the current value of 30 was reached (whether there was a decrease to 30 or an increase to 30) is irrelevant to the future. Let us assume that the process is stationary. A stationary random process has parameters that do not change with time (i.e., the parameters are time-independent). Finally, let us define the random variable as normally distributed with a mean of 30 and a standard deviation of 10. Therefore, in the next time increment, defined, for example, as one year, the value of the variable is drawn from this normal distribution.

8.3.2 Weak-Form Market Efficiency

Using stochastic processes that are Markovian asserts that it is *impossible* to produce consistently superior returns with a trading rule based on the past history of security prices. In other words, technical analysis does not work in a world described by Markovian stochastic processes.

Such a setting is said to be weak-form efficient. The definition of a weak-form efficient market is one where all the information that can be gained from the historical prices, patterns, and volume of information are reflected in the current prices.

For completeness, there are two more forms of market efficiency: (1) A semi-strong efficient market is one where current prices reflect all publicly available information, such as current financial statements, and all financial variables, political, economic, and financial news, as well as all historical information. (2) A strong-form efficient market is one where all information – public and private – are reflected in prices. In a strong-form efficient market, insiders, such as high-level managers (insiders) with first access to private information about their firm, cannot consistently generate extra profits based on their private information. Such strong form efficient markets do not exist anywhere around the world. That is why rules, regulations, and insider trading legislation prevent insiders from using their private information to generate unfair and unethical extra profits at the expense of outsiders.

Markovian stochastic processes and weak-form market efficiency are consistent with each other. Most well-established markets consistently exhibit evidence of weak-form efficiency. Thus, such stochastic processes are applicable to most developed economies around the world.

8.3.3 Continuous-Time Process

In the Markov process example, the time increment was defined as one year. Given the time increment, the probability distribution of the random variable was a normal distribution with a mean of 30 and a standard deviation of 10. Trying to predict values at shorter increments is generally more feasible in stochastic processes. The volatility of the estimation becomes more manageable with shorter time increments. Then the question is, what happens to the probability distribution of the random variable for a time increment of half a year, a quarter, a month, or Δt years?

As predictions become more accurate with shorter time increments, taking limits as Δt goes to 0 redefines the stochastic process as a continuous-time stochastic process. To distinguish between such continuous time and discrete (tangible) time, continuous-time increment is denoted with 'dt', and discrete-time step is denoted with 'Δt'. Continuous-time stochastic processes are more useful in theoretical derivations and proofs. Therefore, it is always more feasible to start with continuous-time settings in developing trading strategies and concepts. Once the derivations are completed and the theoretical model is finalized, the empirical implementation converts continuous-time models into reliable, discrete equivalents.

8.4 STOCHASTIC PROCESSES FOR STOCK PRICES AND STOCK RETURNS

Starting with the 1950s, finance researchers borrowed and implemented various popular processes from mathematics and physics for the description of stock prices and returns.

8.4.1 Wiener Process

The basic stochastic process is the Wiener process. A random variable, z, exhibits Wiener process characteristics if the change of the random variable in a small time interval Δt is normally distributed with a mean of 0 and a standard deviation of $\sqrt{\Delta t}$, or more specifically,

$$\Delta z = \left(\varepsilon\right)\left(\sqrt{\Delta t}\right) = N(0,1)\sqrt{\Delta t} = N(0,\sqrt{\Delta t}), \tag{8.1}$$

where ε is a standard normal random variable, $N(0, 1)$, and the change in the Wiener process, Δz, is a random normal variable, $N(0, \sqrt{\Delta t})$.

The Wiener process exhibits independence over time increments. In other words, for any two non-overlapping periods of time, the values of Δz are independent. Furthermore, Δt, the time increment, is extremely small, such that any power of Δt bigger than '1' would make it become 0. For example, $Dt^2 = \Delta t^{1.5} = 0$. But any power of Δt less than '1' would make it nonzero.

The Wiener process is characterized by a drift rate of 0 per time increment. This means the average change per unit of time is 0. The variance (standard deviation squared) rate is 1 per unit of time. These characteristics have rendered the Wiener process infeasible to describe the change of a stock price process. We know that stock prices change over time. In fact, on average, stock prices tend to increase over time as companies generate profits leading to growth. Thus, the average change of 0 during each time increment is inconsistent with the stock price process. Furthermore, the standard deviation of a stock also varies over time; the variance rate of 1 each time increment is not realistic enough.

In summary, finance researchers trying to incorporate stochastic processes to describe stock price dynamics quickly realized that the standard Wiener process was not sufficient. A more sophisticated model was necessary, and that was the generalized Wiener process.

8.4.2 Generalized Wiener Process

In the generalized Wiener process, the average change (drift rate) and the variance rate for the time increments can be set equal to any chosen constant value based on the return and risk characteristics of the financial security. The specific equation representing the change in the generalized Winer process, Δx, is

$$\Delta x = a\Delta t + b\Delta z = a\Delta t + b(\varepsilon)\left(\sqrt{\Delta t}\right) = a\Delta t + bN(0,1)\sqrt{\Delta t} = a\Delta t + N(0, b\sqrt{\Delta t}), \tag{8.2}$$

where the change in the Wiener process is augmented with an amplification factor, b, and a deterministic drift factor, $(a)/(\Delta t)$. Indeed, the first part of the right-hand side of equation 8.2 is deterministic. This drift factor may be based on the historical mean value of the drift per time increment, the rational expectation of the change in the variable. Therefore, the mean value of the change in the generalized Wiener process (the stock price) per time increment is represented by a. And the standard deviation (variance) of the change in the generalized Wiener process (the stock price) for each time increment is represented by b (b^2).

As in section 8.3.3, when limits are taken as the time increment Δt goes to zero, the infinitesimally small time increment is dt, and the generalized Wiener process equation becomes

$$dx = adt + bdz = adt + b(\varepsilon)\left(\sqrt{dt}\right). \tag{8.3}$$

These very small time intervals and very small changes of the variable denoted with d, instead of Δ, represent continuous-time finance.

The enhanced and more sophisticated process was employed enthusiastically by finance researchers to describe stock returns. However, repeated empirical tests and quantitative fits consistently revealed the shortcomings of the model. The generalized Wiener process was not proper for stock prices. The following numerical example highlights the essential flaw associated with the generalized Wiener process.

Consider a stock's price as $30. The stock's price one year later depends on a random variable normally distributed with a mean of 30 and a standard deviation of 10. If the stochastic process is Markov with no drift to describe the return of this stock, then the model is

$$dS = 10dz, \tag{8.4}$$

where dz is $\varepsilon \sqrt{dt}$, or $N(0, 1) \sqrt{dt}$.

But since most stocks' prices tend to increase over time, assume that the stock price is expected to increase by $6 on average during the year so that the price one year later is based on a random variable normally distributed with a mean of 36 and a standard deviation of 10. The stochastic process for the return of the stock price would then be generalized Wiener process:

$$dS = 6dt + 10dz. \tag{8.5}$$

The first term on the right side of equation 8.5 indicates that the stock price is expected to grow by $6 during the year. The second term on the right-hand side incorporates uncertainty –

that is, the standard deviation of ten times the standard Wiener process dz, which is a normal distribution (with a mean of 0 and a standard deviation of 10) multiplied by $\sqrt{dt}$ (where the unit for the time increment is 'years').

For the dynamics and evolution of a stock's price, we conjecture that the expected change of the price in a short period of time remains constant as a percentage, not as an actual dollar amount. In other words, we generally expect the price to increase by 20%, whether the price is currently $5, $30, or $200 per share. Expressing the change in the price as a percentage would be applicable to any stock with any price. A stochastic model that uses percentages to express changes is more flexible and is applicable to all kinds of stocks with different characteristics. The change in dollars may be different, but the percentage is the same regardless of what the stock price may be. In other words, assuming the percentage change is constant over time makes more sense than assuming the dollar amount change is constant over time.

Unfortunately, the generalized Wiener process uses dollar amounts rather than percentages to express changes. The stock price is expected to increase by $6 in equation 8.5. Such a model does not have the flexibility to be applied to a penny stock with a current price of $0.50. Nor can it satisfactorily express the expected change of stock with the current price of $2,800.

This realization forced finance researchers to search for a better stochastic model that expressed changes in prices as percentages rather than dollar amounts. Such a model would conjecture that uncertainty about the size of future stock price movements would be proportional to the level of the stock price. The search for a better model led to the utilization of the Itô process.

8.4.3 Itô Process for Stock Prices

The Itô process for stock price movements is a significantly advanced version of the generalized Wiener process. The drift rate and the variance rate are functions of time. The drift and the variance evolve dynamically over time. The continuous-time version of the Itô process is

$$dx = a(x,t)\, dt + b(x,t)\, dz, \tag{8.6}$$

and the corresponding discrete-time version,

$$\Delta x = a(x,t)\, \Delta t + b(x,t)\, \varepsilon \sqrt{\Delta t}. \tag{8.7}$$

As Δt tends toward zero in the limit, the discrete version approaches the continuous-time version. The Itô process applied to the description of stock price dynamics is expressed as

$$dS = \mu S\, dt + \sigma S\, dz, \tag{8.8}$$

where μ is the expected return and σ is the volatility, or standard deviation of the stock return. The presence of S in the first and second terms on the right-hand side of equation 8.8 should be noted. The discrete equivalent of the Itô process is

$$\Delta S = \mu S\, \Delta t + \sigma S\, \varepsilon \sqrt{\Delta t}. \tag{8.9}$$

This Itô process for stock prices is also known as the geometric Brownian motion. Equation 8.9 is the price process. The return process for the stock is easily deduced from the price process as

$$\frac{\Delta S}{S} = \mu \Delta t + \sigma \varepsilon \sqrt{\Delta t}. \tag{8.10}$$

The standard stock return is on the left-hand side of the equation: $(S_1 - S_0)/S_0$. This return is equal to the sum of the deterministic return component as the first term of the right-hand side and the random component with ε as the second term of the right-hand side. This random variable represents an uncertainty factor in the economy, financial markets, and political environment.

An important point to note here is that whether the Wiener process, generalized Wiener process, or the Itô process is used for the dynamics of stock prices and stock returns, the uncertainty is described with a normally distributed random variable. Of the three processes, Itô process is by far the superior; and the underlying two theoretical assumptions for the Itô process are: (1) stock prices are normally distributed, and (2) stock returns are normally distributed. The researchers have employed these models to describe stock price and return dynamics starting with these assumptions. Both of these assumptions are *problematic*, as explored shortly.

In more sophisticated versions of the Itô process, multiple uncertainty factors can be integrated into equation 8.10. For each uncertainty factor, a unique Wiener process can be employed. In such an augmented process, one Wiener process can be for interest rate uncertainty, another can be about the uncertainty in G.D.P. growth, and another on the uncertainty in the exchange rate dynamics. Furthermore, uncertainty factors need not necessarily be independent. Suppose dz_1 and dz_2 are two Wiener processes that are correlated. The correlation coefficient $\rho_{1,2}$ would quantify this relationship. Then,

$$\begin{aligned} dz_1 &= \varepsilon_1 \sqrt{\Delta t} \\ dz_2 &= \varepsilon_2 \sqrt{\Delta t}, \end{aligned} \tag{8.11}$$

where ε_1 and ε_2 are random variables coming from a bivariate standard normal distribution where the correlation is $\rho_{1,2}$.

Equations 8.9 and 8.10 in discrete format (or in continuous-time format) represent the stock price and the return processes as applications of Itô. The empirical implementation of the Itô process has been quite well for the stock price and the stock return dynamics. To this day, the Itô process has been one of the two most popular processes to describe stock dynamics.

The second of the two popular processes is based on natural logarithmic returns. This process is less intuitive to grasp and fully understand, but it is more accurate both theoretically and empirically (Itô process assumes normal distribution for the stock price and the stock return, while the lognormal process correctly assumes lognormal distribution for the stock price and normal distribution for the stock return):

$$\Delta log(S) = (\mu - \sigma^2/2)\, \Delta t + \sigma\, \varepsilon \sqrt{\Delta t}. \tag{8.12}$$

This alternative return process is discussed in detail later. For now, the next section is about the empirical implementation of the Itô process with Monte Carlo simulations.

8.5 EMPIRICAL IMPLEMENTATION OF THE ITÔ PROCESS: MONTE CARLO SIMULATIONS

Once a sound theoretical model describing the dynamics of the stock price and the stock return is well-established, the empirical implementation of the model for forecasting follows. Monte Carlo simulations are used to depict stock price movements over time and to make predictions for the future. Random paths for the stock price are generated by sampling (drawing values for ε). Once a price path is generated using step-by-step (for example, weekly time increments) stock price estimations for a future time segment, such as a year, one Monte Carlo Simulation is completed. And a prediction for the stock price one year into the future is obtained. For a reliable forecast, many more Monte Carlo simulations are executed, and many new predictions are generated. By the law of large numbers, the average of those predictions becomes a statistically reliable prediction.

As an example of the generation of one Monte Carlo simulation, the average annual return of a stock is calculated as $\mu = 0.12$ (annual), $\sigma = 0.20$ (annual), and the time increment is 1 week, $\Delta t = 1/52 = 0.0192$ years (always expressed in terms of years). Then the discrete Itô process for the stock price, after some simplification, is

$$\Delta S = \mu S\, \Delta t + \sigma S\, \varepsilon \sqrt{\Delta t}$$
$$= (0.12)(S)(0.0192) + (0.20)(S)(\varepsilon)(\sqrt{0.0192})$$
$$= (0.002304)(S) + (0.027713)(S)(\varepsilon).$$

This expression is used in a recursive manner, starting with the current stock price, S_0. With each iteration, the stock price for the next time increment is calculated after drawing a different value for ε from a normal distribution. With 52 consecutive iterations corresponding to 52 weeks, a price path for one year is generated:

$$S_{t+1} - S_t = (0.002304)(S_t) + (0.027713)(S_t)(\varepsilon)$$
$$S_{t+1} = (1.002304)(S_t) + (0.027713)(S_t)(\varepsilon)$$

The sampling path based on the Monte Carlo simulation starts with the current stock price, for example, $S_0 = \$30$. Then,

$$S_1 = (1.002304)(S_0) + (0.027713)(S_0)(\varepsilon) = (1.002304)(30) + (0.027713)(30)(0.26)$$
$$= 30.29 \text{ (with } \varepsilon \text{ drawn as } 0.26 \text{ from a normal distribution),}$$
$$S_2 = (1.002304)(S_1) + (0.027713)(S_1)(\varepsilon) = (1.002304)(30.29) + (0.027713)(30.29)(0.72)$$
$$= 30.96 \text{ (with } \varepsilon \text{ drawn as } 0.72 \text{ from a normal distribution),}$$
$$S_3 = (1.002304)(S_2) + (0.027713)(S_2)(\varepsilon) = (1.002304)(30.96) + (0.027713)(30.96)(-0.43)$$
$$= 30.66 \text{ (with } \varepsilon \text{ drawn as } -0.43 \text{ from a normal distribution), and so on.}$$

This iterative process ends with the calculation of S_{52}, the stock price one year from today, where S_{52} is the stock price forecast of this simulation. For a really reliable forecast, millions, if not billions, of Monte Carlo simulations must be executed, price paths must be obtained, and averages of the 52-week forecast values must be taken. The result, from the law of large numbers, provides statistically reliable forecast price.

8.6 ITÔ'S LEMMA

The beauty of the Itô process is that it is part of a much larger theoretical structure. The theory developed by Itô is flexible to describe many financial securities simultaneously and consistently. In this section, the theoretical extensions of the Itô process are examined.

If we know the characteristics of a stochastic process for the random variable S (which can be stock price or any other random variable), Itô's lemma determines the stochastic process followed by some function G that is dependent on the random variable, S, and time, t.

Since the price of a derivative security, such as a call option, put option, or a futures contract would be a function of the price of the underlying asset and time, Itô's lemma plays an important role in the analysis of the dynamics of derivative securities. The stochastic processes of these various types of sophisticated derivative securities are obtained with Itô's lemma.

In the mathematical derivations of the stochastic relationships between the derivatives and the underlying financial securities, Taylor series expansion is essential. Taylor series expansions are very useful in simplifying and expressing various complex functions with reasonable approximations. Some examples of Taylor series expansion are

$$e^S = 1 + S + \frac{S^2}{2!} + \frac{S^3}{3!} + \frac{S^4}{4!} + \dots, \tag{8.13}$$

$$\log(1 + S) = S - \frac{S^2}{2} + \frac{S^3}{3} - \frac{S^4}{4} + \dots, \tag{8.14}$$

where n factorial, $n!$, is $(n)(n-1)(n-2) \dots (2)(1)$.

Taylor series expansions also describe changes in functions. The Taylor series expansion of the change in the function $G(x, t)$ is expressed as

$$\Delta G(S,t) = \frac{\partial G}{\partial S} \Delta S + \frac{\partial G}{\partial t} \Delta t + \frac{1}{2} \frac{\partial^2 G}{\partial S^2} (\Delta S)^2 + \frac{\partial^2 G}{\partial S \partial t} (\Delta S)(\Delta t)$$

$$+ \frac{1}{2} \frac{\partial^2 G}{\partial t^2} (\Delta t)^2 + \dots \tag{8.15}$$

It should be noted immediately that the last two terms and every term afterward on the right-hand side will immediately vanish since they contain parameters $(\Delta t)^k$, where $k > 1$ (remember that Δt is such a small time increment that any power bigger than 1 will render it 0).

If the stochastic process of the underlying random variable, S, is well-defined with the general Itô process as

$$\Delta S = a(S,t)\Delta t + b(S,t)\varepsilon\sqrt{\Delta t}, \tag{8.16}$$

and if the goal is to obtain the explicit stochastic process for $G(S, t)$, then according to ordinary calculus, we would end up with

$$\Delta G(S,t) = \frac{\partial G}{\partial S}\Delta S + \frac{\partial G}{\partial t}\Delta t. \tag{8.17}$$

But in stochastic calculus, because ΔS has a component of the order $\sqrt{\Delta t}$, we end up with

$$\Delta G(S,t) = \frac{\partial G}{\partial S}\Delta S + \frac{\partial G}{\partial t}\Delta t + \frac{1}{2}\frac{\partial^2 G}{\partial S^2}(\Delta S)^2. \tag{8.18}$$

Equation 8.18 is the same as equation 8.15 after the terms with Δt having a power larger than 1 are removed (since they are all 0). Further clarifications of the stochastic process $G(S, t)$ are possible depending on the exact stochastic expression for ΔS.

For example, if $a(S, t)$ and $b(S, t)$ equation 8.16 are simply constants, a and b, then

$$\Delta S = a\Delta t + b\varepsilon\sqrt{\Delta t}. \tag{8.19}$$

Ignoring the terms with higher orders with power larger than *1* for Δt, equation 8.18 becomes

$$\Delta G(S,t) = \frac{\partial G}{\partial S}\Delta S + \frac{\partial G}{\partial t}\Delta t + \frac{1}{2}\frac{\partial^2 G}{\partial S^2}b^2\varepsilon^2\Delta t. \tag{8.20}$$

Further simplifications can be accomplished by focusing on the normally distributed random variable, ε, which has a mean value 0 and a standard deviation (and variance) value of 1. These parameters for a normal distribution indicate that

$E[\varepsilon] = 0$ and
$Variance[\varepsilon] = E[\varepsilon^2] - (E[\varepsilon])^2 = 1.$ (8.21)

The second expression in 8.21 is true for any random variable with a finite second moment. Altogether, equation 8.21 leads to $E[\varepsilon^2] = 1$. Referring back to equation 8.20, the last term on the right-hand side simplifies further since $E[\varepsilon^2\Delta t] = \Delta t$ and since the variance of Δt is proportional to $(\Delta t)^2$ and can be ignored – this practically means that the last term behaves like a non-random constant:

$$\Delta G(S,t) = \frac{\partial G}{\partial S}\Delta S + \frac{\partial G}{\partial t}\Delta t + \frac{1}{2}\frac{\partial^2 G}{\partial S^2}b^2\Delta t. \tag{8.22}$$

Substituting equation 8.19 into 8.22, we have

$$\Delta G(S,t) = \left(\frac{\partial G}{\partial S}a + \frac{\partial G}{\partial t} + \frac{1}{2}\frac{\partial^2 G}{\partial S^2}b^2\right)\Delta t + \frac{\partial G}{\partial S}b\Delta z. \tag{8.23}$$

Taking limits as Δt goes to dt, we have

$$dG(S,t) = \left(\frac{\partial G}{\partial S} a + \frac{\partial G}{\partial t} + \frac{1}{2} \frac{\partial^2 G}{\partial S^2} b^2 \right) dt + \frac{\partial G}{\partial S} b dz. \tag{8.24}$$

The discrete equation 8.23 and its continuous-time version, equation 8.24, represent Itô's lemma.

These equations can be utilized for pricing derivative securities dependent on stock prices. For example, if the stochastic process ΔS is as in equation 8.8, the geometric Brownian motion Itô process for the stock price, equation 8.24 becomes

$$dG(S,t) = \left(\frac{\partial G}{\partial S} \mu S + \frac{\partial G}{\partial t} + \frac{1}{2} \frac{\partial^2 G}{\partial S^2} \sigma^2 S^2 \right) dt + \frac{\partial G}{\partial S} \sigma S dz. \tag{8.25}$$

Three specific examples of the function $G(S, t)$ are follows:

Example 1: Forward contracts − the forward price of a stock in continuous-time for a contract maturing at time T is

$$G(S,t) = F(S,t) = S e^{r(T-t)} \tag{8.26}$$

Then, from equation 8.25,

$$dG(S,t) = \left(\mu - r \right) G dt + \sigma G dz. \tag{8.27}$$

Example 2: The natural logarithm of a stock price:

$$G(S, t) = \log(S). \tag{8.28}$$

Again, from equation 8.25,

$$dG(S,t) = \left(\mu - \frac{\sigma^2}{2} \right) dt + \sigma dz. \tag{8.29}$$

Example 3: If an option's price can be expressed as a function of the underlying stock price, then the stochastic process for the option price can be obtained from equation 8.25. This will be explored in the options chapter about the Black-Scholes-Merton equation.

8.7 STOCHASTIC PROCESSES FOR BONDS AND INTEREST RATES

Stochastic processes can be developed for any financial security. Thus far, the focus has been on stochastic processes for stock prices, and two alternative processes have been introduced: the geometric Brownian motion Itô process and the natural logarithm return process. For derivatives, Itô's lemma provides guidelines about how to extract the stochastic processes of derivatives from the underlying security stochastic process. For bonds and interest rates, a reasonable stochastic process for the short-term interest rate has been established and empirically verified as the martingale process.

A martingale is a stochastic process. It has no drift (or zero drift) factors. A variable following the martingale process has its expected future value equal to its current, spot value. This type of random variable has uncertain dynamic movements in the future, just like any other random process, but always tends to revert back to a long-term mean, or an original value. Therefore, martingales are said to be mean-reverting Brownian motions.

Such a mean-reverting process has the negative of the random variable in the drift portion of the process. This ensures that any departure from the long-term mean, however substantial or significant, will ultimately be temporary. In the long term, the variable will come back to the long-term mean. The presence of the negative of the random variable on the right-hand-side drift term renders itself to a specific stochastic process, called the Ornstein-Uhlenbeck process. Interest rates exhibit such behavior, and therefore, stochastic martingale processes are used to describe their dynamic characteristics:

$$dr = \kappa(\mu - r)dt + \sigma dz, \tag{8.30}$$

where r stands for the interest rate, μ is the long-term mean value of the interest rate, κ is the speed of reversion, and σ is the instantaneous volatility.

This particular equation was introduced in 1977 by O.A. Vasicek. One serious drawback of equation 8.30 is that the nominal interest rate can become negative during the drifts. While in extreme crisis periods, negative nominal interest rates can be observed, these are extremely rare occurrences. The Vasicek model was constructed such that negative interest rates were much more likely to occur than in reality. Thus, equation 8.30 has become the basis of dozens, if not hundreds, of stochastic processes developed later by researchers to better explain interest rate movements. The 1985 Cox, Ingersoll, and Ross stochastic process has been an extension of the Vasicek model of equation 8.30 and has avoided the possibility of negative nominal rates.

8.8 LOGNORMAL PROCESS FOR STOCK PRICES

The stock return process based on *geometric Brownian motion Itô process* in equation 8.8 can be used to obtain a recursive expression for the stock price as

$$dS = \mu S\, dt + \sigma S \sqrt{dt}\; \varepsilon \Rightarrow S_{t+1} - S_t = (\mu)(S_t)(dt) + (\sigma)(S_t) \sqrt{dt}\; \varepsilon \Rightarrow$$
$$S_{t+1} = S_t + (\mu)(S_t)(dt) + (\sigma)(S_t) \sqrt{dt}\; \varepsilon. \tag{8.31}$$

The price and return in equation 8.31 are both normally distributed variables. While this implication may be correct for stock returns (which actually is not entirely true; in reality, the tail ends of a stock return distribution are heavier – called a fat-tailed distribution), it cannot be true for stock prices. Normal distribution allows the stock price the nonzero probability of becoming negative. Negative stock prices do not exist; therefore, this implication – as well as, therefore, the geometric Brownian motion Itô process for stock prices and returns – is flawed.

The lognormal process for stock prices fixes the problem of nonzero probability for negative stock prices. According to the lognormal stochastic process for stock prices, the stock price is distributed according to the lognormal distribution. And the natural logarithm of the stock price is a normal distribution corresponding to the stock return. Overall, the lognormal process is theoretically sound and reasonable. The empirical performance of the process in accounting for the stock prices and stock returns has been very good.

Equations 8.28 and 8.29 in example 2 describe the dynamics of the lognormal process. The stock return is described with

$$d \log S = \hat{\mu} dt + \sigma dz \implies \log S_{t+dt} - \log S_t = \hat{\mu} dt + \sigma dz \implies$$

$$\log\left(\frac{S_{t+dt}}{S_t}\right) = \hat{\mu} dt + \sigma dz \implies \frac{S_{t+dt}}{S_t} = e^{\hat{\mu} dt + \sigma dz} \implies$$

$$S_{t+dt} = S_t e^{\hat{\mu} dt + \sigma dz} . \tag{8.32}$$

The stock process in equation 8.32 is a continuous, exponential-based stock price process and natural logarithm stock return process. The price and the return are continuously compounded. The continuously compounded return is lower than the discrete-time return (but generates the same wealth), and the relationship between the two is $\hat{\mu} = \mu - \dfrac{\sigma^2}{2}$ as in equation 8.29.

If returns are small (as is generally the case for small time increments) and volatility is small (as is the case for small time increments), the natural logarithm process and the geometric Brownian motion Itô process tend to converge as dt gets close to 0. With standard deviation tending toward 0, the continuously compounded mean (from the lognormal process) becomes equal to the discrete-time mean (from the geometric Brownian motion Itô process).

8.9 SUMMARY AND CONCLUSION

Stochastic processes are sophisticated equations that accommodate the uncertainties of the dynamic characteristics of variables. The uncertainties are generally due to the random changes in the values of the variables in the future. Such random uncertainties and changes cannot be described by standard calculus. Stochastic calculus is ideal for these variables and parameters.

The history of stochastic processes goes back to the late 1800s. The models introduced and developed in physics eventually found their way into the investment fields to describe the prices and returns of financial securities. Starting from the 1940s and 1950s, under the theoretical framework developed by Kiyoshi Itô, stochastic processes for stock prices and stock returns were introduced. With empirical tests and verifications, the geometric Brownian motion Itô process and the lognormal process for the stock prices became the primary stochastic processes. Stochastic processes for derivative securities were then developed with the help of Itô's lemma. Separately, stochastic processes for interest rates and bond prices were introduced by Vasicek in the early 1970s and subsequently improved by other researchers.

Stochastic processes are used to predict the prices and returns of financial securities in the future. The empirical development is achieved through Monte Carlo simulations for prediction and forecasting purposes. The fundamental tenet of Monte Carlo simulations is to start with a sound theoretical formulation with random variables and then to execute a simulation by drawing values from the statistical distributions of the random variables. Once a simulation is completed, a projection based on the stochastic model is found. The simulations are repeated as many times as possible – ideally with powerful computer frameworks, billions of times. Taking averages of those billions of simulations provide reliable estimates and forecasts of the prices and returns by the law of large numbers.

This chapter introduced various stochastic processes for financial securities. The basics of stochastic calculus were discussed. Itô's lemma was examined. Overall, this chapter focused on the theoretical aspects of stochastic processes. The next chapter on Monte Carlo simulations will focus on the practical and empirical implementation of these theoretical stochastic models to forecast the prices of financial securities.

REFERENCES AND ADDITIONAL READING

Cox, J.C., Ingersoll, J.E., Ross, S.A. 1985. A Theory of the Structure of Interest Rates. *Econometrica*, 53, 385–408.
Itô, K. 1944. Stochastic Integral. *Proceedings of the Imperial Academy*, 20, 519–524.
Itô, K. 1951a. Multiple Wiener Integral. *Journal of the Mathematical Society of Japan*, 3, 157–169.
Itô, K. 1951b. On a Formula Concerning Stochastic Differentials. *Nagoya Mathematical Journal*, 3, 55–65.
Jarrow, R., Protter, P. 2004. A Short History of Stochastic Integration and Mathematical Finance: The Early Years, 1880–1970. *Lecture Notes-Monograph Series JSTOR*, 45, 75–91.
Merton, R.C. 1973. Theory of Rational Option Pricing. *Bell Journal of Economics*, 4, 141–183.
Merton, R.C. 1992. *Continuous-Time Finance*. Oxford, Basil Blackwell, Inc.
Vasicek, O. 1977. An Equilibrium Characterization of the Term Structure. *Journal of Financial Economics*, 5, 177–188.

CHAPTER 9

Monte Carlo Simulations

OBJECTIVES

- Evaluate the history, popularity, and future outlook of the Monte Carlo approach.
- Construct and organize the connections between Monte Carlo simulations and psychology, behavioral science, and economics fields with real-life numerical examples.
- Relate Monte Carlo simulations as the empirical implementation of stochastic models.
- Justify the link between stochastic equations with random variables generating different solutions/patterns through the implementation of Monte Carlo simulations.
- Support the goal of obtaining reliable solutions and patterns through the statistical property of the law of large numbers.
- Develop methodologies for analyzing the Monte Carlo simulation results in projecting and forecasting stochastic processes.
- Formulate software codes to execute multiple Monte Carlo simulations for accurate and precise predictions.
- Design software coding to counter the challenges of the empirical implementation, compare different estimation approaches, and choose successful processes.

9.1 INTRODUCTION

Monte Carlo simulations are computer-based programs that implement repetitions of the random sampling of stochastic equations to reach statistically reliable conclusions. Random sampling draws from probability distributions to quantify random variables for equations that contain such variables. One simulation corresponds to one sampling. The sampling is repeated many times so that the numerical results, when averaged, provide a reliable conclusion by the law of large numbers.

DOI: 10.4324/9781003213697-9

Earlier applications of Monte Carlo simulations go back to the 18th century. Buffon's needle problem by Georges Leclerc is defined as follows: 'if a needle is dropped onto the floor made of parallel strips of wood, each the same width, what is the probability that the needle will lie across a line between two strips?'. The solution to the problem is *probability = (2)(needle)/ (π)(w)*, where *needle* is the length of the needle, and *w* is the width of the strip of wood. This equation has been used by Monte Carlo simulations to calculate the numerical value of π. There have been other Monte Carlo simulations to calculate the numerical value of π, to define neutron diffusions, and other problems, but the official term 'Monte Carlo method' or 'Monte Carlo simulation' was first introduced by researchers at the Los Alamos National Laboratory in the 1940s.

Many different fields in S.T.E.M. (science, technology, engineering, and mathematics) utilize Monte Carlo methods. Computational physics to weather forecasting in physical sciences; microelectronics, geostatistics, wind energy, fluid dynamics, telecommunications, autonomous robotics, signal processing, and groundwater modeling in engineering; climate science; computational biology; computer graphics; applied statistics; design and visuals; law; government search and rescue operations; and artificial intelligence for mass multi-player online video games all use Monte Carlo simulations.

Monte Carlo simulations are used in many areas of finance, such as insurance, option pricing, commodity pricing, interest and exchange rate predictions, labor price determination, sales volume forecasting, evaluation of investment projects, and generation of stock price patterns. The predictions and forecasts based on Monte Carlo simulations are achieved with optimization, integration, and quantification of probability distributions.

In principle, Monte Carlo methods can be used to solve any problem with random components. By the law of large numbers, integrals describing the expected value of a random variable can be approximated by taking an empirical mean (i.e., the sample mean of independent samples of the variable). When the probability distribution of a random variable is parametrized, the equations usually have the Markov process characteristics where past values or patterns are irrelevant. In the limit, these Markov process (or Markov chain) Monte Carlo simulations generate the samples for the desired forecast distribution.

In the previous chapter, stochastic processes were introduced and explored. These theoretical processes are used to predict the prices and returns of financial securities but are not practical unless they are utilized in numerical applications. The empirical implementation is accomplished through Monte Carlo simulations. Monte Carlo simulations start with a sound theoretical formulation with random variables. Then simulations are generated by drawing values from the statistical distributions of the random variables. Finally, projections based on the stochastic models are obtained. The simulations are repeated as many times as possible. Taking averages of those numerous (in the order of billions) simulations provides statistically reliable estimates and forecasts of the prices and returns for the financial securities by the law of large numbers. This approach is used for two of the stochastic processes for stock prices and returns in this chapter: the geometric Brownian motion Itô process and the lognormal process for stock prices and stock returns.

The two processes are compared and contrasted first theoretically, then empirically. The simulation steps will be presented. The iterative equations will be documented. The computer code for the implementation of the iterative process will be developed. Finally, the implementation of the process with Monte Carlo simulations, first as a single sample pattern and then as multiple simulations to find the forecast stock price, will be conducted using both the geometric Brownian motion Itô process and the lognormal process.

9.2 SIMULATION OF THE STOCHASTIC PROCESSES: THE BASICS

The first stochastic process to forecast stock prices and stock returns from the previous chapter is the geometric Brownian motion Itô process. The process in discrete time is described as

$$\Delta S = \mu S \, \Delta t + \sigma S \, \varepsilon \sqrt{\Delta t}. \tag{9.1}$$

Here, S is the stock price, μ is the average return of the stock generally expressed as an annual return, Δt is the time increment in the implementation of the theoretical model for practical application expressed in years, σ is the average volatility (standard deviation) of the stock return expressed as an annual value, and ε is the random variable, specifically a standard normal with a mean of 0 and a standard deviation of 1, therefore, $\varepsilon \sim N(0, 1)$.

The second stochastic process for forecasting stock prices and stock returns from the previous chapter is the lognormal process for stock prices. The process in discrete time is

$$\Delta \log S = \hat{\mu} \Delta t + \sigma \varepsilon \sqrt{\Delta t}. \tag{9.2}$$

As in equation 9.1, S is the stock price, Δt is the time increment in the implementation of the theoretical model for practical application expressed in years, σ is the average volatility (standard deviation) of the stock return expressed as an annual value, and ε is the random variable, a standard normal with a mean of 0 and a standard deviation of 1; therefore, $\varepsilon \sim N(0, 1)$. Additionally, *log* is the natural logarithm and $\hat{\mu}$ is the annual average continuously compounded return of the stock. The continuously compounded return $\hat{\mu}$ and the simple return μ are related to each other as $\hat{\mu} = \mu - \dfrac{\sigma^2}{2}$. The compounded return is smaller because the compounding (earning interest on interest) achieves the same level of wealth during a specific period.

In both equation 9.1 and equation 9.2, the random variable (which makes the equations stochastic) is ε. In empirical implementations, this variable must be drawn from a machine (i.e., a computer software program). From Excel, the formula that generates the value for ε is '=normsinv(rand())'. Two functions are nested within each other here: (1) '=rand()' generates a number between 0 and 1 from a uniform distribution in Figure 9.1. This number is used as the area under the standard normal distribution from .. to the specific ε (i.e., the shaded area in Figure 9.2), and (2) '=normsinv()' inverts the area to that specific ε in Figure 9.2.

Generating random numbers through machines and computers is absolutely essential for implementing stochastic equations and generating Monte Carlo simulations. Human beings have a poor understanding of randomness. Our risk-averse nature and desire for deterministic outcomes make us unable to imagine randomness. Two researchers, Daniel Kahneman and Amos Tversky, have pioneered the field of behavioral finance and behavioral economics by connecting psychology and economics/finance fields together. They showed through

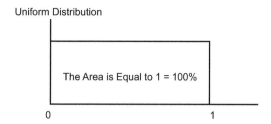

FIGURE 9.1 Uniform Distribution [Excel Function rand() Provides the Number Between 0 and 1]

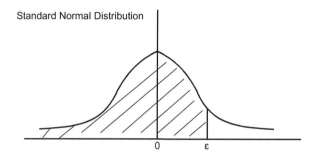

FIGURE 9.2 Normal Distribution [Excel Function normsinv('shaded area') Provides]

hundreds, if not thousands, of experiments that human beings often act irrationally and that human beings cannot imagine randomness even if they try really hard.

For example, one of the experiments Kahneman and Tversky designed was about flipping a coin numerous times to get the outcome heads or tails either, actually, or from the imagination of a human subject. The human was asked to imagine flipping the coin to record the outcome. The human subject never guessed substantially away from the average. After imagining tails three or four consecutive times, the next coin flip would always be imagined as heads and vice versa. In other words, the human subject remembered the history of the flips, and that affected the future imagining of the coin flip, however hard the subject tried to ignore the past.

True randomness does not work this way. The random numbers and outcomes generated by computer programs/machines are totally independent of past outcomes, as they should be. That is why machines/computer codes are absolutely necessary for random number generation.

9.3 SIMULATION FLOWCHART FOR THE GEOMETRIC BROWNIAN MOTION ITÔ PROCESS

The practical implementation of the geometric Brownian motion Itô process for stock prices and stock returns involves three sections:

(1) Expression of the parameters describing the mean and standard deviation of the stock return on an annual basis.

(2) Iterative expressions for the stock price and the stock return.
(3) Coding of the iterative expressions with a software program so that they can be executed to generate the simulation outputs.

In the following simulation steps, the time increment, Δt, is assumed as one day. Access to more powerful computer mainframes would enable a smaller time increment. The historical data used to calculate the average return μ and standard deviation σ for the stochastic process are five years' worth of daily returns. A longer sample would include data when the firm and the stock characteristics would have been different than the current characteristics. Once these two statistics are calculated, they can be adjusted up or down at the discretion of the analyst based on subjective views and/or additional information.

(1) Expressions of the parameters:
  (a) Using daily adjusted closing prices (S_i), find the daily returns: $R_i = \dfrac{S_{i+1} - S_i}{S_i}$.

  (b) Find the arithmetic average of these daily returns, $m = \dfrac{\sum R_i}{n}$, where n is the number of returns (in Excel, the function for this calculation would be '=average()').

  (c) Find the average annual return, $\mu = (252)(m)$, assuming 252 business days in a year.

  (d) Find the standard deviation of the daily returns, s (in Excel, the function for this calculation would be '=stdev()').

  (e) Find the annual standard deviation of the returns, $\sigma = \sqrt{252} \times s$.

(2) Iterative expressions for the geometric Brownian motion Itô process are as follows:
For the stock price,

$$\Delta S = \mu S\,\Delta t + \sigma S\,\varepsilon^{\sqrt{\Delta t}},$$
$$\Rightarrow S_{t+1} - S_t = \mu S_t \Delta t + \sigma S_t \varepsilon \sqrt{\Delta t},$$
$$\Rightarrow S_{t+1} = S_t + \mu S_t \Delta t + \sigma S_t \varepsilon \sqrt{\Delta t},\text{ for } t = 0, 1, 2, \ldots \tag{9.3}$$

For the stock return,

$$\Delta S = \mu S\,\Delta t + \sigma S\,\varepsilon\,\sqrt{\Delta t},$$
$$\Rightarrow \frac{\Delta S}{S} = \mu \Delta t + \sigma \varepsilon \sqrt{\Delta t},$$
$$\Rightarrow \frac{S_{t+1} - S_t}{S_t} = \mu \Delta t + \sigma \varepsilon \sqrt{\Delta t},\text{ for } t = 0, 1, 2, \ldots \tag{9.4}$$

From equation 9.3 and equation 9.4, we notice two important facts about the geometric Brownian motion Itô process. The stock price in equation 9.3 is normally distributed because the only random variable on the right-hand side of the equation, ε, is normally distributed. This is a problematic finding because however small the probability, the normal distribution implies that the stock price can be negative. This is an important theoretical shortcoming of the geometric Brownian motion Itô process. As for equation 9.4, we verify that the stock return is normally distributed. These facts are summarized in Figure 9.3.

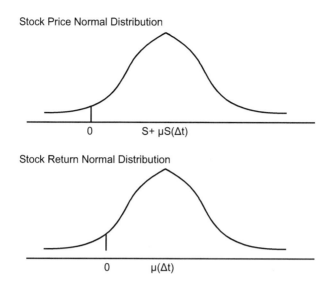

FIGURE 9.3 The Geometric Brownian Motion Itô Process Price and Return Distributions

(3) Computer coding of the iterative expressions:

Any computer programming software can be used to implement the iterative equations into an executable format. Julia, Python, Java, and C++ are some of the popular programming languages that can be employed for this task. Here, Visual Basic, more specifically Visual Basic Applications, is used for coding purposes.

Visual Basic programming language is an integral component of Microsoft software products, including Excel. The earlier version of this programming language was simply called Basic. Going back to the early 1980s, Bill Gates contributed to the development of the Basic programming language. Over the years, Basic programming language was updated with sophisticated versions and was incorporated into Excel. In recent versions, the program has been called Visual Basic Applications (V.B.A.). Anyone can write and computer code using V.B.A. in Excel. The details about access to V.B.A. in Excel are explained shortly. For now, the focus is on the V.B.A. code of the implementation of the iterative equations in Figure 9.4.

Many of the functions in the V.B.A. code in Figure 9.4 are understandable:

(1) '*Sub*' is the term that signifies the beginning of a program (subroutine). The name of the program follows. Any dynamic inputs to the program by the user would be inside the parenthesis. Here, there is no such input from the user.
(2) The cell that contains the number of the periods during the year must be named 'periodsInYear' in the Excel worksheet. This is achieved by choosing the cell, and then from 'Formulas' tab, selecting 'Name Manager' and then 'New', typing the name 'periodsIn-Year', and clicking on 'OK'.

'*Range*' assigns the number in the cell named 'periodsInYear' to the variable '*n*' (for example, 250 as the number of business days representing a year).

```
Sub MonteCarloGBMprice()                                                    '1
n = Range("periodsInYear")                                                  '2
mu = Range("mu")                                                            '3
sigma = Range("sigma")                                                      '4
deltaT=1 / n                                                                '5
Randomize 'This means that the paths won't recur                           '6
ReDim stockPrice(0 To n) As Double                                          '7
stockPriee(0) = Range("S0")                                                 '8

For Iteration= 1 To n                                                       '9
    Static epsilon                                                          '10
    epsilon= Application.WorksheetFunction.Norm_S_Inv(Rnd)                  '11
    'Equation 9.3: the iterative stock price equation:                     '12
    stockPrice(Iteration) = stockPrice(Iteration - 1) + _                  '13
        mu * stockPrice(Iteration - 1)* deltaT _
        + sigma * stockPrice(Iteration - 1) * Sqr( deltaT) * epsilon
Next Iteration                                                              '14

For Iteration= 0 To n
    Range("MCpath").Cells(Iteration + 1, 2) = stockPrice(Iteration)        '15
Next Iteration
End Sub                                                                     '16
```

FIGURE 9.4 V.B.A. Code for the Geometric Brownian Motion Itô Process Stock Price

(3) The parameter *mu* is set equal to the number in the cell named '*mu*'.

(4) The parameter sigma is set equal to the number in the cell named '*sigma*'.

(5) *deltaT* is defined as the time increment expressed in years (for example, 1/250 as a daily time increment expressed in years).

(6) '*Randomize*' is a function that initializes the random number generator, the '*Rnd*' function, and helps produce a new value every time '*Rnd*' is used.

(7) '*ReDim*' defines a variable (stockPrice) as an array (row vector) with the length of the vector specified inside that variable. The elements inside the array are defined '*As*' and '*Double*' (i.e., a wide spectrum of rational numbers).

(8) The first element of the stockPrice array is set equal to the current stock price in the cell defined as '*S0*'.

(9) '*For*' loop has *n* iterations for each time increment (for example, *250*, as the number of business days representing one year).

(10) '*Static*' declares a variable, '*epsilon*', and helps retain its value while the program is running, unless the variable value is specifically changed to another value.

(11) '*Rnd*' randomly generates a number between 0 and 1 from the uniform distribution.
Application.WorksheetFunction.Norm_S_Inv(Rnd) is the inverse of the normal function. It generates the '*epsilon*' value such that the number from the '*Rnd*' uniform distribution function matches the area under the normal distribution from $-\infty$ to '*epsilon*'.

(12) Any line of code that starts with a quotation mark, ' , is skipped during the execution of the program. Such lines are used to provide comments for the coders.

(13) Equation 9.3, the stock price iterations from one-time increment to the next based on the geometric Brownian motion Itô process are provided. This is the most important line of

code in the program. A long statement of code can extend into the next line with '_'. '*Sqr*' is the square root function.

(14) The '*For*' loop ends with the '*Next*' function.

(15) The second '*For*' loop is to record the generated Monte Carlo simulation stock price path as a column starting from the cell in the next row to the one named '*MCpath*'. With each iteration, the next cell below records the price for the next time increment (for example, the next day).

(16) '*End Sub*' concludes the subroutine (i.e., the computer code).

This code is written as a macro program using the V.B.A. language in Excel. The V.B.A. coding window in Excel is usually accessed by simultaneously pressing the Alt+F11 or Fn+Alt+F11, depending on the type of computer. If the window for coding is not directly available as an empty canvas, then 'Insert' followed by 'Module' will open the canvas to code the program. There is generally no need to save the macro program module; it automatically becomes part of the Excel file. Once coding is concluded, the V.B.A. window can be closed.

To execute the program in Excel, 'Macros' is chosen under the 'View' tab. From the list of custom-written V.B.A. programs (subroutines), also called macros, the desired program is selected and 'Run'. Alternatively, after selecting the desired program, choosing 'Options' and then typing a letter from the keyboard, such as 'a', links the program to Ctrl+A. Every time 'Ctrl' and 'A' are simultaneously pressed, the program executes, and the results are observed in the Excel worksheet. A typical price path output after a Monte Carlo simulation is executed using the geometric Brownian motion Itô price process is provided in Figure 9.5.

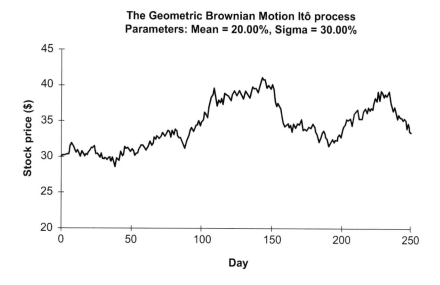

FIGURE 9.5 Monte Carlo Simulation Stock Price Path (Geometric Brownian Motion Itô Process)

9.4 SIMULATION FLOWCHART FOR THE LOGNORMAL PROCESS

The practical implementation of the lognormal process for stock prices and stock returns again involves three parts:

(1) Expression of the parameters for mean return and standard deviation as annual values
(2) Iterative expressions for the stock price and the stock return
(3) Coding of the iterative expressions with a computer program to generate simulation outputs

In the following simulation steps, the time increment, Δt, is assumed to be one day as before. More powerful computers would allow smaller time increments – the discrete process can converge toward a continuous-time process. The historical data used to calculate the average return, $\breve{\mu}$, and standard deviation, σ, for the stochastic process equation is taken as five years' worth of daily returns. Longer, older data would include different characteristics for the firm and the stock. Once the average return and the standard deviation are calculated, they can be adjusted up or down at the discretion of the analyst subjectively and/or with additional information.

(1) Expressions of the parameters:
   (a) Using daily adjusted closing prices (S_i), find continuous daily returns:

$$R_i = \log\left(\frac{S_{i+1}}{S_i}\right) = \log\left(S_{i+1}\right) - \log\left(S_i\right).$$

   (b) Find the arithmetic average of these daily returns, $\hat{m} = \dfrac{\sum R_i}{n}$, where n is the number of returns (in Excel, the function for this calculation would be '=average()').
   (c) Find the average annual return, $\hat{\mu} = (252)(\hat{m})$. This calculation assumes there are *252* business days in a year.
   (d) Find the standard deviation of the daily returns, s (in Excel, the function is '=stdev()').
   (e) Find the annual standard deviation of the returns, $\sigma = \sqrt{252} \times s$.
(2) Iterative expressions for the lognormal process:
   For the stock price,

$$\Delta log(S) = \hat{\mu}\Delta t + \sigma\varepsilon\sqrt{\Delta t},$$
$$\Rightarrow \log\left(S_{t+1}\right) - \log\left(S_t\right) = \hat{\mu}\Delta t + \sigma\varepsilon\sqrt{\Delta t},$$
$$\Rightarrow \log\left(\frac{S_{t+1}}{S_t}\right) = \hat{\mu}\Delta t + \sigma\varepsilon\sqrt{\Delta t},$$
$$\Rightarrow e^{\log\left(\frac{S_{t+1}}{S_t}\right)} = e^{\hat{\mu}\Delta t + \sigma\varepsilon\sqrt{\Delta t}},$$
$$\Rightarrow S_{t+1} = S_t e^{\hat{\mu}\Delta t + \sigma\varepsilon\sqrt{\Delta t}}, \text{ for } t = 0, 1, 2, \ldots \tag{9.5}$$

For the stock return,

$$\Delta log(S) = \hat{\mu}\Delta t + \sigma \varepsilon \sqrt{\Delta t},$$

$$\Rightarrow log\left(S_{t+1}\right) - log\left(S_t\right) = \hat{\mu}\Delta t + \sigma\varepsilon\sqrt{\Delta t},$$

$$\Rightarrow log\left(\frac{S_{t+1}}{S_t}\right) = \hat{\mu}\Delta t + \sigma\varepsilon\sqrt{\Delta t}, \text{ for } t = 0, 1, 2, \ldots \tag{9.6}$$

The natural logarithm of the ratio of the consecutive stock prices, or mathematically equivalently, the difference of the logarithms of two consecutive stock prices, is defined as the continuous–time stock return where earning interest on previously earned interest is assumed on an instantaneous basis. Is this expression of continuous return equivalent to the standard expression for the stock return when the time increments are extremely small (and thus, the discrete returns are extremely small)? This question is addressed using the mathematical series expansion, $log\left(1 + x\right) = x - \dfrac{x^2}{2} + \dfrac{x^3}{3} - \dfrac{x^4}{4} + \dfrac{x^5}{5} - \ldots$, as follows:

Continuous-Time Return = ? Discrete-Time Return

$$log\left(\frac{S_{i+1}}{S_i}\right) = ? \frac{S_{i+1} - S_i}{S_i}$$

$$log\left(1 + \left[\frac{S_{i+1}}{S_i} - 1\right]\right) = ? \frac{S_{i+1} - S_i}{S_i}$$

$$\left[\frac{S_{i+1}}{S_i} - 1\right] - \frac{\left[\frac{S_{i+1}}{S_i} - 1\right]^2}{2} + \frac{\left[\frac{S_{i+1}}{S_i} - 1\right]^3}{3} - \frac{\left[\frac{S_{i+1}}{S_i} - 1\right]^4}{4} + \ldots = ? \frac{S_{i+1} - S_i}{S_i}$$

The higher-order terms on the left side of the equation are all assumed as 0 since the discrete returns are assumed to be extremely small. This leaves only the first term on the left side of the equation, and we verify the equality:

$$\left[\frac{S_{i+1}}{S_i} - 1\right] = \checkmark \frac{S_{i+1} - S_i}{S_i}.$$

Therefore, the natural logarithm of the ratio of two stock prices is indeed the stock return with very short time increments (in the limit, continuous time).

From equation 9.5 and equation 9.6, we note again two important facts about the log-normal process for stocks. The stock price in equation 9.5 is lognormally distributed because the only random variable on the right-hand side of the equation, ε, is in the power of the exponential function:

$$S_{t+1} = S_t e^{\hat{\mu}\Delta t + \sigma\varepsilon\sqrt{\Delta t}} = \left(S_t e^{\hat{\mu}\Delta t}\right) e^{\sigma\varepsilon\sqrt{\Delta t}} \sim (constant)e^{normalDistribution}. \tag{9.7}$$

Since the natural logarithm and exponential are inverse functions of each other, taking the natural logarithm of both sides of equation 9.7 results in the logarithm of the stock price (left side of equation 9.7) being proportional to a normal distribution (right side of the equation):

$$\log\left(S_{t+1}\right) \propto \log\left(e^{normalDistribution}\right)$$

$$\log\left(S_{t+1}\right) \propto normalDistribution \tag{9.8}$$

Thus, taking the log of the stock price turns it into a normal distribution: *lognormal* distribution. Thus, the stock price in equation 9.5 is lognormally distributed. As for equation 9.6, the return of the stock price, expressed as the natural logarithm of the ratio of the stock prices in consecutive periods, $\log\left(\dfrac{S_{t+1}}{S_t}\right)$, is normally distributed since the only random variable on the right-hand side of equation 9.6 is a normal distribution.

Lognormal distribution is an intuitively, statistically, and empirically sensible distribution for the stock price. As summarized in Figure 9.6, the lognormal distribution is never negative (i.e., the stock price can never become negative). Second, as seen in Figure 9.6, the lognormal distribution is skewed to the right. Therefore, a large percentage of the stock price values or a high probability of the stock prices is cluttered within a reasonable range. The stock price can increase dramatically and can have extremely high values, of course, but the probability of these occurrences is quite low. Overall, the lognormal distribution is reasonable for stock prices.

(3) Computer coding of the iterative expressions:

As before, any computer programming software can be used to implement iterative equations into an executable format. Using the Visual Basic Applications (V.B.A.) programming language that is a part of Excel, the code presented in Figure 9.7 implements the lognormal stock price process.

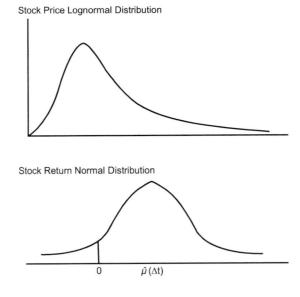

FIGURE 9.6 The Lognormal Process Price and Return Distributions

Most of the functions in the V.B.A. code in Figure 9.5 are similar to those of Figure 9.4 and have been explained there. The only addition here is as follows:

(1) Equation 9.5, the stock price iterations from one-time increment to the next based on the lognormal stochastic process are provided. This is the most important code statement in the program and extends over two lines. 'Exp' is the exponential function.

The program can be executed as before but under the new name for the subroutine *'MonteCarloLogNormalprice'*. A typical price path Monte Carlo simulation with the lognormal stochastic price process is in Figure 9.8.

```
Sub MonteCarloLogNormalprice()
n = Range("periodsIn Year")
muHat = Range("muHat")
sigma = Range("sigma")
deltaT = 1 / n
Randomize 'This means that the paths won't recur
ReDim stockPrice(0 To n) As Double
stockPrice(0) = Range("SO")

For Iteration = 1 To n
        Static epsilon
        epsilon = Application.WorksheetFunction.Norm_S_Inv(Rnd)
        'Equation 9.5: the iterative stock price equation:
        stockPrice(iteration) = stockPrice(iteration - 1) * Exp(muHat * deltaT + _ '1
                sigma * Sqr( deltaT) * epsilon)
Next Iteration

For Iteration = 0 To n
        Range("output").Cells(Iteration + 1, 2) = stockPrice(Iteration)
Next Iteration
End Sub
```

FIGURE 9.7 V.B.A. Code for the Lognormal Stochastic Process Stock Price

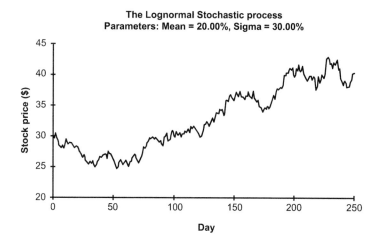

FIGURE 9.8 Monte Carlo Simulation Stock Price Path (Lognormal Stochastic Process)

9.5 MONTE CARLO SIMULATIONS

Monte Carlo simulations start with a sound theoretical model for the future that incorporates stochastic characteristics with random variable(s). The theory is implemented with empirical data and computer code where the random variables are drawn from statistical distributions. Finally, the Monte Carlo simulations are repeated thousands, millions, and given computer power, billions of times, such that by the law of large numbers, the averages provide reliable forecasts.

The computer code here can be expanded so that the program can be executed multiple times. The one-year-ahead stock price is recorded in each simulation. After the Monte Carlo simulations end, the average of the one-year-ahead stock prices is calculated as a forecast. In this example, 1,000 simulations are executed, which can easily be increased for faster computers.

The code for the Monte Carlo simulation is in Figure 9.9. The earlier codes for the lognormal process and for the geometric Brownian motion Itô process are followed by the code for multiple executions – specifically 1,000 times. The 250th-day stock price (one year from today) for each of the 1,000 simulations is recorded. After the simulations, the average of the 1,000 prices one year from today is calculated as the predicted forecast.

In these Monte Carlo simulations, the stock price paths are generated, and price predictions are obtained. The stochastic processes for the stock returns can also be easily implemented. The computer codes for the returns based on the geometric Brownian motion Itô process and based on the lognormal process are as follows:

```
Sub MonteCarloLogNormalprice()
    ⋮
End Sub

Sub MonteCarloGBMprice()
    ⋮
End Sub

Sub MCmultiple()
n = Range("periodslu Year")
For me sim = 1 To 1 000 'This MC executed 1000 times.
        Range("mc_sim") = mc_sim
        'MonteCarloGBMprice 'Pick Ito process: delete quotation beginning of line
        MonteCarloLogNonnalprice 'Pick Lognormal: delete quotation beginning of line
        Range("MCpath").Cells(n+1+1+mc_sim, 2)-Range("MCpath").Cells(n+1, 2)
Next mc_sim
End Sub
```

FIGURE 9.9 V.B.A. Code for the Monte Carlo Simulation (1,000 times)

```
ReDim stockRetum(1 To n) As Double
        ⋮
stockReturn(Iteration) = mu * deltaT +sigma * sqr(deltaT) *epsilon
        ⋮
For Iteration = 1 To n
        Range("MCret").Cells(Iteration, 2) = stockReturn(Iteration)
Next iteration


        ReDim stockReturn(1 To n) As Double
        ⋮
stockReturn(Iteration) = muhat * deltaT + sigma * Sqr( deltaT) * epsilon
        ⋮
For Iteration = 1 To n
        Range("MCret").Cells(Iteration, 2) = stockReturn(Iteration)
Next Iteration
```

FIGURE 9.10 V.B.A. Codes for Stock Returns (G.B.M. Itô Process and Lognormal Process)

9.6 OTHER EXAMPLES OF MONTE CARLO SIMULATIONS

Monte Carlo simulations can be executed for any problem involving uncertainty. In this section, two instances are outlined for more insight: estimating option prices and estimating option Greeks.

Although other and more direct empirical procedures are available for price options, Monte Carlo simulations can also be used. To price European stock options, the simulation process involves:

(1) Using the geometric Brownian motion Itô process, or better, the lognormal process, the underlying stock's price path is simulated. Then the payoff from the option is calculated.
(2) The simulation for the stock price path is repeated many times so that many payoffs are evaluated. The mean payoff is determined.
(3) The present value of the mean payoff is calculated to estimate the price of the option.

This procedure requires a discount rate for the present value calculations. The setting is taken as a risk-neutral world where the risk-free rate becomes the discount rate. The justification for the risk-neutral world is generally easy to establish for the theoretical setting. The theoretical model has been extended to multiple periods and has also been applied to other types of exotic options, such as Asian options, or barrier options. Monte Carlo simulations have been successfully used in evaluating the price of these different types of options.

Just like option price estimations/calculations, Monte Carlo simulations have also been used to determine option Greeks. These variables describe how an option price reacts when one of the parameters (the underlying asset price, time to maturity, interest rate, and volatility of the underlying asset returns) that is used to calculate the option price changes. These option

Greeks are particularly useful in risk management strategies. Theoretically, the option Greek is the partial derivative of the option price with respect to one of the input parameters. Empirically, Monte Carlo simulations are used to figure out the numerical values of these option Greeks.

As an example, one of the option Greeks is delta, $\Delta = \dfrac{\partial Option}{\partial S}$, the partial derivative of the option's price with respect to the underlying security price. For the Monte Carlo simulations to estimate the numerical value of delta, Δ:

(1) Apply a small perturbation in the underlying stock price.
(2) Use Monte Carlo simulations to get the option price given the underlying stock price.
(3) Using the 'same' Monte Carlo simulations, obtain the option price for the perturbed underlying stock price.
(4) Delta, Δ, is estimated as the change in the option price divided by the change in the asset price.

For the other option Greeks, the same process is followed.

9.7 SUMMARY AND CONCLUSION

Monte Carlo simulations help solve problems and equations that have random characteristics and uncertainties. The theoretical formulations are implemented practically using computer code, and a simulation/solution/path is generated. Using new draws from probability distributions governing the random variables each time, the simulations are repeated many times. By the law of large numbers, the averages of the future values and the dynamics become highly reliable projections. The reason the procedure is known as Monte Carlo is the numerous repetitions of the paths from the implementation of the theoretical model with computer code.

Monte Carlo simulations are used in many fields of science, technology, engineering, and mathematics. Specifically, in the finance field, Monte Carlo simulations help to empirically implement the stochastic models designed to describe the price movements and returns of financial securities. Thus, while the previous chapter was about those theoretical models, this chapter focused on the practical implementation of the theoretical models.

The application involves computer coding via Matlab, Mathematica, S.A.S., Python, or another software package. In this chapter, the V.B.A. programming language embedded in Excel is used to code the iterations for the financial security prices and returns based on the stochastic processes. After single simulation codes are created, loops are designed and coded to execute numerous Monte Carlo simulations in order to make projections and estimations about the future characteristics of the financial securities.

The chapter presented the code and the simulation result for stock prices using the geometric Brownian motion Itô process and then using the lognormal process. After single simulation paths, coding was provided for the Monte Carlo simulation of price paths for both stochastic processes. Coding for the return process implementation was also introduced.

Finally, two case examples involving the use of Monte Carlo simulations are outlined, demonstrating the ubiquity of Monte Carlos in different areas of finance: option price calculation and option Greeks calculation.

REFERENCES AND ADDITIONAL READING

Benninga, S. 2014. *Financial Modeling*. 4th edition. Cambridge, MA, MIT Press.

Bodie, Z., Kane, A., Marcus, A.J. 2021. *Investments*. 12th edition. New York, McGraw-Hill.

Isaacson, W. 2014. *The Innovators: How a Group of Hackers, Geniuses, and Geeks Created the Digital Revolution*. New York, Simon & Shuster.

Itô, K. 1944. Stochastic Integral. *Proceedings of the Imperial Academy*, 20, 519–524.

Itô, K. 1951a. On a Formula Concerning Stochastic Differentials. *Nagoya Mathematical Journal*, 3, 55–65.

Itô, K. 1951b. Multiple Wiener Integral. *Journal of the Mathematical Society of Japan*, 3, 157–169.

Kahneman, D. 2011. *Thinking, Fast and Slow*. New York, Farrar, Straus and Giroux.

CHAPTER 10

Value-at-Risk (VaR)

OBJECTIVES

- Formulate an intuitive discussion about the definition and importance of the VaR concept.
- Explain and appraise VaR is an essential part of risk assessment at banks, financial institutions, and investment companies
- Justify VaR as a measure for the financial solvency of a financial institution.
- Develop, distinguish, and implement the two fundamental and independent methods of computing VaR: the historical simulation method and the model-building method.
- Design numerical Excel examples of implementing methods through intuitive discussions.
- Relate and illustrate the connections between the VaR and the international Basel criteria from the Basel I, Basel II, and Basel III global forums.
- Formulate additional testing strategies: stress testing, scenario analysis, and back-testing.

10.1 INTRODUCTION

The fundamental function of banks and financial institutions is to be safe deposit organizations. Individuals, small and medium enterprises, and different forms of businesses deposit their excess funds so that safety and security are assured. Moreover, these deposits provide income for the depositors. Banks provide interest on the deposits and the interest becomes more attractive if the deposit amount is larger and/or stays longer. Thus, rather than 'keeping the extra cash under the pillow', the rational decision is to earn interest from banking institutions.

Banks are willing to pay this interest because the collected deposits are given out as loans to farmers, small and medium enterprises, home buyers, individuals with ideas but strapped for cash to turn them into reality, businesses, and other borrowers. The interest rate charged by the

DOI: 10.4324/9781003213697-10

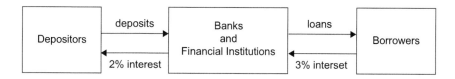

FIGURE 10.1 Fundamental Function of Banks and Financial Institutions

banks to borrowers is always higher than the interest provided to depositors. The difference, 1% in the example in Figure 10.1, is the guaranteed profit for banks and financial institutions.

This arrangement will work well if the bank has complete flexibility in loaning out any portion of the total deposits – if the bank has the ability to loan out the entire deposit amount. There used to be no regulation over how much of the deposits banks could lend out. But lack of regulation contributed to the stock market crash of 1929 and the subsequent Great Depression during the 1930s. When the stock markets started to falter and aggregate panic set in, nervous depositors approached their banks to get their deposits. Banks had no cash to satisfy these customers, and this intensified the panic spreading like wildfire among other customers and then investors in financial markets.

One of the lessons learned after the Great Depression was the importance of keeping some cash within the banking institution. Really nervous customers would contact their banks and get their cash, which would signal to the rest of the market participants that the bank was in sound financial shape and would help restore confidence. The other customers would no longer feel the need to access their deposits anymore. Thus, the Federal Reserve imposed on all banking institutions in the U.S. to keep 10% of the deposits at all times. Over the decades, the 10% reserve requirement has changed up and down due to economic conditions. The Federal Reserve would decrease (increase) the reserve requirement during recessions (expansions) to enable banks to lend more (less) to stimulate (slow down) the economy. Such reserve requirements have been adopted globally.

Although the reserve requirement of about 10% has been a good rule, it is also an arbitrary percentage without any theoretical or mathematical justification and banking institutions have been unhappy. While the importance of keeping some of the deposits with the organization to cool down panic has been accepted, many banks have postulated that the reserve percentage should be lowered for better lending flexibility.

The arguments over the decades gathered the international community to address this issue. Banks, financial institutions, investment companies, central banks (including the Federal Reserve), and other regulatory agencies have met in Basel, Switzerland, over the last four decades to come up with objective and unanimous rules about risk management, liquidity, and capital requirements. Basel I around 1990, Basel II around 2005, and Basel III around 2010 have each provided improvements over these rules, regulations, and procedures. The implementation of some aspects has been enforced, while other aspects have stayed as recommendations. Financial institutions have also been granted flexibility in the implementation mechanisms.

Basel III especially has been an improvement over Basel I and Basel II as the culmination of an internationally agreed set of measures about banking regulation because of the financial crisis of 2006–2009. The purpose of Basel III was to strengthen the monitoring, regulation, and risk management of banking institutions. The regulations were agreed on in 2010, but implementation has been slow: the requirements have remained as recommendations for almost 15 years.

In our context, the focus will be on Basel III agreements and their influence on value-at-risk. Basel III has not been fully implemented due to the delays from the Covid-19 pandemic, and Basel IV is a thought process in development. Therefore, Basel III recommendations in the calculation and implementation of value-at-risk are of great importance. The consensus from Basel III meetings about how value-at-risk can be calculated and what models can/should be used are valuable guidelines for banks, financial institutions, and investment companies.

10.2 DEFINITION OF VALUE-AT-RISK

There are different ways to define or express value-at-risk (VaR). The common tenet is keeping a certain amount of funding within the financial institution such that there is high confidence it will be enough if an economic disaster strikes. Equivalently, there is little chance that the funding kept within the institution will not be enough to survive the disaster. VaR is defined as this funding to be kept within the financial institution. Therefore, VaR is defined in three alternative ways:

(1) VaR is the potential loss in U.S. dollars (or the currency in the country of the financial institution) that must be kept by the financial institution such that the supervisors of the institution, the regulators, and the market participants are H% confident that it will not be surpassed over the next N business days. Here, H% is a high level of confidence, such as 99%, 98%, 95%, or 90%.
(2) The loss from the financial disaster over the next N business days is higher than the VaR amount kept in the institution, with a low loss probability of L%. Here L% is the low loss probability, such as 1%, 2%, 5%, or 10%.
(3) VaR is the worst expected dollar loss that can happen to a financial institution under normal market conditions (including fluctuations) over the next N business days with a high confidence level of H% so that it is kept within for safety and stability.

The general expression is 'a bank calculates its VaR as $1 million with 99% confidence and/or 1% loss probability over the next three business days'. The bank officials are 99% confident that the maximum loss over the next three business days will be at most $1 million. Equivalently, there is a 1% probability that a loss larger than $1 million will happen over the next three business days. The high confidence level and the low loss probability level are linked: they always complement each other to 100%. VaR is the loss level that will not be exceeded with a high level of confidence probability. VaR can be calculated objectively in various different ways so that everyone agrees on the VaR amount suggested by the calculation technique.

There is another variable that can be used instead of VaR, and in some perspectives, it is more informative: expected shortfall or conditional VaR. CVaR is the *specific* expected loss U.S. dollar (foreign currency) amount given that the loss from the financial disaster is greater than the VaR level. The problem with CVaR is that it is not unanimously agreed on. How large will the financial disaster be? What will be the exact loss resulting from this disaster? Researchers, regulators, and officials of financial institutions cannot reach a consensus on these questions, and CVaR calculations remain highly subjective. That is why even though CVaR is informative, specific, and theoretically more appealing, it is the *objective* nature of the VaR that led to its adoption for bank capital recommendations and requirements, such as those in Basel. Ultimately, VaR (1) captures an important aspect of risk management in a single currency amount, (2) is intuitively sensible and rational, and (3) addresses an important issue with a direct answer: it is the funding to be kept in the institution such that when a financial disaster strikes, there is high confidence to ride out the storm.

10.3 HOW TO CALCULATE VAR: HISTORICAL SIMULATION METHOD

One of the most popular methods of calculating the VaR is the historical simulation method. In this technique, the past daily changes in the wealth of the financial institution spanning a long sample period are recorded. These historical daily returns are then simulated in the future.

In each simulation scenario, a past daily return is projected as the daily return for tomorrow. The wealth of the financial institution is calculated based on this projected future return. The profit is calculated as the difference between the wealth of the financial institution the next day and the current wealth. Since VaR is about losses, the negative of the profit (which is, by definition, loss) is recorded.

This historical simulation process is repeated for every historical daily return. Each loss value is recorded. Finally, these losses are sorted from the largest loss to the smallest loss. After the sorting procedure, many losses at the bottom will be negative, indicating actual profits. The focus for VaR is on the large losses near the top. Depending on the provided confidence level and the complementary loss probability, one of the top losses is picked as the 1-day VaR.

As a numerical example, if the past 10,000 daily returns are considered for the wealth of the financial institution, 10,000 historical simulation scenarios will be conducted. The losses from the simulation scenarios will be calculated and then sorted from largest to smallest loss. Then, if the confidence level is set to 99% as the policy of the financial institution, this will correspond to the complementary 1% loss probability. One percent of the 10,000 losses is the 100th loss from the top, which will be designated as the 1-day VaR.

Once the 1-day VaR is figured out, longer horizon VaRs are easy to determine. For example, the 10-business-day VaR will be equal to the 1-day VaR multiplied by the square root of 10. Finally, the Basel III meetings recommended that financial institutions keep three times the VaR for higher security. This issue has remained as a recommendation rather than a requirement:

$$VaR_{N-Business-Day} = \left(\sqrt{N}\right)\left(VaR_{1-Business-Day}\right) \tag{10.1}$$

$$Basel\ III\ Recommendation = (3)(VaR) \tag{10.2}$$

Equation 10.1 implicitly assumes that the daily returns are normally distributed and independent from one another.

10.3.1 Historical Simulation Step-by-Step Flowchart

The step-by-step guidelines to implement the historical simulation method start with identifying the wealth of the financial institution. This wealth can be summarized as an investment, a portfolio, or just the value of the institution itself:

(1) Access and calculate the last M days' returns for the institution's wealth: R_1 through R_M. M should be a large number (for example, 10,000) so that a variety of the impacts of ups/downs of the economy and financial markets is reflected in the wealth of the institution.

(2) In each simulation scenario, tomorrow's return will be one of these M returns. Therefore, there are M scenarios for the next day.

(3) Find the wealth of the institution in each scenario as follows:

(Next Day Wealth)$_1$ = (Current Wealth)(1 + R$_1$)

⋮

(Next Day Wealth)$_M$ = (Current Wealth)(1 + R$_M$)

(4) Find the loss (negative of profit) for each scenario as follows:

− [(Next Day Wealth)$_1$ − (Current Wealth)]

⋮

− [(Next Day Wealth)$_M$ − (Current Wealth)]

(5) Rank these M losses from largest to smallest. The focus will be on the highest losses at the top of the sorted list.

(6) The policy of the financial institution will specify the confidence level and, therefore, the loss probability. If the confidence level is 99% (98%, 95%, 90%), then the loss probability will be 1% (2%, 5%, 10%), meaning 1% (2%, 5%, 10%) of M from the top of the sorted losses should be picked. That is the VaR for the next day, the 1-day VaR.

(7) VaR for N-days is $\left(\sqrt{N}\right)(1day\,VaR)$.

(8) Basel III recommendation is $(3)\left(\sqrt{N}\right)(1day\,VaR)$.

10.3.2 Historical Simulation Method Implementation with Excel

The implementation of the historical simulation method in Excel can best be understood with the following numerical example.

The financial institution has a current wealth of $10 million. The wealth is split into five asset classes: $2 million, $3 million, $1 million, $1.5 million, and $2.5 million. The end-of-the-day values of these five asset classes for the last 3,201 business days (approximately 13 years) are obtained. From these end-of-day values, 3,200 daily returns are calculated. These returns become the 3,200 simulations of potential returns for the next day. In each simulation, the wealth of the financial institution for the next day is calculated. Then, the loss for that simulation is found as the negative of the profit, as summarized in the following figures. Figure 10.2 presents the closing prices of the asset classes for the first ten days. Figure 10.3 depicts the daily returns. Figure 10.4 lists the details of the current wealth of the financial institution. The past returns of the asset classes are potential returns for the next day in

Date	Security A	SecurityB	SecurityC	SecurityD	SecurityE
Day0	28.69	104.16	27.71	47.38	21.9
Day1	29.18	104.16	26.45	45.8	22.2
Day2	32.85	102.12	27.94	44.32	20.74
Day3	32.09	100.09	27.43	45.31	20.77
Day4	32.53	97.3	27.38	46	20.71
DayS	32.19	95.64	25.3	43.93	20.04
Day6	31.81	96.23	25.83	44.72	19.01
Day7	31.54	94.3	24.96	48.96	17.87
Day8	32.63	97.3	24.6	47.97	18.65
Day9	33.18	100.4	25.72	47.77	19.49
Day10	33.4	99.12	26.88	48.27	18.49

FIGURE 10.2 Closing Prices of the Securities (Asset Classes) for the First Ten Days

Date	Returns:				
Day0	Security A	SecurityB	SecurityC	SecurityD	SecurityE
Day1	0.017079	0	-0.04547	-0.03335	0.013699
Day2	0.125771	-0.01959	0.056333	-0.03231	-0.06577
Day3	-0.02314	-0.01988	-0.01825	0.022338	0.001446
Day4	0.013711	-0.02787	-0.00182	0.015228	-0.00289
Day5	-0.01045	-0.01706	-0.07595	-0.045	-0.03235
Day6	-0.0118	0.006169	0.020949	0.017983	-0.0514
Day7	-0.00849	-0.02006	-0.03368	0.094812	-0.05997
Day8	0.034559	0.031813	-0.01442	-0.02022	0.043649
Day9	0.016856	0.03186	0.045528	-0.00417	0.04504
Day10	0.006631	-0.01275	0.045101	0.010467	-0.05131

FIGURE 10.3 Daily Returns of the Securities (Asset Classes) for the First Ten Days

Current Wealth of Financial Institution					
SecurityA	SecurityB	SecurityC	SecurityD	SecurityE	Total
2,000,000	3,000,000	1,000,000	1,500,000	2,500,000	10,000,000

FIGURE 10.4 The Current Wealth of the Financial Institution

Figure 10.5. These returns are used for the wealth of the financial institution. For example, the wealth and the loss in scenario 1 are as follows:

$$Wealth_1 = (1 + 0.0171)\ (\$2\ mil) + (1 + 0)\ (\$3\ mil) + (1{-}0.0455)\ (\$1\ mil)$$
$$+ (1{-}0.0334)\ (\$1.5\ mil) + (1{+}0.0137)\ (\$2.5\ mil)$$
$$= \$9,972,913.$$
$$Loss_1 = -\ Profit_1 = -\ (9,972,913{-}10,000,000) = \$27,087$$

Once all the losses are calculated from these 3,200 scenarios, they are sorted from largest to smallest with the 'Sort' function of Excel under the 'Data' tab. The top ten losses are in Figure 10.6.

After the sorting, the 1–day VaR is determined from the confidence level and the complementary loss probability policy of the financial institution. For example, if the confidence level is 99% (loss probability 1%), then of the 3,200 sorted losses, (1%)(3,200) = 32nd top loss is the 1–day VaR. In this numerical Excel example, the 1–day VaR is $464,312.

With the 1–day VaR as $464,312, it is straightforward to determine a longer horizon VaR: the 1–week VaR (5 business days) is $\left(\sqrt{5}\right)(464,312)$ (i.e., $1,038,233.19). And the Basel III recommendation is (3)(1,038,233.19) = $3,114,700.

Historical Simulations for the Next Day:						Next Day Wealth of	
Scenario	SecurityA	SecurityB	SecurityC	SecurityD	SecurityE	Financial Institution	Loss
1	0.017079	0	-0.04547	-0.03335	0.013699	9,972,913	27,087
2	0.125771	-0.01959	0.056333	-0.03231	-0.06577	10,036,233	-36,233
3	-0.02314	-0.01988	-0.01825	0.022338	-0.001446	9,912,962	87,038
4	0.013711	-0.02787	-0.00182	0.015228	-0.00289	9,957,596	42,404
5	-0.01045	-0.01706	-0.07597	-0.045	-0.03235	9,703,568	296,432
6	-0.0118	0.006169	0.020949	0.017983	-0.0514	9,914,327	85,673
7	-0.00849	-0.02006	-0.03368	0.094812	-0.05997	9,881,471	118,529
8	0.034559	0.031813	-0.01442	-0.02022	0.043649	10,228,926	228,926
9	0.016856	0.03186	0.045528	-0.00417	0.04504	10,281,167	281,167
10	0.006631	-0.01275	0.045101	0.010467	-0.05131	9,907,544	92,456

FIGURE 10.5 The First Ten Historical Simulations, Next Day Wealth, Loss

Scenario	Loss
2196	934078
2228	870547
2184	843983
184	788826
413	703890
175	689797
2192	652165
2216	634580
2190	633303
2201	632322

FIGURE 10.6 The Top Ten Losses After the Sorting Operation from Largest to Smallest

10.4 HOW TO CALCULATE VAR: MODEL-BUILDING APPROACH

The second fundamental method of finding VaR is the model-building approach, occasionally called the variance-covariance approach (because the *VarCov* matrix is needed). This process involves the following steps:

(1) The standard deviation of the daily changes in the wealth of the financial institution is expressed as a currency amount.

(2) The second step is the assumption that the daily returns of the wealth of the financial institution are normally distributed. The normal probability distribution for the returns is the 'model' in this model-building approach. The normal distribution has a mean value of 0 (for very short time increments, the return of the wealth of the institution is/can be assumed to be 0) and a standard deviation value calculated in the first step.

(3) The confidence level percentage and the complementary loss probability percentage are dictated by the policy of the financial institution. The loss percentage is the area at the loss tail end (the left side of the normal distribution) under the normal distribution.

(4) Starting with the *standard* normal distribution with a mean of 0 and a standard deviation of 1, the first calculation is the value on the x-axis that ensures the area under the normal distribution graph from $-\infty$ to that number is equal to the loss probability percentage. The absolute value of this value becomes the amplification coefficient of the actual normal distribution from (2). In practice, the amplification coefficient is easily calculated in Excel as '=abs(normsinv('loss percentage'))'. For example, if the confidence level is *99%* (loss percentage *1%*), then the amplification coefficient is =abs(normsinv(0.01)) = *2.3263* in Figure 10.7.

(5) The product of the amplification coefficient and the currency amount of the standard deviation from (1) is defined as the *1-day VaR* according to the model-building approach:

$$1\text{-}day\ VaR = (Amplification\ Coefficient)(\sigma_{institution}) \tag{10.3}$$

(6) From equation 10.1 and equation 10.2, The N-business day VaR is $\left(\sqrt{N}\right)\left(1day\,VaR\right)$, and the *Basel III Recommendation* is (3)(N-day VaR).

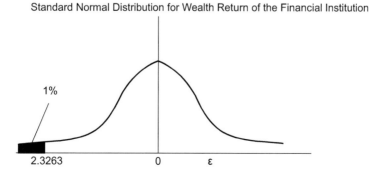

Standard Normal Distribution for Wealth Return of the Financial Institution

1%

2.3263   0 ε

FIGURE 10.7 Amplification Coefficient for 99% Confidence Level, or 1% Loss Probability, Is 2.3263 [from the Excel Function abs(normsinv('shaded area') = abs(normsinv(0.01)]

As this process demonstrates, the important point is the calculation of the standard deviation of the daily returns of the wealth of the financial institution. If the wealth of the institution is tied to only one security, the standard deviation calculation is straightforward. The daily standard deviation of the security would be multiplied by the wealth of the financial institution to get the currency amount of the standard deviation in (1).

Similarly, if the wealth of the financial institution is dedicated to two securities, the standard deviation can be calculated with

$$\sigma_{institution} = \sqrt{w_1^2\sigma_1^2 + w_2^2\sigma_2^2 + (2)w_1w_2\rho\sigma_1\sigma_2} \ , \tag{10.4}$$

where the weights of the securities are expressed as currency amounts, standard deviations as percentages, and ρ is the correlation coefficient between the two securities.

While these calculations are relatively easy, these standard deviations are not realistic. In practice, the wealth of the financial institution is distributed across many different investments, securities, and opportunities. Finding the standard deviation when the wealth is spread across 100 securities, for example, is very difficult using standard calculus methods. Instead, for these realistic investments/portfolios/wealth distributions matrix, algebra is used.

A primer on matrix algebra was provided in the modern portfolio theory and optimization chapter (Chapter 6). The tools and the contents of the primer help us calculate the standard deviation of the wealth of the financial institution with the following matrix equation:

$$\sigma_{institution} = \sqrt{W^T VarCov W}$$

$$= \sqrt{\begin{bmatrix} w_1 & w_2 & \cdots & w_N \end{bmatrix} \begin{bmatrix} \sigma_1^2 & cov_{1,2} & \cdots & cov_{1,N} \\ cov_{2,1} & \sigma_2^2 & \cdots & cov_{2,N} \\ \vdots & \vdots & \ddots & \vdots \\ cov_{N,1} & cov_{N,2} & \cdots & \sigma_N^2 \end{bmatrix} \begin{bmatrix} w_1 \\ w_2 \\ \vdots \\ w_N \end{bmatrix}} \tag{10.5}$$

This is the same expression as in equation 6.10 for portfolios in Chapter 6. The only difference here is that the elements of W (i.e., the weights of the individual securities) are not percentages but rather currency amounts. As a consequence, the matrix generates a currency amount as the standard deviation. In Excel, this formula is the same as equation 6.11 of Chapter 6:

$$\sigma_{institution} = SQRT(MMULT(TRANSPOSE\ (W),\ MMULT(VarCov, W))) \tag{10.6}$$

This linear algebra model assumes (1) the return of the wealth of the institution is linearly related to the returns of the individual securities and (2) the returns are normally distributed.

10.4.1 Model-Building Approach Implementation with Excel

The implementation of the model-building approach in Excel is explained with the same numerical example used for the historical simulation method: As before, the financial institution has a wealth of $10 million, split into five asset classes: $2 million, $3 million, $1 million,

$1.5 million, and $2.5 million in Figure 10.4. The end-of-the-day values of these five asset classes for the last 3,201 business days are in Figure 10.2. From these end-of-day values, 3,200 daily returns are calculated in Figure 10.3.

The returns are used to construct the variance-covariance matrix, *VarCov*. The matrix is obtained in two steps. In the first step, the 'Covariance' function at 'Data Analysis' under the 'Data' tab is applied to the return columns. This generates the partial *VarCov* matrix where only the diagonal elements and the lower half of the matrix are produced. In the second step, partial *VarCov* is 'copy-pasted special values' at a convenient location, followed by a second 'copy-pasted special values' at the same location with 'skip blanks' and 'transpose' boxes checked. The results of these two steps are presented in Figure 10.8.

Using the *VarCov* matrix, the weight vector *W* in Figure 10.9, and equation 10.5 through equation 10.6 in Excel, the standard deviation is calculated as $167,364.77.

If the policy of the financial institution for the confidence level is 99% (loss probability 1%, the amplification coefficient from the normal distribution is 2.3263 [=abs(normsinv(0.01))]. The 1-day VaR from equation 10.3 is

1-day VaR = (2.3263)(167,364.77) = $389,348.68.

It is straightforward to calculate the longer-term 5-day VaR and the Basel III recommendation:

5-day VaR = $\left(\sqrt{5}\right)(389,348.68)$ = $870,610.13, and
Basel III Recommendation = (3)(5-day VaR) = $2,611,830.38.

COVARIANCE					
	SecA	SecB	SecC	SecD	
SecA	0.00045245				
SecB	0.000177284	0.0003175			
SecC	0.000214638	0.0002196	0.0008549		
SeeD	0.000223428	0.0001603	0.0001922	0.0004961	
SecE	0.000256123	0.0001827	0.0002325	0.0002894	0.0008118
VarCov	0.0004525	0.0001773	0.0002146	0.0002234	0.0002561
	0.0001773	0.0003175	0.0002196	0.0001603	0.0001827
	0.0002146	0.0002196	0.0008549	0.0001922	0.0002325
	0.0002234	0.0001603	0.0001922	0.0004961	0.0002894
	0.0002561	0.0001827	0.0002325	0.0002894	0.0008118

FIGURE 10.8 VarCov Matrix Generated in Two Steps

W: weights
2,000,000
3,000,000
1,000,000
1,500,000
2,500,000

FIGURE 10.9 Wealth of Financial Institution Split into Five Securities: Weights in U.S. dollars

STDEV_in institution	167364.77
	Assume Port Mean 0
1% loss probability	2.3263479
One- Day 99% VaR	389,348.68
5-Day 99% Var	870,610.13
Basel III recommend	2,611,830.38

FIGURE 10.10 Model-Building Approach: 1-day VaR, 5-day VaR, Basel III Recommendation

These results from Excel are depicted in Figure 10.10.

10.4.2 Applicability of the Model-Building Approach

The linear matrix algebra method examined here can be used for any wealth portfolio wealth structure. The contents of the portfolio can be from any asset class such as money market, equity, fixed-income, precious materials, options, futures, other derivatives, real estate, and alternatives. Any security from any of these asset classes can be part of the portfolio. As long as the Variance-Covariance matrix can be generated, it can be used along with the weight vector of currency amounts to obtain the standard deviation of the portfolio, and then the VaR for any horizon.

10.5 OTHER ISSUES RELATED TO VAR

10.5.1 Comparison of the Historical Simulation Method and the Model-Building Approach

Both the historical simulation method and the model-building approach are popular techniques. However, neither technique is perfect; both have drawbacks:

The historical simulation method is based on past data getting projected into the future for a (probability) distribution of returns. It is never a good idea to rely purely on the past to make forecasts. But the past market movements and their influence on the wealth of the financial institution are objective starting points. Subjective adjustments can be made afterward as long as a convincing case is made. Another issue about the historical simulation used to be the need for computer power, but the recent advances in chip technology have mitigated this concern.

The model-building approach assumes normal distributions for the returns of the securities making up the wealth of the financial institution. If some of the security returns have non-normal distributions, the VaR results may not be accurate.

In the numerical Excel examples earlier, the 1-day VaR for historical simulation was $464,312, and the 1-day VaR for the model-building approach was $389,3348.68. The fact that the VaR values are not substantially different from each other is considered a good sign. In general, researchers calculate the 1-day VaR from both historical simulation and model building and then present the average of these two results as the final recommendation. Similar average results are also calculated and presented for the long horizon VaR and for Basel III.

10.5.2 Monte Carlo Simulation Technique

There is a third way to calculate the VaR of a financial institution: The Monte Carlo simulation technique from Chapter 9. This is a computationally intense approach, but with the advances in computer power and program execution speeds, this approach has become popular.

In order to compute the VaR using the Monte Carlo simulation technique, the wealth of the financial institution is constructed as a portfolio. The portfolio consists of stocks, bonds, money market instruments, precious materials, real estate, alternative investments, and derivatives, such as options, futures, swaps, and convertible bonds. For each asset class security, stochastic equations governing the dynamics of the price and return are introduced, just like those in Chapter 8. Once the stochastic equations for the change in the value of each security, Δx_i, (i is a representative security in the portfolio), are established, they are unified using the weights of the securities to create the stochastic equation for the change of the portfolio value. Then a large number of Monte Carlo simulations are executed for the change in the value of the portfolio. A distribution of the changes in the wealth of the financial institution is obtained and then ranked from the worst changes (losses) to the best changes (profits).

Finally, given the confidence level percentage and the complementary loss probability percentage, the appropriate loss from the distribution is selected as the 1-day VaR. For example, if ten million Monte Carlo simulations are executed, and if the policy of the financial institution is to have a confidence level percentage of 98% (loss percentage of 2%), then the 200,000th loss from the top of the ranked losses is picked as the 1-day VaR. The N-day VaR is calculated as $\left(\sqrt{N}\right)\left(1day\,VaR\right)$, and the Basel III recommendation would be *(3)(N-day VaR)*.

10.5.3 Tests to Determine the Success of VaR

Once the VaR is calculated for a financial institution, and the currency amount is kept in the institution, how safe is the institution really from a sudden economic or financial disaster? The VaR does not provide 100% protection; there is always a possibility, however small, that the loss probability will materialize and the actual loss of the institution will be larger than the VaR amount. These further analyses are conducted with stress testing and back-testing techniques.

10.5.3.1 Out-of-Sample Testing – Stress Testing

In stress testing, extremely negative financial and economic conditions are evaluated. The survivability of the financial institution is examined under these extreme stress conditions with the ultimate goal of finding out whether the VaR amount is viable or not. These stress conditions are created in different ways.

One approach is using historical data. Economic and financial disasters that have happened in the past are adjusted for future economic and financial conditions, and with these adjustments, plausible catastrophic movements for the future are developed. Testing the success of the VaR against these disasters is one manifestation of stress testing.

The second approach is designing plausible economic and financial disasters. These idea-generation activities are frequently practiced at think tanks, political and economic research organizations, and academic circles. The scenarios created by these professional researchers are then used as stress-testing analyses of the VaR.

The third approach is specific to the financial institution and involves the inspection of the survival-ability of the financial institution against the arrival of financial and economic disasters by experienced and long-term employees of the institution. Is the calculated VaR sufficient to get over the catastrophic financial event, or is there a need for an adjustment of the VaR? The analyses would be for the stress testing of the VaR with a specific focus on institution characteristics.

10.5.3.2 Ex-post Retrodiction

Once the VaR amount is determined by a financial institution, its success can be explored by focusing directly on the past. In ex-post retrodiction, the VaR is compared with the economic and financial disasters in the past. The losses from those past disasters are compared to the VaR. The frequency of the VaR failing to cover the actual losses is recorded. The validity of the confidence level percentage and the complementary loss probability on which the VaR is based are verified. If there is a need for adjustment in the VaR, such recommendations are forwarded to the relevant departments/researchers within the financial institution.

10.6 SUMMARY AND CONCLUSION

Value-at-risk is a very important concept in banking and financial institutions. Keeping the right amount of funds within the organization is a delicate issue. The financial institution should have a fairly high level of confidence that a financial disaster does not cause the demise of the institution. On the other hand, this amount should not be too high to impede lending activity (and reduce profitability). Value-at-risk takes both of these contrasting forces into account in generating an objective and easy-to-understand amount.

There are many different ways to calculate Value-at-Risk. Two of the most popular techniques, the historical simulation method and the model-building approach, are explored here with long numerical Excel-based examples. The third technique of Monte Carlo simulations is also described in detail with connections to the previous two chapters.

The general practice is to obtain the 1-day value-at-risk using two (or three) techniques and then present the arithmetic average as the recommendation. Similar averages are also taken for the longer horizon value-at-risk and for the Basel III recommendation.

The great advantages of value-at-risk are objectivity and simplicity. Discussions and meetings between banks, financial institutions, regulators, and central monetary authorities around the world continue. The Basel agreements evolve and adjust as different perspectives are considered and as consensus shifts due to the dynamic nature of markets and economies around the world. The ultimate goal of a better design for value-at-risk continues.

REFERENCES AND ADDITIONAL READING

Bodie, Z., Kane, A., Marcus, A.J. 2021. *Investments*. 12th edition. New York, McGraw-Hill.
Jorion, P. 2006. *Value at Risk*. 3rd edition. New York, McGraw-Hill.

CHAPTER 11

Fixed-Income Securities, Term Structure of Interest Rates

OBJECTIVES

- Describe the characteristics of fixed-income securities and credit markets.
- Implement the basics of bond calculations using Excel.
- Develop the stochastic expressions of bond prices and returns.
- Relate and establish the link between bonds and interest rates with stochastic equations.
- Analyze the term structure of interested rates from theoretical and practical perspectives.
- Distinguish and differentiate the stochastic equations governing the international relationships between bonds, interest rates, and exchange rates of different countries.

11.1 INTRODUCTION

Bonds constitute a fundamental asset class. They are also known as fixed-income instruments because interest payments or coupon payments are generally fixed amounts paid out at regular intervals. When an entity borrows, the legally binding pieces of paper issued and 'sold' to lenders in exchange for the loan are called bonds. The bond acts as proof of the loan and contains the conditions, such as the length of time of the bond, the interest rate (coupon rate), and the frequency of the coupon payments.

There is a large and active secondary market for bonds, mainly over-the-counter (through computer networks). The most popular bonds are those issued and sold by governments (sovereign bonds). Backed by governments, which have the power to issue cash banknotes, developed country bonds are considered to be very safe because the chance that such governments will go bankrupt is practically zero.

DOI: 10.4324/9781003213697-11

11.2 BOND CALCULATION BASICS

11.2.1 Excel Calculations of the Bond Variables

Typically, a bond is defined with five variables: The maturity (life) of the bond, the face value (principal), which is typically $1,000; the coupon rate (multiplied by the face value to determine the annual coupon); the interest rate of the bond (the discount rate, or yield to maturity per year); and the price of the bond. Given four of these variables, the fifth one can be calculated either with a financial calculator or with Excel. Typically, the price of the bond and the yield to maturity are the variables of interest. The Excel functions are

$$Bprice: =abs(pv(rate, nper, pmt, fv, type)), \tag{11.1}$$

where *rate* is the yield to maturity per coupon period; *nper* is the number of coupon periods; *pmt* is the periodic coupon in dollars (or any other currency); *fv* is the face value, which is typically *$1,000*; and type is *1* for coupons at the beginning of the period or *0* (or skipped) for coupons at the end of the period.

This price is known as the 'clean price' of a bond. In secondary bond market trading, there is also a 'dirty price': the accrued coupon (a portion of the coupon that has accumulated since the last payment) is added to the clean price:

$$Accrued\ Coupon: =(pmt)(\#\ days\ since\ last\ coupon)/(\#\ days\ in\ coupon\ period) \tag{11.2}$$
$$Dirty\ Bprice: =Accrued\ Coupon + Bond\ Price. \tag{11.3}$$

Finally, the yield to maturity of a bond in Excel is

$$Yield\ to\ Maturity:$$
$$r =yield(date(settle), date(mat), couponRate, pr100, fv100, freq), \tag{11.4}$$

where *settle* is the issue/purchase/sale date (format example: 2008,2,15 for February 8, 2008), *mat* is the maturity date (same format as *settle*), *couponRate* is the annual rate expressed as a decimal, *pr100* is the bond price per $100 (if the price is $1,200, the pr100 is 120), *fv100* is face value per *$100*, and *freq* is the number of coupons per year.

As an example, consider a semiannual bond with a coupon rate of 8%, yield to maturity of 6%, face value of $1,000, and 20 years to maturity:

$$Bprice: \ '=abs(pv(0.03, 40, 40, 1000))' = 1231.15$$
$$Yield\ to\ Maturity: \ '=yield(date(2000,1,1), date(2020,1,1), 0.08, 123.115, 100, 2)' = 0.06$$

Assuming that 20 days have passed after the first coupon,

$$Accrued\ Coupon = \ '=(40)(20)/(182.5)' = \$4.38, \text{ and}$$
$$Dirty\ Bprice = \ '=4.38 + 1231.15' = \$1,235.53.$$

11.2.2 Bond Risk: Duration

There are five bond theorems that were formalized by the famed finance researcher Burton G. Malkiel: (1) bond prices and yields are inversely related; (2) the inverse relationship in theorem one is convex; (3) longer maturity bonds are riskier than shorter maturity bonds (all else equal); (4) the third theorem is less pronounced in the longer term (i.e., there is a larger risk difference between 5-year and 10-year bonds compared to that between 20-year and 25-year bonds); (5) smaller coupon bonds are riskier than larger coupon bonds (all else equal).

While these theorems are quite informative, they cannot answer which of the two bonds is riskier: a 10-year, 10% coupon bond or a 5-year, 5% coupon bond. Theorem (3) suggests the first bond is riskier, while theorem (5) suggests the second bond is riskier. The resolution is offered by a bond risk measurement called duration.

Duration (also known as Macaulay's duration) takes both the maturity of the bond and the coupon rate of the bond into account to determine the risk. By definition, duration is the weighted average of the times of future payments of a bond. The weight of each time is the present value of the payment due that time divided by the bond price. Duration is sometimes interpreted as the effective life of the bond; it is also considered as the point in time where all the payments of the bond are concentrated at. The closer that point is to the present, the safer the bond. In other words, bonds with shorter (longer) durations are considered to be safer (riskier). The unit for the duration is 'years', and the formula is

$$D = \sum_{t=1}^{N} \left(\frac{PV(CF_t)}{Bprice} t \right), \tag{11.5}$$

where CF is a future cash flow (coupon) related to the bond, t is the time the cash flow is paid out in years, and N is the number of periods or coupon payments. In Excel, duration is

$$\textit{Duration: } =duration(date(settle), \, date(mat), \, couponRate, \, ytm, \, freq), \tag{11.6}$$

with *settle* as the issue/purchase/sale date (format example: 2008,2,15), *mat* the maturity date (same format as settle), *couponRate* is the annual rate as a decimal, *ytm* is the yield to maturity as a decimal, and *freq* is the number of coupons per year. The duration of the semiannual bond with a coupon rate of 8%, yield to maturity of 6%, face value of $1,000, and 20 years to maturity is

$$\textit{Duration} = \text{'=duration(date(2000, 1, 1), date(2020, 1, 1), 0.08, 0.06, 2)'} = 11.2321 \textit{ years.}$$

The higher the duration, the riskier the bond. The duration of a zero-coupon bond is the maturity of the bond. A coupon-paying bond has a duration less than its maturity. All else being equal, the duration increases with a longer maturity but at a slowing rate, increases with a lower yield to maturity, and decreases with a higher coupon rate. The duration of a portfolio of bonds is the weighted average of individual bonds' durations.

The second use of duration is about the inverse relationship between the bond price and yield to maturity movements, as depicted in Figure 11.1. Duration determines how much the bond price changes when the yield changes, but approximately. The more accurate relation

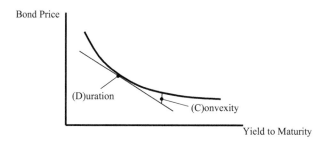

FIGURE 11.1 The Bond Price Versus Yield to Maturity Relationship

between bond price change and yield change is calculated with both duration and convexity – the true convex-inverse relationship.

From a geometric perspective in Figure 11.1, duration is roughly the slope of the change in bond price with respect to the change in yield. That is because, since the bond price is the sum of the present values of the future cash flows, $Bprice = \sum_{t=1}^{N} \left(\dfrac{CF_t}{(1+YTM)^t} \right)$, then taking derivatives,

$\dfrac{\partial Bprice}{\partial(1+YTM)} = \dfrac{1}{(1+YTM)} \sum_{t=1}^{N} \left(\dfrac{-t(CF_t)}{(1+YTM)^t} \right) \dfrac{Bprice}{Bprice}$. This means, $\dfrac{\partial Bprice}{Bprice} = \dfrac{-D}{(1+YTM)}$

$\partial(1+YTM)$, or, $\dfrac{\partial Bprice}{Bprice} = \dfrac{-D}{(1+YTM)} \partial YTM$. Equivalently, $\dfrac{\partial Bprice}{Bprice} = -D^* \partial YTM$, where D^*, modified duration, is defined as the Macaulay duration D divided by $(1+YTM)$.

Duration assumes that the bond price–yield relationship is linear, but as seen in Figure 11.1, the actual relationship is convex. Thus, the second derivative of $Bprice$ with respect to Y.T.M., defined as *Convexity*, *C*, is also necessary. *Convexity C* of a bond is calculated as

$$C = \frac{1}{Bprice(1+YTM)^2} \sum_{t=1}^{N} \left(\frac{CF_i}{(1+YTM)^t}(t^2 + t) \right). \tag{11.7}$$

The Taylor series expansion of the bond price in equation 11.8 is another way to see these links. Dividing both sides by the bond price generates the percentage change in the bond price in equation 11.9.

$$dBprice = \frac{\partial Bprice}{\partial YTM} dYTM + \frac{1}{2} \frac{\partial^2 Bprice}{\partial YTM^2}(dYTM)^2 + \dots \tag{11.8}$$

$$\frac{dBprice}{Bprice} = \frac{\partial Bprice}{\partial YTM} \frac{1}{Bprice} dYTM + \frac{1}{2} \frac{\partial^2 Bprice}{\partial YTM^2} \frac{1}{Bprice}(dYTM)^2 + \dots \tag{11.9}$$

After defining $-\dfrac{\partial Bprice}{\partial YTM} \dfrac{1}{Bprice}$ as modified duration D^*, $\dfrac{\partial^2 Bprice}{\partial YTM^2} \dfrac{1}{Bprice}$ as convexity C, and ignoring the higher order terms, equation 11.9 can be rewritten as

$$\frac{dBprice}{Bprice} = -D^* dYTM + \frac{1}{2} C(dYTM)^2. \tag{11.10}$$

As an example, consider a 20-year, 6% coupon rate, 6% yield to maturity, $1,000 face value, and annual coupon bond. We would like to find D, D^*, C, and the percentage change in the bond price if the yield increases to 8%.

Bprice is $1,000 because this is a par bond. D from equation 11.6 is 12.158 years. D^* is *12.158 / (1+0.06) = 11.47 years*. C is found from equation 11.7 with Excel as 209.24. Finally, when *Y.T.M.* increases from *6%* to *8%*, from equation 11.10, we get *−22.94% + 4.18% = −18.76%* as the decrease in *Bprice* from $1,000 down to $812.40.

Duration is the linear slope or the tangent of the change in bond price with respect to the change in yield. However, since the actual relationship between price and yield is inverse and convex, the convexity variable is also needed to find the percentage change in the bond price more accurately as yield maturity adjusts in Figure 11.1.

11.2.3 Bond Investment Strategies

Bonds are used quite frequently by all investors. Some investment strategies are based on only using different kinds of bonds. Such bonds investment strategies can follow these styles of investment:

(1) Active investment management: The contents of the bond investment are frequently changed and updated. The transaction costs are significant, but the advantages and profits are supposed to outweigh these costs.
(2) Passive investment management: The bond investment portfolio is kept roughly as is. This passive management is sensible for bonds since safety and stability are generally desirable characteristics for both bond investors and passive management. Examples of passive management are (a) buying and holding the bond portfolio; (b) indexing – investing in indexed bond mutual funds and securities that replicate a bond index; (c) immunization, where a bond portfolio is structured to be immune to interest rate movements. The *third function of duration* is to help accomplish this immunization.

11.2.4 Immunization

When an interest rate changes or is changed, there is a ripple effect over all the other rates. In bond investments, such an interest change has two counter impacts:

(1) Price risk: Bond price moves in the opposite direction. If interest rates go up (down), the bond value reacts and goes down (up). The bond investor will be unhappy (happy).
(2) Reinvestment risk: In a pure investment approach, the coupons received from a bond investment are deposited to a bank to earn from reinvestment. If the interest rates go up (down), the reinvestment interest rate also goes up (down), and interest income increases (decreases). The bond investor will be happy (unhappy).

The goal of immunization is to create a portfolio such that these two counter effects perfectly cancel each other. Then, the portfolio will be immune to interest rate changes. Such an immunized portfolio would be a very good passive investment. A bond portfolio is immunized if and only if the duration of the bond portfolio is set equal to the investment horizon of the investor/client. For example, if the client has an investment horizon of seven years, then a bond portfolio with a duration of seven years must be created for this client (such a portfolio would be similar to a zero-coupon bond with a maturity of seven years). This would mean that if two bonds have weights of 20% and 35% and durations equal to four years and six years, the third bond will have a weight of 45% and a duration of [= {7 − (0.20)(4) − (0.35)(6)} / 0.45 = 9.11 years]. As time goes by and the durations of the bonds in the portfolio change, adjustments will be needed; therefore, dynamic management at regular intervals would be the proper approach.

Duration is informative as a risk measurement for developed country government bonds, where maturity and coupon rate are the primary risk sources. Additional sources of risk such as political, country, exchange rate, corporate bankruptcy, and liquidity are appraised by independent rating agencies, such as Moody's, Fitch, Standard & Poor's, and Kroll (Duff & Phelps).

11.3 TYPES OF BONDS

There are different ways to classify bonds. One method of classification is by the issuer:

(1) Sovereign bonds: These are fixed-income securities issued by governments around the world. These bonds generally provide very safe returns since they are backed by the central banks of the governments. However, geopolitical, political, economic, currency, and other risks are appraised by independent rating agencies, and sovereign bonds are rated. Further categorization of these sovereign bonds is possible by the length of the life of the issued bonds. For example, for U.S. government bonds, this categorization is as follows:

    (a) Treasury bills, or T-bills: short-term bonds with maturity less than or equal to one year.

    (b) Treasury notes: middle-term bonds with a maturity longer than one year and less than or equal to ten years.

    (c) Treasury bonds: long-term bonds with a maturity longer than ten years. Traditionally longest maturity has been thirty years for such bonds.

(2) Government agency bonds: Specific agencies within the government regularly issue and sell bonds. For example, in the U.S., Federal National Mortgage Association (F.N.M.A.), Federal Home Loan Mortgage Corporation (F.H.L.M.C.), and Government National Mortgage Association (G.N.M.A.) are some examples of autonomous agencies that influence the mortgage industry.

(3) Municipal bonds are state and local (city) government bonds. In the U.S., such 'munis' provide significant tax advantages in order to attract investors to lend to local governments so that state- and city-based projects can be financed. No federal taxes are paid for the coupon. If the legal residence is that locality, no state or city taxes are paid either.

(4) Corporate bonds are issued by firms when they need to borrow to (a) fund promising projects, (b) straighten the financial conditions, and (c) finance a merger or an acquisition. Short-term corporate bonds with a life of one year or less are known as commercial paper. Corporate bonds provide larger interest or coupon payments but also considered to be riskier − a corporation can always go bankrupt. These bonds are regularly rated by

independent agencies based on the risk characteristics and the financial condition of the firm. Investment grade corporate bonds by strong firms such as I.B.M. or Microsoft are rated high because they are safe, but they provide lower coupon payments. Speculative-grade corporate bonds are rated low because the issuing firms are not financially stable. Bankruptcy risk is significant, but the coupon payments are larger.

(5) Mortgage bonds and mortgage-backed securities are created by home buyers when borrowing from mortgage banks/institutions. These bonds either stay as they are or are repackaged and converted into new securities backed by the mortgage (and, therefore, the house) and sold by mortgage banks to investors.

11.4 BONDS CHARACTERISTICS

There are all kinds of different bonds with different characteristics:

(1) Frequency of coupons: Most bonds are semi-annual. But there are also annual and quarterly bonds.

(2) Fixed coupon versus floating rate coupon: Many bonds have a fixed coupon rate, with the same coupon payments throughout the life of the bond. But there are also bonds whose coupon rate changes according to a pre-specified rule, such as coupon rate is 'the T-bill rate at the coupon payment date + 3%'. One such group of floaters is T.I.P.S. (treasury inflation-protected securities), where the coupon rate is equal to the inflation rate plus a fixed percentage. Such inflation-indexed bonds are popular in inflation-prone countries and provide protection against inflation.

(3) Premium, par, discount: Bond value (Y.T.M.) compared to the face value (coupon rate) leads to the following categorization:
Premium bond: Bond price > $1,000 ⇔ Y.T.M. < coupon rate
Par bond: Bond price = $1,000 ⇔ Y.T.M. = coupon rate
Discount bond: Bond price < $1,000 ⇔ Y.T.M. > coupon rate

(4) Callable bonds: Some bonds can be 'called back' (i.e., purchased back by the issuer before maturity). This can happen any time five years after the issue date. The bondholder must return the bond, and the issuer will pay the original loan plus an extra amount (call premium) as compensation for the inconvenience to the bondholder. For these bonds, the two yields are yield to call (Y.T.C.), assuming a life of five years, and yield to maturity (Y.T.M.), assuming the bond will never be called back. In practice, the majority of callable bonds are purchased back.

(5) Private versus public placements: Many company bonds are issued and sold to market participants. The issue is registered with the government (the S.E.C. in the U.S.), documents such as prospectus (detailed document about the firm finances, sensitive information about the company, future projects and plans) and indenture (characteristics of the bond) are provided to the public (including the competitors). Alternatively, in a private placement, wealthy investor(s) are contacted, and the loan is obtained from them. Nobody, not even the government, would know about this transaction.

(6) Convertible and exchangeable bonds: A convertible corporate bond can be switched into a specific number of equity shares (conversion ratio) of the same company at the choice of the bondholder. An exchangeable bond can be converted into a specific number of shares of another company (for example, exchange the I.B.M. bond for 40 shares of Microsoft). In both cases, the conversion ratio is fixed and known in advance. Moreover, once a conversion is done, there is no going back to being a bondholder. For these bonds, the correct price (floor value) is the bigger one between the regular bond price and the conversion value (the total value of the equity shares).

(7) Junk versus investment grade: Corporate bonds are rated regularly by independent rating agencies such as Fitch, Moody's, and Standard and Poor's. Junk bonds are lowly rated bonds issued directly as such by a company in financial trouble or have become junk over time after their ratings were lowered numerous times. Junk bonds are extremely risky but cheap and have high coupons. Investment-grade bonds are highly rated bonds issued by strong corporations. Such bonds are expensive and very safe and generally have low coupons.

(8) Collateralized versus debentures: A collateralized bond has a specific asset linked to the bond. If there is a failure, the asset is the compensation for the collateralized bondholder. An example is the mortgage bond, where the collateral is the house. A debenture is an ordinary bond without any collateral asset.

(9) Senior versus junior: In case of the bankruptcy of a firm, the senior bondholders will be compensated first from the proceeds of the firm assets. If any funds remain, junior bondholders are compensated. When a bond is issued by the corporation, it is defined as a senior bond or a junior bond. While senior bonds are desirable from this perspective, they generally have lower coupons than those of junior bonds.

(10) Registered versus bearer form: Only the registered person/entity can access the coupons of the registered bond. Bearer form bond does not belong to a specific person/entity. Anybody who has access to the bearer form bond can get the coupons. In the 2002 movie *Panic Room* with Jodie Foster and Kristen Stewart, the thieves breaking into their mansion were trying to find and steal bearer form bonds.

(11) Foreign versus Eurobonds: In foreign bonds, a corporation issues a bond in another country denominated in that country's currency (samurai bond issued by a U.S. company in Japan, denominated in Japanese yen; Yankee bond; bulldog bond; matador bond; Rembrandt bond). In Eurobonds, the corporation issues a bond in a foreign country denominated in the currency of the home country of the corporation.

(12) Covenants: Bonds often have covenants. These are rules that the issuer promises to follow. The issuer must satisfy positive covenants and is prohibited from negative covenants.

11.5 ISLAMIC FINANCE

Islamic finance is about how capital can be raised by individuals and by organizations in tune with the rules and laws of the religion of Islam. There are certain investments and financial securities that are acceptable according to these laws and rules, and these securities are fast becoming a major part of the investment field.

The main tenet of Islamic finance is that wealth can be increased through legitimate investments and trades in assets. These investments should also have social and ethical benefits for society. Increasing wealth through interest (using money only for the purposes of making money) is strictly prohibited. Therefore, lending/borrowing with interest is unacceptable.

When it comes to fixed-income securities, any bond with a coupon is considered unacceptable under Islamic law. This was part of the reason behind S.T.R.I.P.S (Separate Trading of Registered Interest and Principal of Securities). S.T.R.I.P.S. are created by splitting the cash flows of coupon-paying bonds into two parts: a coupon strip where the owner of such a security only receives the coupon payments and a principal strip where the owner of such a security only receives the final principal payment (generally $1,000) at maturity of the bond.

The principal strip is also known as a zero-coupon bond because there are no coupons/ interest payments. The fair price of the principal strip is the present value of the $1,000 payment at maturity. This zero-coupon bond is perfectly acceptable as an Islamic finance security since no interest is involved. Partly because of this reason, zero-coupon bonds became extremely popular starting from the 1970s. Originally created from S.T.R.I.P.S., zero-coupon bonds these days are directly issued by governments, corporations, and other agencies.

11.6 STOCHASTIC MODELS FOR BOND PRICES, BOND RETURNS, INTEREST RATES

In the sophisticated research and analyses of fixed-income securities using stochastic calculus, the bond price (*Bprice*) and yield to maturity (*r*) relationship are established using continuous-time finance (and continuous-time compounding). Whether the bond pays coupons or not, each future cash flow is considered an independent zero-coupon bond. The cash flow payment is normalized to '1', and the discounted value is defined as the bond price. The coupon-paying bond's price becomes the sum of the present values of these zero-coupon bonds:

$$Bprice(t, T) = (1)e^{-r(t)(T-t)} . \tag{11.11}$$

If the interest rate dynamics is structured theoretically and verified empirically, so will the bond price dynamics. The research has intensively focused on the interest rate dynamics throughout the second half of the 20th century, and the first seminal model was introduced by Vasicek in 1977. The model took into account the important mean-reverting characteristic of interest rates. Interest rates may deviate away from the long-run mean, but they cannot stay at high levels for a long time and they cannot become negative. Hence, the rates revert back to the long-term mean:

$$dr(t) = \kappa(\mu - r(t))dt + \sigma dz , \tag{11.12}$$

where dz is the Wiener process, $\varepsilon \sqrt{dt}$, with $\varepsilon \sim N(0, 1)$ a random variable from the standard normal distribution (mean zero and standard deviation one); σ is the volatility of the yield; μ is the long-term average value of the yield; and κ is the speed of reversion.

The Vasicek model was the first to accommodate mean reversion as an important characteristic of interest rates. But the deficiency was the possibility of the nominal yield becoming negative. This deficiency was eliminated by Cox, Ingersoll, and Ross in 1985:

$$dr(t) = \kappa(\mu - r(t))dt + \sigma\sqrt{r(t)}dz \tag{11.13}$$

The additional square root of the interest rate term on the second term on the right-hand side prevents negative yields. When the yield gets close to zero, the variation also becomes very small. The mean-reverting drift takes over and pushes the rate toward the long-term mean.

At that same time, another stochastic interest model by Ho and Lee (1986) was presented:

$$dr(t) = \mu(t)dt + \sigma dz \tag{11.14}$$

According to the model, the yield is normally distributed. Therefore, even with the adjustments to the market conditions using the first term on the right-hand side of the equation, negative rates are possible, and there is no mean reversion characteristic. Because of these two reasons, the Hull and White model of 1990 was preferred over the Ho and Lee model.

$$dr(t) = (\mu(t) - \alpha r(t))dt + \sigma(t)dz. \tag{11.15}$$

The Hull and White model has a mean reversion. If the yield is high (low) in the first term on the right-hand side, then the change in the yield on the left-hand side of the equation is negative (positive), hence the mean reversion. Two more models about the interest rate dynamics are by Black, Derman, and Toy (1990) in equation 11.16 and by Black and Karasinski (1991) in equation 11.17:

$$d\ln[r(t)] = \left(\mu(t) + \frac{\sigma'(t)}{\sigma(t)}\ln[r(t)]\right)dt + \sigma(t)dz, \tag{11.16}$$

$$d\ln[r(t)] = \kappa(t)\big(\mu(t) - \ln[r(t)]\big)dt + \sigma(t)dz. \tag{11.17}$$

The Black, Derman, and Toy model was the first to use the lognormal distribution for interest rates along with mean-reverting characteristics. The mean-reverting characteristic makes .. negative. The model is quite popular and is widely used for the valuation of various interest rate derivatives, such as options on bonds, swaptions, and others.

As for the Black and Karasinski model, there are more flexibilities compared to the Black, Derman, and Toy model because the speed of adjustment ($\kappa(t)$) is not constant but rather time-varying. Moreover, the short-term interest rate volatility ($\sigma(t)$) and the speed of adjustment ($\kappa(t)$) are independent of one another. The interest rate is mean-reverting, and the lognormal distribution is assumed for the short-term interest rate. The model is frequently used for interest rate derivatives, options on bonds (especially Bermudan and American options), and swap options.

There are many more stochastic models for interest rate dynamics. However, the ones explored here are the most popular and most useful models. The stochastic equations covered earlier can be used to drive the expressions for bond prices using equation 11.11. Most of the models presented here are one-factor models. One random variable, and therefore, one economic variable – the short-term interest rate – is the driver of all the interest rates. The single factor is present as a linear factor in all the stochastic equations. As a consequence, the models in equations 11.12 through 11.17 are known also as affine models of interest rates with respect to the random factor.

11.7 TERM STRUCTURE OF INTEREST RATES

The term structure of interest rates, or the yield curve, is a graph of the yields of bonds plotted against their maturities. The bonds have as little frictional risk as possible; by focusing on government bonds, liquidity risks and bankruptcy risks are avoided. The yield curve using only government bonds is typically upward-sloping, as in Figure 11.2, considered indicative and predictive of a healthy economy. On the other hand, an inverted (downward-sloping) yield curve predicts a recession. Humped-shaped or flat-term structures are also possible from time to time.

Researchers are interested in the shape of the term structure of interest rates from two perspectives: (1) *Why* is there a certain shape of the term structure? (2) *How* can the shape of the term structure be predicted so that this predictive power of the term structure over the economy and financial markets helps make advanced and better investment rebalancing decisions?

To address the first perspective, *why* the shape of the term structure, researchers have proposed and tested several term structure theories:

(1) Pure expectations theory: This theory suggests that short-term rates can be used in conjunction with forward rates to predict longer-term interest rates. For example, the two-year bond yield can be determined from the one-year bond yield and the forward rate of a 1-year bond which will be active during the following year:

$$(1 + r_{\text{2-year bond}}) (1 + r_{\text{2-year bond}}) = (1 + r_{\text{1-year bond}})(1 + f_{\text{1-year bond during year 2}}) \qquad (11.18)$$

The one-year bond yield, the one-year bond yield, and the forward rate shift and balance along with the supply and demand such that the equilibrium in equation 11.18 is achieved.

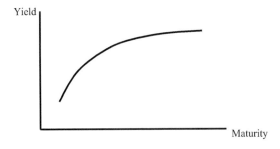

FIGURE 11.2 The Typical Term Structure of Interest Rates in a Normal Economy

The yields and forward rates for all maturities are determined jointly this way, according to pure expectations. Overall, the theory does not predict the typical upward-sloping yield curve.

(2) Market segmentation or preferred habitat theory: According to this approach, each bond is considered in an isolated silo unrelated to other bonds. There are suppliers and investors specifically and only for that particular maturity bond. Whatever the incentives from the other maturity bonds, they are irrelevant. Thus, supply and demand for each specific maturity determine the price and the yield for that bond. This is the essence of the market segmentation theory.

The relaxed version is the preferred habitat theory. If there is enough incentive (huge yield or low price) in the neighboring maturity, the investor will be willing to switch over from the preferred maturity bond habitat to the neighboring bond. Neither market segmentation nor preferred habitat predicts any shape for the term structure.

(3) Liquidity preference theory: This theory conjectures that investors prefer shorter maturity securities rather than longer maturity ones. Longer maturity incorporates more uncertainty and risk about the future, and these are undesirable for investors. Therefore, shorter maturity bonds are actively traded and are liquid, while longer maturity bonds are not actively traded. Those who still invest in them require an additional compensation – extra risk premium – for the inconvenience of illiquidity and for the extra uncertainty due to the longer maturity. This theory does predict the usual upward-sloping yield curve.

To address the second dimension, *how* the shape of the term structure can be predicted, stochastic models of the interest rate from the previous section are used in empirical implementations through Monte Carlo simulations. Most of the stochastic interest rate models use a linear single factor focused on the short interest rate. Extending these models to include the explanation and prediction of longer maturity rates is achieved theoretically by starting with the short-term interest rate and then adding risk premiums for the longer maturities. The stochastic equations are implemented with Monte Carlo simulations to predict the evolution of the term structure of the interest rates, which are then used to forecast the economy and financial markets.

The models have been extended from affine (linear) factor models to quadratic factor models for more flexible and better predictions. Moreover, the models have evolved toward dual-country international term structure of interest rate models in recent years.

11.8 INTERNATIONAL STOCHASTIC MODELS OF BONDS, INTEREST RATES, EXCHANGE RATES

The last three decades have seen significant developments in the design of theoretical and empirical models of the international term structure of interest rates, credit securities, and exchange rates. Researchers such as Ahn, Backus, Constantinides, Dai, Dittmar, Duffee, Duffie, Foresi, Gallant, Singleton, and Telmer have all contributed significantly to this area.

Most of the theoretical models start with a pricing kernel, which is a stochastic discount rate. The pricing kernel is used to establish the link between the stochastic future payments of the securities and current prices. Overall, the pricing kernel is at the core of the pricing structure in an economy. Each country has a unique pricing kernel. Connecting the pricing kernels helps jointly explain the term structure of interest rates, as well as the exchange rate dynamics.

As an example, we can consider the extension of the one-country quadratic term structure model of Constantinides (1992) to an international setting. The pricing kernel, $M(t)$, of each country is an exponential function, representing continuous-time finance. The uncertainties about the future are captured with quadratic state factors that have mean-reverting processes, similar to those in equations 11.12 through 11.17 in section 11.6:

$$M_d(t) = e^{-g_d t + \alpha_{1,d} x_{1,d}^2(t) + \dots + \alpha_{N,d} x_{N,d}^2(t)} \text{ and}$$
$$M_f(t) = e^{-g_f t + \alpha_{1,f} x_{1,f}^2(t) + \dots + \alpha_{N,f} x_{N,f}^2(t)}. \tag{11.19}$$

These pricing kernels generate the pricing equations and the yield equations for zero-coupon bonds of different maturities, T, and paying one unit of currency in country d (f) as

$$P_{d,(f)}(t,T) = E[M_{d,(f)}(T)] / M_{d,(f)}(t) \text{ and} \tag{11.20}$$

$$r_{d,(f)}(t,T) = \frac{-\log\left(P_{d,(f)}(t,T)\right)}{T}. \tag{11.21}$$

Therefore, the term structure of interest rates in each economy is uniquely determined by its pricing kernel. The rich theoretical framework can be used for additional purposes. The influence of one term structure in another economy can be described with correlated state factors or common state factors in both economies. The exchange rate dynamics between the currencies of the two economies can be derived: defining the spot exchange rate as the number of units of domestic currency per unit of foreign currency, $S\_xcr_{domesticCurrency/foreignCurrency}$, pricing kernels uniquely determine the spot exchange rate as the ratio of the pricing kernels of the two countries:

$$S\_xcr(t) = S\_xcr(0)\left[\frac{M_f(t) / M_f(0)}{M_d(t) / M_d(0)}\right]. \tag{11.22}$$

Applying natural logarithms to equation 11.22 and using the definitions in equation 11.19, we can express the exchange rate explicitly as $(log(S\_xcr(t)) = s\_xcr(t))$

$$s\_xcr(t) - s\_xcr(0) = (g_d - g_f)t$$
$$+\{[\alpha_{1,f} x_{1,f}^2(t) - \alpha_{1,d} x_{1,d}^2(t)] + \dots + [\alpha_{N,f} x_{N,f}^2(t) - \alpha_{N,d} x_{N,d}^2(t)]\}$$
$$-\{[\alpha_{1,f} x_{1,f}^2(0) - \alpha_{1,d} x_{1,d}^2(0)] + \dots + [\alpha_{N,f} x_{N,f}^2(0) - \alpha_{N,d} x_{N,d}^2(0)]\}. \tag{11.23}$$

The first term on the right side of equation 11.23 is the difference between very long-term interest rates in domestic and foreign countries. The other terms represent the second term, depending on time-dependent temporal changes of state factors over time.

These stochastic models are calibrated with past data. Then they are used in Monte Carlo simulations for forecasts and predictions.

11.9 SUMMARY AND CONCLUSION

Global fixed-income markets are much larger than global equity markets. In 2021, the worldwide bond market size was roughly $120 trillion, while the worldwide stock market capitalization has been one-third of the bond market, according to the Securities Industry and Financial Markets Association (S.I.F.M.A.). Within the global fixed-income markets, the U.S. dominates and takes up roughly 40% of the entire world's fixed-income market.

The largest fixed-income securities in the U.S. are treasury-, corporate-, and mortgage-based bonds. Municipal, agency, money market, and asset-backed fixed-income securities take up smaller portions of the U.S. bond markets.

The price and risk characteristics of bonds are examined with Excel. Duration is useful for (1) risk measurement in bonds, (2) bond portfolio immunization strategy, and (3) finding the relationship between yield change and price change, with the help of convexity. Different types and characteristics of bonds are investigated. Islamic finance in the context of fixed-income securities is discussed.

Contemporary stochastic models of bond prices and yields, term structure of interest rates, international stochastic features of interest rates, and exchange rates are presented as well.

REFERENCES AND ADDITIONAL READING

Ahn, D.H., Dittmar, R.F., Gallant, A.R. 2002. Quadratic Term Structure Models: Theory and Evidence. *Review of Financial Studies*, 15, 243–288.

Backus, D., Foresi, S., Telmer, C. 2001. Affine Term Structure Models and the Forward Premium Anomaly. *Journal of Finance*, 56, 279–304.

Benninga, S. 2014. *Financial Modeling*. 4th edition. Cambridge, MA, MIT Press.

Black, F., Derman, E., Toy, W. 1990. A One-Factor Model of Interest Rates and Its Application to Treasury Bond Options. *Financial Analysts Journal*, 46, 33–40.

Black, F., Karasinski, P. 1991. Bond and Option Pricing When Short Rates Are Lognormal. *Financial Analysts Journal*, 47, 52–59.

Bodie, Z., Kane, A., Marcus, A.J. 2021. *Investments*. 12th edition. New York, McGraw-Hill.

Constantinides, G.M. 1992. A Theory of the Nominal Term Structure of Interest Rates. *Review of Financial Studies*, 5, 531–552.

Dai, Q., Singleton, K.J. 2000. Specification Analysis of Affine Term Structure Models. *Journal of Finance*, 55, 1943–1978.

Duffee, G. 2002. Term Premia and Interest Rate Forecasts in Affine Models. *Journal of Finance*, 57, 405–444.

Duffie, D., Kan, R. 1996. A Yield-Factor Model of Interest Rates. *Mathematical Finance*, 4, 379–406.

Fabozzi, F.J. 2013. *Bond Markets, Analysis and Strategies*. 8th edition. Upper Saddle River, NJ, Pearson-Prentice Hall.

Ho, T.S.Y., Lee, S.B. 1986. Term Structure Movements and Pricing Interest Rate Contingent Claims. *Journal of Finance*, 41, 1011–1029.

Hull, J.C., White, A. 1990. Pricing Interest-Rate Derivative Securities. *Review of Financial Studies*, 3, 573–592.

Vasicek, O. 1977. An Equilibrium Characterization of the Term Structure. *Journal of Financial Economics*, 5, 177–188.

CHAPTER 12

Options

Introduction

OBJECTIVES

- Identify the fundamental characteristics of options.
- Classify and explore the two most popular option types, call and put options.
- Analyze the pricing of the options through different techniques, such as the Black-Scholes model and the binomial tree model.
- Devise payoff diagrams for options and for option combinations.
- Create a methodical, definitive technique for generating payoff diagrams.
- Discover the most commonly used option strategies and their associated payoffs, and assess how and why they are formed.
- Document and contrast exotic options, why they are created, and what their payoff structures look like.
- Construct and interpret the volatility index (V.I.X.).

12.1 INTRODUCTION

Options are known as derivative securities because the value of an option is dependent on or is derived from the value of another, 'underlying' asset. Even though the underlying asset can be anything in an option contract, typically stocks, indexes, currencies, and futures, contracts make up the bulk of the underlying securities. As in most derivatives, options are zero–sum games; one side of the option trade ends up with profits, and the counterpart on the other side of the trade ends up with losses. The sum of the profit and the loss is zero.

Options are categorized into three groups:

(1) Options as financial securities: These instruments enable the owner the choice but not the obligation to trade the underlying asset at a specific price. Two popular examples are (a) call options that allow buying the underlying asset at a fixed price and (b) put options that allow selling the underlying asset at a fixed price. There are many other types of options, which will be discussed later.

DOI: 10.4324/9781003213697-12

(2) Warrants: These options are provided by firms to their employees as a part of compensation packages. Also known as employee stock option plans (E.S.O.P.s), these options enable employees to purchase shares of their own firms at favorable 'exercise' prices. If the share price of the firm increases in equity markets while the employee has these warrants, it will be advantageous to exercise them and purchase the shares of the firm at the lower 'exercise' price.

(3) Real options: These derivatives are embedded into the operations of a firm. The firm management utilizes such options if the circumstances are favorable. Two examples are (a) tax timing options motivated by the tax code and (b) call provision options in order to pay off a corporate bond earlier than the maturity of the bond.

Options became popular in the mid-1970s, and today, the dollar volume of open interest in organized exchanges is larger than that of futures. There are different options, but calls (the owner has the right but not the obligation to buy the underlying asset by a certain date at a certain price: strike or exercise price) and puts (the owner has the right but not the obligation to sell the underlying asset by a certain date at the exercise price) are the most popular options. Using the choice in the option is called exercising the option. Options do not last forever; the typical life is two years. When an option is created, the maturity date is set (longer or shorter maturity options can be designed by financial engineers). Options are traded as *contracts*. One option contract is 100 options.

Another categorization of options is about when options can be exercised by the owner. An American option can be exercised at any time during the life of the option. European options, on the other hand, can only be exercised on the final, maturity date. These options have nothing to do with physical locations. Both European and American options are traded at all options exchanges around the world. Because of the additional flexibility of the American options, one can correctly expect them to be more expensive than their European counterparts.

Options are expressed with several characteristics. For example, an I.B.M. Sept 100 Call is a call option with a $100 strike price, an expiration date as the third Friday of September (maturity day is always the third Friday of the expiration month), and I.B.M. stock share as the underlying security. The option might be trading at $4.50, but to purchase this option, the minimum to buy would be '1' option contract (100 options) worth $450 plus the transaction cost to the broker.

Options can be in the money, at the money, or out of money. Ignoring the original cost of the option and the transaction cost, if the exercise of the option generates a cash inflow for the owner of the option, this would be an in-the-money option. Suppose the call option's exercise price is $30. If the underlying stock price is $40, then the call option is in-the-money because by exercising the option, the investor can purchase the stock for the exercise price of $30, then sell that stock in the equity exchange for $40, generating a $10 revenue.

If the exercise of an option generates a cash outflow, the option is out-of-money. Since exercising an option is a choice, out-of-money options are never exercised. For instance, if the exercise price of a put option is $30 and if the underlying stock price is $40, the owner of the put option will not buy the stock for $40 from the stock exchange and then sell it for $30 by exercising the put option – these transactions would result in a cash outflow of $10. Finally, an at-the-money option has an exercise that is equal to the underlying stock price. Exercising the option would generate no cash inflow or outflow.

The price of an option is not easy to calculate. A sophisticated equation derived by Fisher Black, Myron Scholes, and Robert Merton in 1973 called the Black-Scholes-Merton equation is used to find the price of European call and put options. Another approach, called the binomial tree, is used to find both American and European call and put option prices. These models are examined in detail in the following chapters. For now, we note that these pricing models require six parameters to determine an option's price:

(1) The underlying asset's price, S (the option price is derived from the underlying price)
(2) The strike/exercise price of the option, E
(3) Time to expiration of the option, T, expressed in years
(4) Volatility, or standard deviation of the underlying asset's returns, σ
(5) The prevailing risk-free rate in the economy, r_f
(6) The yield of the underlying asset, q (e.g., dividend yield of the underlying stock)

12.1.1 Where Are Options Traded?

Chicago has always been the main physical location for options trading since the 1970s. Chicago Board Options Exchange was founded in 1973 in the downtown Chicago area. There have been adjustments over the decades: (1) the merger of the Chicago Mercantile Exchange (C.M.E.) and Chicago Board of Trade in 2006, forming the C.M.E. Group and (2) the inclusion of the New York Mercantile Exchange (N.Y.M.E.X.) into the C.M.E. Group in 2008. However, Chicago has always remained the primary hub for options trading in the world.

The second platform for trading options is over-the-counter markets. Counters refer to computer terminals these days; thus, this trading mechanism is essentially a computer trading network. These networks are accessible only through brokerage firms. Separately, some electronic trading networks accessible only to some traders (at banks, hedge/mutual funds, and corporate treasuries) are used for trading options directly between these traders. Such trading platforms operate simultaneously with other trading mediums.

12.1.2 Size of Options Markets

The size of options markets has increased substantially since the late 1990s. This exponential increase stabilized after the financial crisis of 2007–2008. With the crisis, the increase in open interest has slowed down significantly. However, as confidence returns to markets, the size of open contracts on options is expected to increase in the future.

As far as organized exchanges are concerned, comparing the largest and the most popular two derivatives groups, options and futures, we note that the total size of open interest in notional principals for options is larger than those of futures. In December 2019, for example, the total open interest for options was $60 billion, while it was $35 billion for futures, making the total open interest in organized exchanges for futures and options almost $100 billion. However, it should also be noted that the over-the-counter markets are consistently larger for derivatives markets in terms of the size of outstanding trades.

12.2 OPTION PAYOFF DIAGRAMS

The cash flows generated from exercising options are known as revenues or payoffs. A payoff diagram provides a nice visual summary of the cash flows from the option exercise at different underlying asset prices. Generally, the option payoff diagrams look like hockey sticks. Figure 12.1 (a) is the payoff diagram for a call option with an exercise price of $30, and Figure 12.1 (b) is the payoff diagram for a put option with an exercise price of $30. The x-axis represents different underlying asset prices. Flat portions of the diagrams indicate out-of-money sections where the options are not exercised. The kink points are where the strike price and the underlying stock price are equal to each other (i.e., at-the-money points). The positive regions indicate in-the-money sections where there is a positive cash inflow from the option exercise. The nonzero payoff is always the absolute value of the difference between the exercise price and the underlying asset price. The absolute values of the slopes of these payoff lines are all '1' (45 degrees with respect to the x-axis), indicating that the payoff (vertical) and the exercise price and asset price difference (horizontal) are equal.

In addition to helping find the payoff from an option, the diagrams also reveal the price of an option on its final day. On that maturity day, there is no more time for the underlying asset price to move more/less favorably for the option holder. There is no additional value of the option other than its payoff. Therefore, the option price on the maturity day is directly found in the payoff diagram. On the other hand, before the expiration date, the price of an option is represented by a smoothly curved diagram just above the payoff diagram. The potential price movements of the underlying asset in favor of the option holder make the option more valuable than its payoff for any underlying asset price (there is no increasing downside if the underlying asset price moves against the option holder − the downside payoff is cut off at $0). The price diagrams are the smoothly curved lines in Figure 12.1.

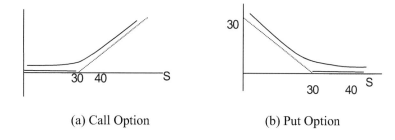

(a) Call Option   (b) Put Option

FIGURE 12.1 Payoff Diagrams for Options Where the Exercise Price Is $30

12.3 OPTION STRATEGIES, PAYOFF DIAGRAMS

Some investors take direct positions in options. Other investors tend to combine options with other securities and create small portfolios called option strategies. With their particular payoffs, these option strategies answer the anticipations of their investors for the future. These strategies are usually designed by financial engineers. There are countless custom-made strategies, but some of them have become popular over the years.

It is important to visualize the payoff diagram of an option strategy. The payoff diagram reveals the reason behind the strategy, shows what the revenue is for different underlying asset prices, and helps obtain the more important profit diagram of the strategy. Given the components of an option strategy, superior visual skills can superimpose the payoff diagram of each component on top of each other to generate the overall strategy payoff diagram. However, not everyone has such visual skills. Moreover, if the strategy is sophisticated, the visual superimposition of the payoff diagrams of many components will lead to mistakes. Therefore, a mechanical approach is necessary to generate the payoff diagram of any option strategy, however complicated. This mechanical approach is described here.

Most option strategies use multitudes of four components: call options, put options, stocks, and bonds. The payoff diagrams of these components must be known by heart. The call and put option payoff diagrams in Figure 12.1 are discussed earlier. The stock and bond payoff diagrams are in Figure 12.2. The stock payoff is a straight line with a slope of '1' (45–degree angle). Whatever the stock price on the x-axis, that would be the revenue/payoff from the stock. The bond payoff diagram is a horizontal line. The underlying stock price on the x-axis has no impact on the bond. Therefore, the bond price is the same as any stock price.

These four payoff diagrams are based on long (buy) positions. The short positions (i.e., selling these securities) would have payoff diagrams that would be mirror images (symmetric) to those in Figure 12.1 and in Figure 12.2 with respect to the x-axis.

The payoff diagrams of these four securities should be known by heart. Any option strategy will be a combination of multiple of these securities. The payoff diagram of an option strategy is obtained by calculating the total payoff at some critical stock prices. The critical stock prices are '0', all the exercise prices in the option strategy, and a large stock price, bigger than all the exercise prices. Once the total payoff (y-coordinate) for each critical stock price (x-coordinate) is determined, these points are marked on the strategy payoff diagram. Connecting these points linearly generates the strategy payoff diagram. Since the last critical stock price is an arbitrarily large value, the payoff continues in the same direction into infinity.

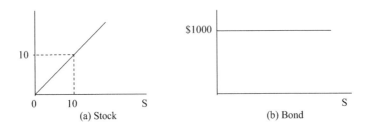

FIGURE 12.2 Payoff Diagrams for Stocks and Bonds

To illustrate, several well-known option strategies are examined to derive their payoff diagrams. The first is 'protective put', the combination of a long position in a stock and a long position in a put option on the same stock (with exercise price of $30 as an example). We can quickly deduce from the individual payoff diagrams the following:

(1) For the stock price of '0', the payoff from the put is $30, and from the stock, $0 – in total, $30.
(2) For the stock price of $30, the payoff from the put is $0, and from the stock, $30 – in total, $30.
(3) For the high stock price of, for example, $50, the payoff from the put is $0, and from the stock, $50 – in total, $50.

These payoff points, the connected dots, and the final payoff diagram for the protective put are in Figure 12.3. An inspection of this diagram quickly leads to the reason behind the name of the strategy. Put options protect the stock investment if the price of the stock goes down.

The second option strategy is 'covered call'. This strategy is a combination of a long position in a stock and a short position in a call option on the stock (with an exercise price of $40). From the individual components and their payoff diagrams in Figure 12.4:

(1) For the stock price of '0', the payoff from the short call is $0, and from the stock, $0; the total is $0.
(2) For the stock price of $40, the payoff from the short call is $0, and from the stock, $40; the total is $40.
(3) For the high stock price of $100, the payoff from the short call is −$60, and from the stock, $100; the total is $40.

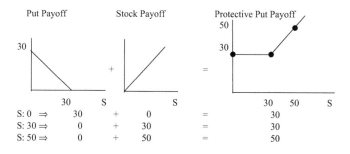

FIGURE 12.3 Protective Put Payoff Diagram

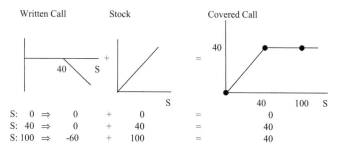

FIGURE 12.4 Covered Call Payoff Diagram

The connected dots in the final payoff diagram for the covered call are in Figure 12.4. This strategy is for the writer (seller) of a call option. If the holder of the call never exercises, the profit for the writer is the selling price. But if the underlying stock price increases, the seller will be covered by the second component, the purchased stock.

Obtaining the payoff diagram of any sophisticated strategy is possible with this mechanical approach. The payoff diagram is useful, but the profit diagram is more important. To get the profit diagram, the payoff diagram is created first. Then the cost of the option strategy is calculated. Finally, using the fundamental definition (from the income statement, net income or profit equals sales or revenues minus all the expenses),

$$\text{Profit} = \text{Payoff} - \text{Cost}, \tag{12.1}$$

the profit diagram is the payoff diagram shifted down (up) because of the positive (negative) cost amount.

This is illustrated with the 'straddle' option strategy. This strategy is a long position in a call and a long position in a put with the same exercise price, $30, and the same underlying stock. The holder of the straddle paid $5 for the call and $3 for the put. Therefore, the cost and the relationship between profit and payoff are

Cost = price of long call + price of long put = $5 + $3 = $8 and
Profit = Payoff − Cost = Payoff − 8.

The profit diagram is a shifted-down version of the payoff diagram by 8 currency units. From the individual components and their payoff diagrams in Figure 12.5, we can deduce the following:

(1) For the stock price of '0', the payoff from the put is $30, and from the call, $0; the total is $30.
(2) For the stock price of $30, the payoff from the put is $0, and from the call, $0; the total is $0.
(3) For the high stock price of $60, the payoff from the put is $0, and from the call, $30; the total is $30.

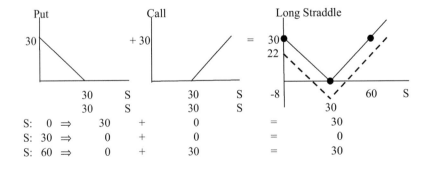

FIGURE 12.5 Straddle Payoff Diagram and Profit Diagram

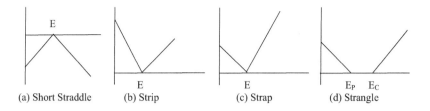

FIGURE 12.6 Different Variations of Straddle-Based Option Strategies

The individual components, connected dots, and the final payoff diagram, as well as the profit diagram (in bold dashed line), are in Figure 12.5. This strategy is for someone who believes that the underlying stock price will be extremely volatile. The price will either significantly go up or down. If the price goes up (down), the call (put) option will help to generate a positive payoff and eventually a profit if the price increase (decrease) is substantial. On the other hand, if the holder of the straddle is wrong about the future and the stock price stays stable around the exercise price of $30, then the strategy payoff will be around zero with a negative profit (loss).

Straddle is a popular option strategy with several variations: (1) Short straddle owner sells a call option and a put option and believes that the underlying stock price will be stable. (2) Strip is a combination of two put options and one call option. Such a strategy places a heavier probability of a declining stock price in the future, while there is still some possibility of an increasing stock price. With multiple options, the payoff and the slope are magnified: With two options, the payoff is twice the difference between the stock price and the exercise price. And the slope is '2'. (3) Strap is a combination of two call options and one put option where the probability of the stock price increase is considered higher. (4) Strangle is composed of a put option with a lower exercise price and a call option with a higher exercise price. The payoff diagrams of these option strategies are in Figure 12.6.

12.4 OPTION TYPES BASED ON UNDERLYING SECURITIES

The underlying security in an option is important because the price, yield, and volatility (standard deviation of the returns) of the security are three of the six parameters that determine the option's price. There are four types of options based on the underlying security: stock options, index options, currency options, and futures options. The underlying security price and yield are different for these option types.

Stock options are plentiful. Actively traded stocks have multiple options. As a matter of fact, stocks such as I.B.M. have dozens of call and put options with different expiration dates and exercise prices. These stock options have the dividend yield and the stock's price as the two inputs for the calculation of the option's price.

Index options have a financial index, typically a stock index as the underlying security. The most popular index options are on U.S. stock indexes: the Standard & Poor's 100 index options, the Standard & Poor's 500 index options, the Dow Jones Industrial Average index options, and the N.A.S.D.A.Q. 100 index options. Typically, index options have the underlying security price as the index value multiplied by 100, and the yield is the average of the index components' dividend yields. All index options are European options. Only the S&P 100 index options also have the American version as well.

Currency options have foreign exchange as the underlying asset. Currency options are actively traded in over-the-counter computer network markets. They are extremely popular and heavily utilized by corporations and multinational firms for hedging purposes when they are faced with foreign exchange exposures. The underlying security price is one unit of foreign currency expressed in terms of the domestic currency; yield is the foreign risk-free rate.

Futures options have futures contracts as underlying securities. They are mostly American options and are identified with the maturity month of the futures contract. The maturity date of these options is between the settlement date (practical expiration date) of the underlying futures contract and a few days earlier. Futures options are attractive because the underlying futures contracts are liquid and easy to trade, and exercising the futures option does not lead to the delivery of the underlying asset (of the futures contract). Futures options and futures contracts are conveniently traded on the same exchange, so transaction costs are low. The underlying security price is the futures price, and the yield is the domestic risk-free rate.

12.5 EXOTIC OPTIONS

Although calls and puts are the most popular options, there are many other types of options. Financial engineers create these exotic options because of client requests. If a certain exotic option is well-received, then it will become popular with a wider group of investors. In this section, we examine some of the popular exotic options.

(1) Packages are the option strategies examined in section 12.3. Examples of these small portfolios are covered calls, protective puts, bull/bear spreads, and straddles.

(2) Non-standard American options can be exercised early but must follow certain rules. For example, Bermudan options (in between European and American options) can be exercised only on certain days before the expiration date, such as the first business day of each month. The second example is an option that can be exercised only after an initial lock-out period – for instance, a two-year option cannot be exercised during the first year but can be exercised during the second year.

(3) Forward start options come into existence at a future date, T_1. When the option starts, the exercise price is set equal to the underlying security price at T_1. These options are cheaper than the exact one that would start immediately. In fact, the forward start option price is e^{-qT_1} multiplied by the option price starting today (q is the yield of the underlying security).

(4) Cliquet option, or ratchet option, is a series of the same at-the-money call/put options. For example, 14 at-the-money consecutive six-month options form a cliquet. When one option expires, the next one comes into existence. Therefore, this cliquet has a total life of seven years.

(5) Compound option has an option as the underlying security. There are four versions: call option on a call, put option on a call, call option on a put, and put option on a put. The prices of these options are quite low when compared with regular options.

(6) Chooser option: starts its life as an unidentified option. At some specific point in their lives, the owner of the option chooses whether the option is a put or a call. Because of this extra flexibility, chooser options are more expensive than regular options.

(7) Barrier option: These types of options experience a substantial event only if the underlying stock price reaches a pre-specified barrier price. The underlying price can reach the barrier from below (up option) or from above (down option). Then the option can come into existence (in option) or may cease to exist (out option). Given that the option can be a call or a put, altogether, there are eight variations ranging from up-in-call to down-out-put.

(8) Binary options are intuitively sensible and very popular. There are two main versions: cash-or-nothing and asset-or-nothing. In the cash-or-nothing binary option, if the underlying stock price is above the exercise price, the payoff is a fixed payment, 'FP'. But if the underlying stock price is below the exercise price, the payoff is zero. The price of this option can be calculated as $e^{-r_f T}(FP)CN(d_2)$.

For the asset-or-nothing option, if the underlying stock price is larger than the exercise price, the payoff is the underlying stock's value, S. And if the underlying stock price is less than the exercise price, the payoff is zero. The price of the option is $e^{-qT}(S)CN(d_1)$.

In the previous equations, r_f is the risk-free rate, T is the time to expiration in years, CN is the cumulative normal function, q is the dividend yield, $d_1 = \dfrac{\log\left(\dfrac{S}{E}\right)+\left(r_f - q + \dfrac{\sigma^2}{2}\right)T}{\sigma\sqrt{T}}$, and $d_2 = d_1 - \sigma\sqrt{T}$. The payoff diagrams of the two binary options are in Figure 12.7.

(9) Shout options essentially allow exercising two times. If the underlying security price moves in a favorable direction leading to a good payoff, the owner 'shouts' and the payoff is recorded even though the option has not been exercised. The owner continues holding on to the option for an even better payoff. If there is indeed a better payoff, the option is exercised and the better payoff is realized. In case there is no better payoff, then the 'shout'

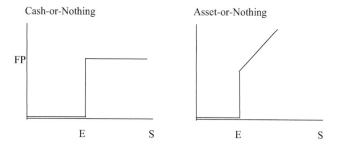

FIGURE 12.7 Payoff Diagrams of Binary Options: Cash-or-Nothing and Asset-or-Nothing

payoff will be the payoff. With their added benefit of an extra payoff opportunity, shout options are more expensive.

(10) Exchange options are used to exchange the underlying asset for another asset. For example, if the option is exercised, the underlying I.B.M. stock might be given up in exchange for Microsoft stock. Clearly, the option will have a positive payoff if the stock that is given up, I.B.M., is of lower value than the stock that is received, Microsoft.

(11) Asian options are highly complex. The payoff is not the typical difference between the underlying security price and the exercise price. Rather, the average underlying security price since the inception of the option is used in the payoff calculation. The calculation of the average can be discrete arithmetic (the average of the closing price of the underlying security every day, for example), continuous-time arithmetic, or geometric average. Another type of Asian option has the exercise price as the average of the underlying security prices. The payoff is then the difference between the underlying security price and this special exercise price.

The advantage of the Asian option is low volatility. The averaging of the underlying security price reduces volatility substantially compared to American or European options. The consequent second advantage of Asian options is their lower price compared to American and European options. On the other hand, Asian option prices do not have a closed-form formula. The price can only be calculated numerically using Monte Carlo simulations with the assumption that the average security price is lognormally distributed.

12.6 VOLATILITY INDEX, V.I.X.

The volatility index is the standard deviation in the S&P 500 index as the underlying security of an index option. The option price formula – for example, the Black-Scholes-Merton equation – is used not to find the option price but to find the standard deviation. The option price is taken from the options exchange with the assumption that the exchange is highly efficient. The option price equation is then used to extract the implied contemporaneous volatility of the index.

The volatility index (the ticker symbol is V.I.X.) is quite informative about markets and is indicative of crises and recessions. Typically, if V.I.X. gets closer to 30 (or goes above 30), this would be an indication of high volatility, uncertainty, and unease in the financial markets.

12.7 SUMMARY AND CONCLUSION

Options became a consistent part of investment portfolios starting in the late 1970s. Even though they are riskier than stocks and bonds, they provide unique characteristics and profit opportunities in investments. Two high-demand options are explored, calls and puts. These options have stocks, stock indexes, foreign currencies, and futures contracts as underlying securities. Options are utilized by financial engineers to design portfolios (option strategies) with payoff structures that clients request. These options strategies, their payoff and profit diagrams, are reviewed. Exotic options, specialized options with unique characteristics, are examined. Finally, the importance of the volatility index is stressed. The following chapters cover binomial trees, the Black-Scholes-Merton option pricing technique, and option Greeks.

REFERENCES AND ADDITIONAL READING

Black, F., Scholes, M. 1973. The Pricing of Options and Corporate Liabilities. *Journal of Political Economy*, 81, 637–654.

Bodie, Z., Kane, A., Marcus, A.J. 2021. *Investments*. 12th edition. New York, McGraw-Hill.

Hull, J.C. 2012. *Options, Futures and Other Derivatives*. 8th edition. Boston, MA, Prentice Hall.

Merton, R.C. 1973. Theory of Rational Option Pricing. *Bell Journal of Economics*, 4, 141–183.

CHAPTER 13

Options

Binomial Tree Model

OBJECTIVES

- Justify the reasons for the necessity of the binomial tree model.
- Develop the binomial tree models.
- Apply the binomial tree model to a variety of options: European, American, and Asian.
- Design and construct computer code in Excel for the binomial tree models.

13.1 INTRODUCTION

Options are some of the most popular derivative securities, and trading them at the correct prices is necessary for an efficient, fair, and ethical market. Moreover, even when an option is in the money with a positive payoff when exercised, it is better to sell the option because the price of the option is higher than its payoff before the maturity date. The time before its maturity date allows the possibility that the underlying security price might move in a favorable direction for the option to generate a higher payoff. This up potential makes the option more valuable than the payoff it would generate if exercised right then. Of course, the underlying security price might move in an unfavorable direction, but the worst that can happen is a zero payoff. Thus, the down potential is limited to zero (but the up potential is not limited). Therefore, before the maturity date, the option price is higher than the payoff. It is essential to know the price of the option.

There are two main ways to find the price of an option: (1) The Black-Scholes-Merton equation is a very popular and convenient closed-form formula; it is only applicable to European options. (2) The binomial tree model is the second way to find option prices and offers far more flexibility.

The binomial tree model can be adapted for pricing many option types. The prices of standard European options, dividend-paying options, American options, Asian options, and path-dependent and exotic options can all be calculated with this flexible option pricing model. The binomial tree model is intuitive to understand, easy to code with a computer software program,

DOI: 10.4324/9781003213697-13

and convenient to implement for price calculation. The binomial tree model and the Black-Scholes-Merton equation converge for European options. In fact, the binomial tree model can be used to prove the Black-Scholes-Merton equation.

13.2 ONE-STEP BINOMIAL TREE MODEL

The option price is higher than the payoff before the expiration date to reflect the up potential in the underlying security price movements. But on the final day of the life of the option, the time advantage no longer exists. Thus, during the last day of the option or on the expiration day, the price of the option is the same as the payoff of the option.

The principle behind the binomial tree is to start from the future and come back to the present step-by-step. The future is the expiration date of the option. Starting from that expiration date, different payoff values (i.e., option prices) depending on a wide spectrum of underlying security prices are calculated. The underlying security prices cover a very large range with a probability distribution of the likelihood of the security having those prices on that day. Using an appropriate discount rate and using the up and down (binomial) branches of the tree based on the probabilities of the underlying security prices at maturity, the option prices at maturity are discounted to the previous nodes of the tree branches. The length of each tree branch represents a time increment between the present and the maturity date. The time increments are supposed to be short for accuracy. Therefore, there are many time increments covering the period between the present and the future expiration date. The resultant sophisticated tree structure enables the accurate determination of the price. Calculating the prior nodes' option prices step-by-step from the maturity date toward to present provides the option price with this binomial tree model.

To fully understand the binomial tree model, we start with the simplest tree structure in Figure 13.1. The call option has an exercise price of $32, time to maturity, $T = 6$ months $= 0.5$ years, and the underlying security is a stock with a price of $30. The stock price at maturity of the option can be $33 or $27. The risk-free rate in the economy, r_f, is 5% per year.

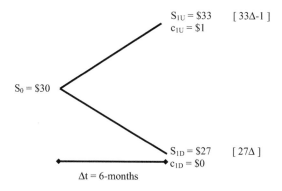

FIGURE 13.1 Numerical Example of the One-Step Binomial Tree Model

Given the stock prices at maturity, the payoff, and, therefore, the price of the call option, is $1 in the up branch, and it is $0 in the down branch. The strategy here is to create a risk-free portfolio with the stock and the option. For this risk-free portfolio, the up branch value and the down branch value will be equal to each other; in other words, it is irrelevant whether the up branch materializes or the down branch materializes for this portfolio – either way, the portfolio value will be the same. Moreover, the present value of this risk-free portfolio will be obtained using the risk-free rate as the discount rate.

We assume the portfolio has Δ shares of stock and one sold call option. In the up branch, as indicated in Figure 13.1, the portfolio value is [33Δ-1]. In the down branch, the portfolio value is [27Δ]. The portfolio is riskless when

$$[33\Delta\text{-}1] = [27\Delta] \Rightarrow \Delta = 0.1667. \tag{13.1}$$

The risk-free portfolio is composed of 0.1667 shares of stock and 1 sold call option. The value of the portfolio at maturity (in the up branch or in the down branch) and at present are as follows:

$$\text{Portfolio value at future maturity date} = (0.1667)(\$27) = \$4.5 \tag{13.2}$$
$$\text{Portfolio value at present} = 4.5e^{-(0.05)(0.5)} = \$4.3889 \tag{13.3}$$

It should be noted that continuous-time discounting is used in equation 13.3 instead of discrete discounting [1 / (1 + 0.05/2)]. Once the price of the portfolio is found at present, the option price can be extracted:

$$(\Delta)(S_0) - c_0 = 4.3889 \Rightarrow (0.1667)(30) - c_0 = 4.3889 \Rightarrow c_0 = \$0.61 \tag{13.4}$$

The strategy and the process flow just described would work to find the option price at any time. However, these steps should be converted into a structured and more direct approach:

In Figure 13.2, U and D are symmetric return relatives with respect to one. For example, if the up branch indicates a 10% increase in the stock price, then U = 1 + 0.1 = 1.1 and D = 1 – 0.1 = 0.9. Or if the up branch indicates a 15% increase in the stock price, then

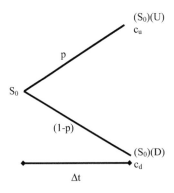

FIGURE 13.2 One-Step Binomial Tree Model

U = 1 + 0.15 = 1.15 and D = 1 − 0.15 = 0.85. As before, the riskless portfolio is Δ shares of stock and one sold call. Equating the up and down portfolios, solving for Δ, discounting the future value of the portfolio to the present, and equating it to the portfolio value at present, $[(\Delta)(S) - c]$, lead to the following:

$$(\Delta)(S_0)U - c_u = (\Delta)(S_0)D - c_d \Rightarrow \Delta = \frac{c_u - c_d}{S_0 U - S_0 D} \tag{13.5}$$

$$\text{Portfolio value at future maturity date} = \left(\frac{c_u - c_d}{S_0 U - S_0 D}\right) S_0 U - c_u \tag{13.6}$$

$$\text{Portfolio value today:} \left(\frac{c_u - c_d}{S_0 U - S_0 D}\right) S_0 - c = \left(\left(\frac{c_u - c_d}{S_0 U - S_0 D}\right) S_0 U - c_u\right) e^{-r_f \Delta t} \tag{13.7}$$

Simplifying, we get

$$c = \left[pc_u + (1 - p)c_d \right] e^{-r_f \Delta t}, \tag{13.8}$$

where

$$p = \frac{e^{r_f \Delta t} - D}{U - D}. \tag{13.9}$$

Equations 13.8 and 13.9 are the essential tools for the binomial tree that is under investigation here. Together (first, equation 13.9 and then equation 13.8), they help determine the option price in the prior, beginning node (at present in this tree structure). Furthermore, a quick inspection of equation 13.8 indicates that the square bracket expression on the right side looks like the expected value of the option at maturity, and the multiplication with the exponential term is indicative of the present value of the expected value of the option. This is all feasible if p in equation 13.9 is interpreted as the probability of the *up* branch in the binomial tree (and *1-p* as the probability of the *down* branch). The value of the option is then its expected value in a risk-neutral world, discounted at the risk-free rate.

When the probability of the up and down movements are p and *1-p*, the expected underlying stock price at a future time Δt is $S_0 e^{r_f \Delta t}$. This means the underlying stock price earns at the risk-free rate, r_f. In the binomial tree model approach, to find the price of the option, it is assumed that the expected return on the underlying security is the risk-free rate, and the discount rate is also the risk-free rate. These are unified under the definition of risk-neutral valuation in the *risk-neutral world*. When the option price is calculated based on the price of the underlying security in the alternative risk-neutral world, the probability of the up and down movements in the *real world* is irrelevant. This is considered by researchers as an example of a more general result which states that the expected return of the underlying security in the real world is irrelevant. Another link between the real world and the risk-neutral world is that volatility is the same in the real world and in the risk-neutral world. Thus, we can measure volatility in the real world using the readily available data and then utilize the volatility measure to build the binomial tree for the underlying security in the risk-neutral world.

In option price calculations using the binomial tree model, the real-world measurements are calculated first. Then the transition from real world to risk-neutral world is completed. The binomial tree structure is constructed, equation 13.9 and then equation 13.8 (repeatedly if the tree structure is more complex) are executed, the option price at present is evaluated, and the transition from the risk-neutral world to the real world is completed.

Revisiting the numerical example in Figure 13.1 and applying equation 13.9 and then 13.8, we find $p = \dfrac{e^{r_f \Delta t} - D}{U - D} = \dfrac{e^{(0.05)(0.5)} - 0.9}{1.1 - 0.9} = 0.6266$ and $(1-p) = 0.3734$. Then the option price is $c = \left[pc_u + (1-p)c_d \right] e^{-r_f \Delta t} = \left[(0.6266)(1) + (0.3734)(0) \right] e^{-(0.05)(0.5)} = \$0.61$ from equation 13.4. It is noted that $U = 33 / 30 = 1.1$ and $D = 27 / 30 = 0.09$. These values are in Figure 13.3.

The only criticism of the one-step binomial tree model is the consideration of only two possible stock prices at maturity. To consider many more potential stock prices at maturity, the binomial tree structure should be more complex. Such more complex structures are explored in the following sections.

13.3 TWO-STEP BINOMIAL TREE MODEL

In the two-step binomial tree model, the time period from the present to the maturity of the option is split into two time steps. At maturity, there are more alternatives for the underlying security price. Thus, the option price calculated from this model will be more accurate compared to the one-step binomial tree model. The visual representation and the numerical example for the two-step binomial tree model are in Figure 13.4.

The European call option has a maturity of six months with two time increments $\Delta t = 0.25$ years, an exercise price of $32, and an underlying stock worth $30 per share, in an economy with $r_f = 5\%$. The positive outlook (up branch) is a 10% increase in the stock price ($U = 1.1$),

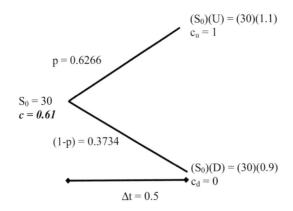

FIGURE 13.3 One-Step Binomial Tree Model with Equation 13.8 and Equation 13.9

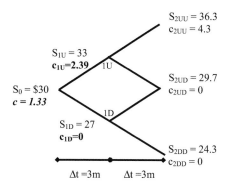

$S_{2UU} = 36.3$
$c_{2UU} = 4.3$

$S_{1U} = 33$
$c_{1U} = 2.39$ 1U

$S_0 = \$30$
$c = 1.33$

$S_{2UD} = 29.7$
$c_{2UD} = 0$

1D

$S_{1D} = 27$
$c_{1D} = 0$

$S_{2DD} = 24.3$
$c_{2DD} = 0$

$\Delta t = 3m$ $\Delta t = 3m$

FIGURE 13.4 Two-Step Binomial Tree Model with Equation 13.8 and Equation 13.9

and the negative outlook (down branch) is a 10% decline in the stock price (D = 0.9). With these pieces of information, we can expect the following:

(1) The stock price at maturity in the U.U. node, U.D. (or D.U.) node, and D.D. node are calculated accordingly. For example, $S_{2,UU}$ = (\$30)(1.1)(1.1) = \$36.3.
(2) Option payoffs and, thus, option prices at maturity are calculated with the exercise price as \$32.
(3) Equation 13.9 is used once, $p = \dfrac{e^{r_f \Delta t} - D}{U - D} = \dfrac{e^{(0.05)(0.25)} - 0.9}{1.1 - 0.9} = 0.5629$ and (1-p) = 0.4371, and equation 13.8 is used thrice to find the option price in each prior node: 1U node option price is $c_{1U} = \left[(0.5629)(4.3) + (0.4371)(0)\right]e^{-(0.05)(0.25)}$ = \$2.3904, 1D node option price is calculated as $c_{1D} = \left[(0.5629)(0) + (0.4371)(0)\right]e^{-(0.05)(0.25)}$ = \$0, and the present time option price is calculated as $c = \left[(0.5629)(2.3904) + (0.4371)(0)\right]e^{-(0.05)(0.25)}$ = \$1.33.

13.3.1 Two-Step Binomial Tree for European Put Options

In this subsection, we determine a put option's price using the two-step binomial tree model in Figure 13.5. Essentially, other than being careful about the maturity date put option payoff values (and therefore, put prices), the process and the formulas are the same as before:

The put option has one year to maturity, the underlying stock price is \$40, and the stock price is assumed to increase by 20% during good economic conditions (up branch, U = 1.2) and decrease by 20% during poor economic conditions (down branch, D = 0.8). The risk-free rate, r_f, is 5%, and the exercise price of the put is \$42. Given these pieces of information, we proceed as follows:

(1) The stock price at maturity in the U.U. node, U.D. (or D.U.) node, and D.D. node are calculated using U and D. For example, $S_{2,UD}$ = (\$40)(1.2)(0.8) = \$38.4.
(2) Put option payoffs (prices) at maturity are calculated with the exercise price as \$42.
(3) Equation 13.9 is used once to get $p = \dfrac{e^{r_f \Delta t} - D}{U - D} = \dfrac{e^{(0.05)(0.5)} - 0.8}{1.2 - 0.8} = 0.5633$ and *(1-p)* = 0.4367.
Equation 13.8 is modified slightly to reflect that the option is a put, and it is used for every prior

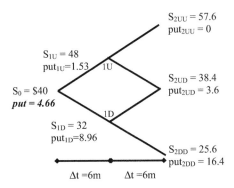

FIGURE 13.5 Two-Step Binomial Tree Model for a Put Option

node: 1U node put price is $put_{1U} = \big[(0.5633)(0) + (0.4367)(3.6)\big]e^{-(0.05)(0.5)} = \$1.5333$; 1D node put price is calculated as $put_{1D} = \big[(0.5633)(3.6) + (0.4367)(16.4)\big]e^{-(0.05)(0.5)} = \$8.9629$; and the current put price is calculated as $put = \big[(0.5633)(1.5333) + (0.4367)(8.9629)\big]e^{-(0.05)(0.5)}$ $= \$4.66$.

13.3.2 Two-Step Binomial Tree for American Put Options

All the examples we have examined thus far have been about European options. Now we examine an American put option. In American options, each intermediate node between the present and the maturity will have a price that is the larger of (1) the payoff at the node (since the American option can be exercised early) and (2) the option price at the node.

The same put option in the previous example is now assumed to be American in Figure 13.6. The up and down branch risk-neutral probabilities and the maturity date option prices are the same as before. The middle-up node price from equation 13.8 is calculated as 1.53. The payoff of the American put at that node is 0; therefore, the option price at the middle-up node is $1.53. For the middle-down node, the price from equation 13.8 is 8.96. The payoff, on the other hand, is 10 (the exercise price is $42, and the underlying stock price is $32). Therefore, the option price at the middle-down node is $10. With this higher value in the middle-down node, the present put price will be higher: $put = \big[(0.5633)(1.5333) + (0.4367)(10)\big]e^{-(0.05)(0.5)}$ $= \$5.10$. The ability to exercise American options early makes them more valuable, and the binomial tree model captures this fact: European put is $4.66; American put is $5.10.

13.3.3 Three-Step Binomial Tree Model

The final version of the binomial tree model we examine is the three-step binomial tree model for an American call option. The option has nine months to expiration; therefore, the three-step binomial tree has three-month ($\Delta t = 0.25$ years) time increments. The exercise price is $32, the underlying stock price is $30 per share, and the risk-free rate in the economy is $r_f = 5\%$. The up branch is a 10% increase in the stock price (U = 1.1), and the down branch is a

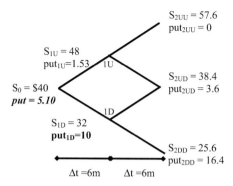

FIGURE 13.6 Two-Step Binomial Tree Model for an American Put Option

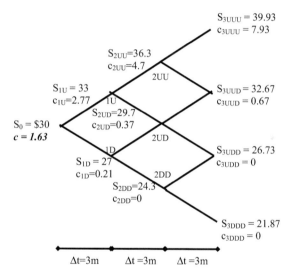

FIGURE 13.7 Three-Step Binomial Tree Model for an American Call Option

10% decline in the stock price (D = 0.9). With these pieces of information, we can assume the following:

(1) The stock price at maturity in the U.U.U., U.U.D. (or U.D.U., D.U.U.), U.D.D., and D.D.D. nodes are calculated accordingly. For example, S_{3UUU} = ($30)(1.1)(1.1)(1.1) = $39.93.

(2) Option payoffs and, thus, option prices at maturity are calculated next with the exercise price of $32.

(3) Equation 13.9 is used once, $p = \dfrac{e^{r_f \Delta t} - D}{U - D} = \dfrac{e^{(0.05)(0.25)} - 0.9}{1.1 - 0.9} = 0.5629$ and *(1-p)* = 0.4371, and equation 13.8 is used repeatedly to find the option price in each prior node:

2UU node option price is $c_{2UU} = \left[(0.5629)(7.93) + (0.4371)(0.67)\right] e^{-(0.05)(0.25)} = \$4.6976;$

2UD node option price is $c_{2UD} = \left[(0.5629)(0.67) + (0.4371)(0)\right]e^{-(0.05)(0.25)} = \$0.3725$;

2DD node option price is $c_{2DD} = \left[(0.5629)(0) + (0.4371)(0)\right]e^{-(0.05)(0.25)} = \$0$;

1U node option price is $c_{1U} = \left[(0.5629)(4.6976) + (0.4371)(0.3725)\right]e^{-(0.05)(0.25)} = \$2.7722$;

1D node option price is $c_{1D} = \left[(0.5629)(0.3725) + (0.4371)(0)\right]e^{-(0.05)(0.25)} = \$0.2071$; and

the current option price is $c = \left[(0.5629)(2.7722) + (0.4371)(0.2071)\right]e^{-(0.05)(0.25)} = \$1.6305$.
Here, the payoffs in the intermediate nodes are never higher than the corresponding prices.

13.4 MULTIPLE-STEP MODELS, U AND D CALCULATIONS, DIFFERENT UNDERLYING SECURITIES

As the binomial tree structure gets more complex, the maturity date consists of a wider range of potential underlying stock prices. This enables the more accurate and precise calculation of the option price. Such sophisticated tree structures cannot be examined by hand calculations; computer coding is necessary for these structures in Figure 13.8.

An even more realistic version of the sophisticated tree structure better chooses U and D. Thus far, the increase and the decrease in the underlying stock price have been subjective approximations. Improvements over the U and D calculations would be (1) assuming continuous-time finance with the exponential function, (2) using the volatility of the underlying security return for the up and down movements, (3) the random

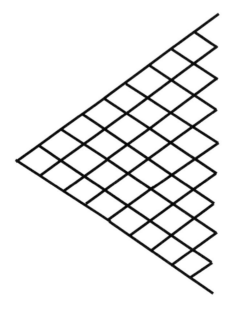

FIGURE 13.8 Multi-Step Binomial Tree Model

portion of the stochastic process. Altogether, the researchers Cox, Ross, and Rubinstein have introduced

$$U = e^{+\sigma\sqrt{\Delta t}} \text{ and } D = 1/U = e^{-\sigma\sqrt{\Delta t}} \tag{13.10}$$

Further improvement of the U and D calculations has been the consideration of the log-normal stochastic process with a deterministic mean return portion:

$$U = e^{\mu\Delta t + \sigma\sqrt{\Delta t}} \text{ and} \tag{13.11}$$
$$D = e^{\mu\Delta t - \sigma\sqrt{\Delta t}} . \tag{13.12}$$

Equation 13.11 and equation 13.12 assume that the binomial tree structure is not symmetric with respect to the x-axis; rather, the tree points upward, reflecting the increase in the underlying security price in a deterministic manner over time in Figure 13.9.

Finally, the underlying security has been non-dividend-paying stocks thus far. For other types of underlying securities, the parameter that needs to be adjusted is equation 13.9 for the calculation of the up-branch risk-neutral probability. The adjustments in equation 13.9 are as follows:

$$p = \frac{e^{(r_f - q)\Delta t} - D}{U - D} \text{ (for stock indexes and stocks with dividend yield } q\text{),} \tag{13.13}$$

$$p = \frac{e^{(r_f - r_{foreign})\Delta t} - D}{U - D} \text{ (for currencies with } r_{foreign} \text{ as the foreign risk-free rate), and} \tag{13.14}$$

$$p = \frac{e^{(r_f - r_f)\Delta t} - D}{U - D} = \frac{1 - D}{U - D} \text{ (for futures contracts).} \tag{13.15}$$

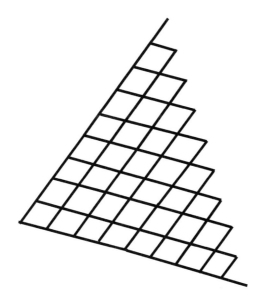

FIGURE 13.9 Multi-Step Binomial Tree Model with Positive Drift

13.5 COMPUTER CODES

With short time increments, the time to maturity of an option will have a sophisticated tree structure with many time steps. This complex tree structure will more accurately determine the option price. Such complex structures can be implemented with computer code. Figure 13.10 presents the binomial tree code for the European call option price function.

The program is relatively easy to understand:

(1) The required inputs to the function are U (UpB); D (DownB); the interest rate per period $e^{r_f \Delta t}$ (IntR); the underlying security price (Security); the exercise price E (ExerPrice); the yield adjustment (Yield) for dividend yield q as $e^{-q\Delta t}$, for foreign currency as $e^{-r_{foreign}\Delta t}$, and for futures contract $e^{-r_f \Delta t}$; and the number of time steps between the present and maturity (NumTimeInc).

(2) Equation 13.9 multiplied with the present value for the previous node $(e^{-r_f \Delta t})$ implemented.

(3) Down branch probability is in line 3.

(4) The 'for' loop finds the European call option price in a recursive manner. Starting from each maturity node at the end, the discounted value to the present is calculated by also considering the number of paths reaching the particular maturity node.

For the European put option price calculation, the same program in Figure 13.10 can be used. The only change would be about the maturity node put option payoff instead of the call option payoff:

(5) Application.Max(ExerPrice − Security $\star$ UpB^TimeInc $\star$ DownB^(NumTimeInc − _TimeInc),0).

The computer code for the American call option price calculation using the binomial tree model would be more complicated since, in each intermediate node, the option price would be compared to the payoff from the exercise at that node, and the bigger of the two values would

```
Function BinomTree_EuroCall(UpB, DownB, IntR, Security, ExerPrice, Yield, NumTimeInc)    '1
        probUp = (IntR * Yield - DownB) / (IntR * (UpB - DownB))                          '2
        probDown = 1 / IntR – probUp                                                      '3
        BinomTree_EuroCall = 0
        For TimeInc = 0 To NumTimeInc                                                     '4
                BinomTree_EuroCall = BinomTree_EuroCall + Application.Combin(NumTimeInc, _
                TimeInc) * probUp ^ TimeInc * probDown ^ (NumTimeInc - TimeInc) * _
                Application.Max(Security * UpB ^ TimeInc * DownB ^ (NumTimeInc - TimeInc) _    '5
                - ExerPrice, 0)
        Next TimeInc
    End Function
```

FIGURE 13.10 V.B.A. Code for the Binomial Tree Model – European Call Option

be picked. Figure 13.11 presents the V.B.A. code for the binomial tree model of the American call option price. The important steps to note are as follows:

(1) The maturity nodes' American call option prices are defined as a vector. The middle nodes' American call option prices are defined as a separate vector.
(2) The 'for' loop is used to calculate the American call option prices at maturity nodes.
(3) The next 'for' loop is actually two for loops nested within each other. The first 'for' loop represents the time steps starting from one before the maturity down to the present. The second 'for' loop is for all the nodes in a particular time step. The American call option prices at each of these intermediate nodes at that time step are calculated one by one. This is not easy because, after the option price is calculated for an intermediate node at a specific time step, it is compared to the option payoff at that same node. Whichever value is bigger, that is picked as the price of the American call option at that particular node for that specific time step.
(4) The binomial tree American call option price is the 0th time step (the present time) intermediate node price.

The code for the binomial tree American put option is exactly the same as that for the American call option in Figure 13.11 except for two points. The payoff should be updated for the

```
Function BinomTree_AmerCall(UpB, DownB, IntR, Security, ExerPrice, Yield, NumTimeInc)
        probUp = (IntR * Yield - DownB) / (IntR * (UpB - DownB))
        probDown = 1 / IntR - probUp

        Dim CP_Ret_Mat() As Double                                              '1
        Dim CP_Ret_Mid() As Double
        ReDim CP_Ret_Mat(NumTimeInc + 1)

        For Node = 0 To NumTimeInc                                              '2
        CP_Ret_Mat(Node) = Application.Max(Security * UpB ^ Node * DownB ^ (NumTimeInc _   '3
        - Node) - ExerPrice, 0)
        Next Node

        For TimeInc = NumTimeInc - 1 To 0 Step -1                              '4
                ReDim CP_Ret_Mid(TimeInc)
                For Node = 0 To TimeInc
                        CP_Ret_Mid(Node) = Application.Max(Security * UpB ^ Node * DownB ^ _ '5
                        (TimeInc - Node) - ExerPrice, probDown * CP_Ret_Mat(Node) + probUp * _
                        CP_Ret_Mat(Node + 1))
                Next Node
                ReDim CP_Ret_Mat(TimeInc)
                For Node = 0 To TimeInc
                        CP_Ret_Mat(Node) = CP_Ret_Mid(Node)
                Next Node
        Next TimeInc
        BinomTree_AmerCall = CP_Ret_Mid(0)                                     '6
End Function
```

FIGURE 13.11 V.B.A. Code for the Binomial Tree Model – American Call Option

American put option from that of the American call option for the maturity nodes ('3') and for the intermediate nodes ('5'). The adjustments for the American put option should be the following:

(5) Application.Max(ExerPrice − Security ★ UpB^Node ★ DownB^(NumTimeInc − Node),0)
(6) Application.Max(ExerPrice − Security ★ UpB ^ Node ★ DownB ^ (TimeInc − Node), _
      probDown ★ CP_Ret_Mat(Node) + probUp ★ CP_Ret_Mat(Node + 1))

These codes are provided in the accompanying chapter13Addentum2_binomialTreeModel. For simpler implementations with arbitrary/flexible choices of U, D, and a number of time steps, chapter13Addentum1_binomTreeFlexible can be experimented with.

13.6 SUMMARY AND CONCLUSION

Binomial tree models are used to price many different types of options. While the most popular option pricing model, Black-Scholes-Merton can solve the price of European options, the binomial tree models can find the prices of European options, American options, and other path-dependent options. The calculation of option prices using up to three time increments is explored first. Then the realistic multi-step complex binomial trees with their computer code implementations for option prices are investigated.

There are additional versions of the binomial tree model. The trinomial tree model has up, middle, and down branches in order to include more underlying security prices at maturity and at previous time steps. However, overall, the binomial tree model of this chapter performs quite well. With computer coding, the number of time steps can be significantly higher, generating complex tree structures and accurate option prices. Most such binomial tree model prices converge to Black-Scholes-Merton prices for European options.

REFERENCES AND ADDITIONAL READING

Black, F., Scholes, M. 1973. The Pricing of Options and Corporate Liabilities. *Journal of Political Economy*, 81, 637–654.
Bodie, Z., Kane, A., Marcus, A.J. 2021. *Investments*. 12th edition. New York, McGraw-Hill.
Cox, J.C., Ross, S.A., Rubinstein, M. 1976. The Valuation of Options for Alternative Stochastic Processes. *Journal of Financial Economics*, 3, 145–166.
Hull, J.C. 2012. *Options, Futures and Other Derivatives*. 8th edition. Boston, MA, Prentice Hall.
Merton, R.C. 1973. Theory of Rational Option Pricing. *Bell Journal of Economics*, 4, 141–183.

CHAPTER 14

Options

Black-Scholes-Merton Model

OBJECTIVES

- Justify the Black-Scholes-Merton option pricing model as one of the most exciting innovations in finance over the last half century.
- Develop and formulate the Black-Scholes-Merton model, and summarize the historical background, the theory, the mathematical model, and the partial differential equation.
- Compare and contrast the Black and Scholes model with the Merton version.
- Construct the formula in Excel as a simple layout and as a custom-written V.B.A. computer code. Demonstrate the advantages of the flexibility of the coding approach with numerical examples.
- Critique and appraise the functionality of implied volatility.
- Contrast implied volatility within the Black-Scholes-Merton formula and implement with V.B.A. coding utilizing examples.
- Investigate and explain the full and rigorous mathematical derivation of the Black-Scholes-Merton formula for the European call option and for the European put option.

14.1 INTRODUCTION

The Black-Scholes-Merton option pricing model goes back more than half a century. Yet it continues to be one of the most interesting formulas in finance. Over the decades, there have been a number of adjustments for better accuracy and for better precision; however, the fundamental version continues to be one of the most widespread models. Introduced in 1973 by Fisher Black and Myron Scholes, it became popular so quickly that the fledging Chicago Board Options Exchange was transformed overnight with rapid demand for trading option contracts.

The Black-Scholes-Merton model is the most widely used option pricing model. It is a sophisticated formula and not easy to fully understand. It is also difficult to formally prove. However, it is relatively easy to use, especially with Excel. The formula can be written in a

DOI: 10.4324/9781003213697-14

single cell, but the better and more flexible approach would be to program the formula as a customized function, as described in subsequent sections.

The original formula is for a non-dividend-paying underlying asset. The five required inputs are the risk-free rate in the economy, the exercise price and time to maturity of the option, and the price and standard deviation of the returns of the underlying asset. The improved version that was introduced at about the same time assumes the underlying asset pays dividends, and the dividend yield is the sixth input to the formula.

An important fact about the Black-Scholes-Merton option pricing formula is that only European call and put option prices can be calculated using the formula. Prices of path-dependent, Asian, American, and exotic options are calculated with the more flexible binomial tree model.

14.2 HISTORICAL BACKGROUND OF THE BLACK-SCHOLES-MERTON MODEL

The derivation of the Black-Scholes-Merton model was pioneered by Fisher Black and Myron Scholes. In the late 1960s, they developed the risk-neutral pricing concept. They believed a dynamic revision approach of a portfolio using the risk neutrality idea would be successful in financial markets. But their practical trading strategies without proper risk management were not successful. They returned to academia and applied their risk neutrality idea to options.

The foundation of the model was based on creating a risk-free portfolio by combining (selling and buying) the option with a proper number of shares of the underlying security such that the change in the underlying security value was eliminated by the change in the option price: a risk-free portfolio. This continuously revised (dynamic) portfolio was first used to calculate the present value of the portfolio and then to extract the price of the option. After extensive efforts on theoretical justification, Black and Scholes finalized and published their famous formula in 'The Pricing of Options and Corporate Liabilities' in the *Journal of Political Economy* in 1973. They made significant use of previous researchers' work in the theoretical derivations from the beginnings of stochastic calculus by Louis Bachelier in the late 1800s to the contributions of Albert Einstein, Kiyoshi Itô (early-to-mid-1900s), and Edward Thorp (1960s).

As these developments were taking place mainly at the Massachusetts Institute of Technology, another researcher, Robert Merton, was in continual collaboration with Black and Scholes. The exchange of ideas between the three researchers helped get the original paper published. And shortly afterward, Robert Merton published another paper on the option pricing formula called 'Theory of Rational Option Pricing' in the *Bell Journal of Economics and Management Science*. His theoretical development and derivation served as an expansion of the understanding and the applicability of the original Black-Scholes model. The original model assumed that the underlying security paid no dividends. Merton's important contribution was the flexibility of the underlying security to pay dividends. This enabled the option pricing model to be used additionally for options with underlying securities, such as currencies, stock indexes, futures, and dividend-paying stocks. Merton had coined the name of the original model as Black-Scholes, but after his significant contributions, Black-Scholes-Merton is the name generally used for the option pricing model.

The Black-Scholes-Merton formula led to an explosion of trading activity at options markets around the world. Over the years, many adjustments and improvements to the model were made, as discussed later. But the Black Scholes-Merton model provides an excellent approximation for European option prices for traders around the world. It continues to be one of the most important concepts in modern financial theory.

Merton and Scholes received the Nobel Prize in Economics in 1997 mainly because of the development and the derivation of the Black-Scholes-Merton option pricing model. Fisher was acknowledged for his part and would have received the prize as well, but he passed away in 1995.

14.3 THE ASSUMPTIONS, INPUT PARAMETERS, PAIRED RELATIONSHIPS

The derivation of the original Black-Scholes-Merton model assumes that

(1) the risk-free rate is constant, r_f;
(2) the underlying security price follows the lognormal stochastic process;
(3) the underlying security pays no dividends (this is removed in the Merton extension);
(4) the option is European and, therefore, cannot be exercised before the expiration date;
(5) there is no arbitrage opportunity: risk-free extra profit (above the risk-free rate) is not possible;
(6) any security can be traded at any amount in any direction;
(7) it is possible to lend and borrow any amount at a risk-free rate; and
(8) there are no frictions (no transaction costs or other fees).

Many of the later extensions of the original Black-Scholes-Merton model were about addressing these restrictive assumptions with the goal of making the formula realistic and practical. For example, the Merton extension made it possible to consider options where the underlying security distributed dividends.

The Black-Scholes-Merton formula requires *six* inputs into the formula:

(1) The underlying asset's price, S
(2) The strike price, or exercise price of the option, E
(3) Time to expiration of the option, T, expressed in years
(4) Volatility, or standard deviation of the underlying security returns, σ
(5) The prevailing risk-free rate in the economy, r_f
(6) The yield of the underlying asset, q (e.g., dividend yield if the underlying is a stock)

The original Black-Scholes formula had the first *five* inputs, and the derivation assumed the underlying was a non-dividend paying security. Merton's extension introduced dividends as a continuous payment expressed as an annual percentage, q.

Each of these six variables impacts the European call/put option in a certain way. The partial derivative of the option formula with respect to the variable helps determine the positive (direct) or negative (indirect) relationship. As a matter of fact, these relationships form the basis

Input Parameter	European Call	European Put
Underlying Security Price, S	+	-
Exercise Price, E	-	+
Time to Maturity, T	?	?
Volatility of Underlying Security, σ	+	+
Risk-free rate, r_f	+	-
Yield of Underlying Security, q	-	+

FIGURE 14.1 The Relationships Between the Input Parameters and Option Prices

of option Greeks, used as important risk management tools, as explored in the next chapter. The effect of each input on the European call/put option value is in Figure 14.1.

While most of the relationships can be verified intuitively, the time-to-maturity relationship is a bit ambiguous. Normally, if the time-to-maturity of an option is long, the option (call or put) should be more valuable because the stock price may move more in the favorable direction generating a larger payoff, while the down potential is limited to zero as the worst case. However, for dividend-paying securities, the underlying security price declines with dividends, and this has a more negative impact on the call option for longer periods to maturity. Thus, the ultimate impact of time-to-maturity is unclear on call options. As for European put options, the payoff at maturity is deferred, and the present value of that payoff gets smaller with longer time-to-maturity. This works against the potential increase in put option value (due to the favorable movement of the underlying security price before maturity). The ultimate impact of time-to-maturity is again unclear on put options.

For American call and put options, most of the relationships in Figure 14.1 are the same. The time-to-maturity affects American option values positively (unless the underlying security yield is high enough to be a detriment to the call option value).

14.4 BLACK-SCHOLES-MERTON OPTION PRICE FORMULA

The Black-Scholes-Merton call option price formula and the corresponding put option price formula are

$$C = Se^{-qT}N(d_1) - Ee^{-r_f T}N(d_2) \text{ and} \tag{14.1}$$

$$Put = Ee^{-r_f T}N(-d_2) - Se^{-qT}N(-d_1), \tag{14.2}$$

where

$$d_1 = \frac{\log(S/E) + \left(r_f - q + \sigma^2/2\right)T}{\sigma\sqrt{T}} \tag{14.3}$$

and $d_2 = d_1 - \sigma\sqrt{T}$. $\tag{14.4}$

In equation 14.1 and equation 14.2, $N(.)$ stands for the standard cumulative normal distribution function, which is the area under the normal distribution from $-\infty$ until d_1 for $N(d_1)$:

$$N(d_1) = \frac{1}{\sqrt{2\pi}} \int_{-\infty}^{d_1} e^{-z^2/2} dz. \qquad (14.5)$$

In Excel, the standard function, '$=normsdist(d_1)$', finds the cumulative normal value.

The put option price can also be expressed using the put-call parity formula. A synthetic stock can be generated with (1) a long bond as the present value of the exercise price of the option, a written put, and a long call with the same exercise price and the same underlying stock. From no arbitrage, this synthetic stock should be equal to the ex-dividend stock price:

$$C - Put + Ee^{-r_f T} = Se^{-qT}, \text{ which leads to}$$

$$Put = C - Se^{-qT} + Ee^{-r_f T}. \qquad (14.6)$$

All of the six inputs to equation 14.1, equation 14.2, and equation 14.6 are relatively straightforward to locate but one: the volatility of the underlying security returns. This volatility measure should be a contemporaneous value, but such a value is not observable. As a proxy, past returns of the underlying security are used to calculate the standard deviation. The historical returns should not go too far back because the risk characteristics of the underlying security should not be too far off from the contemporaneous risk for the proxy to be useful. For example, if daily returns are used, then the past five years' worth of data would be sufficient to calculate the daily standard deviation. The annualized standard deviation would be obtained by multiplying the daily measure with the square root of 252, the number of business days in a year where most of the volatility is generated.

Another avenue of research on contemporaneous volatility utilizes the Black-Scholes-Merton formula. Sometimes equation 14.1 or equation 14.2 is used to figure out the (implied) contemporaneous volatility. The option price in the formula is taken as the trading price from the options market. The volatility implied from the Black-Scholes-Merton formula is calculated. The implied volatility index from stock index options is actually used as a predictor of the near-term economic performance. A high volatility index close to 30 and above would imply pessimistic financial prospects, while a low volatility index of less than 30 would imply a healthy financial environment. There is no closed-form expression for implied volatility. Recursive iterations in computer code determine the contemporaneous implied volatility.

14.5 PRACTICAL IMPLEMENTATION OF THE BLACK-SCHOLES-MERTON FORMULA WITH EXCEL

The Black-Scholes-Merton formula is quite easy to implement using any computer code. In Excel, one approach would be to enter the input parameters, type the intermediate formulas, and finally, the Black-Scholes-Merton formulas in different cells, as in Figure 14.2. While this approach is straightforward, it is also inflexible and inelegant. It is not easy to get the option

UN-12G

	A	B	C	D
1		Black-Scholes-Merton Formula		
2	Underlying Security Price, S	127.98		
3	Exercise Price, E	127.00		
4	Time to Maturity, T	0.2500		
5	Risk-free rate, r_f	1.00%		
6	Yield of Underlying Security, q	1.70%		
7	Volatility of Underlying Security, σ	14%		
8				
9	d_1	0.1198	=(LN(B2/B3)+(B5-B6+0.5*B7^2)*B4)/(B7*SQRT(B4))	
10	d_2	0.0498	=B9-B7*SQRT(B4)	
11				
12	$N(d_1)$	0.5477	=NORMSDIST(B9)	
13	$N(d_2)$	0.5199	=NORMSDIST(B10)	
14				
15	**European Call Option price**	**3.937468**	=B2*EXP(-B6*B4)*B12-B3*EXP(-B5*B4)*B13	
16	**European Put Option price**	**3.183125**	=B3*EXP(-B5*B4)*NORMSDIST(-B10)-B2*EXP(-B6*B4)*NORMSDIST(-B9)	
17	**European Put Option Price (put-call parity)**	**3.183125**	=B15-B2*EXP(-B6*B4)+B3*EXP(-B5*B4)	

FIGURE 14.2 Direct Excel Implementation of Black-Scholes-Merton Formulas

'The intermediate variable d1 is calculated here
Function d1Y(Stock, Exercise, TimeMat, RiskfreeRate, Volatility, Yield)
    d1Y = (Log(Stock / Exercise) + (RiskfreeRate - Yield) * _
        TimeMat) / (Volatility * Sqr(TimeMat)) + 0.5 * Volatility * Sqr(TimeMat)
End Function

'The intermediate variable d2 is calculated here
Function d2Y(Stock, Exercise, TimeMat, RiskfreeRate, Volatility, Yield)
    d2Y = d1Y(Stock, Exercise, TimeMat, RiskfreeRate, Volatility, Yield) - Volatility * Sqr(TimeMat)
End Function

'Black-Scholes-Merton European Call Option Price
Function BSMcall(Stock, Exercise, TimeMat, RiskfreeRate, Volatility, Yield)
    BSMcall = Stock * Exp(-Yield * TimeMat) * Application.NormSDist(d1Y(Stock, _
    Exercise, TimeMat, RiskfreeRate, Volatility, Yield)) - _
    Exercise * Exp(-TimeMat * RiskfreeRate) * Application.NormSDist(d2Y(Stock, Exercise, _
    TimeMat, RiskfreeRate, Volatility, Yield))
End Function

'Black-Scholes-Merton European Put Option Price
Function BSMput(Stock, Exercise, TimeMat, RiskfreeRate, Volatility, Yield)
    BSMput = Exercise * Exp(-RiskfreeRate * TimeMat) * Application.NormSDist(-d2Y(Stock, _
    Exercise, TimeMat, RiskfreeRate, Volatility, Yield)) - Stock * Exp(-Yield * TimeMat) * _
    Application.NormSDist(-d1Y(Stock, Exercise, TimeMat, RiskfreeRate, Volatility, Yield))
End Function

'Black-Scholes-Merton European Put Option Price from the Put-Call Parity Theorem
Function BSMputPCparity(Stock, Exercise, TimeMat, RiskfreeRate, Volatility, Yield)
    BSMputPCparity = BSMcall(Stock, Exercise, TimeMat, RiskfreeRate, _
    Volatility, Yield) + Exercise * Exp(-RiskfreeRate * TimeMat) - Stock * Exp(-Yield * TimeMat)
End Function

FIGURE 14.3 Computer Codes for the Black-Scholes-Merton Formulas Using V.B.A. in Excel

prices in other cells or worksheets. The second approach would be elegant computer coding, such as the V.B.A. macro functions. The macro functions can be used anywhere in an Excel file, or they can be transported to another file with ease.

The Visual Basic Application (V.B.A.) code within Excel is provided in Figure 14.3. There are five functions for the calculation of d_1 (d1Y), d_2 (d2Y), Black-Scholes-Merton call option price (BSMcall), Black-Scholes-Merton put option price (BSMput), and put option price using the put-call parity relationship (BSMputPCparity). As the programs in Figure 14.3 indicate, most of the code is easy to decipher and understand. Some of the clarifications in the code are (1) Log: natural logarithm function; (2) Sqr: square root function; (3) Exp: exponential function; and (4) Application.NormSDist: cumulative normal distribution.

Using these functions, the Black-Scholes-Merton European call and put option prices are easily calculated. The code also includes the alternative put price calculation using the put-call parity relationship. An example of the utilization of the functions is in Figure 14.4.

One more important code application is the implied volatility calculation. In fact, implied volatility can only be calculated using an iterative function that recursively finds the standard deviation of the underlying security returns such that the difference between the trading price of the option and the Black-Scholes-Merton formula option price is minimized. This V.B.A. code for Excel is provided in Figure 14.5.

The code in Figure 14.5 starts with the initial condition as the average of 'up' = *400%* and 'down'= *0%, 200%*, as the volatility of the underlying security. The Black-Scholes-Merton

UN-12G

	A	B	C	D
1		Black-Scholes-Merton Formula VBA		
2	Underlying Security Price, S	127.98		
3	Exercise Price, E	127.00		
4	Time to Maturity, T	0.2500		
5	Risk-free rate, r_f	1.00%		
6	Yield of Underlying Security, q	1.70%		
7	Volatility of Underlying Security, σ	14%		
8				
9	d_1	0.1198	=(LN(B2/B3)+(B5-B6+0.5*B7^2)*B4)/(B7*SQRT(B4))	
10	d_2	0.0498	=B9-B7*SQRT(B4)	
11				
12	$N(d_1)$	0.5477	=NORMSDIST(B9)	
13	$N(d_2)$	0.5199	=NORMSDIST(B10)	
14				
15	**European Call Option price**	**3.937468**	=BSMcall(B2,B3,B4,B5,B7,B6)	
16	**European Put Option price**	**3.183125**	=BSMput(B2,B3,B4,B5,B7,B6)	
17	**European Put Option Price (put-call parity)**	**3.183125**	=BSMputPcParity(B2,B3,B4,B5,B7,B6)	

FIGURE 14.4 Black-Scholes-Merton Call Option Price and Put Option Price Example with V.B.A.

option price is calculated and compared to the trading price from the options market. If the Black-Scholes-Merton option price is higher (lower), that means the volatility is too high (low). Then the 'up' ('down') bound is decreased (increased). The average of the 'up' and 'down' boundary becomes the new volatility, and the Black-Scholes-Merton option price is compared to the option's trading price. This recursive process continues until the difference between the 'up' and 'down' boundaries is less than '1' basis point. Then the implied volatility is finalized as the average of 'up' and 'down'. A numerical example using the V.B.A. code is in Figure 14.6.

```
'Implied Volatility from BSM European Call Option
Function ImpliedVolatilityCall(Stock, Exercise, TimeMat, RiskfreeRate, Yield, OptionTradingPrice)
    up = 4
    down = 0
    Do While (up - down) > 0.0001
    If BSMcall(Stock, Exercise, TimeMat, RiskfreeRate, (up + down) / 2, Yield) > _
        OptionTradingPrice Then
            up = (up + down) / 2
            Else: down = (up + down) / 2
    End If
    Loop
    ImpliedVolatilityCall = (up + down) / 2
End Function


'Implied Volatility from BSM European Put Option
Function ImpliedVolatilityPut(Stock, Exercise, TimeMat, RiskfreeRate, Yield, OptionTradingPrice)
    up = 4
    down = 0
    Do While (up - down) > 0.0001
    If BSMput(Stock, Exercise, TimeMat, RiskfreeRate, (up + down) / 2, Yield) > _
        OptionTradingPrice Then
            up = (up + down) / 2
            Else: down = (up + down) / 2
    End If
    Loop
    ImpliedVolatilityPut = (up + down) / 2
End Function
```

FIGURE 14.5 Implied Volatility V.B.A. Code using Black-Scholes-Merton Call and Put

impliedVolatility

	A	B	F
1	\multicolumn{3}{c} Black-Scholes-Merton Implied Volatility		
2	Underlying Security Price, S	50	
3	Exercise Price, E	51	
4	Time to Maturity, T	0.50	
5	Risk-free rate, r_f	2.00%	
6	Yield of Underlying Security, q	2.50%	
7			
8	Call Option Trading Price	3.00	
9	Put Option Trading Price	2.50	
10			
11	**Implied Volatility (Call Option)**	**25.0824%**	=ImpliedVolatilityCall(B2,B3,B4,B5,B6,B8)
12	**Implied Volatility (Put Option)**	**13.4308%**	=ImpliedVolatilityPut(B2,B3,B4,B5,B6,B9)

FIGURE 14.6 Implied Volatility Example Using Black-Scholes-Merton Call and Put with V.B.A.

14.6 THE THEORETICAL DERIVATION OF THE BLACK-SCHOLES-MERTON FORMULATION

14.6.1 Black-Scholes-Merton European Call Option Price Formula

The derivation of the Black-Scholes-Merton formula conjectures that the option price and the underlying security (taken as a stock) price are impacted by the same source of uncertainty. The goal is to form a portfolio with the stock and the option such that this source of uncertainty is eliminated. This approach is also known as delta hedging. In the continuous-time finance world, the portfolio is continuously risk-free and earns continuously at the risk-free rate. The dividends are paid out continuously at a rate of $q\%$ per year, intuitively implying a decrease in the rate of return of the security. In this risk-neutral world, securities (including the underlying stock) generate returns at the risk-free rate ($\mu = r_f - q$). These concepts lead to the Black-Scholes-Merton differential equation.

The underlying stock price is assumed to follow the lognormal process:

$$\Delta \log S = \left(r_f - q - \frac{\sigma^2}{2} \right) dt + \sigma \varepsilon \sqrt{dt}.$$ (14.7)

Therefore, the stock price is

$$S(t + dt) = S(t)e^{\left(r_f - q - \frac{\sigma^2}{2} \right) dt + \sigma \varepsilon \sqrt{dt}}.$$ (14.8)

However, while the stock price is assumed (correctly) to be lognormally distributed, for instantaneously short time intervals dt, the stock return can be expressed either with the log difference stochastic equation 14.7, or equivalently with the stochastic geometric Brownian motion equation 14.9, as in the derivation of the Black-Scholes-Merton formula:

$$dS(t) = (r_f - q)Sdt + \sigma S\varepsilon\sqrt{dt}$$ (14.9)

The option price (we explore the call option), which is dependent on the underlying stock price and time, follows a stochastic process determined from Itô's lemma in section 8.6 of Chapter 8:

$$dC(S,t) = \frac{\partial C}{\partial S} dS + \frac{\partial C}{\partial t} dt + \frac{1}{2} \frac{\partial^2 C}{\partial S^2} (dS)^2 + \frac{\partial^2 C}{\partial S \partial t} (dS)(dt) + \frac{1}{2} \frac{\partial^2 C}{\partial t^2} (dt)^2 + \dots.$$ (14.10)

This simplifies after the terms of Δt with power larger than '1' are removed (since they are 0):

$$dC(S,t) = \frac{\partial C}{\partial S} dS + \frac{\partial C}{\partial t} dt + \frac{1}{2} \frac{\partial^2 C}{\partial S^2} (dS)^2.$$ (14.11)

Substituting equation 14.9 into equation 14.11 provides further simplification:

$$dC(S,t) = \left(\frac{\partial C}{\partial S}(r_f - q)S + \frac{\partial C}{\partial t} + \frac{1}{2}\frac{\partial^2 C}{\partial S^2}\sigma^2 S^2 \right) dt + \frac{\partial C}{\partial S}\sigma S\varepsilon\sqrt{dt}. \tag{14.12}$$

To create a riskless portfolio by combining the stock (equation 14.9) and the option (equation 14.12), the random variable, E, needs to be eliminated. This is achieved by shorting one call option and buying $\partial C / \partial S$ shares of the underlying stock. Then the combined portfolio, Π, is

$$\Pi = -C + \frac{\partial C}{\partial S}S, \tag{14.13}$$

and the change in the risk-free portfolio value over the time interval, dt, is calculated with $r_f - q$:

$$d\Pi = (r_f - q)\Pi dt, \tag{14.14}$$

$$-dC + \frac{\partial C}{\partial S}dS = (r_f - q)\left(-C + \frac{\partial C}{\partial S}S \right)dt. \tag{14.15}$$

Substituting equation 14.9 and equation 14.12 into the left side of equation 14.15 and simplifying leads to the Black-Scholes-Merton differential equation. This differential equation is also known as the heat equation (about the diffusion of heat). The same structure for the equation is observed in quantum mechanics as well:

$$\frac{\partial C}{\partial t} + \left(r_f - q \right)S\frac{\partial C}{\partial S} + \frac{1}{2}\sigma^2 S^2 \frac{\partial^2 C}{\partial S^2} = \left(r_f - q \right)C, \tag{14.16}$$

with the boundary (initial) condition as $C(S, T) = S(T) - E$ and with the stock price at T being larger than the exercise price.

It is important to note that the differential equation in 14.16 can be for any security whose value function is dependent on the underlying stock. The difference between these securities is the boundary/initial condition, which is uniquely different for different securities. Once the boundary/initial condition is given, the option price can be calculated as

$$C(S,t) = e^{-r_f(T-t)}Expect_{t,S(t)}\left[S(T) - E \right], \tag{14.17}$$

where $Expect_{t, S(t)}$ represents expectation. Here, the stock price at the expiration of the option is from equation 14.8 with $dt = T - t$:

$$S(T) = S(t)e^{\left(r_f - q - \frac{\sigma^2}{2} \right)(T-t) + \sigma\varepsilon\sqrt{T-t}} \tag{14.18}$$

The call option price in equation 14.17 involves the expectation of a normally distributed random variable, ε; thus, the expectation can be re-expressed as

$$C(S,t) = e^{-r_f(T-t)} \int_{-\infty}^{+\infty} \left(S(t)e^{\left(r_f - q - \frac{\sigma^2}{2}\right)(T-t) + \sigma\varepsilon\sqrt{T-t}} - E \right)^+ \frac{e^{\frac{-\varepsilon^2}{2}}}{\sqrt{2\pi}} d\varepsilon. \tag{14.19}$$

The plus sign in the power of the argument in the integral indicates that the payoff for the call option is the larger number between zero and the difference in the parenthesis. In other words, the integral in equation 14.19 is nonzero only when $\left(r_f - q - \frac{\sigma^2}{2} \right)(T-t) + \sigma\varepsilon\sqrt{T-t} > \log\left(\frac{E}{S(t)} \right)$, or

$$\varepsilon > \frac{1}{\sigma\sqrt{T-t}}\left[\log\left(\frac{E}{S(t)} \right) - \left(r_f - q - \frac{\sigma^2}{2} \right)(T-t) \right] \Leftrightarrow \varepsilon > \varepsilon_0. \tag{14.20}$$

Defining the right-hand side of expression 14.20 as ε_0 helps rewrite equation 14.19 as

$$C(S,t) = e^{-r_f(T-t)} \int_{\varepsilon_0}^{+\infty} S(t)e^{\left(r_f - q - \frac{\sigma^2}{2}\right)(T-t) + \sigma\varepsilon\sqrt{T-t}} \frac{e^{\frac{-\varepsilon^2}{2}}}{\sqrt{2\pi}} d\varepsilon - e^{-r_f(T-t)} \int_{\varepsilon_0}^{+\infty} E \frac{e^{\frac{-\varepsilon^2}{2}}}{\sqrt{2\pi}} d\varepsilon. \tag{14.21}$$

Focusing on the first term of the right side of equation 14.21, we define the new variable w as

$$w = -\varepsilon + \sigma\sqrt{T-t}, \tag{14.22}$$

where $dw = -d\varepsilon$, and $w_0 = -\varepsilon_0 + \sigma\sqrt{T-t}$. Using equation 14.20 for ε_0,

$$w_0 = -\frac{1}{\sigma\sqrt{T-t}}\left[\log\left(\frac{E}{S(t)} \right) - \left(r_f - q - \frac{\sigma^2}{2} \right)(T-t) \right] + \sigma(T-t), \tag{14.23}$$

and after simplifying,

$$w_0 = \frac{1}{\sigma\sqrt{T-t}}\left[\log\left(\frac{S(t)}{E} \right) + \left(r_f - q + \frac{\sigma^2}{2} \right)(T-t) \right] \triangleq d_1. \tag{14.24}$$

Furthermore,

$$e^{-\frac{\sigma^2}{2}(T-t) + \sigma\varepsilon\sqrt{T-t} + \frac{-\varepsilon^2}{2}} = e^{-\frac{\sigma^2}{2}(T-t) + \sigma(-w + \sigma\sqrt{T-t})\sqrt{T-t} + \frac{-(w^2 - 2w\sigma\sqrt{T-t} + \sigma^2(T-t))}{2}} = e^{\frac{-w^2}{2}} \tag{14.25}$$

Combining equations 14.22, 14.23, 14.24, and 14.25 into the first term of the right side of equation 14.21 produces

$$C(S,t) = S(t)e^{-q(T-t)} \int_{-\infty}^{d_1} \frac{e^{\frac{-w^2}{2}}}{\sqrt{2\pi}} dw - e^{-r_f(T-t)} E \int_{\varepsilon_0}^{+\infty} \frac{e^{\frac{-\varepsilon^2}{2}}}{\sqrt{2\pi}} d\varepsilon. \tag{14.26}$$

For the second term of the right side of the equation, we define

$$k = -\varepsilon, \tag{14.27}$$

with $dk = -d\varepsilon$, and

$$k_0 = -\varepsilon_0 = d_1 - \sigma\sqrt{T-t} \triangleq d_2. \tag{14.28}$$

Substituting equation 14.27 and equation 14.28 into equation 14.26 leads to

$$C(S,t) = S(t)e^{-q(T-t)} \int_{-\infty}^{d_1} \frac{e^{\frac{-w^2}{2}}}{\sqrt{2\pi}} dw - e^{-r_f(T-t)} E \int_{-\infty}^{d_2} \frac{e^{\frac{-k^2}{2}}}{\sqrt{2\pi}} dk. \tag{14.29}$$

Both integrals in equation 14.29 represent cumulative normal distribution functions, N(.); therefore, we finally reach the Black-Scholes-Merton formula for the European call option price

$$C(S,t) = S(t)e^{-q(T-t)} N(d_1) - Ee^{-r_f(T-t)} N(d_2). \tag{14.30}$$

14.6.2 Black-Scholes-Merton European Put Option Price Formula

The Black-Scholes-Merton European put option price can be derived in a similar manner. The only difference would be the boundary (initial) condition for the European put option as *Put(S, T) = E − S(T)*, with the stock price at *T* being less than the exercise price. The rest of the derivation would follow suit as

$$dPut(S,t) = \left(\frac{\partial Put}{\partial S}(r_f - q)S + \frac{\partial Put}{\partial t} + \frac{1}{2}\frac{\partial^2 Put}{\partial S^2}\sigma^2 S^2 \right) dt + \frac{\partial Put}{\partial S}\sigma S\varepsilon\sqrt{dt}. \tag{14.31}$$

To create a riskless portfolio with the stock (equation 14.9) and the put (equation 14.31), the random variable, E, needs to be eliminated. This is achieved by including one put option and $\partial Put / \partial S$ shares of the underlying stock in the portfolio. Then the combined portfolio Π is

$$\Pi = Put + \frac{\partial Put}{\partial S}S, \tag{14.32}$$

and the change in the risk-free portfolio value over the time interval dt is $r_f - q$:

$$d\Pi = (r_f - q)\Pi dt \text{ and} \tag{14.33}$$

$$dPut + \frac{\partial Put}{\partial S} dS = (r_f - q)\left(Put + \frac{\partial Put}{\partial S} S \right) dt. \tag{14.34}$$

Substituting equation 14.9 and equation 14.31 into the left side of equation 14.34 and simplifying leads to the Black-Scholes-Merton differential equation:

$$\frac{\partial Put}{\partial t} + (r_f - q) S \frac{\partial Put}{\partial S} + \frac{1}{2}\sigma^2 S^2 \frac{\partial^2 Put}{\partial S^2} = (r_f - q) Put, \tag{14.35}$$

with the boundary (initial) condition as $Put(S, T) = E - S(T)$ and with the stock price at T being less than the exercise price. With this boundary/initial condition, the put option price can be calculated as

$$Put(S,t) = e^{-r_f(T-t)} Expect_{t,S(t)}\left[E - S(T) \right], \tag{14.36}$$

where $Expect_{t,\,S(t)}$ represents expectation. Here, the stock price at expiration of the option is expressed again using equation 14.8 with $dt = T - t$

$$S(T) = S(t)e^{\left(r_f - q - \frac{\sigma^2}{2} \right)(T-t) + \sigma\varepsilon\sqrt{T-t}}.$$

The put option price in equation 14.36 involves the expectation of the normally distributed random variable, ε; hence, the expectation can be re-expressed as

$$Put(S,t) = e^{-r_f(T-t)} \int_{-\infty}^{+\infty} \left(E - S(t)e^{\left(r_f - q - \frac{\sigma^2}{2} \right)(T-t) + \sigma\varepsilon\sqrt{T-t}} \right)^{+} \frac{e^{\frac{-\varepsilon^2}{2}}}{\sqrt{2\pi}} d\varepsilon. \tag{14.37}$$

The plus sign in the power of the argument in the integral indicates that the payoff for the put option is the larger number between zero and the difference in the parenthesis. In other words, the integral in equation 14.37 is nonzero only when $\log\left(\dfrac{E}{S(t)} \right) > \left(r_f - q - \dfrac{\sigma^2}{2} \right)(T - t) + \sigma\varepsilon\sqrt{T-t}$, or

$$\varepsilon < \frac{1}{\sigma\sqrt{T-t}}\left[\log\left(\frac{E}{S(t)} \right) - \left(r_f - q - \frac{\sigma^2}{2} \right)(T-t) \right]. \tag{14.38}$$

Defining the right-hand side of expression 14.38 as ε_0 helps rewrite equation 14.37 as

$$Put(S,t) = e^{-r_f(T-t)} \int_{-\infty}^{\varepsilon_0} E \frac{e^{\frac{-\varepsilon^2}{2}}}{\sqrt{2\pi}} d\varepsilon - e^{-r_f(T-t)} \int_{-\infty}^{\varepsilon_0} S(t)e^{\left(r_f - q - \frac{\sigma^2}{2} \right)(T-t) + \sigma\varepsilon\sqrt{T-t}} \frac{e^{\frac{-\varepsilon^2}{2}}}{\sqrt{2\pi}} d\varepsilon. \tag{14.39}$$

The first term on the right side of the equation, by incorporating equation 14.28: $\varepsilon_0 = -d_2$, becomes

$$Ee^{-r_f(T-t)}N(-d_2). \tag{14.40}$$

Focusing on the second term of the right side of equation 14.39, we again introduce w from equation 14.22 as $w = -\varepsilon + \sigma\sqrt{T-t}$, where $dw = -d\varepsilon$ and $w_0 = -\varepsilon_0 + \sigma\sqrt{T-t}$:

$$w_0 = \frac{1}{\sigma\sqrt{T-t}}\left[\log\left(\frac{S(t)}{E}\right) + \left(r_f - q + \frac{\sigma^2}{2}\right)(T-t)\right] \triangleq d_1.$$

Executing the same simplifications using equations 14.22, 14.23, 14.24, and 14.25, the second term of equation 14.39 becomes

$$-S(t)e^{-q(T-t)}\int_{+\infty}^{-\varepsilon_0+\sigma\sqrt{T-t}} -\frac{e^{\frac{-w^2}{2}}}{\sqrt{2\pi}}dw = -S(t)e^{-q(T-t)}\int_{d_1}^{\infty}\frac{e^{\frac{-w^2}{2}}}{\sqrt{2\pi}}dw$$

$$= -S(t)e^{-q(T-t)}\int_{-\infty}^{-d_1}\frac{e^{\frac{-w^2}{2}}}{\sqrt{2\pi}}dw, \tag{14.41}$$

where the last equality step above is due to the symmetry of the normal distribution.

Combining equation 14.40 and equation 14.41 as the two components of the right side of equation 14.39, we get the Black-Scholes-Merton European put option price as

$$Put(S,t) = Ee^{-r_f(T-t)}N(-d_2) - S(t)e^{-q(T-t)}N(-d_1). \tag{14.42}$$

14.7 SUMMARY AND CONCLUSION

The Black-Scholes-Merton formulations for the European call and put option prices are considered to be one of the most innovative and interesting contributions to finance and to the derivatives area. The derivations use stochastic calculus, probability theory, partial differential equations, and statistical distributions. One important innovation of the derivation has been the introduction of risk-neutral transformation from the real world. The real-world return of the underlying security, μ, does not appear in this 'risk-neutral world' Black-Scholes-Merton equation. The equation is also independent of the variables affected by risk preferences.

The derivation and the solution are the same in the risk-free world and in the real world. The risk-neutral valuation assumes the expected return of the underlying security is the risk-free rate. The expected payoff of the option is calculated, then discounted to present with the risk-free rate.

At certain extreme limits, the Black-Scholes-Merton formula becomes the following:

(1) If the underlying stock price is extremely high, the call option price approaches $S(t)e^{-q(T-t)}$ $-Ee^{-r_f(T-t)}$, while the put option price approaches zero.

(2) If the underlying stock price tends to zero, the call option price approaches zero, while the put option price approaches $Ee^{-r_f(T-t)}-S(t)e^{-q(T-t)}$.

(3) If volatility gets extremely high, the call option price approaches $S(t)e^{-q(T-t)}$ and the put option price approaches $Ee^{-r_f(T-t)}$.

While the derivation of the Black-Scholes-Merton equation requires sophisticated mathematics, the application of the formulas is straightforward using Excel and V.B.A. programming. Over the years, the formulas have been modified for more accurate calculations of option prices, but the core formulas continue to be extremely popular.

REFERENCES AND ADDITIONAL READING

Black, F., Scholes, M. 1973. The Pricing of Options and Corporate Liabilities. *Journal of Political Economy*, 81, 637–654.

Bodie, Z., Kane, A., Marcus, A.J. 2021. *Investments*. 12th edition. New York, McGraw-Hill.

Hull, J.C. 2012. *Options, Futures and Other Derivatives*. 8th edition. Boston, MA, Prentice Hall.

Itô, K. 1944. Stochastic Integral. *Proceedings of the Imperial Academy*, 20, 519–524.

Itô, K. 1951a. On a Formula Concerning Stochastic Differentials. *Nagoya Mathematical Journal*, 3, 55–65.

Itô, K. 1951b. Multiple Wiener Integral. *Journal of the Mathematical Society of Japan*, 3, 157–169.

Merton, R.C. 1973. Theory of Rational Option Pricing. *Bell Journal of Economics*, 4, 141–183.

Merton, R.C. 1992. *Continuous-Time Finance*. Oxford, Basil Blackwell, Inc.

CHAPTER 15

Options

Greeks and Risk Management

OBJECTIVES

- Describe the role of option Greeks as a risk management tool in sophisticated portfolios holding derivative securities.
- Assess the functionality and limitations of option Greeks on hedging and on portfolio insurance.
- Evaluate the definitions and the practical interpretations of the core five option Greeks.
- Design detailed (but approximate) examples to intuitively clarify option Greeks.
- Compare and contrast the option Greeks among each other.
- Develop precise formulations of the option Greeks and explain the intuitive steps of the formal derivations.
- Formulate the practical use of option Greeks with accurate equations and with approximate intuitive definitions.
- Construct numerical examples to clarify the meaning and the utilization of option Greeks.

15.1 INTRODUCTION

Option Greeks are useful tools for risk management. Every option has risk components uniquely related to the variables used in the option price calculation. The Greeks measure these risk components. Learning about the risks allows investors and professionals to design correct strategies and select the best derivatives for those strategies.

Each option Greek is a formula that shows the relationship of the change in an option's value with respect to the change in a relevant parameter. That parameter is usually one that is used in the Black-Scholes-Merton formula. Overall, there are five important option Greeks: delta (Δ), gamma (Γ), vega (υ), theta (Θ), and rho (ρ). Additionally, there is a secondary group of about ten option Greeks, which further examines the risk characteristics.

DOI: 10.4324/9781003213697-15

There are different ways to introduce and calculate option Greeks. At its mathematical core, an option Greek is a partial derivative of an option's value (the formula) with respect to the specific parameter. Usually, the partial derivative is a sophisticated formula. The formula is used with the current values of the parameters in order to determine how much the option price changes when that specific parameter changes. The formula and the calculation provide the accurate, correct, and definitive result for the option Greek.

The downside of this approach is that the option Greek formulas are generally quite complex. Unless the formulas are readily available, and unless the necessary computer power is available in the form of a scientific calculator or a software program, such as Excel with customized codes, it is extremely difficult to derive the formulas and use them to calculate the values of the option Greeks.

This issue leads to an alternative way of calculating option Greeks. Since an option Greek measures how much the option value changes with respect to a change in a specific parameter, following an approximate but more intuitive approach, the option value is first calculated using the current values of the parameters. Then the parameter of interest is perturbed a little bit while the rest of the parameters are kept as before. The option value is recalculated. The difference between the recalculated option value and the original option value due to the perturbation of the parameter of interest is the approximate and intuitive option Greek.

This chapter examines the actual and complex formulas for the option Greeks. The intuitive interpretation of each option Greek is provided, along with why/how each Greek is utilized in risk management strategies. The Excel file and the custom-written function codes for each option Greek are provided so that the accurate and precise option Greek is calculated. Additionally, for each option Greek, the intuitive and approximate calculation is described.

The starting point is the Black-Scholes-Merton call and put option price formulas in all the derivations and formulas for the option Greeks:

$$C = Se^{-qT}N(d_1) - Ee^{-r_fT}N(d_2) \text{ and} \tag{15.1}$$

$$Put = Ee^{-r_fT}N(-d_2) - Se^{-qT}N(-d_1), \tag{15.2}$$

where

$$d_1 = \frac{\log(S/E) + \left(r_f - q + \sigma^2/2\right)T}{\sigma\sqrt{T}} \tag{15.3}$$

and $d_2 = d_1 - \sigma\sqrt{T}.$ \tag{15.4}

15.2 THE MOST IMPORTANT GREEK – DELTA (Δ)

The most popular option Greek is delta, which depicts the relationship between an option's price relative to the underlying security price. Therefore, delta is the partial derivative of the option price formula with respect to the underlying security. Formally,

$$\Delta_{call} = \frac{\partial C}{\partial S}, \text{ and } \Delta_{put} = \frac{\partial Put}{\partial S}. \tag{15.5}$$

The partial derivatives of the option price formulas in equation 15.1 and in equation 15.2 with respect to the underlying security price are equal to

$$\Delta_{call} = \frac{\partial C}{\partial S} = e^{-qT} N(d_1) \text{ and} \tag{15.6}$$

$$\Delta_{put} = \frac{\partial Put}{\partial S} = -e^{-qT} N(-d_1). \tag{15.7}$$

In an intuitive, back-of-the-envelope approximate approach, one can find delta as

$$\Delta_{call} = \frac{\Delta C}{\Delta S} \approx \frac{C_{|S+0.01} - C_{|S}}{0.01} \text{ and} \tag{15.8}$$

$$\Delta_{put} = \frac{\Delta Put}{\Delta S} \approx \frac{Put_{|S+0.01} - Put_{|S}}{0.01}. \tag{15.9}$$

In equations 15.8 and 15.9, the option price is calculated at the current stock price and recalculated at the current stock price plus 0.01, while all the other parameters remain same. Then the difference between the option prices is calculated in the numerator.

Delta is also known as the hedge ratio because, using the relationship between the price movements of the option and the underlying security, a risk manager can determine how many call (put) options should be used to hedge (protect), a portfolio based on the underlying security.

Since the call option price and the underlying security price are directly related and move in the same direction, the long security would be hedged with written call options. On the other hand, the put option price and the underlying security price are inversely related and move in opposite directions: if one price increases (decreases), the other price decreases (increases). Therefore, the long security would be hedged with long put options.

The next question is to determine how many options would protect the underlying security. Intuitively, one can think of options as 'little' securities when compared to the underlying security. This would imply that a larger number of options is needed to protect a certain number of the underlying security. The absolute value of delta is always less than 1 both for the call option and for the put option. This implies when the underlying security price changes, the option price does not change as much. Thus, more options are needed to counter the total value change of the underlying security.

Following the previous discussion, one can quickly deduce that the number of options necessary to hedge the underlying security would be $NumberOptions = \left| \dfrac{NumberShares}{\Delta} \right|$, where '$|.|$' stands for the absolute value. Specifically for call options and for put options,

$$NumberCalls = \left| \frac{NumberShares}{e^{-qT}N(d_1)} \right| \text{ and} \tag{15.10}$$

$$NumberPuts = \left| \frac{NumberShares}{-e^{-qT}N(-d_1)} \right|. \tag{15.11}$$

As a quick example, assuming that delta for a call option is 0.8 and that there are 1,000 shares of stock in a portfolio, the number of call options needed to be written in order to hedge the stock portfolio is *1,000 / 0.8 = 1,250.*

For a more comprehensive numerical example, consider call and put options where the underlying stock price is $100, exercise price is $95, time to maturity of the options is 6 months (0.5 years), the risk-free rate is 2%, the underlying security yield is 1%, and the volatility of the stock returns is 25%. With these parameters, we find (using the Excel file accompanying this chapter):

$C = \$9.88123157$
$Put = \$4.43471786$
$d_1 = 0.4068$
$d_2 = 0.2301$
$N(d_1) = 0.6579$
$N(d_2) = 0.5910$

The accurate and precise delta values for the call and the put from equations 15.6 and 15.7 are

$$\Delta_{call} = \frac{\partial C}{\partial S} = e^{-(0.01)(0.5)}N(0.4068) = 0.654653 \text{ and}$$

$$\Delta_{put} = \frac{\partial Put}{\partial S} = -e^{-(0.01)(0.5)}N(-0.4068) = -0.340360.$$

The intuitive calculations would involve finding the call (put) option prices when $S = 100$ and when $S = 100.01$.

$$\Delta_{call} = \frac{\Delta C}{\Delta S} \approx \frac{C_{|100.01} - C_{|100}}{0.01} = \frac{9.887779 - 9.881232}{0.01} = 0.654756$$

$$\Delta_{put} \approx \frac{Put_{|100.01} - Put_{|100}}{0.01} = \frac{(4.4313 - 4.4347)}{0.01} = -0.340256$$

There is not much difference between the actual and approximate delta values. The approximate calculation should not be ignored, especially when the actual formulas are not readily available.

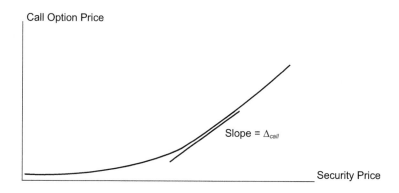

FIGURE 15.1 Graphical Interpretation of Delta

There are two final points to mention about delta. First, sometimes the relationship between the option price change with respect to the underlying security price change is expressed as a percentage. The option Greek for that is referred to as lambda (or omega) as the percentage change in the option price with respect to a percentage change in the underlying security price. For a call option, lambda is $\lambda_{call} = \dfrac{\partial C / C}{\partial S / S} = \left(\dfrac{\partial C}{\partial S}\right)\left(\dfrac{S}{C}\right) = \Delta\left(\dfrac{S}{C}\right)$. Lambda for a put option is also a similar expression. Second, the visual interpretation in Figure 15.1 demonstrates delta as the slope or the tangent of the graph of the option price function against the underlying security price. Given that the smooth option price diagram roughly resembles and just stays above the payoff diagram, delta approaches '1' ('0') for security prices significantly higher (lower) than the exercise price.

15.3 GAMMA (Γ) – FOR THE DYNAMIC HEDGE RATIO

Hedging is a popular risk management strategy among professional investors, investment companies, pension funds, insurance companies, and multinational corporations. After designing sophisticated optimized portfolios, risk managers wish to protect these portfolios against unexpected price movements. Options are used with the proper hedge ratios to provide protection against such shifts.

However, financial markets are dynamic, and as markets conditions, security prices, and option prices change constantly, so do deltas and hedge ratios. This means the number of options necessary for the protection of a portfolio continually changes. For proper risk management, the hedge ratio and the number of necessary options need to be updated regularly. Because of transaction costs, the updates should only be done when there are substantial changes in delta and the hedge ratio. The questions then are how quickly and substantially delta changes and how to measure it.

The second option Greek, gamma (Γ), measures how quickly delta changes. A large gamma value for an option would indicate that a risk management strategy utilizing that option would have to be updated more frequently than a hedging strategy using an option with a lower gamma value. By definition, gamma is the second partial derivative of the option price formula with respect to the underlying security price and shows how much delta changes as the value of the underlying security changes. Using an analogy from physics, if delta is velocity, then gamma would be acceleration. The mathematical derivation for gamma is the same formula for both the call and the put:

$$\Gamma_{call} = \frac{\partial^2 C}{\partial S^2} = \frac{e^{-\left(qT + \frac{d_1^2}{2}\right)}}{S\sigma\sqrt{2\pi T}} \tag{15.12}$$

$$\Gamma_{put} = \frac{\partial^2 Put}{\partial S^2} = \frac{e^{-\left(qT + \frac{d_1^2}{2}\right)}}{S\sigma\sqrt{2\pi T}} \tag{15.13}$$

The approximate way to find gamma would be to calculate the difference between two delta values: one delta at the current underlying security price $+ 0.01$ and the other at the current underlying security price:

$$\Gamma_{call} \approx \frac{\Delta_{call|S+0.01} - \Delta_{call|S}}{0.01} = \frac{\frac{C_{|S+0.02} - C_{|S+0.01}}{0.01} - \frac{C_{|S+0.01} - C_{|S}}{0.01}}{0.01} \tag{15.14}$$

$$\Gamma_{put} \approx \frac{\frac{Put_{|S+0.02} - Put_{|S+0.01}}{0.01} - \frac{Put_{|S+0.01} - Put_{|S}}{0.01}}{0.01} \tag{15.15}$$

Following up on the earlier numerical example, the correct gamma value from equation 15.12 and equation 15.13 for the call and put is

$$\Gamma_{call} = \Gamma_{put} = \frac{e^{-\left((0.01)(0.5) + \frac{0.4068^2}{2}\right)}}{(100)(0.25)\sqrt{2\pi(0.5)}} = 0.020672 \cdot$$

The intuitive approximate calculation using equation 15.14 and equation 15.15 provide

$$\Gamma_{call} \approx \frac{\frac{9.89432876 - 9.88777913}{0.01} - \frac{9.88777913 - 9.88123157}{0.01}}{0.01} = 0.020700 \text{ and}$$

$$\Gamma_{put} \approx \frac{\frac{4.4279148 - 4.4313153}{0.01} - \frac{4.4313153 - 4.43471786}{0.01}}{0.01} = 0.020600 \cdot$$

Again, the approximations are quite close to the actual values, but we note that the option prices need to be more *precise* (with a higher number of decimal places) for the *accuracy* (closeness to the correct value) of gamma.

Finally, the gamma value of an option is highest when the option is at the money (the underlying security price is equal to the exercise price of the option). This is the region of the option price graph in Figure 15.1 where the slope (delta, or hedge ratio) varies a lot as the underlying security price changes. For deep in-the-money options, the delta (slope) is close to '1' and does not change much as the underlying price changes. Similarly, for deep out-the-money options, the delta (slope) is close to '0' and does not change as the underlying price changes. Thus, gamma is close to '0' for in-the-money and out-of-money options.

When trying to decide which options to utilize for risk management, gamma provides a great additional perspective. Options with lower gamma values would have a lower rate of change in the hedge ratio, requiring fewer adjustments or updates in the number of options, saving transaction costs.

15.4 THETA (Θ) – TIME TO MATURITY (T)

The third option Greek, theta (Θ), is about how much the option price changes as time-to-maturity nears. In other words, theta measures the rate of change in the option value as time goes by. For many options (though not for all), the value declines as the time to maturity nears, so theta is usually negative. Indeed, as the expiration date nears for an option where the underlying security price and return volatility remain stable, the price of the call/put option decreases. Therefore, theta is also known as time decay. Formally, theta is

$$\Theta_{call} = \frac{\partial C}{\partial T}, \text{ and } \Theta_{put} = \frac{\partial Put}{\partial T}. \tag{15.16}$$

The partial derivatives of the Black-Scholes-Merton call/put option price formulas with respect to time-to-maturity are equal to the following accurate expressions:

$$\Theta_{call} = \frac{\partial C}{\partial T} = -\frac{S\sigma e^{-qT-(0.5)d_1^2}}{2\sqrt{2\pi T}} + qSe^{-qT}N(d_1) - rEe^{-rT}N(d_2) \tag{15.17}$$

$$\Theta_{put} = \frac{\partial Put}{\partial T} = -\frac{S\sigma e^{-qT-(0.5)d_1^2}}{2\sqrt{2\pi T}} - qSe^{-qT}\left(1-N(d_1)\right) + rEe^{-rT}\left(1-N(d_2)\right) \tag{15.18}$$

These theta values are based on the instantaneous change in time-to-maturity in years. In the approximate approach, theta is calculated as the difference between the option price one time-step closer to maturity and the current option price and then divided by that time-step expressed in years. As an example, the 1-day time step is 1/252 years (since most volatility takes place during business days, the year is assumed to be 252, or 250 business days), and the approximate theta is

$$\Theta_{call} \approx \frac{C_{|T-1day} - C_{|T}}{(1/252)} \text{ and} \tag{15.19}$$

$$\Theta_{put} \approx \frac{Put_{|T-1day} - Put_{|T}}{(1/252)}. \tag{15.20}$$

Of course, ideally, in these approximate calculations, the goal should be to use as small a time step as possible (such as a second) to get the theta value get closer to the correct theta in equations 15.17 and 15.18. However, 1 day is considered as the intuitive time increment.

Using the earlier numerical example, the correct theta values for the call and the put option from equation 15.17 and equation 15.18 are

$$\Theta_{call} = -\frac{(100)(0.25)e^{-(0.01)(0.5)-(0.5)(0.4068)^2}}{2\sqrt{2\pi0.5}} + (0.01)(100)e^{-(0.01)(0.5)}(0.6579)$$

$$-(0.02)(95)e^{-(0.02)(0.5)}(0.5910) = -6.916889 \ and$$

$$\Theta_{put} = -\frac{(100)(0.25)e^{-(0.01)(0.5)-(0.5)(0.4068)^2}}{2\sqrt{2\pi0.5}} - (0.01)(100)e^{-(0.01)(0.5)}(1-0.6579)$$

$$+(0.02)(95)e^{-(0.02)(0.5)}(1-0.5910) = -6.030807.$$

These results mean that the call option will lose roughly $6.92 per year, or lose $0.02745 (=6.92/252) per day. Similarly, the time decay in the put option is $6.03 per year, or $0.02393 (=6.03/252) per day.

The intuitive approximate calculations of theta with the original 126 days to maturity and with 125 days to maturity using equations 15.19 and 15.20 are quite close to the correct values:

$$\Theta_{call} \approx \frac{9.85373400 - 9.88123157}{1/252} = -6.929388 \ and$$

$$\Theta_{put} \approx \frac{4.41073671 - 4.43471786}{1/252} = -6.043250.$$

From theta point of view exclusively, having long positions in options usually hurts. The option holder suffers the loss in the time decay in theta, while the writer benefits.

As final points, looking at the formulas for theta, one can deduce that, first, an option with a long time to maturity has a lower theta compared to an option with a shorter time to maturity, especially when measured for one day to the next. Second, for at-the-money call and put options, theta tends to be the highest/severest. Finally, higher volatility is associated with larger theta values. Higher volatility makes options more valuable. The extra value in excess of the option payoff is larger with volatility; as a consequence, the time decay for the option is higher.

15.5 VEGA (υ) – VOLATILITY OF UNDERLYING SECURITY

The fourth option Greek is vega (υ), which measures the sensitivity of the option's value to the volatility of the underlying security. In general, as volatility and uncertainty increase (decrease), so do the value of the call option and the value of the put option. How quickly do these changes occur? The answer is provided by vega. Formally, vega is the partial derivative of the option price formula with respect to the volatility of the underlying security, σ:

$$\upsilon_{call} = \frac{\partial C}{\partial \sigma}, \text{ and } \upsilon_{put} = \frac{\partial Put}{\partial \sigma}. \tag{15.20}$$

It is interesting to note that there is actually no such Greek letter called vega. The symbol used here, υ, is actually called *nu*. However, because the shape looks like v, related to volatility, this option Greek has the name vega. The mathematical derivations provide the same formula for the call and the put:

$$\upsilon_{call} = \frac{\partial C}{\partial \sigma} = \frac{S\sqrt{T}e^{-qT-0.5d_1^2}}{(100)\sqrt{2\pi}} \tag{15.21}$$

$$\upsilon_{put} = \frac{\partial Put}{\partial \sigma} = \frac{S\sqrt{T}e^{-qT-0.5d_1^2}}{(100)\sqrt{2\pi}} \tag{15.22}$$

The unit for vega is the currency amount per percentage. In other words, the change in volatility is expressed in the denominator as its percentage value. That is why vega formulas in equation 15.21 and equation 15.22 have 100 in the denominator.

The approximate way to find vega would be to calculate the difference between two option values: one option at the current volatility + 1 basis point and the other at the current volatility. The difference is divided by 1 basis point expressed as a percentage:

$$\upsilon_{call} \approx \frac{C_{|\sigma+1bp} - C_{|\sigma}}{(100)1bp} \tag{15.23}$$

$$\upsilon_{put} \approx \frac{Put_{|\sigma+1bp} - Put_{|\sigma}}{(100)1bp} \tag{15.24}$$

Traditionally, the increase in volatility is taken as 1% in these approximations, but using 1 basis point as the increase in volatility would lead to a more accurate result.

Using the earlier numerical example, the correct vega value for the call option and for the put option from either equation 15.21 or equation 15.22 is

$$\upsilon_{call} = \upsilon_{put} = \frac{100\sqrt{0.5}e^{-(0.01)(0.5)-(0.5)\left(0.4068^2\right)}}{(100)\sqrt{2\pi}} = 0.25839445.$$

These results mean that the call option or the put option will gain \$0.25839445 if the volatility increases by 1 basis point.

The intuitive approximate calculations of vega with original volatility of 25% and increased volatility of 25.01% from equations 15.23 and 15.24 are again close to the correct values:

$$\upsilon_{call} \approx \frac{9.88381557 - 9.88123157}{(100)0.0001} = 0.2584$$

$$\upsilon_{put} \approx \frac{4.437330185 - 4.43471786}{(100)0.0001} = 0.2612325$$

Finally, vega is most pronounced for options that are at the money. For an out-of-money or in-the-money option, the impact of volatility change on the option value is lower. In fact, the deeper the option is in-the-money (out-of-money), the lower the vega.

15.6 RHO (ρ) – RISK-FREE RATE IN THE ECONOMY

The fifth major option Greek is called rho (ρ), and it measures the sensitivity of the option's value to interest rate movements in the economy. It has been documented that option prices are least sensitive to interest rate changes compared to the other variables on which option Greeks have been constructed. Therefore, rho is considered less important among the five option Greeks. Formally, rho is defined as

$$\rho_{call} = \frac{\partial C}{\partial r_f} \text{ and } \rho_{put} = \frac{\partial Put}{\partial r_f}. \tag{15.25}$$

The partial derivatives of the Black-Scholes-Merton call and put option prices with respect to the risk-free rate are equal to

$$\rho_{call} = \frac{\partial C}{\partial r_f} = ETe^{-r_f T} N(d_2) / (100) \text{ and} \tag{15.26}$$

$$\rho_{put} = \frac{\partial Put}{\partial r_f} = -ETe^{-r_f T} \left(1 - N(d_2)\right) / (100). \tag{15.27}$$

As with vega, the unit for rho is the currency amount per percentage. In other words, the change in the risk-free rate is expressed as its percentage value in the denominator. That is why equation 15.26 and equation 15.27 have 100 in the denominator.

The approximate way to find rho is to calculate the difference between the option value at the current risk-free rate + 1 basis point and the option value at the current risk-free rate. This difference is divided by 1 basis point, but the denominator is expressed as a percentage:

$$\rho_{call} \approx \frac{C_{|r_f + 1bp} - C_{|r_f}}{(100)1bp} \tag{15.28}$$

$$\rho_{put} \approx \frac{Put_{|r_f + 1bp} - Put_{|r_f}}{(100)1bp} \tag{15.29}$$

Traditionally the increase in the risk-free rate is 1% in the approximations, but using 1 basis point as the increase in the risk-free rate provides a more accurate result.

The earlier numerical example generates the rho value for the call option from equation 15.26 and for the put option from equation 15.27 as

$$\rho_{call} = (95)(0.5)e^{-(0.02)(0.5)}(0.5910) / (100) = 0.27792014$$

$$\rho_{put} = -(95)(0.5)e^{-(0.02)(0.5)}\left(1-(0.5910)\right)/(100) = -0.1924$$

The results indicate that as the risk-free rate in the economy changes by one unit (1 basis point), the call option price increases by \$0.28, and the put option price decreases by \$0.19.

The intuitive but approximate results of changing the interest rate from 2% to 2.01% from equations 15.28 and 15.29 are close to the correct ρ values.

$$\rho_{call} \approx \frac{9.88401096 - 9.88123157}{(100)0.0001} = 0.277939, \text{ and}$$

$$\rho_{put} \approx \frac{4.43279463 - 4.43471786}{(100)0.0001} = -0.192323.$$

Normally, interest rate changes have the least effect on option prices compared to other parameters used in the calculation of option prices. However, significant changes in interest rates are vital. When central banks of governments meet over the new interest rate policy, options investors should pay close attention. Owners (writers) of call (put) options will enjoy an interest rate increase decision, while writers (owners) of call (put) options will suffer from rate increases.

15.7 OTHER OPTION GREEKS

The five option Greeks explored thus far are the most popular among practitioners, academicians, and professional investors. However, there are many more option Greeks that have been developed over the years. Depending on the investment strategy or goal, a specific option Greek may be of significant interest. The remaining group of secondary option Greeks is reviewed only with brief definitions in this section (except for epsilon, the change in the option value as the yield of the underlying security changes).

15.7.1 Epsilon (ε) – Yield of the Underlying Security

The yield of the underlying security is defined as a continuous-time variable according to Merton's extension in the Black-Scholes-Merton formula. Following this approach, the partial derivative of the option price with respect to the yield of the underlying security (dividend yield for the stock, average dividend yield for the stock index, foreign risk-free rate for the currency, or domestic risk-free rate, r_f, for the futures) leads to

$$\varepsilon_{call} = \frac{\partial C}{\partial q} = -STe^{-qT}N(d_1) / (100) \text{ and} \tag{15.26}$$

$$\varepsilon_{put} = \frac{\partial Put}{\partial q} = STe^{-qT}\left(1-N(d_1)\right)/(100). \tag{15.27}$$

Here, the equations are for the price change in the option when the yield changes a certain percentage. That percentage change should be multiplied (without expressing it as a decimal) with the epsilon value to determine the change in the value of the option.

15.7.2 Second-Order Option Greeks

The majority of the remaining option Greeks are based on the second-order partial derivatives of the option prices with respect to the parameters used in the Black-Scholes-Merton formulas. These option Greeks explore further how the parameter impacts the option price. Many of the names of the option Greeks are actually not real Greek letters. They have been picked as consensus from researchers, practitioners, and academicians over time.

Charm is the partial derivative of delta with respect to time-to-maturity and measures how much delta changes (the sensitivity of the option price with respect to the underlying security price) with respect to time-to-maturity. *Vanna* is the partial derivative of delta with respect to volatility and measures the change in delta with respect to the volatility of the underlying security returns. *Vomma* is the second-order partial derivative of the option price with respect to the volatility of the underlying security returns. In other words, vomma is the partial derivative of vega with respect to volatility and measures how much vega changes as volatility changes. *Vera* is the partial derivative of rho with respect to volatility and measures how much rho changes as the volatility of the underlying security changes. *Veta* is the partial derivative of theta with respect to the volatility of the underlying security. These five second-order partial derivatives are used more frequently than other second-order derivatives or third-order derivatives of option prices with respect to the parameters in the Black-Scholes Merton formula.

15.8 HEDGING WITH MULTIPLE OPTION GREEKS

Risk management of a portfolio from multiple perspectives can be achieved using several different options. In section 15.2, delta hedging with an option was explored. In this example here, additional hedging for portfolios is demonstrated by utilizing multiple options.

Consider a portfolio consisting of long 500 calls (A) with delta 0.5, gamma 1.8, vega 0.018, and long 1,000 puts (B) with delta -0.3, gamma 1.5, and vega 0.016, respectively. There are also 250 shares of stock in this portfolio, which is the underlying security for these options. Delta for a long share of stock is always 1.

The option Greeks for the portfolio are

$$\Delta = (500)(0.5) + (1000)(-0.3) + (250)(1) = 200 ,$$

$$\Gamma = (500)(1.8) + (1000)(1.5) + (250)(0) = 2400 , and$$

$$\upsilon = (500)(0.018) + (1000)(0.016) + (250)(0) = 25 .$$

Now let's assume that in the options market, there are two different actively traded call options with the following option Greeks: call 1 with delta 0.48, gamma 1.6, vega 0.03, theta -3, and rho 0.008, and call 2 with delta 0.52, gamma 1.9, vega 0.025, theta -3.2, and rho 0.009.

For this portfolio, delta neutrality can be achieved by shorting 200 shares of stock. As a second, independent question, for gamma and delta neutrality using the first traded option, call 1, we start with gamma neutrality by shorting $2400 / 1.6 = 1{,}500$ call 1 options. This makes delta become $200 + (-1500)(0.48) = -520$. Delta neutrality is achieved with the additional long position of 520 stock shares. Finally, as the third independent question, for delta, gamma, and vega neutrality, we use both traded options and determine their trading numbers from the two-equation system for gamma and vega:

$2400 + (1.6)(x_1) + (1.9)(x_2) = 0$
$25 + (0.03)(x_1) + (0.025)(x_2) = 0$

We can get the answer using matrix algebra in Excel:

$$\begin{bmatrix} 1.6 & 1.9 \\ 0.03 & 0.025 \end{bmatrix}\begin{bmatrix} x_1 \\ x_2 \end{bmatrix} = \begin{bmatrix} -2400 \\ -25 \end{bmatrix} \Rightarrow \begin{bmatrix} x_1 \\ x_2 \end{bmatrix} = \begin{bmatrix} 1.6 & 1.9 \\ 0.03 & 0.025 \end{bmatrix}^{-1}\begin{bmatrix} -2400 \\ -25 \end{bmatrix} \Rightarrow \begin{bmatrix} x_1 \\ x_2 \end{bmatrix} = \begin{bmatrix} 735 \\ -1882 \end{bmatrix}.$$

Buying 735 call 1 options and writing 1,882 call 2 options will achieve gamma and vega neutrality, but the delta of the portfolio is now $200 + (735)(0.48) + (-1882)(0.52) = -425.8$. Therefore, in the final step of delta neutrality, 426 shares of stock should be purchased. Further risk management with more option Greek neutrality is possible using other traded options.

15.9 SUMMARY AND CONCLUSION

One fundamental reason options are used by multinational enterprises, companies, and professional investors is risk management. Controlling the risk exposure, hedging, and risk reduction of a portfolio is possible by incorporating options into that existing portfolio. Greeks help measure different perspectives of risk exposure. Options are then used to minimize the risk exposure to that perspective with the help of these option Greeks.

The most popular option Greeks are delta, which is about the relationship between the option and underlying security prices; gamma, the change in delta as the security price changes; vega, the impact of underlying security volatility on the option price; theta, the time impact on the option price; and rho, the interest rate impact on the option price. Either these relationships are mathematically accurately derived with partial derivatives or they can be found approximately, as explored in the chapter. There are additional option Greeks calculated to measure the sensitivity of the popular option Greeks to other parameters. Some of them were defined in the chapter. Finally, the utilization of option Greeks for risk management and hedging neutrality are demonstrated with examples.

REFERENCES AND ADDITIONAL READING

Black, F., Scholes, M. 1973. The Pricing of Options and Corporate Liabilities. *Journal of Political Economy*, 81, 637–654.

Bodie, Z., Kane, A., Marcus, A.J. 2021. *Investments*. 12th edition. New York, McGraw-Hill.

Hull, J.C. 2012. *Options, Futures and Other Derivatives*. 8th edition. Boston, MA, Prentice Hall.

Merton, R.C. 1971. Optimum Consumption and Portfolio Rules in a Continuous-Time Model. *Journal of Economic Theory*, 3, 373–413.

Merton, R.C. 1973. Theory of Rational Option Pricing. *Bell Journal of Economics*, 4, 141–183.

CHAPTER 16

Forwards and Futures

OBJECTIVES

- Illustrate the characteristics of forwards and futures as derivative financial securities.
- Compare and contrast futures and forwards.
- Appraise the history of the futures and the markets where futures contracts are traded.
- Formulate different types of futures contracts and distinguish the reasons behind investing in futures rather than in the actual underlying securities.
- Construct and develop the relationship between the spot value of the underlying security and the futures contract price through the spot-futures parity theorem.
- Assemble the conditions for normal backwardation and for contango.
- Design examples, representative frictions, and practical applications utilizing futures contracts.

16.1 INTRODUCTION

Forwards and futures are financial securities that are essentially contracts to be fulfilled at a specific future point in time, called the maturity date or the expiration date of the contract. The contract specifies this maturity date, what will be exchanged, between whom (the buyer and the seller), and at what price. The contract price is the futures/forward price. The buyer at maturity is known to have a long position in the contract, and the seller at maturity is said to have a short position in the contract.

Forwards/futures are derivative securities because the contract price – that is, the forward or the futures price is derived from the current spot price of the underlying security – the asset that will be exchanged between the traders at the maturity of the contract.

Studies have consistently shown that the relationship between the futures/forward price and the spot price of the security is highly correlated. Potential investors of the underlying

DOI: 10.4324/9781003213697-16

securities on which futures/forward contracts are written can follow one of two routes: they can either directly invest in the underlying securities, or they can take similar positions in the futures contracts agreeing to pay/receive the futures price at maturity to get/sell the security. As time progresses, the correlation between the futures returns and spot returns remains highly positively correlated. Although this correlation is not perfect and there are dynamic variations, many investors prefer to invest in futures rather than actual assets, which are generally difficult to keep/store. Typical assets in futures contracts are energy items (different grades of oil, natural gas, electricity, etc.), food (corn, wheat, beef, pork, etc.), precious materials (gold, silver, platinum, etc.), and others.

This chapter examines the core subjects of futures and forwards, such as the history of futures/forward contracts, futures exchanges around the world, over-the-counter markets and computer networks, similarities and differences between forwards and futures, the spot-futures parity theorem used to determine futures prices, and contango and normal backwardation characteristics of futures and spot prices.

16.2 HISTORY OF FUTURES/FORWARDS

Even though the interest in derivative products has increased tremendously since the mid-1970s in terms of trading volume and demand for variety, the history actually goes back all the way to the mid-1800s to forward contracts in the Midwest, more specifically in Chicago. Midwest states are the main agriculture production regions of the U.S. Agricultural production is naturally impacted significantly by environmental conditions such as droughts, floods, soil quality or erosion, and rain or scarcity of it. Farmers have always been nervous about these climate conditions since their livelihoods have depended on them. The purchasers of agricultural products (cereal producers, grocery store chains, supermarket representatives) have had similar anxieties as well. There had been an organic desire on the part of both producers and buyers to reduce the uncertainties about agricultural yields and the consequent prices of the products for the next harvest season. This desire started to bring together the farmers and the buyers in Chicago to sign agreements about the price and the quantity of each agricultural product for the next year's harvest. In these contracts, the sellers and buyers would specify ahead of time what would be exchanged (the underlying security, such as corn), at what price, and when. These contracts would be known as forwards. They can be considered as the original derivatives because the value of these contracts depended on the environmental conditions and on the spot values of the underlying securities.

The location of exchange was naturally Chicago because most of the agricultural production in the Midwest states would find its way to Chicago via railroads or river transports. The agreements would be created and honored in Chicago, the products would be traded there, and then, from Chicago, they would be distributed all over the country and even the world through the Great Lakes waterways.

Such forward contracts became ubiquitous in the 1840s and led to the establishment of the Chicago Board of Trade for grain products in 1848. This was followed by the Chicago Produce Exchange for dairy products, such as eggs and butter in 1874. As the underlying securities in these contracts became widespread, the Chicago Mercantile Exchange was formed in 1919.

Over the decades, the contracts started to have more formalized features, such as the size of the underlying asset and the date of the maturity of the contract. With these set features and established trading exchanges, it became possible for a position-holder of a contract to rid of ('sell') the contract to someone else. These types of contracts with standardized features and characteristics are actually called futures contracts, while forward contracts are known as private agreements between buyers and sellers with unique characteristics. Needless to say, these contracts have helped traders and investors enormously with their risk management strategies.

Over time, derivative products other than forwards and futures started to appear, such as options, swaps, real-estate-based structured products, and other alternatives. These types of securities are generally introduced to satisfy the unique need or desire of an investment client. If the security is well-received by a wider group of investment participants, then it becomes a mainstream security for trading purposes.

16.3 FUTURES EXCHANGES

Chicago has been the main physical location for futures/forwards exchanges. The Chicago Mercantile Exchange (C.M.E.) (non-agricultural futures) and the Chicago Board of Trade (agricultural futures) merged in 2006 to create the largest physical exchange for futures trading: the Chicago Mercantile Exchange Group (C.M.E. Group). With the inclusion of the New York Mercantile Exchange and Commodity Exchange, the C.M.E. Group has become the largest marketplace for futures trading. Internationally, Eurex (E-X) in Frankfurt, Germany; London International Financial Futures Exchange (L.I.F.F.E.); Brazilian Mercantile and Futures Exchange in Sao Paulo, Brazil; Tokyo International Financial Futures Exchange (T.I.F.F.E.); and Hong Kong Futures Exchange (H.K.E.X.) are other important futures exchanges.

The second medium of trading derivative securities is through over-the-counter markets. Counters refer to computer terminals these days; therefore, this trading mechanism is essentially a computer trading network. These networks are not directly accessible to individual traders. Some of these electronic trading networks are limited only to traders working for banks, fund managers, and corporate treasurers, who can contact each other directly. Other electronic networks, such as Globex, are more accessible to all the major brokerage firms (and, therefore, indirectly to regular investors).

These trading platforms operate simultaneously. For example, Globex electronic trading continues 24 hours a day. On the other hand, the open outcry system in Chicago is from 10:30 a.m. to 2:15 p.m., eastern time, and overlaps the Globex electronic trading during that period.

16.4 FORWARDS VERSUS FUTURES – SIMILARITIES AND DIFFERENCES

Both forwards and futures are contracts about the future delivery of an asset. There are three key pieces of information on these contracts. The first is about what will be traded. This is the underlying asset. The second is about the contract execution date, which is also known as the maturity date of the contract. The third, and perhaps the most important, is the price at which the trade will be executed on that maturity date, known as the forward/futures price.

These three pieces of information in the contract are agreed on by the parties to the trade, and the contract is signed. The party who commits to buy the underlying asset is known to have a *long position* in the contract. This trader is the buyer/holder of the contract. The counterparty who commits to sell the underlying asset is said to have a *short position* in the contract. This trader is also assumed to have sold the contract.

Forward contracts are generally private agreements, and the three key pieces of information can be anything that the traders agree on. The underlying security in the forward contract is unique and is of interest to only a few investors. For example, the forward contract can be about an antique car to be exchanged in five years for €40,000. Forward contracts are highly *illiquid*; they are not easy to get out of once committed; there is no secondary market.

Futures contracts, on the other hand, are of significant interest to a wide variety of investors all around the world because of the popularity of and demand for the underlying securities. These underlying assets are agricultural commodities, precious materials, and financial securities (indexes, currencies, interest rates). The maturity date and the size of the underlying assets are standardized in the contracts. The standardization makes futures contracts easy to trade in liquid and active secondary markets. Whether it is the over-the-counter Globex computer network or the physical exchange, trading volume is high. Most traders participate for the monetary outcome of their transactions rather than the actual delivery of the underlying asset. In fact, traders only exchange the actual underlying asset in 2% of the transactions. Most long positions are canceled out with an additional opposite short position on or just before the original maturity, leading to a realization of the monetary profit or loss.

Participating in futures trading is encouraged by futures exchanges. When an initial position is taken, minimal funding is required from the trader. The contract price or the spot price of the underlying asset might be substantial, but only a fraction of that amount, around 5% of the contract size, is needed (the specific requirement depends on the length of the relationship between the trader and the brokerage firm). This is called the initial margin, and it is deposited into the account of the futures trader. As the futures price on similar contracts changes during the day and day-after-day, those futures price changes are taken into account with a daily process called marking to market. For example, if the futures price increases (decreases), the long position holder of the original contract will be happy (unhappy) since the original contract allows them to buy at a lower (higher) futures price. This advantage, the profit (disadvantage, loss) is reflected in the account of the trader. If the funds in the trader's account go below a low threshold (maintenance margin), the trader will be contacted (margin call) to increase the funding in the account. If this request is not complied with, the account will be confiscated from the trader.

The low initial margins in futures enable traders to take substantially large positions even with limited funds. Futures exchanges encourage participants to take speculative positions so that the trades initiated by hedgers are met with by these speculators. Small initial margins and the ease of low-rate loans from futures exchanges enable traders to take huge positions in the contracts. If the prices move in favorable directions, the trader ends up with substantial profits. But if prices move against the trader, enormous losses are incurred. This means futures are extremely risky financial securities; in fact, they are the riskiest financial securities among bonds, stocks, and options.

For example, consider a trader with a long position in a gold futures contract where the contract size is 100 ounces and the futures price is $1,800 per ounce. The futures contract is worth $180,000. The trader deposits 5% of this amount, $9,000, into the account. The next day, similar futures contracts have a futures price of $1,805 per ounce. The futures contract is now worth $500 more. This advantage or profit is marked-to-market and is reflected in the account of the trader with a $500 deposit, raising the balance to $9,500.

Let us assume that when the contract maturity date arrives, the futures price on the contract (also the spot price of gold at that time) is $1,700. The contract value at maturity is $170,000. The trader has never been really interested in buying the gold. Instead, the trader engaged in the futures transaction to reap monetary benefits from the belief about gold price movements. Thus, on the maturity date, the trader engages in an additional reverse futures transaction, a short position in gold futures (100 ounces) at the futures price of $1,700 per ounce.

The belief of the trader was that gold would become more valuable during the investment period. That is why the trader had a long (buy) position in the futures contract at the beginning. But the opposite materialized: the gold price has declined. Then, including the offsetting transaction, the trader buys 100 ounces of gold at $1,800 per ounce and, at the same time, sells 100 ounces of gold at $1,700 per ounce. The result is a $10,000 loss. The trader had to commit $9,000 to enter into this futures transaction. That commitment is totally wiped out, and additionally, the trader loses $1,000. Overall, this example demonstrates the significant risks involved in futures trading. Novice traders should be extremely cautious in participating in futures markets.

16.5 SPOT-FUTURES PARITY THEOREM – FUTURES/FORWARD PRICE

The forward/futures price is the most important of the three pieces of information in the contract (the other two are the maturity date of the contract and the underlying security that is to be exchanged). It is often an area of tough negotiation to decide the forward price between the traders.

The determination of the *fair* forward/futures price is through the spot-futures parity theorem. The intuitive justification of the theorem involves two investment strategies, both with the goal of possessing an asset at some future point, T years ahead. The first strategy is to buy the asset right at time 0 at the spot price, S_0. This way, when the future date T arrives, the investor possesses the asset worth S_T at that time. The second strategy is to enter into a futures contract for the asset to be delivered at time T for the price of F_0 to be paid at that T, agreed and signed at time 0. In anticipation of the need for cash of F_0 when the contract maturity date arrives, the investor deposits the present value of this amount, $F_0/(1+r_f)^T$, to a financial institution to earn at the guaranteed risk-free rate, r_f. When the contract maturity date arrives, the investors collect the accumulated F_0 from the banking institution and use it to get the asset worth S_T. Both strategies lead to the same outcome, the possession of the asset worth S_T at the future time T. Thus, the cost of both of these strategies must be equal to each other from the no-arbitrage condition. This would mean $F_0/(1+r_f)^T = S_0$ or, equivalently, $F_0 = S_0(1+r_f)^T$.

The formal derivation of the spot-futures parity theorem considers continuous-time finance and some additional frictions. With continuous compounding, the futures price is

$$F_0 = S_0 e^{\left(r_f + sc - q - cy\right)T},$$
(16.1)

where F_0 is the fair and correct futures price signed on the contract; S_0 is the current spot price of the underlying security to be exchanged in the contract; r_f is the prevailing risk-free interest rate in the economy; sc is the storage costs if the underlying security were held by the purchaser throughout the duration of the contract; q is the yield of the underlying security; cy is the convenience yield – the potential advantages of having the underlying security throughout the duration of the contract; and T is the maturity of the contract expressed in years.

Equation 16.1 implies that a high interest rate, r_f, increases the gap between the spot price and the futures price: the futures price is higher. The yield of the security, q, and the convenience yield of the security, cy, represents the advantages of having the *actual* security. Thus, these parameters reduce the value of the futures contract: the futures price is lower. Finally, storage costs, sc, represent the difficulties of having the actual security throughout the contract duration, which makes the futures contract attractive: the futures price is higher.

The length of the contract, T, makes the futures-minus-spot basis (the difference between the spot price and the futures price) larger. As the contract maturity date nears, the futures price and the spot price converge toward each other. On the contract maturity date, the final day of the life of the futures/forward contract, the spot price and the futures price are equal.

The discrete version of the spot-futures parity formula is used frequently. The equivalent of equation 16.1 for this discrete version is

$$F_0 = S_0 \left(1 + \left[r_f + sc - q - cy\right]\right)^T.$$
(16.2)

Many times, some of the frictions, such as storage costs, yield, and convenience yield, are assumed to be zero. Alternatively, these frictions are all lumped into part of the interest rate as the net cost of carrying. In either case, equation 16.2 can be expressed in a simplified format as

$$F_0 = S_0 \left(1 + r\right)^T,$$
(16.3)

where r is the r_f if the frictions are zero.

As an example, suppose we want to calculate the forward price of gold. If the spot price of gold is S_0, the forward price for a contract deliverable in T years is F_0, and the storage costs, convenience yields, and the gold yield are all assumed zero, then we use the simplified version of the spot-futures parity theorem in equation 16.3, where r would be the annual risk-free rate of interest. If the spot price of gold is $S_0 = \$1,900$ per ounce, the risk-free rate $r = 1\%$, and the contact is for $T = 1\text{-}year$, then the forward price is $F_0 = 1900(1+0.01)^1 = \$1,919$.

16.6 CONTANGO, NORMAL BACKWARDATION, MULTIPLE FUTURES CONTRACTS – TENORS, SPREADS

The relationship between the futures price and the spot price of a security changes dynamically over time, throughout the life of the futures contract. The difference between the spot price and the futures price, which is also known as the basis, shrinks as the maturity date of the futures contract nears. On the final day of the life of the contract, the futures price and the spot price become equal to each other.

The relationship between the futures price and the expected spot price at the maturity of the contract is subject to interest for investors. This relationship manifests itself in two important ways: contango and normal backwardation. Contango is a dynamic situation where the futures price of the contract is higher than the expected spot price at the maturity of the contract (the basis is negative). This is the case where futures investors (long position holders) are willing to pay the higher futures price because the storage costs are extremely crucial and worth the extra premium. The contango will shrink over time as the time to maturity for the contract nears.

Normal backwardation is the opposite situation. When the futures price is less than the expected future spot price at maturity, which intuitively seems to be a rare occurrence, we have normal backwardation (the basis is positive). In this dynamic situation, the carry costs (interest rates and storage costs) are less than the yield of the security along with other convenience yields. In highly stagnant economies where rates can become negative, it is possible to experience normal backwardation. Another example of normal backwardation is when the spot price of a security shoots up dramatically along with the expectation of the spot price in the future due to seasonality or due to negative shocks in supply. In fact, for many commodities, normal backwardation is frequently seen because of seasonality in production. A third example of normal backwardation is for securities where the storage, insurance, and security costs are less than the convenience yield. Consider a unique antique car. The car is so unique and interesting that it is on display and market participants are willing to pay a fee to see it. When the fees collected for the exhibit are higher than carry costs (interest rate), storage costs, insurance costs, and security costs lumped together, normal backwardation is observed; the futures price is less than the expected spot price.

Of course, it should be noted that the expected future spot price is unobservable. Thus, dynamic conditions such as contango and normal backwardation are based on the aggregate expectations of market participants. Sometimes, instead of normal backwardation, the term backwardation is used, which is where the futures price is less than the spot price of the security. Finally, as with contango, normal backwardation diminishes as the contract maturity date nears. Figure 16.1 summarizes the dynamic contango and normal backwardation conditions.

There are multiple futures contracts with different maturities for many underlying securities at any time. Contracts that will mature far ahead in the future are generally not actively traded compared to futures contracts that will mature in the near future. Futures contracts with different maturities for the same underlying asset are known as futures contracts of different tenors. Near-term, short-term, nearby-tenor, and short-tenor (all interchangeable terms) futures contract is the one that has the closest maturity date. When the futures price and spot price relationships are explored, futures contracts with different tenors provide different sorts of relationships. The nearest tenor futures contract is the most popular contract with the highest volume of trade. Therefore, the spot-futures relationship with the nearest tenor contract is considered, as the primary one.

The 'spread' in futures contracts manifests in different ways. For the same underlying security, the futures price differences of different maturities (i.e., price differences in different futures tenors) are known as calendar spreads. Intermarket spread is the price difference of futures contracts with the same maturity date but for different underlying securities. Commodity product spread is about the price difference in futures contracts where the underlying security is not the same but related (e.g., soybean futures and soybean oil futures). These spreads are utilized by traders and speculators for profit opportunities by buying the inexpensive futures and selling the expensive futures in the spread.

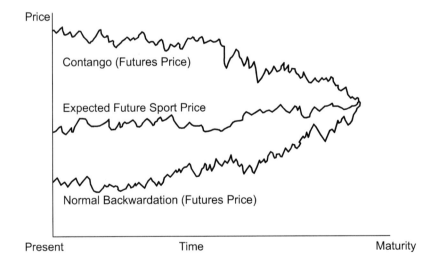

FIGURE 16.1 Contango Versus Normal Backwardation

16.7 RECENT TRENDS IN FUTURES RESEARCH

With recent advances in technology, big data have become easier to manipulate and analyze. Research studies and analyses have moved away from quarterly, monthly, and weekly data toward daily and intraday data. Using high-frequency data studies has revealed the true nature of the relationships between financial and economic variables. The efficiency of markets, lead–lag relationships, and causality relations are more accurately revealed with intraday data.

As examples, two recent studies have used big data in futures markets. The first study investigated the integration of oil spot markets and oil futures markets using intraday data. The evidence indicates highly integrated spot and futures markets where events and shocks in one market quickly transmit to the other market within minutes, consistent with market efficiency. High-frequency data indicate informationally efficient and highly integrated spot and futures oil markets.

The second study explored the currency futures and currency spot basis in predicting currency spot returns and currency futures returns. The study has conjectured that the currency risk premium is an important part of the basis and thus is a proxy for the long tenors but not for the nearest tenors. Using daily data, the study found that the basis could not predict the spot rate changes of long-maturity contracts. However, for these long-tenor contracts, the basis could predict currency futures returns, which are solely determined by the risk premium. On the other hand, the basis of the short-maturity contracts could predict spot rate changes but cannot predict currency futures returns.

The extension of the study has examined near-tenor currency futures returns. In an efficient market with no risk premium, futures returns should not be predicted. Using daily data, the study found the ability of the futures–spot basis as a proxy for the risk premium having predictive power over futures returns in early time subsamples but not in recent time subsamples. Efficiency-enhancing mechanisms in recent decades have reduced the risk premium and eliminated the forecasting power of the basis.

16.8 SUMMARY AND CONCLUSION

The popularity of futures will continue to increase. Precious materials, such as gold, silver, and platinum; energy securities, such as different grades of oil, natural gas, and electricity; food commodities, such as corn, wheat, grain, beef, and pork; financial securities, such as currencies, stock indexes, fixed-income securities/indexes are some of the important and interesting investment alternatives for market participants all over the world. Futures contracts based on these securities are convenient investment opportunities in these assets for all market participants.

Futures contracts became the first type of financial securities to be traded nearly nonstop for 24 hours a day through the Globex electronic trading system. Over the decades, in order to encourage and attract individual and small investors, the contract sizes have been reduced, such as the e-mini futures at the C.M.E. or the 'small contracts' through innovative exchanges (e.g., the Small Exchange – Smalls) and brokerage companies (e.g., Tastyworks). Such innovations will continue in futures markets.

REFERENCES AND ADDITIONAL READING

Benninga, S. 2014. *Financial Modeling*. 4th edition. Cambridge, MA, MIT Press.

Bodie, Z., Kane, A., Marcus, A.J. 2021. *Investments*. 12th edition. New York, McGraw-Hill.

Fama, E.F. 1984. Forward and Spot Exchange Rates. *Journal of Monetary Economics*, 14, 319–338.

Hull, J.C. 2012. *Options, Futures and Other Derivatives*. 8th edition. Boston, MA, Prentice Hall.

Inci, A.C., Lu, B. 2007. Currency Futures-Spot Basis and Risk Premium. *Journal of International Financial Markets, Institutions, and Money*, 17, 180–197.

CHAPTER 17

Alternative Investments

OBJECTIVES

- Justify the existence of and the desire for alternative investments.
- Assess the fundamental characteristics of alternative investments.
- Compare, contrast, and illustrate different types of alternatives: forestry, undeveloped land, art, non-fungible tokens (N.F.T.s), metaverse, and intellectual property.
- Assess the professional organization in this area, Chartered Alternative Investment Analyst (C.A.I.A.) Association.

17.1 INTRODUCTION

Traditional asset classes in the investments area have been (1) cash and cash-like securities, (2) equities, (3) fixed-income securities, (4) precious materials, such as gold, silver, platinum, and diamond, (5) real estate, (6) derivatives – options, and (7) derivatives – futures. As professional/individual investors slowly saturated their portfolios with traditional opportunities such as publicly traded stocks, bonds, and derivatives, such as options and futures, different types of nontraditional investments have started to become interesting.

Nontraditional investments cover a large spectrum of alternatives. They range from diverse opportunities such as college education or crowdfunding/crowdsourcing projects to institutionally preferred prospects. Technological developments, changing trends in sustainability and energy sources, environmental awareness, and scarcity of resources have led to the creation and development of new investment opportunities.

The characteristics of alternative investments are presented next. Popular alternative investments, such as real estate timberland and farmland, infrastructure investments, intellectual property, art and antiques and collectibles, structured products, technology-based non-fungible tokens, and metaverse, are examined. Finally, the organization that is at the center of alternative investments, the Chartered Alternative Investment Analyst (C.A.I.A.) Association, is studied.

DOI: 10.4324/9781003213697-17

17.2 CHARACTERISTICS OF ALTERNATIVE INVESTMENTS

Alternative investments are different from traditional investments from eight key dimensions:

(1) Regulation: The alternative assets are viewed differently by the government in terms of existing rules and taxation. There is often less regulation, and taxation rules are either favorable or not fully established. The majority of the alternatives are newly emerging, or interest in them is recently picking up. The regulatory agencies have not fully understood these investments, and therefore, regulation is generally relaxed until the properties of the new asset are fully understood.

(2) Securitization: The ownership and the cash flows/profits from these assets are usually different from those in traditional assets. Many of the alternative assets may be directly owned rather than through the securitization process. On the other hand, the securitization process may have unique features leading to different return/profit outcomes.

(3) Trading strategies: Many alternative assets have unique sizes and one-of-a-kind features. Finding market participants on the opposite side of the trade is not easy. Consequently, developing correct trading strategies is more important than those for traditional investments. Passive trading strategies might be more reflective of the characteristics, cash flows, and profits of these alternative investments. On the other hand, active strategies may lead to very different return outcomes.

(4) Illiquidity: Many alternatives are highly illiquid. The unique features and characteristics may make an alternative asset attractive to an investor, while other investors may have no interest whatsoever. Therefore, buying or selling these alternative investments at their fair values quickly is quite difficult.

(5) Inefficiency: Alternative investments are new, nontraditional, and used to be obscure. There has not been mass interest in them historically. The number of analysts is limited, and the analysis techniques are not fully developed. Moreover, information is not widely available on these alternatives. With fewer investors, less competition, and higher frictional costs, alternative investments represent an inefficient market. Alternatives also imply information asymmetries and incomplete markets. Experts may be active in these markets, while others only invest a limited portion of their wealth on a long-term basis.

(6) Non-standard returns: The statistical characteristics of alternative investments are different. While the returns of traditional investments can be approximated roughly using normal distributions (with fatter tails), many alternative investment returns exhibit non-normality due to infrequent trading, leverage involved with the alternative, nonlinearities from the linked derivatives, and alternating long-short positions. Non-normal returns of the alternatives affect the statistical techniques for risks, profits, return computations, and risk management strategies. The cash flow streams of the alternatives are also different: some of the alternatives do not have investment outlays or costs. The leverage amounts and margins involved in the alternatives and the additional uncertainties of when and how the future cash flows will materialize render traditional valuation models infeasible.

(7) Arbitrage, return enhancement, risk diversification: Alternatives can be used for multiple reasons. The lack of information and research on these new securities enables knowledgeable

market participants to create arbitrage opportunities using alternatives. Under the ecology of information asymmetries and market inefficiencies, alternatives can also be used in port-folio management as return enhancers with superior returns or as risk diversifiers due to low correlations with traditional securities.

(8) Trading mechanisms, organized exchanges, and financial markets: Alternatives do not have well-established trading mechanisms or organized exchanges. Existing ones are small and not easily accessible to all market participants. Transaction costs and other frictions are quite high. Illiquidity, lack of active trading, limited information about these securities, and lack of substantial interest have all contributed to the underdevelopment of the trading mechanisms and to the underside of the exchanges.

17.3 TYPES OF ALTERNATIVE INVESTMENTS

There are many types of alternative investments. The unique characteristics, risks and returns, and valuation models for some of the popular alternatives investments are explored here.

17.3.1 Intellectual Property: Art

Family trusts, wealthy individuals, and financially stable corporations in different sectors and industries have started to consider the investment value of art, mainly visual art – paintings – over the last quarter century. Acquisition of such artwork is not only for the visual enjoyment of friends, family, coworkers, and business partners but also for the potential increase in the investment value of these unique pieces. The long history of demand for these art pieces, the illiquidity and mispricing because of market inefficiencies, and the lack of transparency in trades and auction markets have made these art items important alternative investments. While the main focus here is art, mainly paintings, others such as jewelry, watches, sculptures, and fashion items are also part of these intellectual property alternatives.

Evidence from investments in visual artwork (paintings) shows that the return performance is not particularly impressive in the long term. The profits are quite stable, and artwork provides an excellent hedge against inflation. Overall, these investments provide wealth maintenance and not necessarily wealth enhancement. Some studies have separated the visual artwork (paintings) into masterpiece (blue-chip), high-quality, medium-quality, and low-quality and have provided some weak evidence of higher profitability of masterpieces. The diversification benefits of artwork are also found to be limited. The additional costs from international art market regis-trations, auction house participations, and transaction commissions indicate that net profits are not necessarily impressive.

Even with these discouraging pieces of evidence against visual artwork paintings as return enhancers or risk diversifiers, interest and investments in these items continue to increase. The aesthetic benefits, the mobility to cross borders anywhere in the world, and the catalyst effects in social and business meetings with customers, suppliers, business partners, and business deals are important benefits and contributions of investing in this group of alternatives. Website plat-forms such as www.masterworks.io provide opportunities for small investors to take positions in masterpiece artworks (blue-chip art).

17.3.2 Intellectual Property: Collectibles

Collectibles, such as stamps, baseball cards, coins, or musical instruments, represent another group of alternatives worth considering. Research suggests that the profitability of these types of investments is not lucrative. While the investment values are retained, and there have been consistent real returns over the decades, these returns are moderate: smaller than equities but larger than those for gold, T-bills, or bonds.

In recent years, the liquidity of these alternatives has increased. Moreover, the correlation coefficients continue to be low with respect to traditional investments, such as stocks or bonds. Including these collectibles in an investment portfolio would provide substantial diversification benefits. Aesthetic utility is an additional benefit.

17.3.3 Intellectual Property: Movies and Music

Investing in movies and movie production has become highly feasible for all investors in recent years with crowdfunding or crowdsourcing practices, through which a project or a venture – in this case, a movie production – is financed by raising small amounts of money from a large number of people. While the majority of movies and television productions continue to be undertaken by professional movie and television studious, a wide variety of investors increasingly participate in this industry as an alternative investment.

In movie/television productions, the story rights are acquired, a movie script is written, and the screenplay is generated. After these initial stages, the preproduction stage starts with the selection of the cast, crew, location, and design. The main production involves the shooting of the movie on location and includes costs due to (1) lodging, (2) catering, (3) costumes, (4) set creation, (5) film equipment, and (5) cast, crew, and employee compensation. The final stage of postproduction is about editing the movie, adding special effects, music score, soundtrack, computer-generated imagery (C.G.I.) effects, and adding titles and credits. All these steps together generate the production costs of the movie. Advertisement, marketing, film prints (digital and physical), and distribution costs added to production costs make up the total cost of the movie.

Financing movies or television productions is through equity financing or debt financing, or both. Examples of equity financing are (1) slate equity financing, where a hedge fund or an investment bank provides the funds for a series of productions of a studio; (2) corporate equity financing, where a private placement or public offering is used to get the funds; (3) coproduction, where several partners get together to share the costs, risks, and returns; (4) third party equity, where wealthy individuals, institutional investors, and others cover the cost not financed through other means. Examples of debt financing are (1) senior collateralized debt by a financial institution, where the collateral can be (a) the purchase of the movie from the producer or a distributor, (b) the distribution rights to foreign territories, and (c) tax credits and/or grants for picking a location in a certain country or state; (2) gap financing, where the difference between the cost of production and the senior secured debt is covered in exchange for selling rights to distributors in certain geographic locations; and (3) super-gap financing where the remaining portion of production costs after senior collateralized debt and after gap financing are covered.

Investments in movies lead to revenues in different stages from cinemas with the initial release, pay-per-view, online rentals, streaming services, cable networks, national network television channels, and syndicated television. Translating revenues to profits is not easy. Movie theaters typically take half of the show revenues as long as the movie is at the cinema.

Research on movie productions has shown that (1) expensive productions generate large revenues but low profits; (2) most movie stars do not have a big impact on revenues, except a few; directors have more influence; (3) sequels generate larger revenues at lower risk; and (4) different genres generate different profits and risks: science fiction, thrillers, and horror generate higher revenues than others.

Music production has similar characteristics as those for movies. A small group of artists, performers, and songwriters gets the bulk of the revenue and profit. The statistical distribution of revenues and profits for music/movie productions is highly non-normal and non-symmetric, with fat tails and extreme outliers. Traditional performance measurement techniques, such as Sharpe ratios and mean and standard deviations, are not successful. On the other hand, with low correlations to traditional investments, these alternatives are excellent for diversification in portfolios.

One distinctive way to measure the return of movie/music/television production/asset is

$$Profit = \left[(0.5)(Dom.BoxOffice) + (0.5)(Intl.BoxOffice)\right] / Costs - 1, \qquad (17.1)$$

where half of the domestic box office revenue and half of the international box office revenue is assumed to be taken by the exhibitor (cinema theater, music store, television channel).

17.3.4 Intellectual Property: Research, Development, Patents

Research and development (R&D) represent intangible assets whose effects are spread over long periods, both in terms of expenditure and in terms of returns. Even with such complications, studies have shown that private investments in R&D provide high profits. R&D also leads to significant social and welfare benefits. Patents are important outcomes of R&D. Profitability of patents is generally minor except for a small group, which is extremely profitable.

The risks in research, development, and patents are (1) the uncertainties in the outcomes of the efforts, (2) regulation and legal risk, (3) expiration or obsolescence risk, (4) technology or industrial risk, and (5) illiquidity risk.

Many investors in R&D are private equity firms. Being part of these private equity organizations had not been easy for small individual investors: large monetary commitments for long and structured periods are typical requirements. However, opportunities have increased for small investors to become part of these types of private equity investments in recent years. Investments in patents can be in different forms – licensing, lending, purchasing, or pooling. In patent pooling, many patents are lumped together and licensed, leased, or loaned to interested investors. Generally, investors in these patent pools are professionals who need the myriad of patents in the pool. In recent years, funds targeting these patent pools started to appear with the goal of marketing to a wider spectrum of investors.

Valuation models of intellectual property are based on the standard present value of the expected future cash flows. The constant growth perpetuity model, better known as the Gordon growth model (developed and published by Myron Gordon in 1956), is typically employed. The intellectual property is successful (positive cash flows) with a probability p_{IP} (and unsuccessful: no cash flows with probability $1-p_{IP}$). Using the first future cash flow ($C_{1,IP}$), the cash flow growth rate (g_{IP}), and the discount rate (r_{IP}), the value of the intellectual property (V_{IP}) is expressed as

$$V_{IP}(t) = \frac{(p_{IP})(C_{1,IP})}{r_{IP} - g_{IP}}. \qquad (17.2)$$

Many intellectual property investments are known as wasting assets. In such assets, the growth rate g is negative; the future cash flows diminish over time, indicating that the intellectual property loses its unique characteristics, its technological innovation, or the ideas become less interesting and become obsolete. Equation 17.2 can be modified to express the return associated with intellectual property investment as

$$r_{IP} = \frac{(p_{IP})(C_{1,IP})}{V_{IP}(t)} + g_{IP}. \qquad (17.3)$$

Equation 17.2 and equation 17.3 both indicate the significant risk associated with intellectual property alternatives. The return and success of the intellectual property depend on the probability of a successful positive cash flow, the rate of 'diminishing' growth of the cash flows, and the first impact (the first cash flow in the future).

As an example, the probability of success in an intellectual property endeavor, a movie project, is 50%; the diminishing growth rate is −20% per year; the first year's total cash flow is $90 million; and the required return is 10%. Then the value of the movie is $150 million:

$$V_{Movie}(t) = \frac{(p_{Movie})(C_{1,Movie})}{r_{Movie} - g_{Movie}} = \frac{(0.5)(\$90 million)}{0.1-(-0.2)} = \$150 million.$$

17.3.5 Agriculture and Farmland

With the increasing desire in developed countries for organic food and local products and with increasing efficiencies in agricultural production all around the world, including emerging countries, agriculture and farmland investments are becoming highly attractive alternatives for a wide range of investors. Farmland investment is an inflation hedge, great for diversification, and represents a *long* position in potentially scarce resources such as food, water, and energy. While U.S. farmlands are stable and mature assets, international expropriation is an added risk.

Farmland investments are highly profitable because of (1) the rise in world population (with higher demand for food), (2) favorable government policies (subsidies and tax breaks), (3) being sources of energy through biofuels (sugarcane and corn for ethanol production, soybeans and rapeseed oil for biodiesel), and (4) increased production efficiency through innovations in technology, chemistry, and farming education. As a consequence, farmland investments have been generating the highest returns, one of the lowest standard deviations, and the highest Sharpe ratios compared to equities, bonds (global/U.S.), and commodities in the 2000s.

There are three ways to invest in farmland and agriculture alternatives: (1) leasing the farmland to a farmer, (2) actually being in the farming/agriculture business (web platforms such as www.farmtogether.com enable small investors to participate in farming and agriculture businesses), and (3) investing in financial securities based on agriculture/farming.

Farmland can be leased to a farmer. This approach reduces risks due to weather conditions and crop prices but increases risks due to problems between the principal (farmland owner) and the agent (farmer) and political decisions (changes in subsidies and taxes or government expropriation). This form of alternative investment provides lease revenues. Net of real estate taxes and insurance is equal to operating income, and subtracting interest expenses makes its net income. In farmland investments, cap rate (capitalization rate) or yield is an important efficiency variable:

$$Cap\ Rate = Yield = ROA = Operating\ Income/Farmland\ Value. \tag{17.4}$$

Many times, the cap rate is used to find the price of the farmland:

$$Farmland\ Value = Operating\ Income/Cap\ Rate. \tag{17.5}$$

The second way of investing is to actually own the farmland for agricultural production. Investors are exposed to shifts in global commodity prices and the demand in specific crops. Additionally, the process of crop production impacts production, yield, revenues, and profitability. Agricultural productivity is expressed as

$$Production = (SolarRadiation)(CropSolarCapture)(Photosynthesis)(Harvest). \tag{17.6}$$

Over the decades, agricultural innovations with technology, agronomy, and chemical inputs have improved harvest production and crop solar capture, which in turn have led to a substantial increase in production and profitability.

The third and perhaps the most practical way of agriculture and farmland investments are D.A.X. Global Agribusiness Stock Index, Global Agriculture Equity Index, and Market Vectors Agribusiness E.T.F. (M.O.O.).

Finally, ideally, having farmland with options would be the best. The ability to plant alternative crops or the ability to transform farmland into residential, industrial, and mining areas would make the investment to be even more profitable. With all these advantages, the potential difficulties in farmland investments are illiquidity and high transaction costs.

17.3.6 Forest Assets, Timber, and Timberland

Forest assets are long-term investments because the rotation from planting to harvest can take up to 25–60 years, depending on the timber species. In the past, the forest industry used to be vertically integrated: companies had forestland, trees, pulp mills, and sawmills. The aggressive leveraged buyout (L.B.O.) activities in the 1980s split the acquisitions into spinoffs of sub-industry companies. Focused investments in timberland are becoming popular alternative investments.

Timberland investments protect from inflation, provide low correlations with equities and fixed-income securities, are perpetually renewable, provide a flexible harvest schedule so that trees can grow until the harvest time for best profits, and are required by various sectors, such as paper, publishing, firewood, pulpwood, and home building. The negatives are the exposure to natural disasters and diseases, the cyclical timber values because of ties to cyclical industries, the non-fixed supply (timberland areas can be expanded) influencing prices, low liquidity, and the declining demand due to the departure from new paper products (electronic media technology and recycling are the culprits).

While the majority of forest areas are owned by the public (governments around the world), in the U.S. roughly 60% of timberland is privately owned. Thus, U.S. forest assets are of primary interest to investors. It is also still possible to invest in timberland internationally because of attractive internal rates of returns, but currency movements and tougher legal requirements/changes are extra sources of risks. Investments in these types of alternatives are (1) E.T.F.s designed to replicate the S&P Timber and Forestry Index; (2) real estate investment trusts (R.E.I.T.S.) – that is, 'mutual funds' focused on timberland; and (3) owning the timberland privately and allowing timber investment management organizations (T.I.M.O.s) to operate for a fee and share of profits. Timberland investments have generated the lowest standard deviations and second highest returns and Sharpe ratios (after Farmland investments) in the 2000s compared to stocks/bonds.

17.3.7 Infrastructure

Investible infrastructures are essential large physical assets/projects that have monopoly characteristics with government influence. They are continually utilized by the public and generate stable inflation-hedged cash flows. They are long-term investments, have low correlations to traditional asset classes, and have higher Sharpe ratios compared to domestic or international equities, international bonds, and futures, but have lower Sharpe ratios than those for domestic bonds. They have high initial capital costs, low operating costs once finished, and help the social welfare of society. Examples are transportation (seaports, airports, railroads, toll roads), utilities (electric, gas, water, communication distribution grids), health (hospitals, hospices, nurseries), and education (schools, colleges, institutions, universities). These alternatives can be new (greenfield) or current that need to be modernized (brownfield). Greenfields are typically riskier than brownfields. Investments in these alternatives can be private or public-private partnership (P.P.P.). P.P.P.s can be privatized when the public (government) sells its share.

The practical ways to invest in these alternatives are becoming a part of private equity, open-end or closed-end mutual funds, and hedge funds, all specialized in infrastructures investments.

17.3.8 Undeveloped Land

Undeveloped land in anticipation of future improvement is another popular alternative investment. These alternatives are becoming very popular with stronger desires for privacy, getting closer to nature, shelter and protection from an environmental or human-made catastrophe, and building an environmentally sustainable dwelling. Acquisition of such land by constructors is actually called 'land banking' in the home-building industry. In addition to location (how far the undeveloped land is from nearby townships), the type of the land lot influences the value: (1) paper lots are land lots just approved for development; (2) blue-top lots are semi-complete with rough grading, drainage, and erosion control finished; and (3) finished lots are fully completed with the infrastructure, ready for home-building.

The expected return of land investment depends on the probability of future development ($Pr_{development}$) and the return such development $E(R_{development})$ or non-development $E(R_{nondevelopment})$ will generate

$$E(R_{land}) = (Pr_{development})(E(R_{development})) + (1 - Pr_{development})(E(R_{nondevelopment})). \tag{17.7}$$

17.3.9 Non-Fungible Tokens and Metaverse

The dramatic technological changes and improvements in mobile and online communications, the tremendous rise in the popularity of the internet starting from the mid-1990s, and online social media applications and platforms have revolutionized and dramatically altered the perceptions, senses, feelings, and interactions of human beings with many art forms. New digital art forms have started to emerge, such as digital imaging, photography, music, paintings, and other fine arts.

Many firsts and originals, such as tweets, memes, posts, pictures, comments, and music tunes, have survived the test of time. In recent years, the desire to tokenize such unique creations has led to the design of non-fungible tokens (N.F.T.s). These digitized art items are protected by copyright and other legal regulations. Traditional art items, sports tokens, and unique and original objects are also being digitized and packaged into exclusive N.F.T.s, which can then be exchanged among enthusiasts, investors, and traders. The digitization and packaging are done in such a way that they could not be replicated or forged, making sure that the created tokens remain unique and the value of the new security is justified.

It will be a process for N.F.T.s to become mainstream securities. While some market participants are tremendously interested in these items, many others participants have no interest or no knowledge of them at all. These new alternative investments will certainly become more popular in the coming years as creativity continues to be tokenized and converted into tradable securities. While currently many cryptocurrencies are used as the medium of exchange for trading N.F.T.s, eventually traditional currencies and easily accessible exchanges/marketplaces will reduce transaction costs and other frictions. The increase in demand and supply for N.F.T.s is certain for the future. Taking positions in these alternative investments at an early stage will be associated with big profit potentials but also significant risks.

Social media platforms, massively multiplayer online role-playing games (M.M.O.s or M.M.O.R.P.G.s), and technological advances in virtual reality (V.R.) – both in hardware and software – have literally led to the foundation of new worlds called metaverse. Participants purchase land and living quarters, pay for exhibitions and art shows, and engage in parties, conversations, and competitions with friends and acquaintances from all around the world. Essentially an alternative, virtual life can be created, where many things that are not possible in real life can be achieved virtually.

Of course, there are many ramifications of the metaverse idea – some adverse. The time, money, and effort spent on V.R. will have negative implications on someone's life in the real world. The psychological and other health consequences for individuals cannot be ignored. However, even with these concerns, the metaverse is fast becoming another alternative investment. A large number of companies are investing huge sums in laying out infrastructures for the metaverse, such as Microsoft, Apple, Facebook (Meta), Alphabet (Google), and others. Taking long positions in the infancy of this new alternative opens up enormous profit potentials but also extremely high risks. If the metaverse takes off, those positions will be huge successes.

17.4 CHARTERED ALTERNATIVE INVESTMENT ANALYST (C.A.I.A.) ASSOCIATION

The C.A.I.A. is an international organization with a presence in more than 100 countries. The C.A.I.A. provides a professional credential in financial investments with a specific emphasis on alternative investments. Since 2002, the association has provided a wide variety of educational programs on alternative investments with the goal of raising awareness for the public, investment participants, and professionals.

The C.A.I.A. is a member-based organization. Successful completion of two exams allows being part of more than 12,000 professionals worldwide. The study materials for the exams cover everything from the characteristics of alternative asset classes to portfolio management concepts central to alternative investments. Some of the information in this chapter is based on the C.A.I.A. Level I and C.A.I.A. Level II official books. C.A.I.A. membership provides rigorous training programs, certifications, network connections, and access to up-to-date information and to strategies.

While the Chartered Financial Analyst (C.F.A.) designation is a general professional title for finance professional, the C.A.I.A. designation is specifically focused on alternative investments. With increasing interest among market participants in alternatives, the C.A.I.A. charter and the educational materials published by the organization are invaluable resources for these new investment opportunities. Detailed information, resources, and free materials are available on the official website of the organization (www.caia.org).

17.5 SUMMARY AND CONCLUSION

In this chapter, new and alternative investment opportunities are introduced and studied. Intellectual properties, such as art (paintings, movies, music), collectibles, antiques, R&D, agriculture and farmland, forest assets and timberland, infrastructure, undeveloped land, N.F.T.s, and the metaverse are explored in terms of profit potential, risk characteristics, and investability.

There are many more alternative investments other than the ones covered in this chapter, such as land with minerals, structured products, and packaged derivatives. Rather than covering the alternatives exhaustively, the focus in the chapter has been on the technological developments, the unique nature of the alternatives, and how to invest in these securities as professionals and small investors.

The alternatives will become more important and mainstream in the coming years with additional innovations and a much wider spectrum of choices. As new alternatives are developed and introduced, some will not be successful, while others will become indispensable in investment portfolios.

REFERENCES AND ADDITIONAL READING

Benninga, S. 2014. *Financial Modeling*. 4th edition. Cambridge, MA, MIT Press.

Bodie, Z., Kane, A., Marcus, A.J. 2021. *Investments*. 12th edition. New York, McGraw-Hill.

Chambers, D.R., Anson, M.J.P., Black, K.H., Kazemi, H.B. 2015. *Alternative Investments: CAIA Level I*. 3rd edition. Hoboken, NJ, Wiley.

Hull, J.C. 2012. *Options, Futures and Other Derivatives*. 8th edition. Boston, MA, Prentice Hall.

Isaacson, W. 2014. *The Innovators: How a Group of Hackers, Geniuses, and Geeks Created the Digital Revolution*. New York, Simon & Shuster.

Kazemi, H.B., Black, K.H., Chambers, D.R. 2016. *Alternative Investments: CAIA Level II*. 3rd edition. Hoboken, NJ, Wiley.

CHAPTER 18

Currency, Cryptocurrency, Blockchain, Fintech

OBJECTIVES

- Identify and analyze traditional currencies, dynamics, and macroeconomic relationships based on currencies.
- Experiment with the forward premium puzzle.
- Develop different utilizations of cryptocurrencies as a medium of exchange, as standalone investment opportunities, and as enhancements of traditional portfolio performance.
- Compare and contrast popular cryptocurrencies.
- Assess blockchain as a decentralized ledger system (1) as processing and recording transactions and (2) as a designed ecology for cryptocurrencies.
- Categorize popular fintech innovations and the associated organizations.

18.1 INTRODUCTION

Traditional currencies have been excellent improvements over barter economies in terms of liquidity, trade execution, and efficiency of economic activity. These traditional currencies are explored as the medium of exchange for goods and services. Central government regulators have a substantial influence on exchange rate dynamics through various currency policies. In the first part of the chapter, the pros and cons of these policies are examined along with traditional currencies as mediums of exchange for goods and services.

Currency dynamics are associated with four fundamental relationships in international economics/finance. The relationships are defined and clarified with a comprehensive numerical example. An important puzzle in this context, the forward premium puzzle is presented.

The power of central governments to print money has made many market participants question the independence of traditional currencies as a proper medium of exchange. These concerns and the technological improvements in online communication infrastructures around the world have led to innovations that decentralize, deregulate, and provide transaction/ownership anonymity in the exchange of goods and services. These innovations are (1) digital

DOI: 10.4324/9781003213697-18

currencies: cryptocurrencies and (2) ecologies within which cryptocurrencies operate: blockchain online ledger systems. These innovations are investigated in detail.

The cryptocurrency market is one of the largest unregulated markets in the world. While the illegal use has declined substantially with rising mainstream interest, practical problems related to investing in cryptocurrencies include high volatility, theft, fraud, hacking, and ransom attacks.

Lack of regulation is problematic because it leads to a lack of protection, but increased levels of constrictive regulation disrupt the attractiveness of cryptocurrencies to users, which could initiate illiquidity and drastic declines in their value.

Cryptocurrencies and blockchain ledger technologies are becoming viable mainstream alternatives to traditional currencies. Other fintech initiatives mentioned in the chapter also bring together technology and finance for superior solutions in banking, investments, education, data management, insurance, trading, and financial advising.

18.2 EXCHANGE RATES AND CURRENCY DYNAMICS

Currencies are used as a medium of exchange in the trade of goods and services. While in a cashless barter economy goods are exchanged directly at agreed-upon rates, in an economy with an established formal and traditional currency, banknotes and cash bills are used during the purchase and sale of goods and services. Needless to say, currencies make trading more convenient, streamlined, efficient, effective, and faster.

Traditional currencies are maintained by the central banks of the governments. The volume of the currency in circulation is one of the important economic tools of the central bank in influencing economic variables. Interest rates, inflation rate, the growth of the economy, international economic relationships, imports and exports, trade surpluses, and deficits are all influenced by currency decisions.

Governments follow different currency policies. For a long time, the norm was the gold standard in currencies. This monetary system fixed the value of one unit of the currency to a certain amount of gold. The gold standard was followed by most governments from the mid-1850s until 1944. During the Bretton-Woods meetings (New Hampshire, U.S.A.), many governments agreed to fix the U.S. dollar to a specific value of gold, and the other currencies were pegged to the U.S. dollar.

The Bretton-Woods system was eventually terminated by the U.S. government during the recessionary period of the early 1970s. Since the mid-1970s, four exchange rate policies have emerged: (1) many currencies, including the U.S. dollar, have become freely floating, where the currency value is determined by independent market forces; (2) soft currency pegs, where the currency is free-flowing in general but the central bank intervenes from time to time; (3) hard currency pegs, where the central bank frequently intervenes to keep the currency within a narrow band; and (4) merged currency where the value is set equal to that of another currency all the time.

International firms, investments, and export and import activities use exchange rates and currency conversions constantly. When an American company imports from Switzerland, Swiss francs are needed by the supplier. The American company resorts to foreign exchange markets.

There are central locations around the globe for foreign exchange trading, but most trading and business transactions are conducted by telephone or through computer networks without the use of a central marketplace.

In foreign exchange markets, principal dealers are larger commercial banks and investment banks. Local businesses and firms and multinational corporations conduct their foreign exchange operations through these institutions. There is enormous turnover daily in the exchange of currencies. Bank for International Settlements (B.I.S.) surveys indicate an average daily turnover of about $6.6 trillion in 2019–2020. The turnover has increased steadily over the last two decades from roughly $1.9 trillion in the early 2000s. London is the most important central location for foreign exchange markets, where the daily turnover has been $2.4 trillion.

18.2.1 Exchange Rates

Exchange rates are quoted in two different ways. The *direct quote* indicates the number of domestic currencies needed to buy one unit of foreign currency for a domestic investor. The direct quote is essentially the price of the foreign currency – how much does it cost to buy £1 or €1? The other type of exchange rate quote is the *indirect quote*. This is the number of foreign currency units needed to buy one domestic currency; for example, ¥110 is needed to buy $1 (if the U.S. is the domestic country). The direct quote and the indirect quote are reciprocals of each other. If the direct quote is $1.4 for £1, the indirect quote is £0.71 for $1. Similarly, if the indirect quote is ¥110 for $1, then the direct quote is $0.009 for ¥1.

18.2.2 Calculating International Returns with Foreign Exchange

Exchange rate movements need to be taken into account when calculating the returns from international investments. The domestic currency is converted into foreign currency just before the investment, and at the end of the investment period, the foreign currency is converted back to the domestic currency. The conversion rates are different in the beginning and at the end, and both need to be considered in order to compare the international return with the domestic return. The domestic equivalent of the international return is calculated as

$$1 + r_{domesticEquivalent} = [1 + r_{foreign}]\frac{xcr_1}{xcr_0}, \tag{18.1}$$

where $r_{domesticEquivalent}$ is the return of the foreign investment in domestic currency (comparable to the returns of other domestic investments), $r_{foreign}$ is the regular return of the foreign investment, and xcr_0 (xcr_1) is the beginning (end) of the investment period exchange rate in a direct quote.

As an example, consider an investment in a British security purchased for £40 and later sold for £44. This means that the return from this foreign investment, $r_{foreign}$ was *(44–40)/40 = 0.1 = 10%*. The initial conversion rate between the U.S. dollar and the British pound was $2 per British pound, and the final exchange rate was $2.10. The domestic equivalent of the foreign investment return is

$$r_{domesticEquivalent} = \left[1 + \left(\frac{44 - 40}{40}\right)\right]\frac{2.10}{2.00} - 1 = 0.155 = 15.5\%.$$

In this instance, the exchange rate between the pound and the dollar moved in the investor's favor. After the conversion from the U.S. dollar, the British pound gained value. And this contributed to a higher overall return for the investor. The British pound appreciation is *(2.10–2.00) / 2.00 = 5%*. Combined with the foreign security return of 10%, the total return is not the sum of these two components (15%) but rather 15.5%. The reason for this is the compounding impact of these two financial securities. The currency return and the foreign security return complement and fuel each other to generate a compound return of 15.5%.

18.3 EXCHANGE RATES AND INTERNATIONAL FINANCIAL/ ECONOMIC RELATIONSHIPS

The overview in the chapter is from finance and financial markets perspectives. But international economics and international finance are intertwined. Therefore, it is warranted to examine some of the most important relationships in international economics.

Theories on international economics start from the rationality of markets and participants. Rational expectations lead to equilibrium conditions in terms of supply, demand, prices, and production. A perturbation of a parameter away from equilibrium has a ripple effect over other variables until a new rational expectations equilibrium is reached. Under the umbrella of rational expectations, there are four fundamental relationships that drive international economics:

(1) Covered interest parity: This is the relationship between spot and forward exchange rates and foreign and domestic interest rates. The relationship answers the question 'Why are the interest rates of two countries different from each other?' with exchange rate movements. Using direct quotes for exchange rates, the equation governing the relationship is

$$\frac{f\_xcr_{domesticCurrency/foreignCurrency}}{s\_xcr_{domesticCurrency/foreignCurrency}} = \frac{1+r_{domestic}}{1+r_{foreign}}, \tag{18.2}$$

where f_xcr is the forward exchange rate, s_xcr is the spot exchange rate, and $r_{domestic}$ and $r_{foreign}$ are the domestic and foreign interest rates with matching maturities with the forward contract. The gains from interest income are offset by the decline in the currency value according to this relationship.

(2) Uncovered interest parity (U.I.P.): This relationship clarifies what the forward contract value of the exchange rate is supposed to be. The question answered by the relationship is 'Why is the forward exchange rate different from the spot exchange rate?' The answer is the clarification of the forward exchange rate as the expected future spot rate of the currency. Using direct quotes, the governing equation for this relationship is

$$f\_xcr_{domesticCurrency/foreignCurrency} = E[s\_xcr_{domesticCurrency/foreignCurrency}(t=1)], \tag{18.3}$$

where the right side of the equation indicates the expected spot exchange rate on the maturity date of the forward contract.

(3) Purchasing power parity: This relationship is about exchange rate movements and inflation rates in two countries. The main question about this relationship is 'What influences the currency dynamics?' Inflation rates in the two countries drive currency movements as

$$\frac{s\_xcr_{domesticCurrency/foreignCurrency}(1)}{s\_xcr_{domesticCurrency/foreignCurrency}(0)} = \frac{1+\inf_{domestic}}{1+\inf_{foreign}}, \tag{18.4}$$

where the left side of the equation is the ratio of the future and spot exchange rates, and the right side is the ratio of the one plus domestic to one plus foreign inflation rates. This formulation is known as the relative purchasing power parity relationship, with the left side as the change in the exchange rate (in the absolute purchasing power parity, the exchange rate reflects the ratio of the price levels in two countries). Higher inflation rates are linked to weaker future currencies.

(4) International Fisher effect: This relationship is about the inflation rates and interest rates in two countries. The real rates in the two economies are assumed to be the same. As a consequence, the governing equation is

$$\frac{1+r_{domestic}}{1+E(\inf_{domestic})} = \frac{1+r_{foreign}}{1+E(\inf_{foreign})}. \tag{18.5}$$

Therefore, the expected real return is the same in all countries.

As a comprehensive numerical example, consider the U.S. and Swiss economies. The interest rate in Switzerland is 1 basis point (0.01% since 100 basis points is defined to be equal to 1%), and the interest rate in the U.S. is 100 basis points (1%). The spot exchange rate between the U.S. dollar and the Swiss franc as a direct quote is 0.9091. To address the covered interest parity, we calculate from equation 18.2 the forward exchange rate 1 year ahead as

$$f\_xcr_{\$/SF} = 0.9091\ (1 + 0.01)/(1 + 0.0001) = 0.9181.$$

The higher forward rate is indicative of the depreciation of the U.S. dollar against the Swiss franc. The second relationship, uncovered interest parity, verifies this as $E[s\_xcr_{\$/SF}(1)] = 0.9181$ – that is, the expected spot direct quote one year ahead is 91.81 cents (compared to the spot 90.91 cents.

Further examination of the two economies reveals that the inflation rate in the U.S. is anticipated as 2% and in Switzerland as 1% for the coming year. Are the rates consistent with rational expectations? The third purchasing power parity relationship answers with the verification of equation 18.4: $\frac{0.9181}{0.9091} = \frac{1.02}{1.01}$. Thus, the equilibrium condition is valid. Finally, focusing on the international Fisher effect, given that the U.S. and Swiss inflation expectations are 2% and 1% and that the U.S. interest rate is 1%, what should the Swiss interest rate be? From equation 18.5, we find $\frac{1+0.01}{1+0.02} = \frac{1+r_{SW}}{1+0.01} \Rightarrow r_{SW} = 0.0001 = 0.01\%$. This is indeed the Swiss interest rate the numerical example started with. Thus, all four relationships are consistent with each other and that the rational expectations equilibrium holds between the U.S. and Switzerland.

18.4 THE FORWARD PREMIUM PUZZLE (F.P.P.)

The uncovered interest parity relationship combined with covered interest parity has been of empirical interest for researchers for many years. Equations 18.2 and 18.3 jointly indicate that currency movements are influenced by the interest rates of the two countries:

$$\frac{E[s\_xcr_{domesticCurrency/foreignCurrency}(1)]}{s\_xcr_{domesticCurrency/foreignCurrency}(0)} = \frac{1 + r_{domestic}}{1 + r_{foreign}}. \tag{18.6}$$

To test the validity of equation 18.6 empirically, the standard approach has been to take the natural logarithm of both sides. Ratios turn into differences in natural logarithms, and the natural logarithm of one plus a small number is approximately that small number. With these two properties, the currency return results in

$$\ln(E[s\_xcr(1)]) - \ln(s\_xcr(0)) = r_{domestic} - r_{foreign} \text{ or}$$

$$q\_xcr = r_{domestic} - r_{foreign}, \tag{18.7}$$

where q_xcr is the currency return calculated as the natural logarithm difference of the exchange rates. In the empirical regression tests, uncovered interest parity and rational expectations hold if the intercept coefficient $A = 0$ and the slope coefficient $\beta = 1$:

$$q\_xcr = \alpha + \beta(r_{domestic} - r_{foreign}) + \varepsilon. \tag{18.8}$$

Since the Eugene Fama research in 1984, hundreds of studies using various exchange rates, interest rate differentials, time periods, and country pairs have consistently shown the slope estimate $\hat{\beta}$ to be statistically significantly less than 1 – in fact, many times less than 0. This is clear evidence of the failure of the uncovered interest parity relationship and also the failure of the rational expectations equilibrium.

Rational expectations equilibrium posits that high-interest-rate currencies are supposed to lose value and maintain equilibrium. That is why interest rates are high in the first place: to compensate investors for the upcoming depreciation of the currency and to preserve equilibrium. The empirical evidence strongly exhibits the opposite: high-interest-rate currencies actually gain value. The failure of the rational expectations equilibrium is called the forward premium puzzle (F.P.P.), or the forward premium anomaly. One explanation of the puzzle is a highly variable exchange rate risk premium, which (1) is negatively correlated with currency change and (2) has higher variation compared to the variation of currency change. Some studies have also proposed that if the currency return horizon is long (e.g., ten years), the anomaly is not seen long term. Therefore, the short-term and long-term relationships between currencies and interest rates seem to be different. Research to understand and account for the F.P.P. continues at an exciting pace.

18.5 CRYPTOCURRENCIES AND BLOCKCHAIN

The cryptocurrency concept is based on the desire for a universal medium of exchange of goods and services that is not controlled by any government or regulatory agency. With the popularity and access to the internet globally, such a system became feasible. Unfortunately, the initial applications of such mediums of exchange were for purchasing and selling questionable and illegal products from the dark web. However, increased general interest in these cryptocurrencies has transitioned them over to the transparent, reliable, and legal realm of commerce and commercial activities.

One way to define cryptocurrency is cash for the internet. Cryptocurrencies are digital pieces of information that have value as long as no one else has access to the information and the keys that provide the value. The entity that holds the information at that point in time is also the holder of the value of that cryptocurrency.

The creation of cryptocurrencies has been based on the need for internet cash combined with the desire for anonymity in internet transactions. Those concerned with privacy and personal liberty have experimented with and eventually invented the cryptocurrency as (1) decentralized, (2) unregulated, and (3) anonymous system of transactions directly from user to user (peer-to-peer) without a bank account or credit card.

The first characteristic of decentralization has been possible because of the ecology of cryptocurrency transactions. In his manifesto, Satoshi Nakamoto – the developer of bitcoin – highlighted the problems with lack of privacy and safety in transactions and proposed the solution of the blockchain ledger system. The decentralization of cryptocurrencies is through blockchain technology. In a distributed ledger operated within peer-to-peer networks, the data and information contained on the blockchain platform reside in thousands of computers all over the world so that the entire data cannot be accessed only by one specific user, miner, or bystander. This makes the system highly unlikely to be hacked compared to a centralized organization, such as a bank, where there is one central repository of information susceptible to breaches in security. Blockchain technology and its utilization through cryptocurrencies provide decentralized consensus entailing the distribution of information to alter the information space. Smart contracts through the blockchain ecology mitigate informational asymmetry and improve social welfare through enhanced competition.

The second attractive characteristic of cryptocurrency is the lack of regulation. No government or organization has any control over any cryptocurrency. Because there is no government monitoring, transactions are not regulated and are not subject to sales tax. Moreover, no intermediary (lawyers, banks, payment providers) is needed in the user-to-user system, reducing frictional costs further. However, these characteristics also make cryptocurrencies susceptible to potential fraud and to potential government intervention in the future.

The third characteristic of cryptocurrencies is anonymity and the untraceable nature of the transactions. When a transaction takes place on the blockchain network, each user involved in that transaction has a specific personal key, similar to a user name. Once the transaction is completed and verified, those personal keys are also completed and can never be used again. Every time a user engages in a transaction, a unique and untraceable personal key is generated. No bank account or credit card is used for the transaction either, ensuring anonymity.

Cryptocurrencies can be deployed in three essential ways:

(1) Their original purpose – as a medium of exchange. The reason cryptocurrencies were originally created was for consumers to have the means to buy and sell goods and services all around the world using the same (crypto)currency exchange without any interventions, frictions, or regulatory controls. Various companies, such as Tesla, Subway, Starbucks, Microsoft, Home Depot, Rakuten, Whole Foods, PayPal, and A.M.C. Theaters, have already welcomed the idea of selling their goods and services in exchange of cryptocurrencies. This trend will continue with more companies, especially for internet-based transactions.

Employees and individuals have also started to prefer their compensation in cryptocurrencies. The mayor of New York City, Eric Adams, has his salary converted into cryptocurrencies (bitcoin and ethereum), as does Miami Mayor Francis Suarez (bitcoin). One reason these mayors have pushed for cryptocurrency compensation has been to encourage bringing cryptocurrency securities markets to their cities. Sports stars Odell Beckham Jr. and Aaron Rogers of the N.F.L., Klay Thompson of the N.B.A., and others have signed contracts to receive cryptocurrencies.

(2) An independent investment asset class. Cryptocurrency as a medium of exchange has a fundamental problem. Because the value of the cryptocurrency is not backed by an authority or denominated to a standard, such as gold, there are wild fluctuations compared to other traditional currencies or other asset values.

Cryptocurrencies have failed thus far to be the universal currency free from any government control because they have not managed to be a consistent short-term or long-term store of value, have not been a reliable inflation hedge, and have not managed to become a safe haven for investors. The speculative wild variations in the prices of cryptocurrencies are exactly opposite to how a true numeraire must be: one of minimum variance with respect to an arbitrary basket of goods and services in order to be a true inflation hedge and be a reliable store of value. Cryptocurrency value can drop to 0 in the extreme case of absolutely no interest.

Such characteristics reduce the role of cryptocurrencies as a stable medium of exchange but would make them an interesting new asset class for investment purposes. Indeed, a large number of market participants have invested in a variety of cryptocurrencies as alternative assets.

Most cryptocurrencies have been created as a finite quantity (21 million units, or coins, for bitcoin). The existing quantity of a cryptocurrency is increased toward that finite quantity through mining operations by interested investors. Mining refers to using computer power to solve complex problems, including the operations necessary for the decentralized blockchain ledger. Sophisticated investors around the world have built large mining/farming facilities with enormous computer mainframes for the sole purpose of mining cryptocurrencies. The electricity used for these operations and the heat generated from the hardware have reached such levels that concerns about the environmental consequences have increased. As the existing quantity increases, mining the cryptocurrency becomes more difficult. The limited supply of cryptocurrencies makes them valuable. But the value fluctuates with demand. The dynamics of cryptocurrency prices make them a useful and independent asset class for investment purposes.

(3) Augmentation of traditional investment portfolios to provide enhanced returns and reduced risks. Cryptocurrencies have independent risk and return characteristics. As the demand evolves dynamically over time, so do the profits and risks. This makes cryptocurrency returns have low correlations with those of traditional investments and financial securities. As a consequence, augmenting traditional portfolios with cryptocurrencies will help obtain better optimal portfolios with higher returns and/or lower risks.

Studies have consistently documented that adding cryptocurrencies to traditional portfolios results with better return and risk combination. Bitcoin has been the most useful cryptocurrency in this regard in the 2000s, compared to other popular cryptocurrencies like ripple or litecoin. The different risk and return characteristics between bitcoin and the Dow Jones Industrial Average index are apparent in Figure 18.1. Which cryptocurrency contributes best for optimality varies because of the evolving nature of risk and returns within the crypto.

The cryptocurrency crashes at the end of December 2018, at the end of April 2021, at the end of October 2021, and in the spring/summer of 2022 have reduced the attractiveness of cryptocurrencies as investment alternatives, but the dynamic characteristics warrant their future demand in investment portfolios. Popular cryptocurrencies have had a useful role in portfolio construction and investments, in addition to their original purposes.

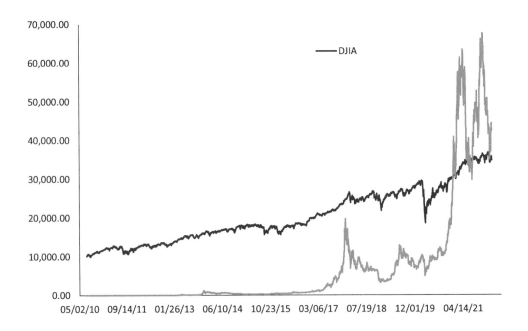

FIGURE 18.1 Dow Jones Industrial Average Index (Darker Line) Versus Bitcoin (Thin Line)

18.6 POPULAR CRYPTOCURRENCIES

There are thousands of cryptocurrencies. Every day new ones are introduced with a unique set of rules and protocols. The success of a cryptocurrency almost always depends on the interest in and demand for it by market participants. Although the list changes and is highly subjective, some of the popular cryptocurrencies are bitcoin, ethereum, ripple, litecoin, and dogecoin. A wide spectrum of market participants invests in these cryptocurrencies through trading platforms such as Coinbase and Robinhood.

18.6.1 Bitcoin (B.T.C.)

The first cryptocurrency, bitcoin, was introduced in 2008 by an unknown person under the pseudonym Satoshi Nakamoto in a white paper, 'Bitcoin: A Peer-to-Peer Electronic Cash System', with publicly available software. Bitcoin has been defined with a limited supply of 21 million units (coins). These units are in the process of being created through mining (computers solving complex problems and verifying the blockchain ledger) and are the most commonly used medium of exchange for goods and services. Even though highly criticized for (1) environmental harm of large electricity use through mining, (2) use in illegal transactions, (3) insecurity and potential for theft, and (4) high volatility, it has become the most popular cryptocurrency. Bitcoin is accepted by many companies as payment for their services, by employees as compensation, and in September 2021 by El Salvador as legal tender (the first country to do so).

18.6.2 Ethereum (E.T.H.) and Cardano (A.D.A.)

Ethereum is a network created by programmer Vitalik Buterin in 2013 and was activated in 2015. It is an online programming ecology where it is possible for anyone to create and run decentralized applications, smart contracts, and a broad range of financial services without intermediaries such as brokers or banks. Within the ethereum blockchain, N.F.T.s and a myriad of cryptocurrencies can be created. The ethereum blockchain is validated with a frequency that is 50 times faster than that of the bitcoin blockchain. Ether is the official cryptocurrency within this framework and it is the second most popular crypto after bitcoin. Ether is mined just like bitcoin but there is no finite supply.

Cardano is another cryptocurrency platform with A.D.A. as the official cryptocurrency. It was created by ethereum co-founder Charles Hoskinson in 2015, became functional in 2017 with venture capital (thus, not a not-for-profit platform), and rising in popularity.

18.6.3 Ripple (X.R.P.)

Ripple was created by Jed McCaleb in 2005 as an online secure global payment platform. The official cryptocurrency X.R.P. has been the facilitator allowing financial institutions to complete immediate transfers without any transaction costs. The popularity of the platform had started to challenge the S.W.I.F.T. code bank wire transfer system of the Society for Worldwide Interbank Financial Telecommunication. But concerns over security, lack of regulation, and arbitrary issuance of X.R.P. coins (which actually had to be strictly generated for the transfer of payments) led to a class-action lawsuit by the U.S. Securities and Exchange Commission (S.E.C.). While the platform has lost its allure, the X.R.P. cryptocurrency is still considered a popular crypto.

18.6.4 Litecoin (L.T.C.)

Litecoin network was released in 2011 because of the assumptions of increasing difficulty in accessing the bitcoin blockchain platform. With four times the number of coins (84 million) compared to that of bitcoin, and with four times faster speed of transaction confirmation compared to bitcoin, litecoin increased in popularity and has been included as one of the cryptocurrencies in the PayPal system.

18.6.5 Dogecoin (D.O.G.E.)

Dogecoin was introduced in 2013 as an alternative crypto with the aim of providing access to a wider group of participants. With continuous interest in social media and online communities, such as Reddit, Twitter, and Twitch, cryptocurrency has been very popular. The number of coins was limited to 100 billion, a substantially larger number compared to other cryptos. Since 2015, five billion more coins have been created beyond the original limit. With a large number of coins and increasing supply, the goal is to keep the value of the cryptocurrency relatively stable. From this aspect, dogecoin satisfies the original goal of having a 'medium of exchange' much more successfully. The dogecoin blockchain confirmation speed of one minute is ten times faster than bitcoin and two and half times faster than litecoin. Elon Musk and Mark Cuban have been some of the important supporters of dogecoin.

18.7 FINTECH INNOVATIONS

Financial technology (fintech) is a newly emerging industry where technology and financial services/operations are synthesized to provide efficient and effective solutions in banking, investments, education, data management, nonprofits, insurance, trading, and financial advising.

Machine learning, artificial intelligence, robo-advising, big data analysis, application program interfaces (A.P.I.s), and smart contracts are some examples of the methodologies and techniques used to bridge technology and finance.

States and city governments around the world have embraced the notion of innovation hubs to become fintech innovation centers. Santiago, Dublin, Singapore, Tallinn, Helsinki, Vilnius, Zurich, Bangalore, Berlin, and Tel Aviv are some examples, in addition to London, San Francisco, and Boston.

There are many areas where fintech initiatives are taking hold. Fundraising for start-ups by crowdfunding Kickstarter and Indiegogo; peer-to-peer insurance by Lemonade, SureApp, Cuvva, and Trov; saving incentives by Digit, Rise, Acorns, Mint, Y.N.A.B., Stickk, Long Game, and Prize-Savings; lending services by SoFI and GreenSky; currency transfers by Wise; financial services by Stripe, Credit Karma, Ant Group, Robinhood, Klarna, Ferratum, and Northmill; online security systems by BioCatch; blockchain analysis systems by Elliptic; and cloud-based human resources by Zenefits are just some examples of the fintech innovations from around the world.

18.8 SUMMARY AND CONCLUSION

Traditional currencies have long been the medium of exchange for goods and services. Central banks of governments follow different exchange rate policies (free-floating, soft peg, hard peg, fixed/merged) in order to influence the export/import imbalance, inflation rates, economic growth, or the budget surplus/deficit. The power of governments to print money has made many market participants uncomfortable about the independence of traditional currencies as a proper medium of exchange.

These concerns, the rise of the global online communication infrastructure, and the interconnected computer networks have led to the introduction of unregulated, decentralized, and anonymous ledger platforms (blockchains) and digital currencies (cryptocurrencies), starting around 2010. The popularity of and familiarity with cryptocurrencies increase continually. The blockchain technology with which cryptocurrencies are linked is becoming mainstream for corporations and institutions.

Cryptocurrencies have been among the largest unregulated markets in the world. While illegal use has declined substantially with rising mainstream interest, practical problems related to investing in cryptocurrencies include high volatility, theft, fraud, hacking, and ransom attacks. Since cryptocurrencies are unregulated, decentralized, untraceable, and anonymous, there are no protections, liabilities, or insurers. Although the lack of regulation is an important problem, increased levels of regulation could pose an even bigger problem. Government regulation could disrupt the nature of cryptocurrencies leading to illiquidity and drastic declines in demand and value.

With the positives and the negatives, cryptocurrencies and blockchain ledger technologies are becoming viable alternatives to currencies. Other fintech initiatives bridge together technology and finance for superior solutions in numerous areas of finance.

REFERENCES AND ADDITIONAL READING

Bodie, Z., Kane, A., Marcus, A.J. 2021. *Investments*. 12th edition. New York, McGraw-Hill.

Chambers, D.R., Anson, M.J.P., Black, K.H., Kazemi, H.B. 2015. *Alternative Investments: CAIA Level I*. 3rd edition. Hoboken, NJ, Wiley.

Fama, E.F. 1984. Forward and Spot Exchange Rates. *Journal of Monetary Economics*, 14, 319–338.

Inci, A.C., Lagasse, R. 2019. Cryptocurrencies: Applications and Investment Opportunities. *Journal of Capital Markets Studies*, 3, 98–112.

Inci, A.C., Lu, B. 2007. Currency Futures-Spot Basis and Risk Premium. *Journal of International Financial Markets, Institutions, and Money*, 17, 180–197.

Kazemi, H.B., Black, K.H., Chambers, D.R. 2016. *Alternative Investments: CAIA Level II*. 3rd edition. Hoboken, NJ, Wiley.

Nakamoto, S. 2008. *Bitcoin: A Peer-to-Peer Electronic Cash System*. https://bitcoin.org/bitcoin.pdf.

Solnik, B., McLeavey, D. 2003. *Global Investments*. 6th edition. Boston, MA, Pearson – Prentice Hall.

19

Artificial Intelligence in Finance

OBJECTIVES

- Give an overview of the history of artificial intelligence (A.I.), the development parallel with the innovators and innovations in computers, and A.I.'s present state and future outlook.
- Explore and evaluate the influence of A.I. in different areas of finance, including research, personal finance, corporate finance, and investments.
- Analyze the benefits, challenges, and ethical perspectives of A.I.

19.1 INTRODUCTION

One of the cutting-edge innovations with limitless potential has been the introduction and development of artificial intelligence (A.I.). Its applications in different areas of science have begun to generate tremendous leaps and advancements. Machine learning and A.I. have opened up new areas of research and innovations in the fields of finance and investments.

This chapter will be an overview of the history of artificial intelligence. The A.I. development parallel with the innovations and innovators in computers, past, present, and future are explored. After the broad introduction, the specific impact in different areas of finance will be investigated, including research in finance, personal finance, corporate finance, and investments. The benefits, challenges, regulation needs, and skewed impact of A.I. on economies around the world will be considered.

19.2 HISTORY OF COMPUTING

The introduction of the first computer both as hardware and as software go back to the 1830s United Kingdom. Charles Babbage is credited with the hardware. The great poet Lord Byron's daughter, Ada Lovelace, is credited with the software – the development of the flowcharts and programs for coding. Through her contributions, Ada Lovelace transformed the first computer

DOI: 10.4324/9781003213697-19

by Babbage from the original 'difference engine' to the 'analytical engine'. Over the next two centuries, there have been extensive developments both in hardware and in software toward attaining the sophistication of replacing humans in many areas of science, technology, engineering, and business.

Inventors John Atanasoff, Presper Eckert, and John Mauchly developed the E.N.I.A.C. (Electronic Numerical Integrator and Computer) in 1945, the first computer that was completely electronic and digital and ran on binary language, and it was a general-purpose machine able to manage a number of different tasks. Bardeen and Brattain introduced the transistor in 1947 to help reduce the size of the hardware components. The microchip was invented by Jack Kirby, Robert Noyce, and Gordon Moore in 1958, and the microprocessor was developed by Ted Hoff in 1971. The microchip and the microprocessor jointly paved the way for modern computer hardware. Powerful mainframes and terminals were established by governments and by firms, such as I.B.M. Personal computers were introduced and have been upgraded by Ed Roberts, Bill Gates, Paul Allen, Steve Wozniak, and Steve Jobs.

On the software front, women have led the way. Following the footsteps of Ada Lovelace, Grace Hopper, Jean Jennings, Betty Holberton, and Dorothy Vaughan were among the primary developers of Cobol and Fortran computer software languages. John von Neumann had tremendous contributions to the theoretical development of software architecture. Higher-level computer languages, such as Basic by Ed Roberts, Bill Gates, and Paul Allen; C++ by Bjarne Stroustrup; Java; and open-source languages starting with Linux by Linus Torvald, followed by others such as Python and Julia, have empowered software programmers with the means to write highly sophisticated code to grant autonomy to computers toward the direction of A.I.

Finally, communication and exchange of information between users and computers formed the third dimension of computing. The interconnected network (the internet) was envisioned by Vannevar Bush in the late 1940s. John Licklider, Bob Taylor, and Larry Roberts initiated the Advanced Research Projects Agency Network (A.R.P.A.N.E.T.) in 1966 to enable access to remote computers. Originally designed for the U.S. Department of Defense, the network was expanded to include the National Science Foundation in the early 1980s. Eventually, A.R.P.A.N.E.T. was decommissioned and transformed into today's internet after (1) the launch of supercomputing centers at several universities, (2) the partnerships with the telecommunications industry and the computer industry, (3) the private sector expansions, and (4) the commercialization of the worldwide online networks.

Alan Turing introduced the concepts of A.I. and the Turing test in the 1940s. The Turing test has been used as the critical threshold in A.I. for the determination of whether a computer has the capacity to think like a human. In the Turing test, a computer is supposed to use written communication to try to deceive a human interrogator into thinking that it is another human. Innovators Douglas Englebart (inventor of the computer mouse) and Stewart Brand have researched A.I. from the perspective of human and machine interactions and laid out important foundations in the late 1960s and early 1970s at the Stanford University A.I. laboratory. Despite major advances in A.I. over the decades, no computer has passed the Turing test as of the early 2020s.

A.I. examples such as Siri (Apple), Alexa (Amazon), Cortana (Microsoft), Google Assistant, and Bixby (Samsung) are getting more sophisticated with each iteration and new version, but there is a long way for such systems to be truly interactive human-like entities.

19.3 A.I. IN FINANCE

Artificial intelligence is continually used at greater frequency and capacity in many areas of finance. Credit decisions (mortgage loans, small business lines, credit cards); quantitative trading (automated trades, limit/stop order combinations, portfolio management); financial risk management; personalized banking; financial security (fraud detection, fraud prevention, cybersecurity); the design of blockchain ecologies and associated cryptocurrencies; and predicting cash flow events through machine learning are some examples of where A.I. is utilized. The finance industry is assisted by A.I. in optimizing all these different kinds of processes and in transforming the way customers and clients interact with money.

The use of A.I. in the design process and analysis process of financial decisions provide significant cost advantages by reducing the human workforce and by training employees for better efficiency and for higher quality output. Security measures developed with A.I. can be more effective and less costly. Businesses incorporating A.I. would be progressing successfully in the technologically advanced and innovation-driven world of today and the future.

The benefits of A.I. in finance are immense. From task automation and fraud detection to providing customized client recommendations, all financial institutions benefit from A.I. in their interactions with their customers and clients:

- A 24-hour-day, 7-day-a-week customer interaction is now possible for most institutions (granted that the scope of these interactions – chat-bot assistants – needs significant enhancement).
- Reduction of tedious and repetitive work (such as checking the balances of accounts, creation of receipts and bills, collection of payments, matching the collection dates, and determination of fees and costs).
- Lowering the number of human mistakes, clerical errors, and false positives.
- Savings through streamlined communications and connections (lower frictions, lower transaction costs, and faster execution of services).

Automation of tasks through machine learning and with A.I. is estimated to generate cost savings worth trillions of U.S. dollars in the future for financial institutions around the world. The adoption of A.I. by financial institutions will be accelerated by adjustments and moderation in regulations, advances in technology, and familiarity with the customers/consumers/clients.

The numerous applications of A.I. in different areas of finance can be categorized into four groups:

(1) Personal finance: The ability to manage financial wealth through 24/7 financial guidance with A.I. equipped with natural language processing (N.L.P.) tools and personalized insights helps customers attain financial independence. Erica (Bank of America), Eno (Capital One), Ally Assist (Ally Bank), Citi Bot S.G. (Citibank), and Clari (T.D.) are some of the primary good-quality A.I. chat-bots. These A.I. mechanisms provide account information, conduct spending/savings analyses, transfer funds, execute trades, activate/notify card activities, and warn of suspicious activities.

(2) Banking: A.I. helps banks manage and correctly interpret large quantities of high-speed data for valuable insight. Many bank features such as digital payments, biometric fraud detection systems, and other high-quality services are enabled with A.I. systems for a wide spectrum of customers. Moreover, banks utilize A.I.-powered systems to appraise customer credit histories more accurately in order to avoid default situations. Mobile banking applications track and analyze the financial transactions of users. These help banks anticipate the risks associated with issuing loans (such as customer insolvency).

(3) Consumer finance: Prevention of fraud, cyberattacks, or theft of accounts is of paramount importance in consumer finance. A.I. is used to develop and implement tools and algorithms that analyze consumer transactions, detect irregularities, notify consumers, and take preventive actions. Security and reliability are the main benefits of A.I. in the consumer finance field.

(4) Corporate finance: A.I. is particularly useful in two areas of corporate finance. The first is for analyzing projects. Evaluation of a project's profitability by correctly considering its costs and by accurately predicting future cash flows are essential for the financial strength of a firm. A.I., through its machine learning ability, can predict cash flow events and can conduct base-, best-, and worst-case scenario analyses, as well as break-even tests, in order to determine the net present value and the profitability of a project. The second useful area of A.I. in corporate finance is predicting/assessing loan risks. A.I. has the ability to detect more accurately the credit quality of applicants and applications. This ability improves loan underwriting and reduces the financial risk of corporations. A.I. can also reduce corporate financial crimes through advanced fraud detection and through unusual activity detection, encouraging company treasurers, accountants, and financial analysts to focus on long-term growth.

19.4 COMMON EXAMPLES OF A.I. IN FINANCE

Risk assessment: A.I. can be used to determine the risk characteristics of an applicant in an unbiased manner. Financial institutions increasingly utilize machine learning techniques to evaluate the creditworthiness of an individual, small business, a project, or an organization. These applications are evaluated expeditiously, more accurately, and depending on the inputs provided, in an unbiased manner.

Risk management: A.I. techniques are applied to collect data, analyze the performance of a portfolio from both return and risk perspectives, and provide suggestions and adjustments to fit the investment portfolio with the investment goals of investors. The optimization procedures normally designed by quant researchers are being streamlined toward the A.I. direction.

Cybersecurity and fraud detection and prevention: A.I. systems are employed by financial institutions to constantly monitor the banking, investment, and credit card accounts of clients. Out-of-the-ordinary behaviors and transactions are designed to trigger immediate notifications and warnings to clients and financial institutions. In many cases, suspicious transactions are not implemented unless additional confirmations are supplied by clients.

Financial advice: A.I. machine learning algorithms nowadays have the ability to analyze client portfolios and provide suggestions and investment advice based on economic conditions, client's investment trends, and up-to-date financial data.

Trading: A.I.-based algorithms analyze data, patterns, and existing conditions much faster than human analysts. The analyses lead to trading recommendations, and subject to an additional layer of permissions, the algorithms execute the suggested trades in a fast and accurate manner, saving time and avoiding transaction costs and other frictions.

Managing personal banking: As mentioned in the applications section, a common example of A.I. in finance is the utilization of virtual assistants for numerous banking functions such as checking balances, setting up payments, transferring funds, and verifying activities. Significant time is saved, and human error is literally eliminated compared to the alternative of speaking on the phone with a customer service representative.

Superior prediction and assessment of loan risks: A.I.-based connections, communication systems, and applications can better analyze a loan applicant's savings patterns, spending patterns, and digital footprints and consequently predict the repayment behavior of that customer. The application process is faster, more informative, and generally more successful.

Continuous service: Many banks and financial institutions use A.I. systems to present virtual assistants and chat-bots for 24 hours every day. Productivity increases, most issues are resolved in a satisfactory manner, time is saved, efficiency increases, cost reductions are achieved, customers are better satisfied, and the resources of the financial institution are used more effectively.

The additional advantages of the A.I. examples in finance are the automation of repetitive tasks, the minimization of human errors, the reduction of costs, and savings in time and money. Once automated and initiated, A.I. can accomplish any task of any length of time.

19.5 ETHICS AND A.I. IN THE FINANCE SECTOR

A.I. in the finance field is associated with a number of ethical issues that need to be addressed comprehensively. These ethical issues can be categorized under five headings: (1) one-dimensional goals, (2) openness/transparency, (3) responsibility/accountability, (4) impact on the workforce, and (5) misuse.

A.I. is based on machine learning algorithms: computer programs written by coders where the programs can update over time and reach decisions by learning in a self-sustained intelligent manner. But these learning processes can get out of control without proper checks and balances. For example, in order to generate the maximum profit for the financial institution, the A.I. process may offer products to customers who do not really need them. In other words, A.I. may become aggressive in offering products and services to customers that are not necessary, even worse, that manipulate the investment portfolios of customers to generate extra profits for the financial institution at the expense of customers (through transaction costs and unnecessary trading activities). The A.I. systems must be designed to avoid such one-dimensional goals, and the systems should take into account many different concerns. While the technology is improving dramatically, the current A.I. systems are not as sophisticated to address multitasking.

The second important issue with A.I. systems is openness and transparency. Mainly because of proprietary reasons, the algorithms and codes written for A.I. systems are not revealed and stay as black boxes. This results in confusion when an A.I. system generates a certain decision. The reasoning is not always clear, and that makes market participants, regulators, and other interested parties uncomfortable. This issue is not easy to solve because A.I. designers do not want to reveal their sophisticated codes to the public (and, therefore, to the competitors).

The third issue is about responsibility. The decisions taken by A.I. systems have consequences. If a decision makes every related party happy, then there would be no problem. Unfortunately, that is rarely the case. Who would be responsible if the A.I. system makes the wrong decision or if a decision hurts certain participants? This issue is again not easy to resolve because the original code might have been designed by certain programmers at a certain financial institution, but with gained experience and machine learning, at some point, the A.I. system starts to adjust the decisions that would not necessarily be consistent with the intentions of the original programmers/financial institution. The responsibility and accountability become vague in those circumstances. This is an important issue that must be clarified for all customers and relevant participants.

The fourth issue is the impact on the workforce once A.I. starts to dominate different businesses and industries. That has been the common fear with A.I. and robotics: that robots will replace humans. While this is indeed a concern, the potential solutions would be to educate individuals about more sophisticated jobs and professions or to provide a universal basic income to everyone. These potential solutions must be improved and must become concrete for this issue to be properly resolved.

Finally, the possibility that A.I. can be misused to access the private information of clients, sell client information to others, and blackmail clients for ransom is a serious ethical concern. Proper protection mechanisms must be established. A.I. systems must be developed with codes to prevent unethical extensions. Severe penalties and legal consequences must also be in place such that unethical behavior is discouraged/prevented.

The feedback systems setup for ethical checks and balances in A.I. must make sure that (1) only unbiased data are used in the A.I. decision process; (2) the confidentiality of applicants (data collaborators) is protected; (3) data processes and decision mechanisms are continually reviewed internally; (4) the A.I. conclusions can be satisfactorily explained; and (5) transparency is maintained, accountability is clear, and regulatory policies are complied with.

19.6 THE FUTURE OF A.I. IN FINANCE

A.I. is becoming more widespread across all sectors and industries, including the financial sector.

A.I. has already had a profound impact on finance through the restructuring of tasks, automation, consolidation of responsibilities, and analyses of data faster than the alternatives. These developments will continue in an intensified manner in the future.

It is easy to forecast that virtual assistants and chat-bots will represent a much larger proportion of the interactions with clients, enhanced with more responsibilities and tasks. The role of A.I. in the financial services industry and financial services will be a dominant one in the future. As a matter of fact, we can also predict that A.I. will have a more substantial role in all areas of finance. The finance-related activities will become cheaper, leaner, faster, more efficient with fewer frictions, more effective, and more satisfactory for all parties involved. In addition to such enhancements, A.I. will enable financial services to make more accurate and more informed decisions about their clients and about client needs.

Do these developments mean that A.I. will replace the human element completely? Will there no longer be human financial consultants, advisors, C.F.A.s, and C.A.I.A.s? Will financial analysts become obsolete? We can predict that the answer to all these questions is *no*. There will always be the human element in finance-related functions. A.I. will be an enormous enhancement in covering the groundwork of conducting accurate analyses, in taking over mundane and time-consuming repetitive tasks, but A.I. will never be fully intelligent in an independent way. Human-like intelligence, called general artificial intelligence (G.A.I.) or artificial general intelligence (A.G.I.), where a machine/computer/robot reaches a consciousness level such that it understands and learns any intellectual task like a human is predicted not to be possible in the near future – perhaps ever.

Human beings have an intelligence level that is *analogous*. Human consciousness is not purely based on rationality. There are emotions, decisions, feelings, actions, and tasks that cannot be based on rationality or based on pure reason. That is what makes humans different from machines. That higher level of connection can only be understood and only make sense between human beings and through human interactions. Therefore, in the field of finance, the final decision of an investment, a project, the formation of a portfolio, and getting a loan will boil down to that human element which cannot be a subset of the realm of artificial intelligence.

Thus, A.I. will not be able to replace the role of human financial advisors. Human advisors will have the intelligence quotient (I.Q.) and the emotional quotient (E.Q.) to truly connect with their clients. C.F.A.s and C.A.I.A.s will continue to be only human because, in addition to the deep knowledge that they will possess (which can be replicated by A.I.), they will also have the cognitive ability to think outside the box, consider irrationality, and take into account the emotional nature and emotional randomness of their clients (which cannot be replicated by A.I.). A.I. will be better suited to handling the day-to-day ordinary, time-consuming, and mundane tasks.

Finance professionals, analysts, and advisors will not become obsolete. But they will have to change and adapt. They will have to embrace A.I. and learn how to control, manipulate, and delegate to A.I. systems. There will be new career paths in A.I. banking and A.I. finance with significant emphasis on ethics, security, privacy, and moral and social responsibility in designing A.I.-enabled systems. The human mind and the A.I. mind are different. The goal should be achieving a symbiosis between humans and A.I. rather than replacing/replicating one with the other. Finance professionals will get new quantitative skills in coding, computing, statistics, mathematics, analyses, and new qualitative skills in psychology, communication, and human behavior. The new finance professional will be more customer-focused in order to enhance the wealth, value, and ultimately, the utility of the client.

19.7 DEVELOPING A.I. FOR DECISION-MAKING – HOW TO DESIGN A VIRTUAL ASSISTANT

Regardless of sector and industry, firms are embracing A.I. and are going through the process of hyper-automation, which means aggressively embracing automation in their business and information technology processes. The goals are to cut costs, optimize operating activities, reduce inefficiencies, and delegate repetitive tasks to A.I. technologies/platforms without human interactions.

Specific areas of hyper-automation, according to Gartner research and consulting, are (1) R.P.A.s (robotic process automations); (2) A.I. and machine learning; (3) process mining for optimization; (4) integration platforms connecting cloud processes, services, and data within a business organization; (5) intelligent document processing and manufacturing using machine vision, optical character recognition, speech recognition, natural language processing; and (6) no-code frameworks for easy automation of processes and tasks.

These hyper-automation activities are also called artificial intelligent process automations (A.I.P.A.s). The A.I.P.A. has three broad steps: In the first step, the R.P.A. is recognized. In the second step, the process or the data are analyzed. In the third step, reports and visual outputs are generated. These three steps are explained further with descriptions of their practical implementations.

In this day and age, it is no longer necessary to be a software engineer or a sophisticated computer programmer to develop R.P.A.s and apply them to financial processes. There are helpful automated organizers that generate flowcharts to be filled out by the individual to accomplish the R.P.A. In the first step, the R.P.A. is depicted and clarified by identifying each and every repetitive task (however small or unimportant a step may be) for the process, such as data collection. Once the flowchart is clearly depicted, a readily available software tool is programmed to implement the flowchart. There are numerous software packages, such as Workfusion, Uipath, Microsoft, Blue Prism, Nice, Kryon, Pegasystems, Automation Anywhere, and S.A.P.

Once the R.P.A. is implemented using the software package, the second step of the A.I.P.A. is the analysis of the data. Again, readily available software packages are utilized for this purpose, such as Alteryx, Matlab, Microstrategy, Tableau, Tibco, S.A.S., Tiger Analytics, Trifacta, and Talend. However large and complex the data may be, these software packages help analyze, interpret, and summarize the data.

The final step of the A.I.P.A. is the reporting of the data analyses to clients, customers, and other interested parties. The report and the visual presentation are again created using readily available software packages, such as Tableau, Microstrategy, I.B.M. Cognos, Power B.I., and Qlik. The reports and the visual presentations complete the R.P.A. and data analysis steps and justify the A.I. decision process. The three-step process fully implements the artificial intelligent process automation A.I.P.A.

19.8 SUMMARY AND CONCLUSION

Artificial intelligence is leading the way to limitless innovations in all areas of science, technology, engineering, and business. The applications in these different fields are generating tremendous leaps and advancements. Machine learning and artificial intelligence have opened up new areas of research and innovations in finance and in investments. Efficiency, cost cuts, optimization, faster speed of financial processes, cybersecurity, fraud detection/prevention, credit analyses, decisions underwriting, intelligent document processing, predictive analytics, and overall better customer experiences are the results of A.I. applications in finance.

REFERENCES AND ADDITIONAL READING

Chambers, D.R., Anson, M.J.P., Black, K.H., Kazemi, H.B. 2015. *Alternative Investments: CAIA Level I.* 3rd edition. Hoboken, NJ, Wiley.

Isaacson, W. 2014. *The Innovators: How a Group of Hackers, Geniuses, and Geeks Created the Digital Revolution.* New York, Simon & Shuster.

Kazemi, H.B., Black, K.H., Chambers, D.R. 2016. *Alternative Investments: CAIA Level II.* 3rd edition. Hoboken, NJ, Wiley.

Lewis, M. 2014. *Flash Boys.* New York, W.W. Norton & Company.

CHAPTER 20

Big Data Analytics

OBJECTIVES

- Describe and discuss the background and evolution of big data and big data analytics.
- Critique the technologies utilized in big data and their application in different industries.
- Categorize and contrast big data analytics tools.
- Apply big data analytics to financial markets for price discovery, market efficiency, and international integration of spot and futures markets.
- Analyze information asymmetry and intraday insider trading with big data.
- Investigate intraday insider trading and intraday price behavior using big data analytics.

20.1 INTRODUCTION

There have been spectacular advances in technology, computer power, and processing ability over the last 50 years. Moore's law (based on the observations of Gordon Moore, co-founder and former C.E.O. of Intel, during the late 1960s) states that the speed and capability of computers will double every 18 to 24 months, suggesting exponential growth, while costs will decrease. This observation has held since the mid-1970s and is now referred to as a 'law'. The pace of growth has facilitated all kinds of technological innovations over the last several decades. The exponential growth in computer processing power is so fast that it cannot sustain itself because of the limits in quantum mechanics. Critics claim that the rate of growth has started to slow down, and the peak power will be reached over the 15- to 50-year horizon. On the other hand, while Moore's law is still valid, its relevance has diminished because of the introduction of new ways of attaining and measuring processing power.

The increase in computer power has opened many doors for new data collection and storage opportunities, new analysis techniques, and new decision tools. In the past, researchers collected, used, and analyzed data with annual, quarterly, monthly, or weekly frequencies. These

DOI: 10.4324/9781003213697-20

low-frequency datasets would lead to certain results and conclusions presented in research papers. With the recent technological developments, datasets that were unthinkable to collect, store, and analyze because of their enormous size and high frequency are now possible to cope with. For example, in finance, intraday and tick-by-tick data from financial markets and financial securities are nowadays easier to obtain, handle, and analyze. These high-frequency data mirror the realities of continuous, analog life much more accurately. Investigation of these high-frequency data often leads to new insights and new conclusions. Many times, previous conclusions from earlier studies with low-frequency data are refuted. At the same time, enormous technological advancements have been integrated into the trading infrastructures of financial markets over the last two decades. Trading platforms now execute trades at the speed of light through fiber optic communication networks. Nowadays, ultra-high-speed intraday trading is widespread.

In this chapter, the tenets of big data are explored. The tools to analyze such data are introduced. Two examples of big data applications in finance employing intraday high-frequency tick-by-tick prices are presented. The first example is about intraday trading and price discovery relationships between the spot and futures markets in an international setting involving many time zones. Big data analytics leads to new and more accurate insights into the efficiency of financial markets and energy markets. The second example is information asymmetry and intraday insider trading, where the rules and regulations for an equal, fair, and ethical trading environment are surveyed. Information asymmetry and stock price behavior around intraday insider trading are discussed and documented with new conclusions, again with the help of big data analytics.

20.2 BIG DATA AND BIG DATA ANALYTICS

20.2.1 Big Data

The collective quantity of information is constantly increasing as time passes. While there were five billion gigabytes of data globally in 2003, more than two and a half quintillion (2.5 billion billion) gigabytes of data are created in a single day currently. As the quantity of data created, recorded, and stored these days is at truly baffling levels, the utilization of the data have evolved as well.

Big data represent datasets whose sizes and/or types are beyond the ability of traditional databases to manage and process with low latency (delay). Big data characteristics are large-*v*olume, high-*v*elocity, and wide-*v*ariety – known as the three Vs. These data are so voluminous, so complex, and from so many different data sources (A.I., social media, mobile devices, the internet, etc.) that traditional data processing software just can't manage them.

Data exist in a structured format (e.g., in an Excel file), semi-structured format (e.g., in an email message), or unstructured format (e.g., pictures and videos). All these massive volumes of data constitute big data and can be used to address and solve business problems that were not possible to identify, address, or solve before. The development of open-source frameworks, such as Hadoop, Spark, Cassandra, and others, starting in 2005 has been essential for the growth of big data because these frameworks have made it easy to work with and cheaper to store big data.

Big data and big data analytics are actively used in numerous sectors, such as e-commerce (for customer trends and optimal prices), marketing (for improved sales and return on investment), education (to develop new courses and programs), healthcare (to collect and analyze medical histories to predict future health problems), arts and entertainment (to analyze customer demands and deliver personalized visual/audible fine arts productions), finance (to analyze customer savings/spending patterns and offer more appropriate products), communications (to forecast networking requirements and better customer experience), and local and federal government agencies (for law enforcement, tax collection, and budget design).

20.2.2 Big Data Analytics

Big data analytics evaluate very large volumes of data to discover patterns, trends, correlations, and various other insights. With the current technology, tools, and techniques, the analyses are fast, and the answers to problems are rapid. Almost every industry, from banking, healthcare, and utilities to local/federal government, is in the process of utilizing the technologies to solve challenges and problems and make better decisions. Open-source free software help with data mining, cleaning, integration, visualization, and improving the process of analysis to generate cost-effective outcomes.

Big data analytics tools utilize the collaboration of several technologies to get the most out of large volumes of data. Some of the forefront technologies are (1) cloud computing as the ecology and the framework for big data on the internet; (2) data filtering and cleaning for quality and for reliable analyses; (3) data mining for discovering patterns, trends, and relationships in the data; (4) text mining for analyzing text data from large scale sources with machine learning or natural language processing; (5) data storage in the form of complementary data lakes (for raw and unstructured data in original format) or data warehouses (for storing large amounts of filtered and structured data for the quick access, analyses, and resaving) in a central database; and (6) machine learning as a subset of A.I. to learn and to analyze large scale volumes of complex data by quickly producing quantitative models.

Big data analytics can be categorized into descriptive, diagnostic, prescriptive, and predictive analytics:

(1) Descriptive analytics is the first step in analyzing raw data with simple statistical operations for financial reports, comparison metrics, surveys, and social media initiatives. This way, firms interpret large amounts of data and compare current business situations with those in the past.

(2) Diagnostic analytics are for understanding the reasons that certain events, changes, and behaviors happen to firms, organizations, customers, employees, and products. Businesses better understand their customers by diagnosing data through regressions, filtering, and pattern identifications.

(3) Prescriptive analytics find optimal solutions to business problems through Monte Carlo simulations and other simulations. These initiatives lead to improved strategies, production processes, marketing campaigns, and services.

(4) Forecast analytics use predictive statistical models, machine learning tools, and A.I. techniques to reliably forecast the demand, supply, inventory, shipping needs, business trends, sales, and profits.

Big data analytics help companies gain value in different ways. Risk management, cost reductions, more accurate product development and innovations, faster and better decision-making, and improved customer experience are some of these add-ons. These benefits help companies identify new opportunities, achieve more efficient operations, generate higher profits, and increase the number of happier customers.

20.3 INTRADAY TRADING AND PRICE DISCOVERY IN FUTURES MARKETS

In this section, we comprehensively examine a study in financial markets, specifically the futures market, using big data. The intraday price discovery and market efficiency in energy markets are explored from an international perspective. Big data and big data analytics lead to different, more relevant, and more accurate results and conclusions.

Futures are contracts for the delivery of an underlying security at an agreed-upon price on a specific future date. The futures price and the current spot price of the underlying security roughly move in a similar fashion. Therefore, investors interested in the underlying security can have the choice of either investing directly in that security or having long positions in the futures contracts on that security. The big advantage of investing in futures is convenience. Instead of actually buying gold, silver, beef, oil, or gas, one can long futures contracts on these securities. Later, with an additional opposite position (short position) in the futures contract on the same underlying security, the profit (or loss) from the difference in the long futures and short futures prices would be obtained.

Futures markets are unique in the sense that they are truly global. The Globex electronic trading system operates 24 hours a day, 6 days a week. But an important issue is about how closely spot and futures markets are integrated intraday. When a shock (arrival of new information, positive or negative) happens in spot markets, how quickly is it propagated to the futures markets and vice versa? The intraday characteristics of price movements between spot and futures markets oil futures would provide useful information about efficiency and international integration of energy markets.

The integration of energy markets is an important issue for producers and consumers, as well as for speculators, arbitrageurs, and policymakers. Well-integrated spot and futures markets indicate that oil markets function well in discovering new, important, and relevant information. The pricing and the transfer of information, quickly and fully, to all related markets is necessary for market efficiency. Moreover, closely integrated oil markets perform the risk transfer function that is essential to hedgers, speculators, and arbitrageurs.

Such a research study must be careful about the frequency of data used for the investigation. Many former studies have provided evidence of daily lags in the statistical causality from spot oil prices to futures oil prices, as well as in the statistical causality from futures prices to spot prices. These findings imply market inefficiency because daily lags of past spot (futures) price changes can be used to predict futures (spot) price changes days ahead. If either spot oil prices or futures oil prices can be predicted using past daily data, this would suggest that it takes days for a price shock in spot (futures) markets to be incorporated into futures (spot) markets. In today's fast-moving prices and trades, this means a highly inefficient energy market in general and oil markets in particular.

The fundamental problem with the former studies has been the use of low-frequency daily data in the statistical tests. Given the geographic dispersion of oil markets and almost continuous trading activity, daily data do not match benchmarks in real time and do not allow for adjustments in time zone differences between different oil markets. Important oil-related production and/or inventory news that arrives late in the afternoon in the U.S. impacts global markets. But this information would be recorded in West Texas Intermediate (W.T.I.) prices that day and recorded in the Brent benchmark or Dubai benchmark the next day. Even if the information appeared on the same day, nonsynchronous closing times would reduce the degree of correlation between the different series: while the electronic trading on C.M.E. Globex, C.M.E. Clearport, and the I.C.E. in London continues for more than 22 hours every day, N.Y.M.E.X. daily closing price for W.T.I. is at 2:30 p.m., New York time. The cutoff for the daily closing oil price data would create timing-mismatch problems.

A recent paper by Inci and Seyhun (2018) investigates the integration of oil spot and futures markets using big data. Working with precisely matched customized intraday data for the first time in order to avoid non-synchronous trading issues in futures markets, specifically oil futures, they find evidence of highly integrated spot and futures markets. Economic shocks that arise in spot (futures) markets are quickly transmitted to the futures (spot) markets approximately one-for-one. Most of the reaction takes place within minutes. Their findings indicate well-functioning, well-integrated spot and futures oil markets that accomplish price discovery, risk transfer, and informational efficiency.

The researchers have provided intraday oil futures data that were time-stamped in milliseconds. They also used daily Dated Brent data for the spot prices of physical oil, announced precisely at 4:30 p.m., London time. Using the intraday, time-stamped futures data and the Dated Brent prices, they created daily, 2-minute, and 30-minute customized price series. They matched the announcement of the spot price data at around 4:30 p.m., London time, to the exact futures contract trading time. Consequently, using intraday, time-stamped oil futures data and precisely timed Dated Brent data, they bypassed difficulties arising from timing mismatches and time zone differences between spot and futures data.

More specific sources of the data used by the researchers constituted two spot indices for the physical oil prices to obtain their results. The first is the Brent Index, the average of the trading prices in the 25-day North Sea Brent Blend, Forties Blend, Oseberg, and Ekofisk crudes, known as the B.F.O.E., computed at 7:30 p.m., London time. The second oil spot price index is the Dated Brent index mentioned previously, the benchmark for a large proportion of the crude oil that is traded internationally, where dated Brent is for the cargo of the North Sea Brent blend crude oil that has an assigned date for loading onto a tanker. The third data component of the study was the I.C.E. Brent futures contracts based on the Brent Crude of the North Sea B.F.O.E. market. Brent Crude price is a trading arrangement of light sweet crude oil that functions as a major benchmark for purchases/sales of oil globally and is also called Brent Blend, London Brent, or Brent petroleum. The I.C.E. Brent became the world's largest crude oil futures exchange in 2012 in terms of volume.

The critical issue in the research was the timing of the Dated Brent physical oil spot price at 4:30 p.m., London time, to precisely match with futures prices. Given the availability of the trading prices of futures contracts continually intraday, futures prices at 4:30 p.m., 4:32 p.m., and 5:00 p.m., London time, were picked for the custom-constructed price series with

2-minute, 30-minute, and daily frequencies around the announcement of Dated Brent spot price each day.

With their more accurate and precisely matched big data of intraday oil futures prices, the researchers have confirmed the previous findings that spot and futures markets are highly integrated. However, in contrast to the previous literature, they have found that using time-matched intraday data, the typical daily lead-lag relations between spot and futures markets mostly disappear. Economic shocks that arise in spot (futures) markets are typically transmitted to the futures (spot) markets approximately one-for-one, within the day, usually within minutes.

The new evidence from the big data analytics utilizing the appropriate intraday big data of the study indicates that futures and spot prices are better integrated than previous studies suggested. The high-frequency big data evidence correctly extracts the conclusion that no profitable trading opportunities are available when the more precise big data are used for the analyses. Information travels between spot and futures markets and within futures contracts of different maturities (tenors) within seconds and minutes, not days.

Overall, the findings indicate well-functioning, well-integrated, and informationally efficient spot and futures oil markets. The markets transfer information between spot and futures prices as well as different tenors of futures prices very quickly. This high speed of information transfer is consistent with oil markets that perform the functions of both price discovery and risk transfer efficiently. Such accurate and precise results are only possible with big data analytics for fast-moving markets, ultra-high-speed trading, and fast information propagation.

20.4 INFORMATION ASYMMETRY, INTRADAY TRADING ACTIVITY OF INSIDERS

We explore another finance study comprehensively: information asymmetry and intraday insider trading using big data and big data analytics. An insider is someone who is in the mid- to upper-level management of a company and who has access to private and material information about the company. Legally, officers, directors, and owners of more than 10% of the shares of a company are considered insiders. Such people possess asymmetric private information, and they are not legally permitted to trade using their private information. Such trades would surely generate profits but at the expense of other investors who do not possess insider information. This is unfair and unethical, and there is legislation going all the way back to 1934 to prevent insiders from using private information.

This does not mean that all insider trading is illegal. If the insider trades shares of their own company without using private information, that would be legal. Perhaps the insider needed money for a vacation and sold some shares of their own company. Or the insider had excess cash and simply decided to purchase extra shares of their own firm. For such trades, the S.E.C. requires the reporting of the date, whether it was a buy or sell, how many shares were traded and at what price, the name and position of the insider, the name of the firm, and the characteristic of the trade (open market, gift, option exercise, etc.).

Dozens of studies of these S.E.C.-reported insider trades have conclusively shown that the aggregate of these trades are related to the private information possessed by insiders. Even after taking risk premium factors, such as size, book-to-market, and others, into account, the reported insider trades still generate excess profits. Studies document that the insider purchase (sale) on aggregate takes place on a date where the price had been decreasing (increasing) to the lowest (highest) level over the last 30 business days. After the insider purchase (sale) at the lowest (highest) level, the price trend reverses and increases (decreases) over the next 30 business days. Most such studies have used daily data to examine insider trading reactions.

In a recent paper by Inci, Seyhun, and Lu (2010), the researchers used big data intraday, identified the insiders' specific trades during the day, and examined what happened to the share price of the firm before and after the insider trade. The motivation was the famous T.V. personality Martha Stewart. She was convicted for selling 4,000 shares of ImClone for $230,000 following a recommendation by her Merrill-Lynch broker, Bacanovic, who had learned about the demise of ImClone from another client of his, Sam Waksal, the C.E.O. of ImClone. Sam Waksal knew before others that a drug under development was not approved by the F.D.A. His sale was triggered by this private piece of information, which was actually illegal to act on. The sequence of transactions showed that the insider trade was recognized by the market maker, and a piggyback of trades followed.

The intraday insider trading study identified the reported insider trade from background trades on the same day recorded in the Trade and Quote (T.A.Q.) database. The primary matching criterion was price and volume. An insider buy of 100 shares of a firm for $30 per share on a specific date could only be matched with a trade from the T.A.Q. database if and only if there was only one such unique trade for that firm on that day. If there were two (or more) similar trades in the T.A.Q. database at two different time points on the same day, the insider trade could be either one of them. Since a unique match could not be made in that situation, the insider trade had to be discarded. Ultimately, roughly 180,000 uniquely matched trades from 1988 through 2002 were used in the study.

The cumulative average abnormal returns are given in percentages during an intraday one-day window in figure 20.1, from 60 trades before to 60 trades after the insider trade. The solid line represents trades around insider purchases, where the price reactions are more pronounced. The stock price decreases before the insider purchase. The order is recognized as coming from an insider because, along with the immediate price increase with the insider buy order, the

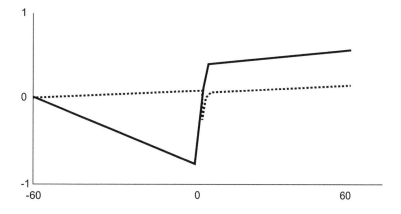

FIGURE 20.1 Trade-by-Trade Intraday Excess Price Reactions Around the Insider Trade

stock price continues to go up in the follow-up trades after the insider trade. On the other hand, for trades around insider sales in the dashed line, there is an increase in the stock price before the insider sale. The sale is again recognized by the market maker as originating from an insider. However, the immediate price decline with the insider sale is temporary. In the follow-up trades, the price recovers to a similar trend before the insider sale.

Some of the unique findings of big data analytics from the intraday price movements around privately informed insider trades are summarized as (1) insiders' presence is discovered at the time of trade; (2) there is no evidence of front-running, but there is evidence of piggybacking on insiders; (3) insiders are contrarian – they buy when prices are declining and sell when prices are rising; (4) insiders' purchases have an immediate and permanent price effect; (5) insiders' sales tend to have a temporary price effect and limited permanent impact; and (6) insiders profit regardless of trade volume but more from larger trades.

20.5 SUMMARY AND CONCLUSION

Big data and big data analytics are bringing about new insights into all areas of science, technology, engineering, and business. High-volume data representing the high frequency of trades intraday and the analytical tools for these big data variables better inform us about important financial markets issues, such as market efficiency, global integration of markets, information asymmetry, and the use of private information, as examined in the chapter. Advancements in the storage, access, and analyses of big data help firms with innovation, risk management, cost reduction, and improved customer experience.

REFERENCES AND ADDITIONAL READING

Inci, A.C., Seyhun, N. 2018. Degree of Integration between Brent Oil Spot and Futures Markets: Intraday Evidence. *Emerging Markets Finance and Trade*, 54, 1808–1826.

Inci, A.C., Seyhun, N., Lu, B. 2010. Intraday Behavior of Stock Prices and Trades Around Insider Trading. *Financial Management*, 39, 323–363.

Isaacson, W. 2014. *The Innovators: How a Group of Hackers, Geniuses, and Geeks Created the Digital Revolution*. New York, Simon & Shuster.

Kazemi, H.B., Black, K.H., Chambers, D.R. 2016. *Alternative Investments: CAIA Level II*. 3rd edition. Hoboken, NJ, Wiley.

Schwartz, R.A., Francioni, R. 2004. *Equity Markets in Action: The Fundamentals of Liquidity, Market Structure and Trading*. Hoboken, NJ, Wiley.

Seyhun, N. 1998. *Investment Intelligence from Insider Trading*. Cambridge, MA, MIT Press.

Bibliography

Ahn, D.H., Dittmar, R.F., Gallant, A.R. 2002. Quadratic Term Structure Models: Theory and Evidence. *Review of Financial Studies*, 15, 243–288.

Aragon, G.O. 2007. Share Restrictions and Asset Pricing: Evidence from the Hedge Fund Industry. *Journal of Financial Economics*, 83, 33–58.

Backus, D., Foresi, S., Telmer, C. 2001. Affine Term Structure Models and the Forward Premium Anomaly. *Journal of Finance*, 56, 279–304.

Bank of International Settlements Statistics. 2021. *BIS Derivatives Statistics.* www.bis.org/statistics/.

Benninga, S. 2014. *Financial Modeling.* 4th edition. Cambridge, MA, MIT Press.

Black, F., Derman, E., Toy, W. 1990. A One-Factor Model of Interest Rates and Its Application to Treasury Bond Options. *Financial Analysts Journal*, 46, 33–40.

Black, F., Karasinski, P. 1991. Bond and Option Pricing When Short Rates Are Lognormal. *Financial Analysts Journal*, 47, 52–59.

Black, F., Scholes, M. 1973. The Pricing of Options and Corporate Liabilities. *Journal of Political Economy*, 81, 637–654.

Bodie, Z., Kane, A., Marcus, A.J. 2021. *Investments.* 12th edition. New York, McGraw-Hill.

Bollen, N.P.B., Juha Joenväärä, J., Kauppila, M. 2021. Hedge Fund Performance: End of an Era? *Financial Analysts Journal*, 77, 109–132.

Burmeister, E., Roll, R., Ross, S.A. 1994. A Practitioner's Guide to Arbitrage Pricing Theory. In *A Practitioner's Guide to Factor Models.* Charlottesville, The Research Foundation of the Institute of Chartered Financial Analysts.

Carhart, M.M. 1997. On Persistence in Mutual Fund Performance. *Journal of Finance*, 52, 57–82.

Chambers, D.R., Anson, M.J.P., Black, K.H., Kazemi, H.B. 2015. *Alternative Investments: CAIA Level I.* 3rd edition. Hoboken, NJ, Wiley.

Chen, N.F., Roll, R. and Ross, S.A. 1986. Economic Forces and the Stock Market. *Journal of Business*, 59, 383–403.

Constantinides, G.M. 1992. A Theory of the Nominal Term Structure of Interest Rates. *Review of Financial Studies*, 5, 531–552.

Cox, J.C., Ingersoll, J.E., Ross, S.A. 1985. A Theory of the Structure of Interest Rates. *Econometrica*, 53, 385–408.

Cox, J.C., Ross, S.A., Rubinstein, M. 1976. The Valuation of Options for Alternative Stochastic Processes. *Journal of Financial Economics*, 3, 145–166.

Dai, Q., Singleton, K.J. 2000. Specification Analysis of Affine Term Structure Models. *Journal of Finance*, 55, 1943–1978.

Dodd, C., Frank, B. 2010. *Dodd – Frank Wall Street Reform and Consumer Protection Act.* www.cftc.gov/sites/default/files/idc/groups/public/@swaps/documents/file/hr4173_enrolledbill.pdf.

Duffee, G. 2002. Term Premia and Interest Rate Forecasts in Affine Models. *Journal of Finance*, 57, 405–444.

Duffie, D., Kan, R. 1996. A Yield-Factor Model of Interest Rates. *Mathematical Finance*, 4, 379–406.

Fabozzi, F.J. 2013. *Bond Markets, Analysis and Strategies*. 8th edition. Upper Saddle River, NJ, Pearson-Prentice Hall.

Fama, E.F. 1984. Forward and Spot Exchange Rates. *Journal of Monetary Economics*, 14, 319–338.

Fama, E.F., French, K.R. 1992, The Cross-Section of Expected Stock Returns. *Journal of Finance*, 47, 427–465.

Fama, E.F., French, K.R. 2015. A Five Factor Asset Pricing Model. *Journal of Financial Economics*, 116, 1–22.

Fama, E.F., French, K.R. 2015. Incremental Variables and the Investment Opportunity Set. *Journal of Financial Economics*, 117, 470–488.

Fama, E.F., French, K.R. 2016. Dissecting Anomalies with a Five-Factor Model. *Review of Financial Studies*, 29, 69–103.

Fama, E.F., French, K.R. 2017. International Tests of a Five-Factor Asset-Pricing Model. *Journal of Financial Economics*, 123, 441–463.

Fernandez, P., Bañuls, S., Acin, F. 2021. Survey: Market Risk Premium and Risk-Free Rate Used for 88 Countries in 2021. *IESE Business School Working Paper*, IESE.

Hasanhodzic, J., Lo, A.W. 2007. Can Hedge Fund Returns be Replicated?: The Linear Case. *Journal of Investment Management*, 5, 5–45.

Ho, T.S.Y., Lee, S.B. 1986. Term Structure Movements and Pricing Interest Rate Contingent Claims. *Journal of Finance*, 41, 1011–1029.

Hull, J.C. 2012. *Options, Futures and Other Derivatives*. 8th edition. Boston, MA, Prentice Hall.

Hull, J.C., White, A. 1990. Pricing Interest-Rate Derivative Securities. *Review of Financial Studies*, 3, 573–592.

Inci, A.C., Lagasse, R. 2019. Cryptocurrencies: Applications and Investment Opportunities. *Journal of Capital Markets Studies*, 3, 98–112.

Inci, A.C., Lu, B. 2007. Currency Futures-Spot Basis and Risk Premium. *Journal of International Financial Markets, Institutions, and Money*, 17, 180–197.

Inci, A.C., Ozenbas, D. 2017. Intraday Volatility and the Implementation of a Closing Call Auction at Borsa Istanbul. *Emerging Markets Review*, 33, 79–89.

Inci, A.C., Seyhun, N. 2018. Degree of Integration between Brent Oil Spot and Futures Markets: Intraday Evidence. *Emerging Markets Finance and Trade*, 54, 1808–1826.

Inci, A.C., Seyhun, N., Lu, B. 2010. Intraday Behavior of Stock Prices and Trades around Insider Trading. *Financial Management*, 39, 323–363.

Isaacson, W. 2014. *The Innovators: How a Group of Hackers, Geniuses, and Geeks Created the Digital Revolution*. New York, Simon & Shuster.

Itô, K. 1944. Stochastic Integral. *Proceedings of the Imperial Academy*, 20, 519–524.

Itô, K. 1951. Multiple Wiener Integral. *Journal of the Mathematical Society of Japan*, 3, 157–169.

Itô, K. 1951. On a Formula Concerning Stochastic Differentials. *Nagoya Mathematical Journal*, 3, 55–65.

Jarrow, R., Protter, P. 2004. A Short History of Stochastic Integration and Mathematical Finance: The Early Years, 1880–1970. *Lecture Notes-Monograph Series JSTOR*, 45, 75–91.

Jorion, P. 2006. *Value at Risk*. 3rd edition. New York, McGraw-Hill.

Kahneman, D. 2011. *Thinking, Fast and Slow*. New York, Farrar, Straus and Giroux.

Kazemi, H.B., Black, K.H., Chambers, D.R. 2016. *Alternative Investments: CAIA Level II*. 3rd edition. Hoboken, NJ, Wiley.

La Porta, R., Lopez-de-Silanes, F., Shleifer, A., Vishny, R.W. 1998. Law and Finance. *Journal of Political Economy*, 106, 1113–1155.

Lewis, M. 2014. *Flash Boys*. New York, W.W. Norton & Company.

Lintner, J. 1965. The Valuation of Risk Assets and the Selection of Risky Investments in Stock Portfolios and Capital Budgets. *Review of Economics and Statistics*, 47, 13–37.

Markopolos, H. 2010. *No One Would Listen: A True Financial Thriller*. Hoboken, NJ, Wiley.

Markowitz, H.M. 1952. Portfolio Selection. *Journal of Finance*, 7, 77–91.

Merton, R.C. 1969. Lifetime Portfolio Selection Under Uncertainty: The Continuous-Time Case. *Review of Economics and Statistics*, 51, 247–257.

Merton, R.C. 1971. Optimum Consumption and Portfolio Rules in a Continuous-Time Model. *Journal of Economic Theory*, 3, 373–413.

Merton, R.C. 1972. An Analytical Derivation of the Efficient Portfolio Frontier. *Journal of Financial and Quantitative Analysis*, 7, 1851–1872.

Merton, R.C. 1973. Theory of Rational Option Pricing. *Bell Journal of Economics*, 4, 141–183.

Merton, R.C. 1992. *Continuous-Time Finance*. Oxford, Basil Blackwell, Inc.

Mossin, J. 1966. Equilibrium in Capital Asset Markets. *Econometrica*, 34, 768–783.

Nakamoto, S. 2008. *Bitcoin: A Peer-to-Peer Electronic Cash System*. https://bitcoin.org/bitcoin.pdf.

Sadka, R. 2010. Liquidity Risk and the Cross-section of Hedge-Fund Returns. *Journal of Financial Economics*, 98, 54–71.

Sarbanes, P., Oxley, M.G. 2002. *Sarbanes – Oxley Act*. www.govinfo.gov/content/pkg/PLAW-107publ204/pdf/PLAW-107publ204.pdf.

Schwartz, R.A., Francioni, R. 2004. *Equity Markets in Action: The Fundamentals of Liquidity, Market Structure and Trading*. Hoboken, NJ, Wiley.

Seyhun, N. 1998. *Investment Intelligence from Insider Trading*. Cambridge, MA, MIT Press.

Sharpe, W.F. 1964. Capital Asset Prices: Theory of Market Equilibrium. *Journal of Finance*, 19, 425–442.

Sharpe, W.F. 1966. Mutual Fund Performance. *Journal of Business*, 39, 119–138.

Solnik, B.H. 1974. Why Not Diversify Internationally Rather than Domestically? *Financial Analysts Journal*, 30, 48–54.

Solnik, B.H., McLeavey, D. 2003. *Global Investments*. 6th edition. Boston, MA, Pearson – Prentice Hall.

Stulz, R.M. 2007. Hedge Funds: Past, Present, and Future. *Journal of Economic Perspectives*, 21, 175–194.

Treynor, J.L. 1962. *Toward a Theory of Market Value of Risky Assets*. Unpublished manuscript.

Vasicek, O. 1977. An Equilibrium Characterization of the Term Structure. *Journal of Financial Economics*, 5, 177–188.

Index

Note: Numbers in *italic* indicate figures and numbers in **bold** indicate tables on the corresponding page.